Letters from Filadelfia

Writing the Early Americas

Anna Brickhouse and Kirsten Silva Gruesz, Editors

Letters from Filadelfia

Early Latino Literature and the Trans-American Elite

Rodrigo Lazo

University of Virginia Press
Charlottesville and London

University of Virginia Press
© 2020 by the Rector and Visitors of the University of Virginia
All rights reserved
Printed in the United States of America on acid-free paper

First published 2020

9 8 7 6 5 4 3 2 1

Names: Lazo, Rodrigo, author.
Title: Letters from Filadelfia : early Latino literature and the trans-American elite / Rodrigo Lazo.
Description: Charlottesville : University of Virginia Press, 2020. | Includes bibliographical references and index.
Identifiers: LCCN 2019015596 (print) | LCCN 2019980184 (ebook) | ISBN 9780813943541 (cloth) | ISBN 9780813943558 (paperback) | ISBN 9780813943565 (ebook)
Subjects: LCSH: Spanish literature—Pennsylvania—Philadelphia—History and criticism. | Spanish literature—18th century—History and criticism. | Spanish literature—19th century—History and criticism. | Hispanic Americans—Intellectual life—18th century. | Hispanic Americans—Intellectual life—19th century.
Classification: LCC PQ7078.5. P45 L39 2019 (print) | LCC PQ 7078.5. P45 (ebook) | DDC 860.9/97481109033—dc23
LC record available at https://lccn.loc.gov/2019015596
LC ebook record available at https://lccn.loc.gov/2019980184

Cover art (clockwise from top): Plan of the city of Philadelphia and adjoining districts (Philadelphia: H. S. Tanner, 1830; Library of Congress); letter from Fray Servando Teresa de Mier to Mery and Charlotte Stephenson, 20 June 1821 / letter from Jean-François Hurtel to Fray Servando Teresa de Mier, 7 August, 1821 / letter from Manuel Torres, 24 September 1821 / letter from Vicente Rocafuerte, 31 July 1821 (Nettie Lee Benson Latin American Collection, University of Texas Libraries, The University of Texas at Austin)

Contents

	Acknowledgments	vii
	A Note on the Spanish Language	xi
	Introduction	1
1	La Famosa Filadelfia	25
2	The Trans-American Elite	70
3	Faith in Print	110
4	Anonymously Yours: Republican Man	156
5	Leaving Filadelfia, or Archival Dislocations	192
	Notes	231
	Bibliography	261
	Index	281

Acknowledgments

Numerous people and institutions helped in the development and eventual completion of this book. It began as an essay, "La Famosa Filadelfia: The Hemispheric American City and Constitutional Debates," in *Hemispheric American Studies* (New Brunswick, NJ: Rutgers UP, 2008), aspects of which appear in chapter 1 of this volume. The editors of that collection, Caroline Levander and Robert S. Levine, were early supporters. Thank you, Bob, for being a longtime mentor and friend; you will always be my dissertation director.

At the University of Virginia Press, the series editors—including Anna Brickhouse, whose scholarship charted these paths before me—inspired me to finish. Editor in chief Eric Brandt helped me get through the publication process. My thanks to all at the press for your work on this project, especially with the editing. My appreciation to the anonymous readers and to the not-anonymous Samuel Otter, who knows Philadelphia and has been a friend for years.

Aspects of chapter 5 appeared originally as "The Invention of America Again," *American Literary History* 25 (2013): 751–71, used with permission from Oxford University Press. A couple of pages of the introduction appeared in different form in "Before LatinX: X and *Cartas de un Americano*," *ELN* 56, no. 2 (2018): 48–51, used with permission from Duke University Press. Research was conducted at the following, among others: the American Antiquarian Society, the Historical Society of Pennsylvania, the Nettie Lee Benson Latin American Collection at the University of Texas at Austin, the Library Company of Philadelphia, the Library of Congress, the New-York Historical Society, the Huntington Library, the University of Maryland Special Collections and University Archives, and the Langson Library at UC Irvine. My thanks to all who helped, especially the Interlibrary Loan staff at UCI, who kept the books coming.

Important sources of institutional support must start with the Historical Society of Pennsylvania and the Library Company of Philadelphia, which provided a Balch Institute fellowship that allowed me to start this work. The UCI School of Humanities provided a course release so that I could devote time to finishing the book; the UCI Humanities Commons provided publication support. I also thank the following institutions for inviting me to make presentations that drew from parts of the book: Boston College, Bryn Mawr College, University at Buffalo (SUNY), University of Colorado Boulder, Duke University, Haverford College, Loyola Marymount University, University of Maryland at College Park, Penn State University, and University of Warwick. During these visits and others, I benefitted from conversation with Mary Pat Brady, Carrie Tirado Bramen, David Luis Brown, Rebecca Earle, Jennifer Harford Vargas, Adam Lewis, Anthony McFarlane, Owen Stanwood, and many other friends.

Over the years, certain people have stood out for nourishing me with encouragement and friendship. Susan Gillman is one of the most generous readers, and I have benefited from her mentorship. I thank Raúl Coronado for asking me to be part of a keynote panel at a Latina/o Studies conference. Ivy Wilson gathered a lively group at a remarkable seminar hosted by Notre Dame University. I also had the opportunity to work with a great group as part of C19, where I was inspired by the energy and brilliance of Karen Sánchez-Eppler, Hester Blum, and Dana Luciano. I thank the following for reading and conversation: Ralph Bauer, Leonard Cassuto, Chris Castiglia, Russ Castronovo, John M. González, Sean X. Goudie, Sandra Gustafson, Gordon Hutner, Carrie Hyde, Jennifer James, Laura Lomas, Joseph Rezek, Xiomara Santamarina, and Kyla Tompkins.

To all of the scholars who contributed to *The Latino Nineteenth Century*, your thinking about historical Latinidades raised important questions for me. Carmen Lamas's generosity in matters related to Cuban history and culture is remarkable. Emily García's work on Manuel Torres served as a guide for my second chapter. I learned a lot from Robert McKee Irwin, John Alba Cutler, José Aranda, Alberto Varon, Gerald E. Poyo, and Nicolás Kanellos. The Recovering the US Hispanic Literary Heritage Project conferences at the University of Houston have always been important gatherings providing an opportunity to interact with scholars. Thanks to my friends on the LatinX circuit (and visitors of famous houses), you're a hoot Marissa López, Maria Windell, and Claudia Milian.

Closer to home at UCI, former humanities dean Vicki Ruiz is a mentor and friend who has come through for me many times. Julia R. Lupton is a great colleague and helped me on many fronts. I was lucky to find my way into a couple of writing groups with Victoria Bernal, Erika Hayasaki, Lilith Mahmud, Laura Mitchell, and my good friend Arlene Keizer. Jennie Jackson is wonderful and a keeper of my narrative. Jerry Christensen, you will always be my chair. Martin Harries regularly reminds me that I can enjoy Crystal Cove without running six miles. Other colleagues whose work and engagement are nourishing include Sharon Block, Carol Burke, Richard Godden, Jayne Lewis, Laura O'Connor, Rachel O'Toole, R. Radhakrishnan, and James Steintrager. My Disneyland buddies Jami Bartlett and Jim Fujii! I still miss at UCI Elisa Tamarkin, who listened to me early on when I started talking about Filadelfia. I appreciate the opportunity to work with outstanding graduate students—some of them on to successful careers in and out of academia—including Erin Pearson, Cristina Rodríguez, Judith Rodríguez, Michelle Neely, Chris Varela, Ian Litwin, Annie Yaniga, Jennifer Geraci, Brian Flores, Dennis López, Brian Fonken, Erin Sweeney, Austin Carter, Brandon Wild, Sharon Kunde, and Jessica Collier. The Humanities Core Program survived my crankiness as I completed the manuscript, and I thank Tamara Beauchamp, Giovanna Fogli, Amalia Herrmann, Susan Morse, Dawn Jenison, Laura Swendson, and all the outstanding teachers and scholars in the program.

My brother Robert Lazo gave me a ride to college when I was a freshman. Thank you for everything, Bob! My sister, Martha Delucca Lazo, is a good friend and reminds me that I have a great job. Siempre llevo en mis pensamientos a mis hermanos Pancho Lazo y Marcelo Lazo. Por todo su amor a mi mama, Grace Pombar, que llegó a los 92. My nieces Bianca Martin, Vanessa Lazo, Kristine Lazo Carpenter, and Michele Cataruozolo are a source of enjoyment. A todos los Lazos en Puerto Rico: Javier, Dennis, VaneMo, Marcelo, Emmanuel y Paco. I draw a lot of strength from my sons, el alemán Gabriel Lazo and oh-so-wise Francisco Lazo. My deep affection to Amy DePaul for many great years. My appreciation to Corinne DePaul. I have wonderful friends, including Jack Galindo, George Ordonez, Ben Mis, "the Rev." Doug Harsch, John Troccoli, Kathy Bronstein, Sandi Thomas, Kevin O'Connor, and the Saturday morning crew. Special thanks to Chris Philipp.

My deepest gratitude and love go to the Trans-American Study Group, whose meetings were a tremendous source of cariño and intellectual energy for this project. Sara Johnson reminds me to unravel the contradictory politics of historical research (and is a generous host). To mi hermano Jesse Alemán, eres un great friend, feisty interlocutor, and hilarious colaborador. Keep it sassy! And most of all, I am grateful for an epistolary correspondence—papel, pluma, y tinta—with mi amiga poética, Kirsten Silva Gruesz, an awesome series editor, energetic colaboradora, and tough reader whose scholarship is an inspiration, Q.S.M.B.

A Note on the Spanish Language

Many of the materials analyzed in this book were written in Spanish. Unless otherwise noted, all translations are by me. In cases where materials published in other centuries are quoted, I have not modernized or corrected the original text, and thus the accent markings or punctuation may not correspond with contemporary Spanish-language orthography. I have avoided the use of *sic* unless it is absolutely necessary. In cases where a more recent edition of a text is cited, material is quoted as it appears in the newer edition. In translations, whenever possible, I have attempted to stick to the Spanish-language diction and sentence structure so as to provide a feeling for the source language and to allow non-Spanish speakers to trace the correspondence. This at times can lead to clunky English, or what some might call "bad translation" because it does not re-create the text in the target language. The charge of bad translation has an entire politics around it, as chapter 1 shows, and the point of offering translation here is to bring this material to readers who might otherwise not have access to the language in which something was written or published. Translation here is intended as support for the book's argument. In some cases, modern idioms and English-language phrasing have been added to create a flow in the prose.

Letters from Filadelfia

Introduction

The book went out as a letter. Opening with the intimate salutation "Amados paisanos mios" (My beloved countrymen), the prologue assumed a brotherhood of readers not only in the editor's country but also in other parts of the Americas. The year was 1821, and the book was titled *Ideas necesarias á todo pueblo americano independiente, que quiera ser libre* (Essential ideas for all independent American countries that want to be free). Published in Philadelphia, it contained translations into Spanish of US documents from the time of the revolution, including Thomas Paine's *Common Sense,* the Declaration of Independence, the Articles of Confederation, and the US Constitution.[1] The editor was Vicente Rocafuerte (1783–1847), a dashing intellectual who traversed the Atlantic and made his way around the Americas in search of ideas and political connections supporting the cause of independence (and his own business ventures). Best known historically as the second president of Ecuador, Rocafuerte sent out his collection of translations to make a case against monarchical rule while calling for changes in the economic protectionist policies that Spain's colonial government favored.

His audience was both particular and general. On the one hand, the "countrymen" were compatriots in Guayaquil, a territory that had declared independence from Spain on October 9, 1820, only months before the book's appearance. Rocafuerte said that he had felt joy in his heart upon learning that "the glorious standard of independence" waved over the shores of the mighty gulf of Guayaquil. On the other hand, a more general readership could be found in other countries fighting their own struggles against colonial rule. "All American countries" included those to the south of the United States moving from war toward independence. Jaime Rodríguez O. has shown that republicans in Mexico fighting against monarchical tendencies in their country had asked Rocafuerte to publish material against the establishment of a new form of monarchy in the wake of victories against Spanish colonial forces.[2] *Ideas necesarias* implicitly spoke to the future of

Mexico's governmental organization, and the book made its way to that country. A second edition was published in Puebla in 1823.[3]

But if Mexico was a place with potential readers, and if the book addressed itself to "all American countries," why did Rocafuerte open by invoking what sounds more like a local group, namely, countrymen in Guayaquil? Both the words chosen for the salutation and the deployment of an epistolary opening in the prologue suggest a recourse to intimacy. Rocafuerte wants to retain a domestic *fraternité* even as he publishes a document for an audience that is public throughout multiple countries. Thus the presumed intimacy (proximity) responds to the inverse: Rocafuerte is far from his readers. The book is small, 3¾" × 5", suggesting that it was meant to travel and circulate, perhaps in a pocket.[4] Rocafuerte seeks to cross the great distance from Philadelphia to Guayaquil and Mexico, releasing his book as a bridge between an enlightened hemispheric and transatlantic discourse and a local need for change in governmental organization. This is what scholars of epistolary fiction have noted as an important contradiction: the letter simultaneously records distance and seeks to build a bridge across it.[5] This contradiction, along with Rocafuerte's investment in translation, in this case a transfer from the English language to Spanish, makes his collection exemplary of books and periodicals published by writers from Spanish America who settled in or passed through Philadelphia in the early nineteenth century.

Philadelphia was the most important Spanish-language printing center in the early United States. This is a largely unknown dimension of a city that has long offered associations with US independence and the founding of the country. But as Spanish-language materials show, Philadelphia was an international center that influenced movements far beyond its local parameters and the US Revolution. Therefore, this book presents Philadelphia as a site where hemispheric political movements and Spanish-language writing were in dialogue with Anglophone US cultural and political currents. The city became a crucial intersection for Caribbean, South American, US, and European intellectual commerce and did so through the active participation of its printers. *Letters from Filadelfia* contributes to a view of American literature and print culture that includes one of the important languages of the United States, Spanish. In doing so, this book reminds us that Philadelphia and the revolution it came to represent were connected to major trends in world history. In their most exuberant moments, the writers in this study saw Philadelphia not as a national city but as an inspiration for the world.

Philadelphia emerged as a space of liberation for revolutionary intellectuals in the decades that saw Spain dislodged from most of its colonial holdings in the Americas. Starting in the 1790s, Philadelphia became a new home for Spanish Americans who went into exile after participating in revolutionary causes, and it also became a stopping point and travel destination for intellectuals seeking ideas and books to remake their home societies. Some settled in the city for years, engaging with local culture and institutions, and others passed through, pausing long enough to write or publish materials. With the word *Filadelfia* appearing often on title pages, dozens of Spanish-language titles were published in the city in the second and third decades of the nineteenth century, including political tracts, economic treatises, novels, poetry books, histories, periodicals, and texts that defy usual generic classification (e.g., a Masonic manual).

In important Spanish-language writings from the early nineteenth-century United States, Philadelphia became Filadelfia, a site of symbolic importance both for its political imagination and its economic vigor. If Philadelphia was the physical city, then Filadelfia was its Hispanophone imaginative potential. For Spanish American intellectuals, the city functioned as both a living lab of republicanism and a symbol of possible futures for the Americas. It was also a refuge and a place where they could print books that would have been prohibited in Spanish colonial territories. As early as 1799 the revolutionary Francisco de Miranda, who passed through Philadelphia to raise support for his revolutionary project, had written, "Dos grandes ejemplos tenemos delante de los ojos: la revolución americana y la francesa. Imitemos discretamente la primera; evitemos con sumo cuidado la segunda" (We have two great examples before our eyes: the American Revolution and the French. Let us imitate discreetly the first and avoid with the utmost care the second).[6] The Spanish *imitar* (to imitate) emerges in numerous Filadelfia writings and thus records the depth of the political exchange that took place in the late eighteenth and early nineteenth centuries.

By the time Rocafuerte published his collection, Filadelfia was intricately bound with a history of revolutionary writing, so that Rocafuerte notes enthusiastically in *Ideas necesarias:* "¿Y en dónde puedo encontrar recuerdos mas sublimes, lecciones mas heróicas, mas dignas de imitacion, y ejemplos mas análogos a nuestra actual situacion política, que en esta famosa Filadelfia?" (And where would I find memories more sublime, lessons more heroic and more worthy of imitation, and situations more analogous to our actual political situation than in the celebrated Philadelphia?).[7]

Thus he turns to historical interpretation with a purpose. Filadelfia could travel across distance, carrying forward constitutional theory. It offered not only debates about the federal form of government but also sites (situations) with potential for imitation. For Rocafuerte, Philadelphia was an important inspiration for urban organization, a model so vibrant that it could be translated to other places. And part of what he sought to convey through translation was the city's commercial strength, which would contribute to the history of Hispanophone US publications and motivate Philadelphia printers' participation in a world economy.

The imaginative Filadelfia was first and foremost a site of translation, in the sense of a transference from one person or place to another, that manifested itself in printed materials. The Spanish *traducir* also includes among its meanings *explicar* and *interpretar,* both references to interpretation, and certainly Filadelfia texts attempted to interpret US writing and republican forms of government.[8] Rocafuerte claimed Filadelfia because he sought to participate in what he and others conceived as a hemispheric American political tradition leading to independence. *Filadelfia,* appearing on the title page of Rocafuerte's book, leaves him exuberant, and he describes it as the model city of the model republic, "asilo de los oprimidos, centro de las luces, baluarte de la libertad, el genio de la independencia" (asylum of the oppressed, center of lights, bastion of liberty, spirit of independence).[9] This enthusiasm reflects Philadelphia's importance as a place where intellectuals on the run, sometimes from incarceration and even the penalty of death, could gather to forge plans for overthrowing Spanish colonialism in the southern Americas. Spanish Americans were by no means the first or only refugees from political turmoil who turned to the city during the revolutionary era that began in the late eighteenth century. As François Furstenberg has shown, Philadelphia in the 1790s was "awash with French people, French goods, and French culture" as a result of its economic and political entanglement with the French Atlantic.[10] Revolutions that spread from France to the Caribbean informed the military and political movements in various Spanish American colonial settings, and Philadelphia became an attractive destination for people from various European countries and the Caribbean.

Decades ago, the Venezuelan historian Pedro Grases characterized Rocafuerte and his fellow travelers as "el círculo de Filadelfia" (the Philadelphia circle) and situated the city alongside London as a crucial site for Spanish American independence.[11] Luis Leal and Rodolfo Cortina, considering the publication of the novel *Jicoténcal* (Philadelphia, 1826), called attention to the city as a "center of conspiracy."¹² Their phrase approximated the title of the fictional *Filadelfia: paraíso de conspiradores* (Philadelphia: Paradise of conspirators), by the twentieth-century Mexican novelist Martín Luis Guzmán.¹³ Nicolás Kanellos noted Philadelphia as one of the important sites for a community of Hispanophone writers in the early United States who smuggled their work "to fellow colonials in Cuba, New Spain, New Granada, and points south."¹⁴ Rafael Rojas has argued that materials from Philadelphia contributed to a republican pedagogy in Spanish America from which emerged strategies for building nation-states and "los primeros intentos de constitución de una ciudadanía moderna" (the first attempts to constitute a modern citizenry).¹⁵ As Rojas and others read it, the diffusion of republican principles across the Americas marked a rupture with a monarchical dynasty and a move toward representative government. More recently, scholars such as Raúl Coronado, Nancy Vogeley, and Emily García have focused on the importance of Philadelphia in relation to print and the production of US Spanish-language materials as well as to a nascent Latino community.¹⁶

The writing from early nineteenth-century Latino Philadelphia shows that the US Revolution was not only a national event but part of a hemispheric historical process that challenges the myth that Philadelphia was the first city of a monolingual Anglophone and monocultural Anglocentric US nation-state. The Spanish language circulated in North America before the borders of the present-day United States were conceived, and returning to *Filadelfia* today helps us develop a fuller picture of the multilingual dimensions of US history and culture. This study adds to significant scholarship on Philadelphia's lesser-known voices, which have drawn the attention of historians such as Gary B. Nash and Erica Armstrong Dunbar and literary critics such as Laura Rigal and Samuel Otter.¹⁷ "The city became the destination for waves of European immigrants, especially from Ireland, Germany, and England, for Africans escaping from the American South or taken from the Caribbean (in the 1790s, many planters fled to the city with their slaves from Saint Domingue during the hemisphere's other late-eighteenth-century revolution), and for those already in the North seeking a new space for freedom," writes Otter, who describes Philadelphia as a "city of porous boundaries" that created stories about the US nation, particularly about race and the belief in freedom.¹⁸ Otter does not include Spanish American connections to Philadelphia, but his emphasis on how writers narrated the city are important to this study. In addition, Otter's emphasis on race presents important questions about the way Hispanophone Filadelfia writers grappled with racialized hierarchies in their home countries even as they largely ignored the question of slavery in the United States, topics to which we return in succeeding chapters.

With Filadelfia as both an aspiration and a rhetorical opportunity, Spanish American writers were reluctant to criticize US conditions, instead celebrating the country as an anticolonial example of great success outside Europe. Emerging before the United States and Latin America were clearly divided along geopolitical lines, Filadelfia was conceived as a symbolic cityspace that harked back to its onomastic classical implications and offered the potential of organizing new countries with a promise of greater equality. Filadelfia precedes the type of North-South tensions that will become codified in retroactive readings of the Monroe Doctrine, in the emergence of an idea of Latin America as distinct from Anglo-America, and in José Martí's division between the United States and "nuestra América."[19] Writers who made their way to Filadelfia were attracted to principles of equality articulated in the documents that constituted the United States; however, aspirations to spread those principles did not always extend to a direct consideration of the large numbers of indigenous and slave populations in Central and South America and the Caribbean. Imbedded in Filadelfia, as will become clear in this book, is the failure of American governments north and south to extend notions of equality and economic opportunity to populations suffering from racial and gender hierarchies. Filadelfia evokes both potential and pitfall.

Spanish American intellectuals viewed Filadelfia favorably before the United States committed itself fully to imperialist aggression in the Americas and other parts of the world. While the war against Mexico leading to the acquisition of territories in 1848 and the blatant imperialism of 1898 made the US geopolitical posture in the Americas more lucid, the first three decades of the century presented a more ambivalent US attitude toward the southern Americas that at times veered into popular, though not necessarily governmental, support for revolutions against Spain. Caitlin Fitz, analyzing US–Spanish American interactions into the 1820s, writes, "It was an age of American revolutions, in other words, not only because Latin Americans were themselves casting off colonial rule, but also because so many people in the United States saw those efforts as a continuation of 1776."[20] The principles stated by President James Monroe in his 1823 speech to Congress, which would only later become known as the Monroe Doctrine, originally echoed a type of anti-Europeanism that could be found in the writings of the Filadelfia group. Who among the anticolonialist Filadelfia writers would argue with the proposition that "the American continents, by the free and independent condition which they have assumed and maintain, are henceforth not to be considered as subjects for future colonization by any European powers"?[21] Nevertheless, the phrase preceding that statement—"as a principle in which the rights and interests of the United States are involved"—betrays the nationalist impetus behind the US opposition to Europe in that speech. As critics have argued, it was only later, through a process of interpretation and restatement—and its association with later historical events—that Monroe came to be the imperialist "doctrine" of other centuries.[22] In the years preceding Monroe's address, Filadelfia intellectuals such as Manuel Torres were in conversation with his administration, advocating the recognition of new American republics emerging to the south. The hemispheric affiliation that emerges in Filadelfia writing was less about a misreading of US intentions than about a revolutionary historical moment in which the possibility of new nations emerging in South as well as North America led to a convergence of anticolonial perspectives. As Fitz notes, US residents looked south and saw a version of themselves—"republicans, revolutionaries, Americans"—at least until sectional strife and racial differentiation led to a North-South opposition both inside the United States and across the Americas.[23]

Keeping hemispheric political contexts at the forefront, *Letters from Filadelfia* is primarily a study of writing, most of it in Spanish, from the 1790s to the 1830s and takes its title from a confluence of epistolary apparitions that range from the Cuban poet José María Heredia's personal letter from Filadelfia to a variety of publications that claim an epistolary starting point.[24] Filadelfia publications include numerous books and other documents with the word *cartas* (letters) in their titles addressed to presumed public audiences across numerous countries. Among these are Manuel Lorenzo de Vidaurre's Philadelphia publication *Cartas americanas, políticas y morales* (American letters on politics and morals, 1823), two volumes of reflections on constitutional debates and philosophical questions intertwined with personal missives regarding an extramarital affair; the collection *Cartas de un americano sobre las ventajas de los gobiernos republicanos federativos* (Letters of an American concerning the advantages of federal republican governments, 1826), which was published in London and contains documents written in Philadelphia and New York; and Félix Varela's *Cartas a Elpidio* (Letters to Elpidio, 1835–38), a moral and theological treatise that he wrote during years working as a parish priest in New York. Some publications were not overtly labeled "letters" but were published with the epistolary agency evident in *Ideas necesarias.* Other books and publications that invoke *cartas* and epistolary documents provide a window into how personal relationships among an elite group motivated personal exchanges.[25]

Epistolary Effects

The epistolary overture conveys a sense of *Ideas necesarias* not as operating solely within a local print culture but rather as a communication that crosses national and colonial boundaries as well as languages. By opening with a salutation, Rocafuerte tempers the formality of decades-old constitutional US documents with a word, *amados,* that goes back to the Latin *amare,* whose lexical family includes the Spanish *amigo* (friend). Who are these beloved friends that make up part of the broader hemispheric address? Rocafuerte is speaking to a cadre of educated men interested in the collection's foundational US documents and their attendant political issues. While dispersed across a vast geographic territory, the audience is exclusive (like that of a personal letter) because its recipients are for the most part upper-class men.

Filadelfia brings us a convergence between personal letter writing and the print-culture world of communication through published *cartas.* The word *letters* implies both materials of higher learning in the humanities and any written or printed form of communication. It can also refer to signs without an apparent context; I use it as bilingual play on the Spanish *cartas* and *letras.* The latter shares with its English lexical partner a reference to alphabetic signs. Like *letters, letras* can also refer to literary culture or the study of written texts. The Spanish *carta* refers to an epistolary document as well as pieces of paper, maps, or even playing cards. With the English *letter* in dialogue with both *cartas* and *letras,* the connection to Filadelfia invokes a lettered terrain of analysis as well as a range of epistolary connections. In discussing the early modern period, Walter Mignolo associates epistolary communication with "a fundamental instrument of administrative control and government" in the process of colonization. In other words, the social interaction and intellectual exchange facilitated by private letters was part and parcel of humanism and its colonial investments.[26] In that vein, Angel Rama's "lettered city," to which we turn in chapter 1, also proposes the relationship of educated men to the Spanish colonial project. The use of the word *cartas* in the Filadelfia context is an indication of how the lettered battle waged by anticolonial writers was intertwined with European intellectual visions that supported colonial effects. Filadelfia writers had come of age under the aegis of the colonial system they sought to displace, and they were participants in the discursive formations of their historical period.²⁷

But if letters could be used as an instrument of colonial control, they also introduced in the wake of a hemispheric American Enlightenment the potential for crossing cultures, intellectual traditions, and languages. More generally, they became a way to foment anticolonial liberation. Elizabeth Hewitt has emphasized how epistolary communication registers "myriad social attachments" and "speculative maps." As we will see in chapter 1, a speculative map of Philadelphia helps emphasize distinctions between Europe and hemispheric America while positing connections among different parts of the Americas, the latter precisely through the work of highly educated intellectuals. "Any individual letter is located at a communicative node—not only at a point of intersection between particular correspondents, but also within the larger system of correspondence into which these readers and writers have entered," Hewitt writes.²⁸ That system involves not only printers but also reading publics, and in the case of Filadelfia, Spanish-language readers were spread across the Americas.

The important connection in Filadelfia between epistolary writing and published books called *cartas* is a result of the fruitful interaction between the different registers of personal communication and public address. The discourse of letters (*cartas*) signals a historical difference between, on the one hand, materials published in the late eighteenth and early nineteenth centuries, what I am calling *early Latino literature,* and, on the other hand, a notion that becomes dominant in the twentieth century, of literature as tied to particular genres of fiction, poetry, and drama. Scholarship on the history of Latino literature has shown the inadequacy of contemporary literary forms for considering much of the material from these revolutionary decades. And yet I retain a sense of *literature* (which can also mean printed matter) so as to avoid an imbalance in which some people have literature and others have writing.²⁹ It is important not to relinquish "literature" to a contemporary historical formulation that emphasizes certain literary genres in the twentieth century. A more capacious sense of literature comes closer to the notion of letters circulating in Filadelfia in the early nineteenth century; these materials call attention to the way the notion of literature changes historically. These points are not new to the field of early American literature, which has for decades included pamphlets, sermons, and autobiography in its corpus.

The use of the Spanish *carta* in many publications resulted from an Enlightenment fascination with epistolary claim as a way to approach a broad reading public. Voltaire's *Lettres philosophiques* (1734), Montesquieu's novel *Lettres persanes* (Persian Letters, 1721), or closer to the United States Hector St. John de Crevecoeur's *Letters from an American Farmer* (1782) were among thousands of books in various languages that deployed "letters" to name a heterogeneity of forms and to tackle a plentitude of topics. Here André Magnan's gloss on the heterogeneous use of "letters" in titles published in eighteenth-century France is instructive: "they consisted of works dealing with facts and ideas: in other words, they encompassed 'literature' as it was understood at the time, meaning history, knowledge, erudition, criticism and discussion ... Today, we would probably consider these writings 'essays' or 'manifestos,' but in the 18th century the word 'letter' was used uncritically throughout the larger discourse devoted to presentations or reviews."[30] Thus, letters provide not a form but a communicative address taking up various topics across a vast geographic space. More than a metaphor, letters (*cartas*) provided for Filadelfia writers a way to comprehend the transmission of ideas and conceptions of changing social structures.

The deployment of *cartas* in titles reflects a transatlantic and trans-American movement through print centers that included London, New York, and Mexico City; thus the notion of letters as traveling books is analogous to personal epistolary communication crossing various oceans. This circulation across vast geographic areas complicates a notion of the public sphere as tied to a nation-state or a local territory. Jürgen Habermas's influential work has been approached by critics who take up questions of transnational or international public spheres, a matter to which we will turn in chapter 3. For Filadelfia writers, what we might characterize as a public sphere was inextricable from trans-American and transatlantic circulation and the belief that writing for a public in another country (the sending of letters) was in and of itself part of a "cultural meaning of printedness," to use Michael Warner's phrase.[31] In this case, the meaning is informed by European political philosophy, struggles for independence from colonial rule, and the movement of intellectuals from various countries to Philadelphia. But the implications were also that a community of intellectuals was being formed across the Americas.

By fostering the exchange of ideas among an educated readership, epistolary writing facilitated an intimate (proximate) exchange. Dena Goodman writes about the French Enlightenment, "Correspondence made collaboration across Europe, and even across the Atlantic, possible and bound the citizens of the republic into a cooperative network of intellectual exchange.

Through correspondence, men of letters overcame distances that would otherwise have kept them from fruitful discussion and access to scholarly resources."[32] Goodman goes on to note that the formality of letter writing also expressed a respectful friendship that de-emphasized animosity and confrontation and mediated differences, even those of social rank. In other words, epistolarity presented a communications process that minimized the types of disagreement that would halt collaboration.

The important Enlightenment concepts of brotherhood and friendship informed these relationships. Within this domain, affection entered the personal letters and printed books in that these texts sought to unite political actors despite the distances separating a place of publication from its presumed readership. Given the importance of the foundation of new independent nations in these processes of communication and print culture, expressions of affection could cross into intimacy in that relationships came to express familiarity and a deep friendship. The shared ideas of Filadelfia letters stem from personal interaction as well as public proclamations. The importance of intimacy—here recall Rocafuerte's "Amados paisanos mios"—spoke both to a traversal of vast distances and to republican notions of affiliation leading to nationhood. While this was part of a shift from the hierarchies of monarchical social structures toward a more lateral organization of a republic, Filadelfia letters at times veer toward an extravagant emotional expression that suggests the problematics of intimacy. Lauren Berlant's work on sentiment and fantasy in culture as being intertwined with intimacy emphasizes how this process leads to notions of citizenship. In the following passage, Berlant suggest theoretical starting points for a consideration of intimacy: "To intimate is to communicate with the sparest of signs and gestures, and at its root intimacy has the quality of eloquence and brevity. But intimacy also involves an aspiration for narrative about something shared, a story about both oneself and others that will turn out in a particular way. Usually, this story is set within zones of familiarity and comfort: friendship, the couple, and the family form, animated by expressive and emancipating kinds of love. Yet the inwardness of the intimate is met by a corresponding publicness. People consent to trust their desire for 'a life' to institutions of intimacy."[33] In the case of Filadelfia letters, the spare signs are sometimes in the intrusion of words such as "Don querido mio de todo mi corazón" (Dearest beloved who holds all of my heart). The narrative they often produce is about a shared anticolonial storyline and a growing sense of hemispheric friendship. Berlant notes that the relationship between intimacy and public modes of identification is historical, and while the types of connections in Filadelfia letters are more representative of Habermas's account of a public sphere than of twentieth-century public modes of identification, the intimate address in many Filadelfia texts cannot be extricated from the development of a male-centered, masculinist, and even homosocial discourse. We turn to that in chapter 2 in an analysis of the trans-American elite that shows how Filadelfia letters are part of a gendered normativity influenced by social restrictions on women's travel to the United States. Among the contradictions of this trans-American process is a lettered domain that is both revolutionary and exclusive.

The types of "institutions of intimacy" that emerge in the early nineteenth-century trans-American context are mediated by translation and printed material, and that mediation is not available to all the presumed modern liberal subjects for which Filadelfia letters supposedly speak. In other words, intimacy is linked to an elite discourse. Lisa Lowe has invoked intimacy to foreground "liberalism as a project that includes at once both the universal promises of rights, emancipation, wage labor, and free trade, as well as the global divisions and asymmetries on which the liberal tradition depends, and according to which such liberties are reserved for some and wholly denied to others."[34] Thus Lowe uses intimacies as a reference to the circuits and connections of laboring people and commodity production that cut across continents. This analytic approach differs from my focus on elite expressions of brotherhood. The intention of Lowe's project is to consider residual and peripheral economic and social processes that are part of the condition of elite discourses (e.g., liberal individualism). In relation to Filadelfia letters, we might consider both racialized labor and the gendered division of labor in the southern Americas as factors sustaining the publication and circulation of material. Filadelfia shows how Spanish American hierarchies sustained the ability of elite writers to travel to and publish materials in the United States, plugging into a US-based print-culture context sustained by shifting forces in the book market. As chapter 1 shows, the production and circulation of commodities in Philadelphia are part and parcel of the publication of Spanish-language materials. Filadelfia becomes both an imaginative and a material site for intellectuals to gather and develop intimate conversations about anticolonial movements and the establishment of new governments.

The importance of intimacy emerges also in direct address, pointing to affective friendship and closeness, sometimes in homosocial ways. An example of this intimate turn appears when letters are signed with the initialism Q.S.M.B. (*que su mano besa*), which can be translated word for word as "who kisses your hand," or s.s.s. (*su seguro servidor*), which means "your trusted servant." More colloquially, and no less affectionately, these phrases approximate "yours truly," but they speak to a faith in epistolarity as a medium of affect and a desire to be close to someone. Rebecca Earle, considering how epistolary correspondence can provide insight into emotional relationships between men and women, notes that letter writing in the colonial "Spanish world was an art governed by established formulae, in which the correct heading and closing played no small part."[35] In Filadelfia materials, the intimacy of personal epistolary exchange is accompanied by the reality of a distance from material conditions, both in terms of correspondents being far from each other and in terms of the topic of *cartas*, especially books on political economy and republican theory, being distant from actual living conditions for people under colonial Spanish rule. While the letters did not go as far as outright expressions of love, they skirt the bounds of affectionate address, and those intimations make it into print.

The initialism Q.S.M.B. appears in the letters of the aforementioned *Cartas de un americano sobre las ventajas de los gobiernos republicanos federativos*, a book otherwise aiming for analytic detachment in its content. *Cartas de un americano* is presented as a collection of documents that "by coincidence" landed in the hands of the unnamed editor, a self-described "true, independent and free American." The book consists of nine letters, written in New York and Philadelphia between October 1825 and January 1826 and signed with an *X*, which emphasizes anonymity. The editor presents the letters as explicating "las teorías presentadas por los autores del Federalista, que sirven de base al sistema republicano federativo que se admira en Washington, y que los habitates de Méjico y de Goatemala han tenido el feliz acierto de introducir en su patria" (the theories presented by the authors of *The Federalist Papers*, which serve as the foundation for the republican federal system that is admired in Washington and that the inhabitants of Mexico and Guatemala have had the wisdom to introduce in their nations).[36] Despite their abstract bent, the letters close with lines such as "your affectionate friend and servant"—including the abbreviation *afmo* for *afectísimo* (most affectionally). As such, the kiss of a hand inserts what Berlant calls "zones of familiarity and comfort" in a book that seeks to bridge the distance from Philadelphia, New York, and London to readers in Spanish America. More than a mode of address, epistolary affect, whether in personal correspondence or print, spoke to the urgency of communicative attempts to touch people and change their minds so they would transform their local societies and do away with colonial rule.

Before Latinx: Early Latino Literature

X, the signee of the *Cartas de un americano,* presents himself as an anonymous writer who circulates an abstract notion of a republican political subject. In chapter 4 we look at the importance of anonymous publication for Filadelfia writers, who composed their work at a time when the notion of individual authorship was not as important as it is today. *X (equis)* offers a different notion of subjectivity than the recent invocation of the letter *x* to name a nongendered population through the term *Latinx.* While both uses of the letter *x* emerge from attempts to rise above the situated grounding of name and identity, the *X* in *Cartas* is part of a historical context, as we will see in chapter 4, connected to a trans-American and transatlantic public sphere. In this case, *X* is deployed as a substitute for the name of a political actor in a representative government, whereas the contemporary use of *Latinx* registers gender fluidity.

The distance from *X* in *Cartas de un americano* to *Latinx* points to the challenges of historical scholarship and literary history, which are always in dialogue and tension with the conceptual frames of the present. *Latinx,* which sometimes sounds like *Kleenex* but is also pronounced by joining *Latin* and the English *x,* has become an important label in debates about identification of the self and the group.[37] And yet deploying it historically calls forth the discomfort of potential anachronism and thus raises important questions about the terminology we use in historical recuperation. *Latinx* is an attempt at an inclusive term that bypasses the gendered *Latino/a,* which is often used in English as a noun rather than the Spanish adjectival forms (e.g., *Latino América* or *América Latina*). *Latinx* recognizes the crossing of gendered experiences and respects what Gloria Anzaldúa might call *los atravezados,* people who identify as neither one gender nor another, as well as those who are transgender or prefer a fluidity between the traditional notions of Latino and Latina. And yet using the gender-neutral term *Latinx* in the contemporary arena for all Latino/a/x people appropriates the power of those who choose to identify as Latinx because of their own queer sexuality or complicated relationship to gender. The tension between using *Latinx* as an umbrella ethnic label and using it as a label for cross-gender identity returns us to the problem of what term to use in the United States to unite people of Latin American descent under one banner for the purposes of civil representation.

For scholars working historically, the problem with *Latinx* is that it turns the Spanish *Latino/a* into an English neologism. In Latin America, some might consider *Latinx* an Anglophone imposition (or worse, language imperialism). Considering the historical disavowal of the Spanish language as a dimension of US culture (including in US states that are former colonial territories of Spain), the word *Latinx* linguistically situates Latinidades in the Anglo wing of the United States and de-emphasizes or even shuts down the trans-American and Spanish-language dimensions and movements of Latino culture. As always, Latinidades and their terminology are affected by personal identifications (or preferences) as well as by social contexts, a point other critics have made.

It is unclear whether *Latinx* will continue to circulate or go the way of the now passé *Latin@*, but I invoke *X* versus *Latinx* to make a literary historical claim for letters from Filadelfia as part of an early *Latino* literature. This is in part a recognition that letters are often written between and among men and are part of a homosocial discourse. The gendered *Latino* as an umbrella ethnic label is a misnomer, a masculine term that supposedly encompasses women and any other gendered identifications. Here it is used both to register the gendered dimensions of Filadelfia letters and also as a reminder that a misnomer can emphasize the impossibility of naming a very large and heterogeneous group of people. More importantly, the significant terms of identification shift across history. In his *Cartas de un americano*, X (the signatory) takes an explicit anticolonial and anti-European posture. This position is exemplary of Filadelfia writing and shows how early Latino literature is defined in part by articulations in relation to colonial processes. The opposition to empires, first Spain and later the United States, continues in the anti-imperialist writings of the mid- and late nineteenth century, including those of José Martí. In the twentieth century, post-1960s Latino/a/x literature is developed with the decolonial sensibilities and politics that accompany various Third World movements and particularly revolutionary governments in Cuba, Chile, and Nicaragua. This is not to say that everything included in Latino/a/x literature engages with the dynamics of empire, but resistance to colonialism and imperialism is a topos that opens the potential for analytic frames spanning the centuries; it also brings forward the importance of hemispheric connections to Latino/a/x studies.

The *X* in *Cartas de un americano* furthermore reminds us that Latino literary history, as different from national Latin American literary history, necessarily passes through the United States. What begins in the nineteenth century as a Spanish-language print-culture process attempting to connect US printing centers with Spanish America offers continuities with and breaks from post-1960s Latino/a/x literature, which consists predominantly of fiction and poetry written in English. Even as the forms of printed materials can be radically different, the connections relate to certain political sensibilities, such as the anticolonialism noted above, and the presence of the United States as a contested site (immigrant destination, print-culture center, exilic shore, or home with another home).

The historical interpretation of Latino literature presents a series of challenges related to the temporal index of the past within contemporary configurations of knowledge, particularly as they relate to notions of Latinos as a people. The claim to a Latino subject that appears across the centuries, which motivates anthologies such as *The Norton Anthology of Latino Literature*, misses important economic conditions and international sociohistorical shifts that are part and parcel of the printed materials. Although the nineteenth-century historical record suggests commonality among populations through terminology such as *Spanish American, Hispanoamericano,* or *Latinoamericano,* that century gives us only gestures toward the type of pan-national and pan-ethnic US-based subjectivity of the type regularly associated with contemporary Latino/Hispanic communities. Much recent scholarship attempts to navigate the historical difference of earlier centuries by offering terms that complicate the notion of a Latino subject, including *errant* Latino, *almost* Latino, *migrant* Latinos, or a Latino *continuum*.[38]

Latino was not a term in circulation in Filadelfia, and the notion of an entity called Latin America emerges later in the nineteenth century in relation to what comes to be called *la raza Latina*.[39] Which is to say that the past offers overtures toward common experiences but not toward a transhistorical identity even if the aspiration toward a common terminology uniting populations goes back centuries. In terms of self-identification, the men who made their way to Philadelphia most often referred to themselves as *americanos* or *americanos españoles* and, depending on the year and context, in relation to their home countries. As John Charles Chasteen has noted, patriots "constructed a binary divide separating all americanos, on the one hand, from *europeos* (Europeans, meaning European-born Spaniards)," thus marking a pivotal shift in the history of independence movements in the Americas.[40] For example, Manuel García de Sena addresses his compatriots as "AMERICANOS ESPAÑOLES" in two epistolary prefaces that precede his books of translation, to which we turn in the next chapter.[41] Along this line, Anglophone writers of the period would have characterized the Filadelfia group as "Spanish American," as when William Cullen Bryant, in his review of the novel *Jicoténcal,* refers to the book as part of "the literature of Spanish America."[42] I use *Spanish American* in reference to writers in this study and the territories from which they come, but I retain the term *Latino* in reference to texts (literature/letters) and situate these texts within literary historical trajectories. In other words, *Latino* in this case is not a noun but an adjective referring to politically progressive movements, speaking contextually, from the southern Americas to the United States.

Among the challenges of reading Latino literature before the 1960s is excavating contexts that can provide insight into the content of materials, whether letters or published pages, that differ in important ways from a twentieth-century corpus of Latino/a/x literature (predominantly English-language novels, poems, and plays). The types of exchanges that emerged in Filadelfia letters led to a multiplicity of textual production, a variety of writing that engaged with a range of topics, from political organization to religious conceptions. In terms of print forms, these included pamphlets, economic treatises, translations, periodicals, and gift books. Novels and poetry books also appear, but they are part of an eclectic mix of texts, among them Juan Germán Roscio's captivating *El triunfo de la libertad sobre el despotismo* (The triumph of liberty over despotism, 1817), an argument for the right of popular sovereignty using the Latin Vulgate, to which I turn in chapter 3. Most of these texts were produced by intellectuals involved in political movements rather than writers in the twentieth-century sense of the term. In Filadelfia, a writer could be the future president of a nation-state or a priest.

Excavating the US roots of letters from Filadelfia tells only part of the story. These texts are also part of intellectual traditions, political movements, and local concerns in other countries. This is particularly apparent in some of the writing by Cubans, who continue to grapple with a colonial government in the 1820s after many countries in Spanish America have declared independence. Thus early Latino literature calls for interdisciplinary approaches that delve into the histories of specific Latin American countries and their colonial antecedents. Filadelfia can become an opportunity for opening an avenue of research rather than offering a single narrative that closes interpretive possibilities. As I argue in chapter 5, Filadelfia complicates the separation between US American studies and Latin American studies, thus opening archives to new routes for research.

From American Literature to Filadelfia Letters

Filadelfia letters come to us today as epistolary communications about idealistic notions of hemispheric and universal rights. They precede the ossification of nation-states in the Americas in the mid-nineteenth century; they circulate before the United States plays its hand overtly as an imperialistic power; and they present conceptions of political organization that are often implicitly about men. Letters from Filadelfia engage in intellectual conversations that cross vast geographic ranges; thus, following Edward Said, I would say that a Filadelfia text is "connected both to its specific historical and cultural situations as well as to a whole world of other literatures and formal articulations."[43] Said here is talking about a kind of intellectual work that is broad in scope and speaks to audiences across geographic and temporal settings. For Said, engaging across cultures is a way to create types of *worldliness* that allow works to enter a broad conversation. In this case, that worldliness is related to the utopian longings of revolutionary projects. While I agree with Raúl Coronado that texts in the discursive war against Spain allowed for imaginative possibilities that did not have to lead to nationalism and a revised hierarchy of domination, I focus on the fact that abstract tendencies in political projects and an emphasis on American republican organization did not address sufficiently power hierarchies that affected the very people who were supposed to be liberated.[44] In chapter 2, I emphasize that the Filadelfia circle was part of an *elite*. I do so not to offer a deterministic economic reading or overlook the way migration to the United States for these intellectuals was often the result of hardship and political danger but rather to approach the contradictions inherent in a discourse of independence. Those contradictions emerge not only in and through intellectual history but also in the materiality of print culture as it emerges in a specific site.

The economic underwriting of Rocafuerte's book, for example, is inextricable from the production of his print epistolarity. Rocafuerte traveled to the United States in part to publish *Ideas necesarias*. He probably paid for a run of the book from his prodigious personal coffers. Later in life, Rocafuerte described the process in a memoir: "Yo fui a los Estados Unidos a publicar un opúsculo que compuse y lleva por título *Ideas necesarias*" (I went to the United States to publish a tract that I composed and is titled *Ideas necesarias*). The sentence is direct in its claim to a definite agency that displays tremendous psychological, intellectual, and economic resources.

The Spanish *compuse* (compose) can refer to the writing or editing of a book, and in printer's lingo it means to set type. Rocafuerte makes it sound straightforward, a part of his work as a man of letters.

Rocafuerte can afford to go from one country to another, and thus the book is a product of socioeconomic relations in his territorial home of Guayaquil, where his family of birth had commercial and political power. Rocafuerte's family on both his mother's and his father's sides were leaders in the military and administrative colonial governance and had the type of resources that sent the young Vicente to be educated in Spain and France, where he studied multiple languages and read Rousseau's *Social Contract,* Montesquieu's *The Spirit of the Laws,* and Guillaume Thomas (Abbé) Raynal's *The Revolution of America.*[45] Aided by inherited wealth, Rocafuerte developed his "essential ideas" in a broad political and educational space. We see in Rocafuerte's book how a trans-American print economy, including the personal resources to publish a book and the availability of printers in the United States, is intertwined with multinational effort to reach readers.

Filadelfia letters challenge the fields of American literature, Latin American literature, and US Latino literature. For American literature, the recognition that Spanish-language cultures of print were in operation in the United States during much of the nineteenth century complicates an excessive monolingualism that has traditionally defined the field. When one of the centers of US history and culture becomes Hispanicized as Filadelfia, we enter into a realm that allows for a consideration of multiple points of analytic entry. Considering print culture that moves across the Americas, a Spanish-language anticolonial public sphere emerges in the early nineteenth century that differs in important ways from the Anglophone texts that presented a local iteration of the US republic. For Latino studies, Filadelfia letters offer an example of texts in Latino literary history that are intertwined with hemispheric movements and supranational concerns. The spatial dimensions of these texts, often sent to audiences in other countries, work against the notion of a single destination or national closure. Letters from Filadelfia offer a view of a print network that is connected to the multiple economic and print-culture conditions motivating textual formation in the early nineteenth century. To frame these as Latino literature is to recognize the capacious, contradictory, and insufficient dimensions of the term *Latino,* which is less descriptive than it is a way to convey a set of associations or concerns. The inadequacy of the term *Latino* is indexed through the ongoing reformulations, most recently in the term *Latinx*.

Trans-American movements do not offer an alternate field of study but rather a set of conditions that challenge a nationally bounded field. In past decades, complicated trans-American relationships were not always admitted into a view of Latino literature that sought to emphasize minority populations in the United States. Juan Bruce-Novoa, for example, distinguished between US-based minority writers and Latin American travelers, among whom he included José Martí: "There is a centuries-old tradition of Hispanic writing done in and about the United States, written by Latin Americans deeply concerned with the implications of the U.S.A. and who viewed the country and its people from the perspective of sojourners. Moreover, they usually wrote for readers in their home countries. The literature which concerns us here [in his study] was written by permanent residents of this country, insiders in spite of being an ethnic and linguistic minority often excluded from the mainstream; and their literature is, for the most part, directed at and read by other permanent residents of the United States."[46] Bruce-Novoa's points are not without merit, as he draws important distinctions in terms of perspective, audience, and context. But the past offers complicated scenarios in which certain distinctions, including that between insider and outsider, are not evident; nor is it always clear who counts as a resident.

For Latin American studies, Filadelfia challenges the geographic demarcation and the reading of figures in terms of nationalist histories. As Carmen Lamas has argued, historical Latinidades are often on a continuum that suggests different types and degrees of connection to Latin America and thus do not allow for an easy severance between North and South America.[47] The resources of Filadelfia writers sometimes allowed them to adopt the cultural and publication capital that we might associate with insiders, and their residency in the United States was sometimes lengthy. Thus they formed part of another tradition: one of fluidity in movement and publication across the Americas intertwined with the trans-American circulation of texts, transatlantic intellectual currents, and economic world systems.

The interconnections presented by Filadelfia are at odds with the type of dualistic thinking that has structured fields of study in relation to the Americas: the presumed divide between the United States and Latin America, a separation that has become increasingly reflective of the militarized

US-Mexico border. Both Latin American studies and (US) American studies developed in tandem with Cold War academic-area studies that divided the world into geographic regions with supposed cultural and historical commonality. The division valorizes two archives of purported knowledge, and its dualism reinforces a historical distinction both racial and cultural between Anglo- and Hispanic America. The division sometimes closes off potential analytic frames, so that when US scholars use shorthand references to the early decades of the nineteenth century they invoke "the early republic" or "early American republic" (United States); it appears that historical events in the United States moved solely or primarily along national lines and in distinction to a different set of events called the "wars of independence" (Latin America). But in the last two decades, literary scholars and historians have sought to shift the frame of discussion toward hemispheric connections and comparative approaches.[48] The importance of trans-American movement for nineteenth-century Latino textual production cannot be overstated. As will become clear in succeeding chapters, the production and circulation of letters from Filadelfia move far beyond local and national politics and are intertwined with international economic conditions and intellectual movements.

Filadelfia letters are the product of a conjunction between the collective political aspirations of individual actors such as Rocafuerte, discourses of revolution and independence, and the robust commerce of print in Philadelphia. Trade between US cities and Spanish American territories grew significantly in the first decades of the nineteenth century, and books were not exempt. Philadelphia became part of a Hispanophone system of publication that included production across the Atlantic (London) and the Americas (Mexico City and sites with new presses). A Hispanophone system gestures toward Immanuel Wallerstein's "world-system," which does not necessarily encompass the globe but rather implies activities outside or before the nation-state.[49] Wallerstein writes, "We are dealing with a spatial/temporal zone which cuts across many political and cultural units, one that represents an integrated zone of activity and institutions which obey certain systemic rules."[50] World-systems theory, committed as it is to an interdisciplinary and multiregional focus on capital accumulation and production processes, helps us make sense of the investment of US printers and publishers in the international movement of books that might otherwise be read primarily as the result of intellectual currents. As we will see in chapter 1, the purchasing power of wealthy Spanish American intellectuals allowed for the commissioning of printing in Philadelphia at a time when publishers and booksellers were developing a Hispanophone book trade partly connected to language learning.

The five chapters that follow emphasize tensions between a local site (Philadelphia) and trans-American movements, between individual writers and discursive formations, and between an approach that emphasizes the United States (Latino literature) and the necessity of considering the various contexts of trans-American print culture. Methodologically, the book seeks historically specific conditions, particularly in relation to print, while emphasizing the type of close reading of documents that is often associated with literary interpretation. Because the Filadelfia circle as a group is not particularly well known, the biographical background of writers offers both a look at print-culture processes and a view of the interconnection between economic conditions and discursive formations in textual production. The first two chapters present the historical panorama, the what and why of Filadelfia and the who of the Spanish American intellectuals who contributed to Filadelfia letters. Chapter 1 introduces the print culture of Filadelfia and shows how a Hispanophone system was the result of hemispheric and transatlantic capitalist processes that gained momentum with the wars of independence against Spain and the political actions of Spanish American intellectuals. The importance of translating concepts across languages in relation to political movements is developed through a reading of Manuel García de Sena's translation work. Chapter 2 turns to the personal fortunes of the trans-American elite, not to emphasize individual experiences but as an indication of how their work was tied to macroeconomic forces. The chapter shows the role of class and educational privilege in the formation of a homosocial and racialized exclusive brotherhood and interprets selected texts in light of these economic considerations. Focusing on Manuel Torres and Félix Varela, this chapter presents the term *trans-American elite* as an alternative to other descriptions, such as *creoles,* and seeks "to abolish the lines between economic, political, and sociocultural modes of analysis."[51]

The next two chapters together provide an overview of the range of politically oriented materials printed in Filadelfia, from the periodical *El Mensagero Semanal* to the pamphlet *El amigo de los hombres* (1812). These chapters track the various uses of print to develop a trans-American public sphere that was simultaneously revolutionary in its claim of sovereignty in the people rather than in monarchs and insufficiently attentive to racialized and gender hierarchies of the Americas. Chapter 3 considers the importance of print to the building of a public sphere that crossed the Americas and the Atlantic. Focusing on the religious argument in *El triunfo de la libertad sobre el despotismo,* the chapter shows how intellectuals entered various debates, including that on the Bible's relationship to monarchy and what counts as poetic achievement, to offer a liberatory print model that was trans-American and transatlantic. As part of this process, writers situated sovereignty within an imagined demos that did not necessarily overlap with specific countries; chapter 4 shows how changing notions of sovereignty led to the development of an abstract political subject reflected in anonymous publication. Focusing on a variety of pamphlets as well as on the anonymously published novel *Jicoténcal,* the chapter argues that anonymity, although in keeping with an Enlightenment discourse of equality and brotherhood, helped promote an abstract notion of the people that did not account for social hierarchy.

The final chapter focuses on the work of Fray Servando Teresa de Mier and Manuel Lorenzo de Vidaurre, two colorful figures whose publications break out of the limitations imposed by the divisions of contemporary academic fields and disciplines. This chapter presents the notion of archival dislocation to show how important it is to trace the movements of trans-American intellectuals outside the spaces of inquiry that structure academic fields and that we can associate with a bounded archive. Most importantly, the final chapter presents two examples of dislocated letters, one a love letter and the other a set of letters form a dying man, to argue that interdisciplinary, trans-American research should not be contained by a specific delimited academic vein. Filadelfia, as will become apparent, offers opportunities for unforeseen routes of scholarly inquiry. So let us begin with Filadelfia as it was conceived by some of the prominent figures of early Latino letters: a city that was at once an example of republican success and a translatable model for countries in the Americas.

1

La Famosa Filadelfia

By the 1820s, Philadelphia was known among revolutionary intellectuals from Spanish America as "la famosa Filadelfia," a symbol of American liberation from European colonialism and a city full of printers that could help produce pro-independence publications. When José María Heredia—poet, conspirator, and trans-American intellectual—sent a letter to his uncle describing a walk through "la famosa Filadelfia" in 1824, Heredia was self-conscious of repeating certain conventions: "Mil veces habrás oído decir que es una de las ciudades más regulares del mundo, y es verdad" (A thousand times you might have heard it said that it is one of the most orderly cities in the world, and it is true).[1] Other Spanish Americans had indeed come before him, including the Venezuelan Manuel García de Sena, who had translated and published Thomas Paine's writing in 1811; the Mexican priest Fray Servando Teresa de Mier, who had published several titles in 1821; and the political theologian Juan Germán Roscio, who had escaped from prison and published the impressive *El triunfo de la libertad sobre el despotismo* (The triumph of liberty over despotism) in 1817. Vicente Rocafuerte had also used the phrase *la famosa Filadelfia* in his *Ideas necesarias á todo pueblo americano independiente* (1821). *Famosa,* lexically close to *famous* but perhaps closer in translation to *celebrated,* shows that Philadelphia had become an important political location in the ongoing Spanish American wars for independence; the books and pamphlets coming out of the city showed that it was a Spanish-language print-culture hub.

Spanish Americans viewed Filadelfia as a trans-American city because they saw it not primarily as a national (US) site but rather as a model that could inspire other republican urban centers across the hemisphere. While printers facilitated the publication of texts that could circulate in a public sphere, the city itself offered cultural and social institutions, commercial and financial activity, and approaches to governance that could be adopted in new countries. Because of Philadelphia's association with the drafting of the Declaration of Independence and the US Constitution, revolutionary writing and urban topography became intertwined in the imagination of Spanish American intellectuals, who saw the city as an inspiration for the world. The attention to la famosa Filadelfia shifted the discourse of independence toward the Spanish language and offered a new translocal horizon of anticolonial work.

The dissemination of Filadelfia as a representative city for all of the Americas was an attempt to invert the colonizal gaze of European empires that had seen American territories as colonial outposts since the sixteenth century. Spanish American travelers, exiles, and immigrants promoted Filadelfia as a rival to Europe and a model whose revolutionary history could be emulated. "This great city founded by William Penn, inhabited at first by a few Quaker families, today has the appearance of an illustrious European city, with greater beauty and much greater hope for prosperity," wrote the Mexican politician and journalist Lorenzo de Zavala in his *Viaje a los Estados Unidos del Norte de América* (Journey to the United States of North America, 1834).[2] As we will see, Zavala was not the only one to compare Philadelphia favorably with European capitals.

Considering Filadelfia's trans-American print culture and symbolism, this chapter depicts how the work of publication—which included composition, printing, and circulation—cut across multiple countries. Philadelphia, which was home to dozens of printers in the early nineteenth century, offered an alternative to the censorship and strict licensing controls on printing in Spanish colonial sites. The participation of Philadelphia printers in Spanish-language publishing was an offshoot of Philadelphia's evolution as a print center. The city's printers and booksellers increasingly approached their business not solely in relation to local readers but as a commercial process that cut across the economies of North and South America and other areas. We begin with a panorama of Spanish-language publishing in early nineteenth-century Philadelphia. In the second part of the chapter, we turn to Philadelphia's symbolic implications outside the United States. Letters about Filadelfia show how Spanish American intellectuals framed the city as representing political and commercial principles that could influence new countries, even as they papered over social problems and racial politics, including slavery, in the United States. For an example of the types of materials emerging from Filadelfia, we turn to Manuel García de Sena's *La independencia de la Costa Firme justificada por Thomas Paine treinta años há* (The independence of the Spanish Main justified by Thomas Paine thirty years ago, 1811), which offered translations of Thomas Paine and other US revolutionary-era documents in an attempt to influence political movements in Venezuela and elsewhere. García de Sena's book calls attention to the important politics of translation across the Americas in early Latino literature. But first let us begin with a print job that registers the growing investment of Philadelphia printers in Spanish-language publishing.

Spanish-Language Books and "Men of Capital"

On July 24, 1821, about the time Rocafuerte was making his way to the United States to publish *Ideas necesarias,* the Philadelphia printer Thomas H. Palmer printed pages of a Spanish translation of Thomas Paine's *The Rights of Man* (1791) for Mathew Carey's publishing house. According to the house's account books, Carey paid Palmer $95.76 for printing "forms," the body of type that had been set, and went on to make up pages of the book, which was published by "Matias Carey é Hijos" (Mathew Carey and sons) as *El derecho del hombre* (1821).[3] This small detail of the workings of the Carey publishing house is important because it depicts the commercialization of Spanish-language materials in the early United States and displays the publisher's imperative to capitalize on Spanish-language books. The Carey house contracted a job to Palmer in order to see the book into print—with a view to markets outside the country. It was neither the first nor the only time that Carey produced Spanish-language books. While Rocafuerte and intellectuals in Mexico envisioned the printing and sending of *Ideas necesarias* as an epistolary intervention in the political changes taking place in the Americas, Carey saw an opportunity for international profit in such publications. As an example of this thrust into other markets in the Americas, *El derecho del hombre* was among materials in a cache of Spanish-language books sent by the Carey house to Mexico in 1822 via an agent whom Nancy Vogeley has called a "bookrunner."[4]

The production of Spanish US writing was not isolated from changes in the US book market in the first three decades of the nineteenth century. Carey's translation of *The Rights of Man* provides us an opportunity to consider changes in the market that are connected to the commercial potential of Spanish-language materials. To trace these changes, we need to consider not only the increase in the number of Spanish-language titles that appeared in the 1820s United States but also the change from subscription publishing toward market investment; we can do so by comparing Carey's 1821 Paine translation with an earlier publication by its translator, Santiago Felipe Puglia, an immigrant from Italy who had ushered in Spanish-language publishing in Philadelphia decades before with a self-authored book. In 1794, Puglia had published his *El desengaño del hombre* (Man undeceived), a 257-page energetic argument along philosophical, political, and religious lines against divine sanction for monarchs that was clearly aimed at readers in Spanish America. As Emily García has noted, "To *desengañar* is to un-deceive, and this is Puglia's main goal in the work: to try to render Spanish and Spanish American populations 'undeceived' of their allegiance to the monarchy, to bring his readers to the light of reason."[5] Probably the first Spanish-language book out of Filadelfia against Spanish colonial rule, it was banned by the Spanish Inquisition, a point to which we will return.

El desengaño del hombre was a result of sponsored publication rather than an investment in a product that could sell on the market. Unlike Carey's 1821 Paine book, *El desengaño del hombre* followed a subscription-based publication approach. A year before its printing, Puglia had circulated a call for subscribers by publishing a pamphlet with the following appeal:

> The Author conceives that the greater part of the Friends of Liberty in this country having no knowledge of the Spanish, will become Subscribers merely to encourage the publication, without wishing to have all the copies they may subscribe for. . . . The generous light of Democracy which eminently shines forth in the American Stars, will in the publication of this work find a favourable opportunity of shewing how inclined it is to the propagation and support of the Rights of Man.[6]

By asking people who themselves probably could not read Spanish to subscribe to this book, Puglia was in effect requesting a donation for a publication that would be distributed in places with Spanish readers. This attempt to circulate outside the United States was a manifestation of a process that I have characterized as epistolary.

The publication conditions of Puglia's *El desengaño del hombre* show not only that other intellectuals in the city shared a sense of "cause" in the Americas; more to the point here, the call for subscriptions demonstrates that the book's publication was partly the result of sponsorship. Puglia's call was handed out on Philadelphia street corners, and it took several months before Puglia could collect enough money to persuade someone to print the book.[7] When five hundred copies of the book were published, the list of subscribers included "Alexandro Hamilton," "Tomas Jefferson," "P. Freneau," and "one true friend of liberty and independence for all nations who paid for 130 copies."[8] That true friend, Puglia revealed later, was Edmond-Charles Genet, a.k.a. "Citizen Genet," French ambassador to the United States during the French revolutionary period. It was the antimonarchical warrior Genet, according to Puglia, who made the publication possible.⁹ Through his subscription book, Puglia ushered Spanish into the languages of the revolutionary United States, to the consternation of Spanish colonial authorities.

The subscription-based model, not uncommon in the US colonies, was tied to the dominant local language, making a Spanish-language subscription book all the more eventful. Subscription allowed authors and printers to collect money to cover the costs of printing up front and helped gauge interest in a particular work. Some proposed books never made it into print owing to a lack of subscriptions. In *Printers and Men of Capital,* an impressive study of Philadelphia's book market from the late eighteenth to the early nineteenth century, Rosalind Remer argues that the new century ushered in a change from local printer-based publication of books, including subscription publishing, to a new, more diversified production process in which publishing houses invested in books but did not print those books, even as they sought markets in other parts of the United States.¹⁰ Publishers who committed to a project financed the books (paper and printing) through credit networks. And this approach became linked to expanding markets. "By selling books to the countryside, publishers hoped to relieve the financial pressure of overstocked shelves while acting to unify the growing nation through the distribution of the printed word," Remer writes.¹¹

For Spanish American intellectuals in the United States, the shift away from publication driven by subscription meant that certain books could move into world markets rather than having to be financed by those who wanted them printed. Or to put that another way, self-publication gave way to the marketplace of letters. Two examples that demonstrate the shift from self-publication to printing for profit are books by Valentín de Foronda and Manuel Torres, published thirteen years apart. Foronda's *Carta sobre lo que debe hacer un principe que tenga colonias á gran distancia* (Letter regarding what a prince should do when he possesses colonies at a great distance, 1803) is a product of coterie publishing with connections to the American Philosophical Society. Foronda's *Carta* does not include information about publisher or printer, and the title page says only "Philadelphia: ANO DE MDCCCIII."¹² It was published anonymously. I refer to coterie publishing because it appears that Foronda or someone else paid for the run, which was done by a lower-end print shop. Foronda's "letter," which looks like a pamphlet, is printed without type for the letter *s*. In its place, the printer used the letter *f*, known as a "descending s" or a "long s." By 1803, the long *s* was only being used by printers who could not afford to modernize with new type. Generally speaking, this means that Foronda went to a lower-quality printer.

Foronda's *Carta,* which delves into political economy, precedes by several years instances when a publication on economics and the Spanish American colonial setting would be attractive to a for-profit publisher. In 1816, Manuel Torres's *An Exposition of the Commerce of Spanish America,* a book clearly appealing to commercial interests, was both printed *and* published by George Palmer, whose shop on Chestnut Street also printed other Spanish-language titles. We turn to that book and to Torres, an important editor and activist who helped build a pro-independence intellectual circle in Filadelfia, in the next chapter. The point here is that the exposition's connection to the Palmer house showed that intellectuals had greater access to a budding publishing industry in 1816. The difference between Foronda's letter and Torres's exposition illustrates the shift from private printing to publishing for a market of readers interested in Spanish America. Potential readers of Torres's book would have included merchants and ship captains trading in Spanish American ports.

By the 1820s there was a Spanish-language print culture in the US Northeast, supported in part by increasing economic trade with the southern Americas and growing interest in the history and culture of Spanish America. Scholars have studied different aspects of the growing interest in the Spanish language, Spanish-language publishing, and Spanish American history occurring on both sides of the Atlantic. Focusing on intellectual history, Iván Jaksić has shown that starting in the 1820s US academics such as the Harvard professor George Ticknor and the historian William H. Prescott turned to the "Hispanic world" and developed the antecedents of fields of study that would later focus on Spain and Latin America. This development, he argues, was intricately connected to efforts to shape US national identity in contradistinction to Spanish "national character." Richard Kagan has argued that in the 1820s negative associations related to the Black Legend gave way to a romantic view of Spain that included associations with the picturesque. Nancy Vogeley has characterized the rise of publications out of Philadelphia about Spanish America in both English and Spanish as a "Hispanic vogue" tied to a greater commercial and diplomatic interaction. Mar Vilar García has studied the growing interest in Spanish-language instruction in the nineteenth-century United States.[13] Rather than focusing on the US gaze and retaining the US–Latin American divide in scholarly approach, I emphasize the intricate intersection of, on the one hand, conditions for a for-profit print culture in Philadelphia and, on the other hand, the political goals of trans-American intellectuals who were drawn to Philadelphia. The work of these intellectuals moved in tandem with changes in the commerce of Philadelphia printing and political changes brought on by anticolonial battles in Spanish America. As a result of this activity, we see the emergence of early Latino literature in a northeastern US city.

The printing of some Philadelphia books coincided with the opening of new markets and competition among publishers, including the Carey house's attempt to make inroads into various markets in a world system of publishing. For the Carey house, expanding markets came to include not only other parts of the United States but also Canada and various international sites—and thus the firm's interest in the Spanish-speaking world.[14] Mathew Carey (1760–1839), an immigrant from Dublin, was one of the most important publishers in early Philadelphia, putting out eleven hundred books in the period 1785–1821 (the years when he ran the firm). These included Bibles, atlases, and novels; among the latter was the first US edition of Susanna Rowson's *Charlotte Temple,* in 1794.[15] Carey's political views, and particularly a dislike for England, drew him into the battle between the Federalists and Jefferson, with Carey publishing several titles in support of the Jeffersonian side. For decades, Carey also published books in languages other than English, including Greek and Latin texts for study. "Foreign language books were usually printed for use in schools, and Carey published many grammars, dictionaries, and study texts in not only the classical languages but also French and Spanish," James Green writes.[16] For example, in 1811 Carey published the spelling and grammar book *El director de los niños* (A guide for children), as well as a pocket-size edition, *El pequeño director de los niños, para aprender á deletrear y leer* (A small guide for children learning to write and read). The latter contains thirty-six pages and measures $3\frac{1}{2}'' \times 5''$, small enough to fit in a pocket. The full title tells us that it offers a "Metodo para facilitar los progresos de los niños quando se mandan por la primera vez á la Escuela" (method to help children progress when they are sent for the first time to school). The book opens with instructions on learning the Spanish alphabet and includes illustrations; toward the end, the book shifts to religious topics, including "El padre nuestro" (the Our Father) and "El persignarse" (making the sign of the cross), and concludes with the Ten Commandments. It was Mathew Carey who registered the book in the district court, suggesting that this was first and foremost a moneymaking effort.

For Philadelphia's printers, the 1820s brought enthusiasm for international markets and multilingual books. During that decade, the Carey house passed from the aging Mathew to his son, Henry, who took on as partner his brother-in-law, Isaac Lea, and publications began appearing with imprints such as Carey & Sons and Carey & Lea. The younger publishers embraced participation in a world system of books and included Spanish-language titles, extending credit to booksellers in other parts of the Americas. In 1821 Carey saw fit not only to translate and publish Paine's *The Rights of Man* but also to put out a new edition of Puglia's 1795 subscription book, *El desengaño del hombre*. The 1821 and 1822 account books for the firm show that the Carey house was trying to set up a regular export business with Chile, Brazil, Puerto Rico, Haiti, and "Buenos Ayres," among other destinations in the Americas and Asia. Shipments of books and other merchandise were listed as "Adventures" in the accounts books, such as "Adventure to Brazil," and consigned to particular merchants abroad.[17] In 1824 the Carey house sent a representative to Europe and arranged for the Philadelphia store to receive a large shipment of books in French, Italian, and Spanish.[18]

For printers, the book trade was clearly a commercial enterprise with a profit motive. Sometimes payment for materials sent out by the Carey house came back in goods that could be exchanged on the Philadelphia market. Such was the case with business done with Louis Castagnino, a merchant based in Havana who was one of Carey's successful traders. Letters from the Carey house to Castagnino in 1822 show enthusiasm for merchandise received as payment for books and stationery. "We are advised by one of our friends who is in the mercantile business," one letter says, "that either sugars or coffee would answer better than anything else. We mean Brown sugar."[19] In November 1821 Castagnino had sent payment in cigars, and Carey was eager for more. "If you can procure segars of the manufacturer of Cabanas, they will always sell without difficulty at a fair price," one letter says. And in a sentence showing that early nineteenth-century Philadelphians had discriminating taste in Cuban cigars, the letter urges, "It is necessary that they be genuine [Cabanas] as we are informed that many imitations of them we make but they will not sell here."[20] Exchanging books for tobacco would not have been unusual given that many printers and publishers worked in a system of exchange for goods, and publishers would sometimes be paid not in cash but in other books, paper, or goods in trade. The intricacies and challenges of a trading system in which the Carey firm invested in books sent out as "adventures" to sell in other countries are discussed in Nancy

Vogeley's book *The Bookrunner*, which offers meticulous detail about the work of a book agent in Mexico named Thomas W. Robeson.[21]

The investment of printers (and particularly the Carey house) in selling materials in the southern Americas as independence was ushered in explains the variety of subjects in Spanish-language titles out of Philadelphia and other US cities. That includes manuals for Freemasons with information on secret rituals and how to run lodges. Between 1800 and 1830 at least ten Spanish-language titles dealing with Masonry were published in the northeastern United States.[22] Among these was *Reflexiones imparciales sobre la franc-masonería* (1818), which has been attributed to a liberal Spanish priest in exile, Miguel Cabral de Noroña. (Although the book is published anonymously, the initials "C.N." appear on the last of its thirty pages.) These reflections, written from the perspective of a reformer of the Masonic order, display intimate knowledge of the rites and degrees. Manuel Hernández González notes that while it is unclear whether Cabral de Noroña was a Mason, he clearly had an investment in improving the order.[23] Cabral de Noroña refers to the "Supremo Arquitecto del Universo" (supreme architect of the universe) and writes the following recommendation: "La Masonería, despojandose de todas sus quimeras y momerias, y reduciendose á los objetos sencillos de la beneficiencia y caridad, no deberia admitir estatutos, ni ceremonias ó practicas que fuese extrañas ó inutiles para el exercisio generoso y puro de estas virtudes" (If Masonry were to dispose of its chimeric foolishness and focus on benevolence and charity as its goals, it would not adopt regulations, ceremonies, or practices that were unnecessary and alien to the liberal exercise of those virtues).[24] The appearance of this type of work in Philadelphia shows that Masonic lodges in that city were in conversation with lodges in other parts of the Americas, including Cuba and Mexico, with the latter drawing the interest of Carey's trade.[25] Masonic lodges throughout the hemisphere were involved in independence movements, and in some cases Masonic membership facilitated connections for intellectuals going from one country to another.

Despite the commercial interests of printers, the mainstay of Filadelfia publication was books and pamphlets commissioned by Spanish American intellectuals. In 1821, the house of Jean-François Hurtel printed an edition of the Dominican friar Bartolomé de las Casas's *Breve relación de la destrucción de las indias*. Originally published in 1542, this book appeared with Hurtel's imprint with the following line: "IMPRESA EN SEVILLA, REIMPRESA EN LONDRES, Y AHORA EN FILADELFIA" (Printed in Seville, reprinted in London, and now in Philadelphia).[26] Thus the title page announced the type of transatlantic circulation that fed Spanish-language publishing in Philadelphia. This edition was brought to print by Servando Teresa de Mier and paid for with support from Manuel Torres, as I discuss in chapter 5.[27] In this case, as in many others, Jean-François, who specialized in Spanish and French books, printed the Spanish-language title under the Hispanicized name Juan F. Hurtel.

Like Hurtel, many printers and publishers involved in the Hispanophone book trade were immigrants (or second generation) and thus brought international perspectives to Philadelphia publishing. Some of the most active in Spanish-language publication were those of French descent. Sara E. Johnson's work on the bookseller and printer Médéric-Louis-Élie Moreau de Saint-Méry shows the importance of French-language print culture in Philadelphia and its connections to elites affected by revolutionary upheaval. "Eighteenth-century observers and contemporary scholars have acknowledged the importance of Moreau's bookshop as a centre of French life for people fleeing revolution in France and the Antilles, particularly Saint-Domingue," Johnson writes. "Patrons viewed the store as a vital information hub and psychic refuge."[28] More importantly, Johnson points out that some took refuge after losing fortunes, which plunged the upper-class, slave-owning Moreau into work as a bookseller. The growing French community, whose temporary residents included the Enlightenment philosopher and traveler Constantin-François de Chasseboeuf, comte de Volney, created enough of a demand that in the 1790s at least five French-language newspapers circulated in Philadelphia.[29] Some printers were among the elites fleeing from revolution, and in succeeding decades printing became an option for livelihood. Hurtel, who also published Manuel Lorenzo de Vidaurre's *Cartas americanas, políticas y morales* (1823), hailed from a French family that had left Saint Domingue after the slave rebellion of the 1790s.[30] Another Frenchman contributing to Filadelfia publications was Andrés Josef Blocquerst, the printer of the controversial pamphlet *El amigo de los hombres* (1812), who may have been the first Spanish-language printer in Saint Domingue before making his way to Philadelphia.[31] (We will return to *El amigo de los hombres* in chapter 4.)

Other immigrant printers included Thomas and George Palmer, from Kelso, Scotland, who did everything from the aforementioned job printing for Carey to printing titles such as the anonymously published *Manual de un republicano, para el uso de un pueblo libre* (1812). Thomas Palmer offers one example of how the capacious intellectual interests, multilingual commitments, and international connections of publishers and printers contributed to the rising number of Hispanophone publications. Thomas published the *The Historical Register of the United States* (1812–14), and after George's death in 1817, Thomas went on to publish a variety of titles that included education books, travel books, an atlas, and a medical dictionary. Like most publishers, the Palmers ranged far and wide in their titles, and Spanish-language materials were only a part of their work. In 1813 Thomas Palmer wrote a letter to Thomas Jefferson with a query about amendments to state constitutions; Palmer was writing a work tentatively titled "Tabular View of the Constitution of the US and of the Several States." "Although the constitution framed by Virginia in 1776 does not contain provision for amendments, yet I thought it possible it might have undergone a change notwithstanding," Palmer wrote.[32] Jefferson responded several days later: "In answer to the inquiries in the letter of Feb. 22, I have to observe to you that the constitution of Virginia has undergone no formal change, nor recieved [*sic*] any formal amendment since the date at which it was passed."[33] Jefferson wished Palmer success with his work.

The exchange between Palmer and Jefferson clarifies that for printers like Palmer, the Spanish language played a small part in their work. The limited archival materials from presses that published Spanish-language materials makes it difficult to determine exactly how these books fit into their stock. The Carey house has always received more attention than other printers in early Philadelphia, not only because of its importance but also because account books and other materials are held in US repositories. Archives do not have similar holdings for the Hurtel house, for example. The result is that the history of Spanish-language publishing in the United States inevitably confronts certain archival silences. Often the most revealing textual remains are in the books themselves. Such is the case with the novel *Jicoténcal* (Philadelphia 1826), whose pages offer clues about print-culture conditions.

Jicoténcal has been discussed by critics because of its political content, its authorship, and its genre; however, its publication appears to have been tied to an emerging Spanish-language bookselling market in New York and Philadelphia.[34] In the 1820s, bookshops in northeastern US cities began to promote Spanish-language books, and some even got into the publication side of the business. *Jicoténcal* was published in two small volumes, measuring 5¾" × 3¼", with the participation of a bookseller. The book's author remained anonymous, but the book was copyrighted by Frederick Huttner, who a few years later ran the Foreign and Classical Book-Store at

32 S. Sixth Street in Philadelphia. While Luis Leal and Rodolfo Cortina note that Huttner lived on the same street as the purported author of *Jicoténcal,* Félix Varela, the more important point is that Huttner was involved in bookselling and may have commissioned this book to make money.[35] (I return to the questionable attribution of the Varela authorship in chapter 4.) Huttner's shop, which opened in 1831, was described at the time as "a book and fancy print store, the windows of which are so attractive to the multitude as to make the footpath barely passable. Mr. H's assortment of *foreign books* is very extensive and complete, while all the popular and standard works of the day are to be found on his shelves."[36] Huttner's shop was an outpost of New York's Foreign and Classical Book-Store, run by Charles de Behr, a French immigrant who was active in publishing and bookselling. The Foreign and Classical Book-Store emphasized German titles and advertised itself as having made arrangements with houses in "Hamburgh, Leipzig, Frankfort and Brussels." "Books can be imported with the least possible delay, and at the lowest prices," it promised.[37] Given the role of international exchange, the circulation of Spanish-language books in Philadelphia was part of expanding markets.

The New York bookseller with an interest in *Jicoténcal* was Lanuza & Mendía, which specialized in Spanish titles. On the page facing *Jicoténcal*'s copyright, several lines advertised that the book would be for sale in New York at Lanuza & Mendía and in Philadelphia at the home of Félix Merino, a teacher and translator of Spanish and French; at the merchant and bookseller John Laval's shop, 118 Chestnut; and at the Franklin Institute, which had recently opened at 15 S. Seventh Street as a center for the promotion of science and technology.[38]

These book-market conditions show that *Jicoténcal* was produced not only because of the politico-literary aspirations of its anonymous author but also to sell along a New York–Philadelphia corridor, which William Charvat identified as an important publishing artery that had increasing influence on literary taste and promoted expansion of bookselling into the interior of the United States. These cities, Charvat wrote, "close together and connected by an abundant ocean, river, and road transportation, formed what I shall call the publishing axis."[39] This publishing axis influenced not only Anglophone literary culture, as Charvat argued, but also the movement of Hispanophone publications and Spanish-speaking intellectuals between the two cities. (Two periodicals, *El Habanero* [1824–26] and *El Mensagero Semanal* [1828–29], began publishing in Philadelphia and then moved to New York.)

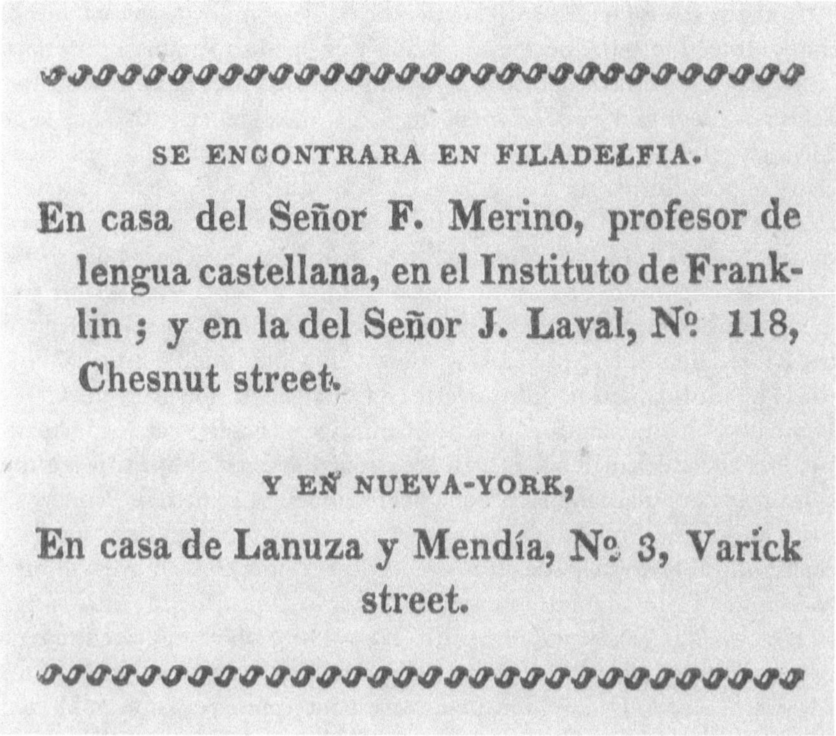

> SE ENCONTRARA EN FILADELFIA.
> En casa del Señor F. Merino, profesor de lengua castellana, en el Instituto de Franklin ; y en la del Señor J. Laval, N? 118, Chesnut street.
>
> Y EN NUEVA-YORK,
> En casa de Lanuza y Mendía, N? 3, Varick street.

Fig. 1. Advertisement in the opening pages of *Jicoténcal* (1826). (Courtesy of the American Antiquarian Society)

Jicoténcal is one example of how printers and booksellers not only in Philadelphia but also in New York and Boston began to publish Spanish-language materials that could appeal to Spanish readers in the United States and other parts of the Americas. The advertisement announcing that *Jicoténcal* was for sale in the two cities speaks to Huttner's New York connections and the entrance of booksellers with shops into the publishing market. William Stavely, identified on the title page as having printed *Jicoténcal* at the Imprenta de Guillermo Stavely, Stavely printing house, most likely functioned solely as printer and not as publisher. With book printers in the northeastern United States and London keeping an eye on Spanish American markets and *Jicoténcal*'s author presumably in touch with Spanish-speaking intellectuals who sent missives to other countries, the novel could sell to readers in both the United States and Spanish America.

In the years immediately following the publication of *Jicoténcal*, bookshops jumped into the business of publishing Spanish-language materials. The New York bookseller Behr & Kahl published translations of Walter Scott's *Ivanhoe* and *The Talisman* in 1827 and, together with Lanuza & Mendía, published an edition of *Fabulas literarias*, by the Spanish neoclassical poet Tomás de Iriarte, in 1826.[40] In addition, Lanuza & Mendía sold numerous Spanish-language titles at its store, some of them listed on the back page of the second volume of *Jicoténcal*.[41] These bookstores were reaching out to readers hemispherically while at the same time trying to tap into a growing market for students of the Spanish language in the United States. In April 1815, Mathew Carey published a list of almost thirty Spanish-language titles advertised for sale.[42] And in 1825, the Carey house listed more than thirty Spanish-language books in a catalog of Spanish, French, and Italian books "just received from Paris."[43] Spanish was the third most popular language, behind French and German, in Pennsylvania schools, and Philadelphia saw some of its Spanish American intellectuals publish Spanish-instruction books. In the next chapter, we will turn to Manuel Torres's language-instruction book, *Dufief's Nature Displayed in Her Mode of Teaching Language to Man* (1811), which appeared in new editions in 1817 and 1826. Charles LeBrun, who worked as a translator for Mathew Carey and gained a reputation as an interpreter, possibly published a book on Spanish and English grammar, and Edward Berry, who also translated books into Spanish, published *The Elements of Spanish and English Conversation* (1822).[44]

The imperative to publish for Spanish-language learners fueled the production of an important book in the history of US Spanish-language publishing: José María Heredia's *Poesías* (1825), which included his well-known poem "Niágara." This book, published by the bookseller Behr & Kahl, shows the intricate connections between the emergence of a hemispheric literary culture and the commercial dimensions of US-based print culture. Heredia, whose Filadelfia letter we consider shortly, traveled around the United States and composed poems about sites he visited. The 1825 collection included some of his early pieces previously published in periodicals in Cuba but also featured more recent work, which was increasingly inflected by the pain of exile.

In the United States, we see Heredia following two tracks of writing, his poetic conceptions and his letters describing the sites he visited. Such is the case with the visit to Niagara Falls, which produced "Niágara" as well as a letter describing the trip to upstate New York. "Niágara," which was translated and admired by William Cullen Bryant, intertwines Heredia's exilic vision, his longing for Cuba, with a meditation on the sublime.[45] Publishing what would become a canonical poem in the context of Behr & Kahl's selling of books, Heredia taps into the growing commercial interests in the Spanish language in the northeastern United States. The conjunction of his literary aspirations and commercial viability is evident in the following introductory note containing both Spanish and English text:

> Se notará en esta obrita profusion de acentos; pero há sido necesario emplearlos, para hacerla útil á los Americanos que estudian el Español, y desean adquirir una buena pronunciación.
>
> The author has paid particular attention to the accents, to make these poems useful to Americans learning the Spanish language. Nothing is better calculated to give them a practical knowledge of the true pronunciation of words, than the habit of reading poetry. May they receive this little service of an exiled youth, as an expression of gratitude for the asylum he has found in this happy country.[46]

Heredia emphasizes poetry as being "useful" to language learners and also apologizes for a "profusion" of accents to help with pronunciation.[47] But *profusion* might be a strong word, because the poems are not heavily accented. Or the statement speaks more to the goals of the publisher than to the actual accents in the poems. (In his letters, Heredia had noted upon first arriving in the United States that English was alien to him. It may be taken as a sign of his own language-learning process that he could write a note in which he presented his poetry as an expression of gratitude to the United States.)

A similar imperative to address the interests of Spanish-language learners appears in a note at the front of Domingo Del Monte's collection of poetry *Versos de J. Nicasio Gallego, recogidos y publicados por Domingo Del Monte* (Philadelphia, 1829), a book to which we will return in chapter 3. Del Monte specifies that he intends to circulate Gallegos's verses among all those in "America" who are dedicated to poetry and also to make them available to "foreigners" who study "Spanish literature."[48] Del Monte's publication of the verses of a Spanish poet whose literary sensibilities were in keeping with liberatory politics in Cuba shows how anticolonial political projects could tap into a budding market for Spanish-language books.

The apogee of Spanish-language printing for profit was the appearance of three gift books offering romantic fare. Their appearance illustrates the emergence of the book as a luxury commodity. In 1828 and 1829, the Carey house published *El Aguinaldo para el año de 1829* (Philadelphia, 1828), *El Aguinaldo para 1830* (Philadelphia, 1829) and *Presente las damas* (Philadelphia, 1829). By introducing the book itself as an object of desire, with gilded pages and illustrations, the Carey house inserted an aesthetic dimension into circulation, and did so with an appeal to women readers. The title *Presente las damas* (Ladies are here) made a direct overture to readers who might have been attracted to that book's series of engravings, which drew from work by landscape painters. The thirty-two plates are accompanied by poems. *Presente las damas* includes an opening graphic with the words "Presentado a" (Given to), which allows the purchaser to fill in the name of the gift recipient.[49] In printing these three gift books, Carey ensured that the Spanish language was represented in the gift-book vogue that started in the 1820s. Ralph Thompson notes that gift books "appealed to the eye and the heart rather than to the mind; they were handsome and costly; they were 'artistic' and 'refined.'"[50] Known as souvenirs and keepsakes and sometimes labeled "a gift for the holiday," these books were published as elegant editions meant to be kept as tokens of affection. Sometimes bound in leather, the volumes featured a variety of poetry, essays, and miscellaneous writings, but what distinguished them was the ornate pictures, known as "embellishments," which were engravings inserted between the pages of writing. In his discussion of the rise of the US novel in the early nineteenth century, Stephen Shapiro has argued that its popularity was intertwined not only with a market for sentimental cultural productions but also with the expansion of Atlantic bourgeois trade and an international market that supported sensational consumption.[51] In this case, the appearance of Spanish-language books definitely speaks to the proliferation of books as an expensive commodity.

El Aguinaldo para el año de 1829 is self-conscious in its promotion and connotation of various types of affection, and the content situates it alongside other luxury items that someone might purchase at a store. It is an impressive book, with lovely engravings and thick gilded pages. The copy at the American Antiquarian Society has a green hardback cover with an illustration of a nymph playing a lyre. It measures 3¼" × 5½", and its 248 pages contain miscellaneous offerings of poetry, essays, and travel pieces. After a brief preface, the volume opens with a poem titled "El Aguinaldo," which explains various meanings of the term.[52] With an assertion that the

Spanish language lends itself to multiple signification—un "idioma" "que encierra sentidos varios" (a language that contains many senses)—the poem concludes:

> Y no como quiera, corre,
> Sino que se vá buscando
> Como se buscaban antes,
> Los abanicos y lázos.

> (And it does not circulate on its own,
> Rather it is sought
> Like once were sought,
> Hand fans and ribbons.)

Buyers who seek adornment will now display the book, which becomes a fashion statement or something in vogue. (The word *aguinaldo* is still used today in various parts of the Americas to refer to a holiday gift or work bonus.)

While expensive gift books are distant from the politically loaded tracts published by Filadelfia's politically minded writers, they indicate how the nineteenth century saw the coming together of interest in Spanish-language reading in the United States and the political and cultural goals of intellectuals who sought to circulate their materials across the Americas. Poetry, for example, could provide language that could resist colonial rule, in the case of Heredia by situating him within a nascent literary culture in Cuba, a point to which we turn in chapter 3. But while Filadelfia became an attractive print center, another factor needs to be considered: the push from colonial sites in Spanish America that made it difficult or even impossible to publish politically charged materials.

Banned Books and Printing Presses in the Americas

The attraction of Philadelphia's print shops for Spanish American intellectuals and the role of censorship in the uneven distribution of printing opportunities across the Americas is best told through the experiences of the Mexican priest and political operative Fray Servando Teresa de Mier. Mier was one of the most colorful figures of the era, on the run for decades after coming into conflict with the Catholic Church as a result of his views on theology. When he returned from Europe in 1817 to the territory that would become Mexico, three crates of books were seized from him. Mier had arrived on an expedition led by Francisco Javier Mina to fight for the country's independence. The expedition failed. Mier was captured, and so were his books. The crates contained a variety of pamphlets, manuscripts, personal letters, newspapers, and stationery, as well as books whose topics ranged from ecclesiastical matters to republicanism, American independence, and constitutional reform. (Among the titles was the practical *Nuevo estilo y formulario para escribir cartas y responder a ellas* [Madrid, 1810], an epistolary writing manual.)[53] Mier's cache includes many texts that would have been of interest to the Filadelfia circle, including Guillaume Thomas Raynal's history of the US revolution, Humboldt's *Essai politique sur le royaume de la Nouvelle Espagne* (*Political Essay on the Kingdom of New Spain*), and Las Casas's book on the destruction of the Indies. Four books and three pamphlets in his confiscated crates had been published in Philadelphia.[54] After his books were taken, Mier was subjected to another series of detentions that took him to Havana.

In 1821, he made his way to Philadelphia, where he published *Memoria politico-instructiva, enviada desde Filadelfia en agosto de 1821* (An instructive political account, sent from Philadelphia in August 1821), a book to which we will turn in chapter 5. Mier could not have published his *Memoria* in Spanish America, where printing jobs were restricted by the colonial government. By contrast, Philadelphia had at least fifty printers and more than a dozen booksellers in 1805.[55] These offered publishing opportunities, especially for someone who could afford to pay for a run of books. While Mier was broke, his Philadelphia benefactor, Manuel Torres, footed the bill for *Memoria politico-instructiva*.

Across Spain's American colonies, the production of books, pamphlets, and periodicals was uneven. In general, most of Spanish America was affected by three factors that prevented publication: few presses, colonial censorship, and prohibitions from the Inquisition. Prior to the eighteenth century, much of the printing activity had taken place in two major cities that had numerous presses, Lima and Mexico City. In 1640 and 1660, presses had arrived in Puebla, Mexico, and then Guatemala, but other locations throughout Spanish America did not get presses until the eighteenth and nineteenth centuries. The bibliographer José Toribio Medina has established the following dates for the arrival of presses: Mexico City, 1539; Lima, 1584; Havana, 1707; Quito, 1760; New Orleans, 1769; Buenos Aires, 1780; and Caracas, 1808.[56]

Restrictions on printers in Spanish America limited the output of these presses. Before printers in Spanish colonies could operate, they needed to be licensed by colonial authorities, and this authorization usually came with the understanding that they would print mostly approved religious texts. In Lima, for example, a license was required from Spanish authorities not only for printing but also for selling a particular book.[57] In reference to Spain's administrative council and courts, Eugenia Roldán Vera writes that "under Spanish rule, every book had to be examined by the *Consejo de Indias* or the *Real Audiencia* before it went into print, and the publication of popular religious books was monopolized by a few printers who were granted the royal privilege to do so."[58] Many of the books published were elementary readers intended to convert indigenous populations, devotional manuals, and selected law books.[59] In addition, authorities could seize books from printers and from travelers transporting materials. The Inquisition was particularly active in certain areas and kept a tally of prohibited books, meaning that an individual person with a copy of a banned book could be fined or excommunicated. These print-culture conditions helped push writers toward Philadelphia and London, which also became an important center for Spanish-language publishing outside Spain and its colonies. The result was a trans-American and transatlantic network of print and circulation, as we will see in more detail in chapter 3.

On the eve of the wars of independence, revolutionaries adopted the symbolic claim that Philadelphia was the place for printing material against the Spanish Crown. In turn, *Filadelfia* sometimes appeared as the place of publication in false imprints. In one important example, a pamphlet by the exiled Jesuit Juan Pablo Viscardo y Guzmán, *Lettre aux Espagnols-Américains* (Letter to Spanish Americans) was published in London in 1799 with a false "Philadelphie" imprint.[60] Viscardo did no less than call for the people's right to choose their own government and developed a case for independence based on people's right to govern themselves; his pamphlet is considered one of the most important documents in the history of Spanish American independence movements. The letter was an important contribution to London's print culture and inspired interest among intellectuals in England about the revolt in Spanish America.[61] The agent behind its publication was Francisco de Miranda, a revolutionary who toured the United States on two separate occasions to build support for an armed attack on Spain's colonial holdings. Miranda inherited Viscardo's papers when the Jesuit priest died in 1798 and then proceeded to circulate copies of the pamphlet among prominent figures in London and the United States, including Alexander Hamilton. Miranda then had the French version of the *Carta* published and followed up with the Spanish version.[62] According to Karen Racine, Miranda decided to insert a Philadelphia imprint to avoid antagonizing the English prime minister, William Pitt, whom Miranda hoped to recruit to the cause of Spanish American independence.[63]

False imprints sometimes were used to circumvent local censors, and they were also a material manifestation of an imagined association between the United States and the independence movements of Spanish America. Scholars have proposed that the book *Bosquejo ligerisimo de la revolucion de Mégico* (Brief sketch of Mexico's revolution, 1822), which appeared with a Philadelphia imprint, was actually published in Havana, where such a publication would have been forbidden.[64] In other cases, the inspiration for the use of false Filadelfia imprints may not have been censors but the symbolic connotations of the city, which would imply that books were following in the US revolutionary tradition. That is why Rocafuerte is adamant about emphasizing the city as the site of composition and publication on the title page and in the prologue to *Ideas necesarias,* even though the book was probably printed in New York City.[65]

In Spanish America, with the Catholic Church sometimes serving as an institutional vanguard for the Spanish monarchy, the Inquisition could limit the circulation of dangerous ideas through its disciplinary mechanisms. The Inquisition went after one of the earliest Filadelfia books. On October 24, 1794, about eight months after Puglia's *El desengaño del hombre* was published, the Inquisition in Mexico issued an order of excommunication for anyone holding a copy of the book. A broadside with the order, signed and sealed by five church authorities, was posted on church doors in Mexico City. It critiqued Puglia's use of the Spanish language, calling him a "merchant turned pedantic writer," and then accused him of inciting rebellion among Spain's colonies:

> SABED: QUE CON ASOMBRO, Y GRAVE dolor de nuestro corazon, hemos leído y exâminado, y hecho exâminar â nuestros zelosos, y sabios Calificadores un Libro en octavo, intitulado: Desengaño del Hombre, impreso en Filadelfia en este presente año, su Autor D. Santiago Felipe Puglia. Este infame autor se manifiesta por su Obra, orgulloso, altivo, inobediente, blasfemo, traidor, y con todos los demás caractéres con que describe San Pablo en la segunda Carta á Timoteo, capítulo tercero, aquella casta de hombres que aparecerán en los

último dias, que segun parece se acercan, é instan yá, â vista de tantos monstruos, como ha producido este siglo, quienes despues de blasfemar de toda Religion natural, y revelada: despues de destronar á la Suprema Magestad de Dios del Solio de su divino Poder: y a la Católica Religion, de su divina Autoridad, ê institucion, calificandola de fanatismo, han emprehendido ultrajar, hacer odiosa, y aun arrancar desde los cimientos la Autoridad, y Magestad Real.[66]

(Let it be known that with great pain in our hearts and amazement we have read and examined and asked our wise and zealous theological censors to examine an octavo volume titled *Man Undeceived,* printed in Philadelphia this year, its author Don Santiago Felipe Puglia. In this work the infamous author shows himself to be proud, haughty, disobedient, blasphemous, treacherous, and to have all of the other traits that Saint Paul, in his second letter to Timothy, third chapter, attributes to that class of men that appeared in the days before judgment, which it appears is imminent when one considers that this century has produced so many monsters who after desecrating all Religion—after disenthralling the Supreme Majesty of God from the throne of his Divine power and the Catholic Church from its divine authority, calling the latter fanaticism—have undertaken to disdain, to inspire hatred against, and to tear out from its roots the ruling authority and his royal majesty.)

The Inquisitors took the opportunity to renew an earlier edict of 1790 banning any book focusing on France and, more generally, any book that could inspire sedition. They then pointed to *El desengaño del hombre* as the most seditious of all. Anyone with a copy of the book who did not turn it in within six days would be sentenced to excommunication, and in case that was not enough of a deterrent, they would also be fined five hundred ducats, to be paid to the church. In addition, the Spanish government sent a letter of protest to President Washington demanding that Puglia and the printer of the book be punished. Washington replied that he could not interfere with freedom of the press in the United States.[67] Antonio Saborit has argued that the vehement opposition to *El desengaño del hombre* was the result of local colonial governors feeling insecure about their ability to protect militarily areas such as Florida, Texas, and New Orleans.[68]

How did restrictions on publishing in Spanish America affect writers who made their way to Philadelphia? Rocafuerte's home, Guayaquil, did not get its first printing press until 1810, so publication was extremely restricted in that city.[69] As such, Rocafuerte found it more expedient to travel elsewhere to publish his books. Medellín, in what would become Colombia, did not see a printing press until 1814, and by then Manuel Torres had been in Philadelphia publishing and doing his revolutionary work for almost two decades. Prior to 1811, books published in Spanish America on political topics were for the most part friendly to colonial rule. Victor Peralta Ruiz has shown that in Lima between 1808 and 1810, an increase in the publication of books with political content were of a loyalist orientation, and it was not until the succeeding decade, as the military battle against Spain became more intense and Spain loosened some restrictions over the colonies, that political titles appeared with a more polemic position in relation to colonial rule.[70] Nevertheless, restrictions continued into the 1820s, and intellectuals continued to suffer repercussions for having certain books, not to mention writing and printing them.

Filadelfia offered an anticolonial position from which to conceive of the possibilities of publication. While contemporary readers might be tempted to see the distinction drawn in this chapter between the commercial presses of Philadelphia and the restrictions of Spanish America as presenting a sense of US exceptionalism (or at least an evaluative preference based on freedom of the press), the Filadelfia circle was more likely to see print culture in the United States not as a nationalist manifestation but as part of a revolutionary hemispheric Americanism. One of the effects of colonial subjection was uneven development, so that as Philadelphia attempted to move into the center of economic production in the early nineteenth century, parts of Spanish America still had a peripheral status within a Spanish imperial economy. My goal is not to situate Spanish America within an ideology of underdevelopment but rather to draw a distinction between different print-culture conditions that explain why in symbolic terms, *Filadelfia* came to name for certain intellectuals not only a place of print but also a political and economic potential for the future.

Letters about Filadelfia: The Athens of America

Filadelfia has left us a trove of Spanish-language letters, political books, and travel accounts that position the city as representing a postmonarchical future and a living lab of republicanism in the Americas. The economics of print culture, linked to commercial activity in Philadelphia, cannot be divorced from the political symbolism of Filadelfia and the way intellectuals experienced the city's institutions, urban planning, and architectural wonders. Invoking associations with classical democracy and at times referring to the city as "the Athens of America," Spanish American intellectuals participated in a Hispanophone version of Philadelphia's mythmaking as a revolutionary site. The claim to Athens was a story that Philadelphia told about itself early on.[71] As Gary B. Nash has noted, the telling and retelling of Philadelphia's history has been linked to "the two most important documents in the history of the United States, the Declaration of Independence and the Constitution of 1787," as well as to its role as capital until 1800 and its myriad contributions to the new republic, being "the site of the first American paper mill, hospital, medical college, subscription library, street lighting, scientific and intellectual society, bank, and government mint."[72] But Nash also emphasizes the different ways that Philadelphia's past is remembered, particularly by the city's "rich variety of ethnic, racial and religious groups," and how that reflects on the present.[73] For Spanish American intellectuals, Filadelfia was representative of political currents beyond the United States. The Declaration and the Constitution were models to be considered alongside European constitutional theory, and the city's urban accomplishments were seen as inspiration for new countries. Thus, Filadelfia writers circulated a memory of 1776 with universal implications. They thought of the city as having hemispheric connections.

As a space motivating independence, Filadelfia offered an alternative not only to Europe but to colonial thinking. The role of cities in the colonizing mission has been of interest to Latin American studies scholars, who have argued that urban organization was intertwined with imperial forms of domination and Euro-inflected notions of civilization. "To impose order on vast empires, the Iberian monarchs created precocious urban networks, carefully planned with pen and paper, their geometrical layout standardized by detailed written instructions," writes John Charles Chasteen in his introduction to the English-language translation of Angel Rama's *La ciudad letrada (The Lettered City)*.[74] Rama emphasizes the importance of writers to urban organization: "New cities housed both the institutions of state power and the writers who dealt in edicts, memoranda, reports, and all the official correspondence that held the empire together."[75] Influenced by Michel Foucault, Rama argues that urban organization imposed social order on Spanish colonial territories. From another vantage point, critics approaching urban sites in relation to economic questions have emphasized the urban-rural inequality created by capitalist world systems. Andre Gunder Frank, Theotonio Dos Santos, and others working on dependency theory in Latin America argued that urban centers served as sites where a national bourgeoisie could manipulate local economies to feed world capitalist expansion, whether through the plantation system of the colony and early independence or through later practices of industrialization.[76]

While such arguments remind us that Philadelphia in the early nineteenth century was an active participant in an economic world system, the concept of Filadelfia was also movable, deployed for rhetorical effect during the wars of liberation from Spanish colonialism. The connection of Filadelfia to Athens, which could be marshaled as classical inspiration for a democratic future, drew directly from the experience of writers who walked around the city. The point was made most directly in descriptions of architecture, especially examples of the Greek classical revival. The name Philadelphia was etymologically connected to the Greek *philos* (beloved, dear) and *adelphos* (brother) and thus the city of brotherly love. In the 1780s, Philadelphians claimed a connection to Athens as they established the first city of the new republic. The architect Benjamin Henry Latrobe, arguing for the importance of fine arts in the United States, proposed in 1811 that "the days of Greece may be revived in the woods of America, and Philadelphia become the Athens of the Western world."[77] Using *Western* in a hemispheric sense distinct from Europe, Latrobe presented a vision that would materialize in the city's Greek revival architecture, at which Spanish American travelers would later marvel.

That sense of Athens is evident in *Viaje por los Estado Unidos del Norte, dedicado á los jovenes mexicanos de ambos secsos* (1834), part travelogue and part epistolary exchange between two Mexican statesmen, Rafael Reynal and Carlos Gastelú.[78] According to the book, Reynal was forced into exile and traveled from 1832 to 1834 to New Orleans, Cincinnati, and New York, with a month-long stop in Philadelphia.[79] These letters, written after Mexico had gained independence, relate his interest in "las diferentes maneras, habitos, y costumbres de un pueblo que por la simpatia de su gobierno con el nuestro nos llama tanto la atencion" (*V* 4; the different manners, habits, and customs of a people who interest us so much because of their government's similarity to ours). The building that catches Reynal's attention is the Greek-inspired Philadelphia Merchants' Exchange, constructed not long before his arrival in the city: "Ese edificio es enteramente igual al que los modernos Ateniences nombran: La Linterna do Demostenos, el cual fué levantado 330 años antes de la era cristiana; cuenta 150 pies ingleses de longitud y 95 de latitud, y los muy hermosos chapiteles de sus columnas asi como los adornos de bronce de su cupula fueron construidos en Ytalia por los mejores artistas de esta epoca" (*V* 97; This building is identical to the one modern Athenians call the Lamp of Diogenes, which was erected 330 years before Christ; it measures 150 English feet in length and 95 in width, and the very beautiful chapiters of its columns as well as the bronze engravings of its dome were constructed in Italy by the best artisans of this era). Also known as the choragic Monument of Lysicrates, the Lamp of Diogenes was indeed emulated by the Merchants' Exchange's architect in accordance with the Greek revival style that influenced numerous buildings, including the US capitol, which Reynal visited prior to making his way to Philadelphia.[80] For Reynal, who comments on hospitals, prisons, and other buildings devoted to public beneficence, the Merchants' Exchange is the most captivating structure in Filadelfia. The passage above emphasizes size and beauty and connects the building to learning by celebrating its reading room, which offered newspapers from throughout the United States and other countries.[81] The emphasis on Greek architecture and Reynal's reference to artisans in Italy at once propose a connection to a strain of European political tradition (democracy) and its production of aesthetic value. Herein lies a contradiction: Philadelphia simultaneously motivates a continuation of European political thought and suggests anticolonial urban accomplishments.

The invoking of continuities with Athens comes with an emphasis on an anticolonial hemispheric Americanism. A notable example of a writer touting Philadelphia architecture against that of Europe emerges in Heredia's 1824 letter. In his walk through the city, Heredia lingers at the building housing the First Bank of the United States and writes: "Sin duda es el más bello que he visto sobre la tierra; y me gozo en pasearme debajo de su pórtico, donde siempre reina una deliciosa frescura. Creo que en esta fábrica se tomó por modelo el Partenón de Atenas; pero dudo que éste, aun en tiempo de su mayor lustre, igualase en sencilla elegancia y belleza al edificio americano" (Without doubt it's the most beautiful [building] I have seen on earth; and I enjoy strolling under its portico, where a delicious breeze reigns at all times. I believe that in its makeup it took the Parthenon in Athens as its model; but I doubt that the latter, even in its moment of greatest luster, can rival the American building in simple elegance and beauty).[82] Heredia was correct that the bank had been modeled on the Parthenon, albeit with marble from the quarries of Montgomery County, Pennsylvania.[83] Heredia echoes the Athens-of-America discourse, which included praise of the city's classical architecture. Contrast Heredia's celebratory perspective with the Eurocentric and colonial vision of elite French émigrés, who, François Furstenberg suggests, felt in Philadelphia as if they "had landed in the marchlands of European civilization."[84]

By elevating the hemispherically American building (a bank) over its predecessor, Heredia offers economic power as a part of the competition with Europe. In doing so, he reminds us that Filadelfia symbolism was inextricable from economic liberalism. Heredia calls the Bank of the United States a "triumphant achievement of human ingenuity," thus refuting notions of European superiority. And he notes the importance of withdrawing money: "El salón principal donde se despacha y paga, es suntuoso, aunque sin ningún adorno extraño; ¿pero acaso lo necesitan aquellas seis columnas que sostienen una bóveda tan vasta y resplandeciente?" (The main lobby, where business is transacted, is magnificent, although without excessive décor, which is unnecessary for the six columns that support a vault that is so vast and resplendent).[85] Noting the simplicity of the bank's grandeur, Heredia emphasizes that its power is in monetary reserves. The marble beauty represents the economic power of a growing nation, and Heredia finds the breeze blowing through the bank's columns salutary.

Greek revival could refer not only to classical democratic processes; it could also refer to Philadelphia's economic power. Rocafuerte, for one, frames Filadelfia as offering an economic model. After celebrating the

Fig. 2. First Bank of the United States, *Views of Philadelphia and Its Environs* (1830). (Library Company of Philadelphia)

merits of Thomas Paine's work and the other translated documents in his collection *Ideas necesarias,* Rocafuerte plays his economic hand. He proposes an analogy (and a potential influence) between Filadelfia and his native Guayaquil, which he describes as an important commercial port on the "west coast of America." Like Philadelphia, he argues, Guayaquil's natural advantages and resources are at the roots of its impending economic success: "La provincia de Guayaquil por su situacion geográfica, por la feracidad de su suelo, por la riqueza de sus producciones, por la actividad de su industria, por la variedad de sus maderas, y por la abundancia de sus aguas, y facilidad de transporates y conducciones, está destinada por la naturaleza á ser el centro mercantil de la costa occidental de la América" (The province of Guayaquil, because of its geographic location, the fertility of its soil, the richness of its products, the bustle of its industries, the variety of its woods, and because of its abundant ports and ease of transport and access, is destined by nature to be the economic center of the West Coast of America).[86] With the two cities as counterparts on opposite coasts, Rocafuerte suggests comparative political-economic scenarios across the continent. His focus on natural resources such as wood suggests the gaze of a capitalist vanguard seeking profitable resources. When Lorenzo de Zavala visited Philadelphia and stayed at the exclusive Mansion House, he offered several pages on banks, noting that "Philadelphia is the city of capital as New York is of commerce."[87] In this panorama, Filadelfia comes to stand in for liberal economics, which supposedly offers an effective response to the stultifying limits of colonial protectionism under Spanish rule.[88] Thus, the anticolonial symbolic potential of Filadelfia and its economic vibrancy feed a macroeconomic vision that does not account for particularities in Spanish America, a point we take up in succeeding chapters. In this case, the Athens of America was inextricable from a capitalist economy and the financial institutions established to promote economic growth, which is to say that Filadelfia freedom was intertwined with a profit motive.

The celebration of America's Athens had its limit and could serve as cover for certain omissions. Despite references to banks and commercial vigor in the United States, letters from Filadelfia say very little about economic hierarchies in the United States or the conditions under which people live. Although they contain references to Quakers and the city's major figures (William Penn and Benjamin Franklin), letters from Filadelfia do not focus on the everyday people actually living there. The treatment of American Indians in the early US republic is rarely considered, and Filadelfia writing is largely devoid of commentary on race relations between blacks and whites in Philadelphia. The latter is notable considering the prominence of free blacks in Philadelphia, which Erica Armstrong Dunbar has called "a leading example of black freedom in the nation."[89] As she has shown, in the early nineteenth century Philadelphia offered a picture of the movement from black servitude to personal freedom. While some publications, which we will discuss in chapters 3 and 4, discuss slavery in Spanish America, the topic rarely comes up in relation to the United States.

The lack of attention to free blacks and a lack of engagement with slavery in the United States suggest blindness, willful disregard, and/or an attempt to overlook aspects of Philadelphia that made it seem less than the pinnacle of freedom and independence. Even in discussions of the US Constitution, the question of slavery is not taken up. This is the result of an inclination among Filadelfia writers to view the political change to which they aspired in terms of universal abstraction in US foundational documents and European writings such as the Declaration of the Rights of Man and of the Citizen. In addition, references to racial hierarchies in the United States would have complicated the notion of Filadelfia as a model city for the Americas. Writing decades before US–Latin American relations would come to be defined in terms of different interests and military conflicts, Spanish American intellectuals could conceive of Filadelfia not in relation to uneven development along a North-South divide but rather as a site possibly emerging horizontally with other markets, including the emerging major ports of South America and Mexico.

One book that does discuss slavery in the United States is Lorenzo de Zavala's *Viaje*, which suggests that Spanish Americans viewed Philadelphia as a contrast to the southern US slave states. Zavala wrote and published his travel account in the 1830s, after Mexico and most Spanish American countries had achieved independence and abolished slavery. Zavala, an opponent of slavery, offered a brutal account of his travel through the US South, noting an intense contrast to his home country:

> A mi pasada por Nueva-Orleans habia en venta mas de un mil esclavos. Esta pobre gente es tratada con mucha severidad en la Luisiana. Ellos hacen el servicio de las casas y posadas, y generalmente duermen en el suelo. Cuando un amo quiere castigar á su esclavo ó esclava, los manda á la cárcel con un billete que contiene la órden del número de azotes que debe darles el carcelero.... Muchas veces se oyen los gritos y lamentos de estos infelices, al pasar por las cárceles por la mañana.[90]

(Passing through New Orleans I saw more than one thousand slaves for sale. These poor people are treated very cruelly in Louisiana. They work in houses and inns but are in most cases forced to sleep on the ground. When a master wants to punish a male or female slave, he sends the slave to jail with a note specifying the number of lashes to be administered by the jailer.... Often the screams and cries of these suffering people can be heard when one passes by a jail in the morning.)

Zavala's scene of terror stands in contrast to the celebratory tone and more abstract consideration in Filadelfia letters. And yet, Zavala is talking about the slave-based economies of the US South, which he distinguishes from Philadelphia.

José María Heredia's Spatial Practice

The connection between Filadelfia's symbolism and the writing produced by Spanish American intellectuals emerges in various ways. In epistolary documents and travel accounts, the city itself is a topic of discussion. In other printed materials, most often *Filadelfia* emerges only as a place of publication on the title page. Let us look at examples of writing that show very different approaches to the city. In one, the interesting personal letter written by José María Heredia (1803–1839), Philadelphia offers an opportunity for him to work through questions about the city's role in anticolonial thinking: Heredia offers a vision of la famosa Filadelfia as an alternative to the colonial condition of hemispheric America vis-à-vis Europe.

Heredia is a major figure of Latin American letters, claimed by Cuban nationalist literary history in the early twentieth century. Critics in the United States connect him to the island despite his movement in and out of various countries. "His soul had the scar of Cuba on it," writes Enrique Anderson Imbert. "He had lived only for a short time on the island and for this reason idealized it."[91] Having escaped from Cuba after he was accused of taking part in a conspiracy against Spanish rule, an experience he described as being torn away from a land with many objects of love, Heredia went from being part of a potential uprising in a specific location (Cuba) to the dislocation of travel and exile. His twenty-two months in the United States would take him from Cape Cod to New York to Monticello to Niagara Falls and ultimately on to Mexico, where he faced the clichéd early death of a romantic poet.[92] His epistolary production during these travels, which includes his Filadelfia letter dated April 15, 1824, presents a chronicle of the movement leading to the publication of his notable collection *Poesías* in New York in 1825.

Heredia's Filadelfia letter offers a walking tour of the city and thus can be read as a "spatial practice," to use Michel de Certeau's phrase, that intertwines walking and writing in a display of hemispheric anticolonialism. Penned for his uncle and benefactor, the letter emphasizes movement and objection to fixity. The turns and ruptures in his walking present Filadelfia in its relation to a mythic past, a glorious present, and an auspicious future. Heredia is a walker in the city much in the vein that de Certeau describes a writer/walker creating new routes: "The art of 'turning' phrases finds an equivalent in an art of composing a path."[93] As writer-walker, Heredia must contend with a tension between a panoptic desire for a controlling vision and a series of turns that bring forward Filadelfia as a site that cannot be contained by the absolute space of the city. De Certeau described this tension as follows: "The city becomes the dominant theme in political legends, but it is no longer a field of programmed and regulated operations."[94] In turning to Filadelfia, Heredia infuses it with symbolic capital. "A *migrational*, or metaphorical, city thus slips into the clear text of the planned and readable city," de Certeau writes.[95] That metaphorical slip comes forward in Heredia's turn away from the regularity with which Philadelphia is associated in the early republican period.

Before him is Philadelphia's well-known grid of streets, and Heredia seems compelled to send a map to his uncle, almost as a lettered version of F. Drayton's 1824 *Plan of the city of Philadelphia*.[96] Like Heredia's letter, Drayton's map emphasizes right angles, regularity, and the importance of water framing the city plan. Mapping the layout of Filadelfia, Heredia notes the importance of the Delaware and Schuylkill Rivers, one providing the port and the other water for the population. At various points in the letter he notes streets and buildings. The Water Works. The theater on Chestnut Street. The Masonic Hall. These form a parade attesting to success in construction. He is methodical (if less than enthusiastic) in noting the plane of the streets: "Todas sus calles están tiradas a cordel, y se cortan en ángulos rectos. Las que corren paralelas con los ríos se llaman primera, segunda, etc. hasta la décimatercia; y terminan en la magnífica plaza que se llama Central Square. . . . Las dos principales calles, que son más anchas que las otras, se cortan en Central Square; y se llaman calle Ancha y calle Alta o del Mercado" (All of its streets are paved in straight lines, which are crossed at right angles. The ones that run parallel with the river are called First, Second, etc., until Thirteenth, and they end at the magnificent plaza called Central Square. . . . The two main streets, which are wider than the others, meet at Central Square, and they are called Broad Street and High [or Market] Street)."[97] This account is not particularly original. As Samuel Otter has noted, numerous visitors to Philadelphia in the antebellum period, including Charles Dickens, used the grid as both an orienting and a disorienting mechanism. "Figurative play with the grid helped to structure literary responses to Philadelphia, as writers charted the gap between abstract and actual space," Otter writes, and he relates that gap to race and access to freedom.[98] For Heredia, a type of gap emerges when it becomes clear that he harbors a longing for epistemological uncertainty, the type of disconcerting feeling he experiences in the sublime vision of Niagara Falls rather than in the orderliness of the streets.

In response to the map, Heredia turns to imaginative musings and the potential for disorientation. This shift stems from a suspicion of an orderly city as part of a colonial regime. Angel Rama's Foucauldian reading presents an association between order, knowledge, and domination as structuring elements of Spanish American colonial cities, which have their own "ubiquitous checkerboard grid."[99] And thus it is no surprise that as he walks, Heredia experiences discomfort with the city's regularity, exclaiming, "Sin embargo, aquella misma regularidad de sus calles y casi completa igualdad de sus edificios, causan no sé qué fatiga al que los contempla; y como que me abrumaba el cúmulo de esfuerzos reiterados e iguales, que debió costar a los hombres la erección de aquellas filas de casas tan uniformes e inmensas" (Nevertheless, the same regularity of its streets and almost total uniformity of its buildings bring on some type of fatigue to those who behold them; I was exhausted from thinking about the repetitive effort it must have cost the men who erected those lines of houses at once uniform and grand).[100] Heredia confesses that he prefers the brilliant irregularity of New York, another indication that his spirit seeks to flee from the tethers of straight lines. In turn, Heredia composes a path that veers away from regularity, at least temporarily.[101] Romantic longing takes over Enlightenment accounting of knowledge.

The opportunity presents itself in Heredia's encounter with the skeletal remains known in the early US period as the "incognitum" (species unknown). Heredia steps into Peale's Museum, located on the second floor of what was then the Pennsylvania State House but would become known as Independence Hall.[102] The museum's greatest attraction (with its own room) was the mastodon's skeleton, which inspires Heredia to use a Spanglish phrase, *el esqueleto de mammoth*. While today science distinguishes between the mastodon and the mammoth as distinct species, in the early nineteenth century the two terms were interchangeable, and Peale's exhibition had ushered into general usage the sense of *mammoth* as enormous in size. Heredia writes that after he saw it, all his previous impressions disappeared.[103] Part museum spectacle, part revolutionary-era curiosity, the mastodon evoked the wonders of paleontology and debates in the early United States about the strength of the nation. "For many Americans," Paul Semonin writes, "the great beast had become a symbol of the new nation's own conquering spirit—an emblem of overwhelming power in a psychologically insecure society."[104] Unearthed by Charles Willson Peale in a swampy terrain in southeastern New York, the reconstructed skeleton had drawn gawkers for more than two decades by the time Heredia arrived.[105]

The mastodon also became an exhibit in debates over the strength of Europe versus that of the Americas, which extended from scientific to literary considerations.[106] Comte de Buffon and other Europeans had argued that animals in the Americas were smaller than those in Europe, which drew a refutation from Thomas Jefferson in *Notes on the State of Virginia:* "The skeleton of the mammoth (for so the incognitum has been called) bespeaks an animal of five or six times the cubic volume of the elephant, as Mons. de Buffon has admitted," Jefferson wrote, emphasizing that these remains differed from the skeletal structure of elephants.[107] This type of anticolonial response, although nationally inflected in the United States, would have appealed to those in Heredia's circle of intellectuals. Debates over the sizes of animals tapped into notions of environmental underdevelopment, the belief that Europe was superior to other territories because of environment. To refute these claims was a way to defend hemispheric Americas' political awakening and even growing economic power. Ultimately, Heredia presents the mammoth as an example of the natural hemispheric strength of America in contradistinction to Europe.

Heredia's initial response is to the skeleton's size, which shifts the focus from the immediate surroundings of Philadelphia and the museum to more abstract realms: "La presencia de los restos enormes de un animal monstruoso, que ha desaparecido de la tierra, a la vez de llenar de admiración con su grandeza, que asi pasa de los limites de lo posible, no puede menos de llevar al espectador a hondas cavilaciones, precipitarle en el abismo insondable de los tiempos y hacerle buscar alguna luz en su oscuridad con la formación de sistemas" (The presence of the enormous remains of a monstrous animal that has disappeared from the earth, while inspiring admiration with an immensity that surpasses the possible, can do no less than transport the spectator to deep meditation, tossing him into the unfathomable abyss of time and forcing him to seek light in such darkness through the development of [scientific] systems).[108] Here his language (writing) matches his desire as a walker; he speaks of surpassing the possible, the unfathomable abyss of time, and the need to escape from darkness. In other words, he picks up on the quandary presented by the mastodon: where did it register in relation to the presence of humans on earth?[109]

Baffled by these temporal questions, Heredia turns to the indigenous past. "'Ha como diez mil lunas,' dicen ellos, 'que cubría la tierra una raza de seres invencibles y maléficos . . .'" ("Ten thousand moons ago," they say, "a race of invincible and evil beings spread across the earth . . .").[110] He goes on to retell a legend about how the Great Spirit rained lightning on these prodigious beings and wiped them from the earth. Heredia says he does not remember where he read this, but it is no less than a loose translation of the handbill circulated to publicize the exhibition of the mammoth: "Ten thousand moons ago, when nought but gloomy forests covered this land of the sleeping Sun . . . The Bolts of Heaven were hurled upon the cruel Destroyers alone, and the mountains echoed with the bellowings of death."[111] By the 1820s, this legend had become an oft-repeated part of the mammoth viewing. It had even made its way into Jefferson's account, in which he quotes a Delaware saying, "That in ancient times a herd of these tremendous animals came to the Big-bone licks, and began an universal destruction of the bear, deer, elks, buffaloes, and other animals, which had been created for the use of the Indian: that the Great Man above, looking down and seeing this, was so enraged that he seized his lightning."[112] Those visions of supernatural battles against earthly giants appeal to Heredia, and he revels in "regiones de conjeturas en que se pierde el entendimiento, y se fatiga en vano la misma imaginación, y se detiene con espanto" (regions of conjecture where one loses understanding and even the imagination tires from its vain attempts and stops itself in fear).[113] But they are visions of a mythic past, an indigenous trace that implies absence. Heredia is drawn to a mythological vision at a time when Spanish American revolutions should confront the very real indigenous populations in the new nation-states. The repetition of the legend shows the extent to which Philadelphia generates oft-told stories and reproduces conventional perceptions. In some ways, Filadelfia allows writers to paper over socioeconomic conditions in the southern Americas. That is to say, it becomes *famosa* in retellings, even as it offers a new route for venturing into unknown realms and imagining responses to colonialism's effect on the Americas.

Translating Philadelphia: Manuel García de Sena's Target-Territory

More than a decade before Heredia drew inspiration from the city and its symbolic possibilities, Manuel García de Sena turned to Philadelphia for its revolutionary documents and printing presses. In one of the early published translations of Thomas Paine into Spanish, García de Sena titled his book with a phrase that made it sound as if Paine was calling for the independence of Spanish America, ascribing a position that Paine did not take directly in the selected passages. *La independencia de la Costa Firme justificada por Thomas Paine treinta años há* (The independence of the Spanish Main justified by Thomas Paine thirty years ago, 1811), printed by Thomas and George Palmer, deployed US revolutionary documents as an intervention in movements for independence.[114] *Costa Firme,* or mainland (Spanish Main), refers to the region in northern South America and, moving north, on the coast around the Gulf of Mexico and inclusive of García de Sena's home in the country that would become Venezuela. While Paine does not address Spanish America in the selections chosen by García de Sena, the translation is an attempt to transfer Paine's ideas from one context to another. In doing so, it applies the universalist tendencies of *Common Sense* across space and time. García de Sena becomes a ventriloquist, making Paine's writing and additional US constitutional documents speak to and about Spanish America in 1811.

La independencia de la Costa Firme shows that the circulation of Filadelfia ideals was premised on a temporal (historical) conflation between 1776 and the second decade of the nineteenth century and a geographic connection between the northeastern United States and Spanish America.[115] While Lester Langley has called the period from 1776 to the 1820s a "revolutionary age," this temporal period also has geographic dimensions that reach across various transatlantic and trans-American urban centers, thus the invoking of *la Costa Firme.*[116] Heredia's spatial practice of writing the city so as to draw connections with other parts of the Americas has a print-culture counterpart in the circulation of materials across the territories of the hemisphere. A notion of a geographic revolutionary age encompasses military activities and print-culture networks that stretch from the United States to Saint Domingue (and France) and on to Spanish American territories.

García de Sena's work challenges a view that the primary consideration of a translation is how well it captures the source. Translation studies usually distinguish between *source* (originating language and text) and *target* (the language of the translation), but as we will see, in this case the target is also the intended destination of the printed materials. Historically, literary-translation studies have emphasized the evaluation of the move from source to target language, taking up the following types of questions: How good is a translation? How does it change not only the language but also the accomplishments of the originating text and its author? Lawrence Venuti suggests that in some circles when translation "aims to address a different audience by answering to the constraints of a different language and culture," it "provokes the fear of error, amateurism, opportunism—an abusive exploitation of originality."[117] The bogeyman here is none other than excessive veneration of an author's original creation. In an article considering literary texts that straddle the "translational" middle ground between source and target, Waïl S. Hassan explains the dynamic: "This relation is often conceived in the Platonic terms of *original* and *copy:* the original is viewed as sacrosanct (especially when it is a sacred text but also when it is not), while the translation is seen, at best, as imperfect and deficient and, at worst, as an adulteration, a profanation, and a betrayal that is captured in the Italian phrase *traduttore traditore.*"[118] In contrast to this perspective, García de Sena is working in a tradition of translation as a response to political crisis, and thus he privileges the circulation of ideas over aiming for what will be deemed a quality translation.

Before proceeding with an analysis of García de Sena's translation work, and particularly its emphasis on a politics of urgency, let us consider how he came to spend several years in Philadelphia. The historian Pedro Grases has shown that García de Sena came from a prominent military family in La Victoria, a city in northern Venezuela. García de Sena was a cadet in a battalion; his father and his brother Ramón also held military posts. After Ramón was sentenced to jail for taking part in a fight, Manuel asked to be released from military duty. The permit was granted.[119] Over the first two decades of the century, the García de Sena family joined the cause of independence, and Ramón eventually died fighting against Spanish forces. Manuel made his way to the United States on what can be described as a mission of translation.

Shipping records show that García de Sena arrived in Philadelphia on the ship *Mary Ann* from La Guaira, Venezuela, on July 8, 1809. With him were his brother Domingo, a man named Juan José Torro, and "their two servants." Manuel also brought with him 183 bags of coffee, no doubt to trade or sell on the Philadelphia market.[120] The arrival with servants and goods to trade indicates that García de Sena had resources to settle himself in Philadelphia, making him one of the Filadelfia group with the economic ability to carry out printing projects, a point to which we will turn in the next chapter. In December 1810, García de Sena wrote the dedication to *La independencia de la Costa Firme*, which was published the following year. He followed this book with another translation, this time of John M'Culloch's *A Concise History of the United States, From the Discovery of America till 1807*. The second book, *Historia concisa de los Estados Unidos, desde el descubrimiento hasta el año de 1807*, published in 1812, displays García de Sena's investment in circulating information about the historical dimensions of US political institutions.

García de Sena offers an important early example of Filadelfia translations' goals: to combat monarchical government, to make a case for independence in Spanish America, and to promote the US economic model as one that can be adopted in other countries.[121] For García de Sena, Filadelfia produces a situation in which materials in the English language can be marshaled through Spanish into contested colonial sites with the goal of changing governmental structures in other parts of the hemisphere. In organizing the table of contents for *La independencia de la Costa Firme*, García de Sena selected what he believed would speak to Spanish America without running afoul of the Catholic Church: the introduction and first two sections of *Common Sense, Dissertation on First Principles of Government,* and *Dissertations on Government; the Affairs of the Bank; and Paper Money*. These share a focus on moving away from monarchy and despotism toward representative government. In addition to selections from Paine, the collection includes the Declaration of Independence, the US Constitution, the Articles of Confederation, and five US state constitutions. The volume opens with an antimonarchical call for representative government and shifts into samples of constitutional practice.

In its paratextual insertions, García de Sena's translation does no less than challenge the fetishization of the source text. He self-consciously shifts the question of translation away from the evaluation of how well it offers a rendering of a source text, de-emphasizing the importance of an impressive stylistic reworking into a target language. Instead he makes a case for translation as the product of and a material response to colonial subjection. He writes, "Ni lo fastidioso del estilo ni los muchos defectos, que se encuentren en la traduccion, serán capaces de desfigurar los hechos que me propongo trasmitir al Español para aquellos á quienes no sea posible obtenerlos de otro modo" (Neither my bothersome style nor the many defects that can be found in the translation will be capable of defacing the accomplishments that I propose to transmit into Spanish for those who would not have access to them otherwise).[122] García's *hechos* (accomplishments but also actions) connotes both the documents translated and the establishment of the US government. In addition, *trasmitir*, which can be translated as "to transmit" but also "to transfer," shows how that process is inextricable from the practice of *traducir* (translate). García de Sena here is anticipating attacks from Spanish authorities about the quality of the translation as a way to discredit his project. He also deflects criticism by perhaps facetiously saying that readers will not encounter the beautiful language that can be found even in ordinary publications. As Anna Brickhouse has noted, "The distinction between successful and failed projects of translation is, of course, an artificial and unstable one, as demonstrated by a venerable genealogy of translation studies."[123] Nevertheless, García de Sena feels the weight of how his translation will be received and knows that Spanish authorities can invoke proper use of language as a rhetorical tool to discredit the ideas in the book.

The table of contents is in keeping with García de Sena's attempts to avoid detection by the censors of the Inquisition. The issue here is not only the right of heredity but also the Spanish monarchy's claim to divinely sanctioned rule. García de Sena navigates this by translating documents that do not address the Catholic Church or religion in general; he avoids Paine's writing on religion. In *Common Sense* Paine offers an attack on monarchy without taking up the question of divine right directly. This allows García de Sena in the dedication to his brother to claim that his book does not "contain a single word against our Religion" (de no contener una sola palabra contra nuestra Religion). García de Sena, it appears, hoped his paratextual claim would get the book past the Inquisition, which did not happen. *La independencia de la Costa Firme* was banned by the Inquisition in Mexico City and appears on a list of prohibited books.[124]

In terms of the actual translation, García de Sena remains close to Paine's writing, following along paragraph by paragraph with a few exceptions. This is not surprising considering that, as Edward Larkin has written, Paine's simple, plain, and common prose opened political language to a wide spectrum of readers without dumbing down the argument. "By insisting that truth is by its nature simple and universal," Larkin writes, "Paine both manipulates and politically enfranchises a new popular audience by presenting what are actually complex and rhetorically sophisticated arguments as simple facts."[125] In addition to explaining Paine's rhetorical efficacy,

Larkin's point can help us understand part of Paine's appeal to intellectuals seeking to reach audiences across the Americas in Spanish. In his version of *El sentido común,* García de Sena's sentence construction is so close to Paine's that it appears driven by a theoretical inclination to replicate the sentences of the source text. This is apparent in the following paragraph, which emphasizes the universalist dimensions of Paine's writing and stands alone on a page in the 1811 edition:

> La Causa de America es sobre manera la causa de todo el genero humano. Muchas circunstancias han ocurrido, y ocurrirán, que no son locales sino universales, por medio de las quales son atacados los principios de todos los amantes del genero humano, y en cuyos acontecimientos se halla interesada su afeccion. Un país desolado á sangre y fuego, una declaracion de guerra contra los derechos naturales de todo el genero humano, y la extirpacion de los defensores de ellos sobre toda la haz de la tierra, es del interes de todos los hombres, á quienes la naturaleza ha dado la facultad de sentir.[126]

> (The cause of America is in a great measure the cause of all mankind. Many circumstances hath, and will arise, which are not local, but universal, and through which the principles of all Lovers of Mankind are affected, and in the Event of which, their Affections are interested. The laying a Country desolate with Fire and Sword, declaring War against the natural rights of all Mankind, and extirpating the Defenders thereof from the Face of the Earth, is the Concern of every Man to whom Nature hath given the power of feeling.)[127]

García de Sena tends toward a word-for-word translation: "all mankind" (todo el genero humano), "universal" (universal), "all Lovers of Mankind" (todos los amantes del genero humano), "natural rights" (derechos naturales), and "every man to whom Nature hath given" (todos los hombres, a quienes la naturaleza ha dado). Paine's universalist diction allows García de Sena to pull the text out of its stated particular place and time (indicated by Paine in the introduction as "Philadelphia, February 14, 1776") and present it as relevant to Spanish America, and particularly Venezuela, in the second decade of the nineteenth century.

With its geographically expansive version of Paine, *La independencia de la Costa Firme* enters a type of circulation that Susan Gillman and Kirsten Silva Gruesz have connected to the concept of "text-network," which "elevates the role of translation to active participant in, rather than mere footnote to, the production of literary and cultural meaning."[128] Text-network scrambles the binary consideration of the source and target toward a multiplicity of influences and textual reappearances. In the case of this translation, the intended meaning is less about cultural reproduction than it is about proposing (and replicating) governmental reorganization. Paine remains important as the writer of a source document, as emphasized in García de Sena's decision to place his name in the book's Spanish-language title, but the point is circulation around various places in the Americas where people are fighting for independence. Thus the translation is not about glorifying Paine as author but about supporting political change. This text-network does not start or end with Paine or García de Sena, since the version of the US Constitution in *La independencia de la Costa Firme* is based on the twenty-eight-page pamphlet *Constitucion de los Estados Unidos de América traducida del Ingles al Español por Don Jph. Manuel Villavicencio,* published in Philadelphia in 1810. (José Manuel Villavicencio's decision to Anglicize his name to "Joseph" in the title indicates an engagement with the English language.) The circulation of García de Sena's Paine was in keeping with other efforts to translate and make available US documents going back to the eighteenth century. As early as 1777, material out of Philadelphia circulated in Venezuela in an unpublished translation into Spanish of documents produced by the first Continental Congress prior to the signing of the US Declaration of Independence.[129]

On the other side of the text-network, sections of García de Sena's translation of *Common Sense* are published in the Venezuela newspaper *La Gazeta de Caracas* in January 1812 with a headline that Hispanicizes Paine as "Tomás Payne."[130] García de Sena's collection also influences Rocafuerte's *Ideas necesarias,* which includes similar selections, albeit with Rocafuerte's paean to Filadelfia in his prologue. As late as the mid-nineteenth century, exiled Cuban writers in the United States such as Miguel T. Tolón will turn to Paine to argue against colonialism. In other words, many texts are connected to *La independencia de la Costa Firme.*

Translation becomes an important mode for transferring ideas across the Americas, and García de Sena calls attention to the importance of what I would call *target-territory,* a term that emphasizes the historical geographic dimensions and goals of a translation project that responds to a colonial set of power relations. The targeting of a territory is as much about transferring political ideas across geographic areas as it is about moving from one language to another. A consideration of target-territory presents an alternative to the excessive valorization of the source text and moves toward a descriptive approach to translations, emphasizing the context of the target text. As Theo Hermans has noted, "A target-oriented approach is a way of asking questions about translations without reducing them to purely vicarious objects explicable entirely in terms of their derivation. In countering an ideology which views translation exclusively as replication, this approach contextualizes the translator's activity in functional terms."[131] Paul Cahen has argued that García de Sena "ultimately re-contextualized or 'rewrote' *Common Sense* for a different audience, for the Venezuelan lawmakers, politicians, and fellow activists who were thirsty for democracy" by trying to "reach his target readers at their own level, and in a 'language' that would speak to their moral and political views."[132] In the case of translations coming out of Philadelphia, the concept of target-territory introduces a spatial practice that should move our analysis toward the translator's sociopolitical intention. The movement of materials across geographic areas is more important than the stylistic force of a translation, although the two considerations are not mutually exclusive. Furthermore, materials out of Philadelphia remind us that in certain target-territories, governmental and religious restrictions can affect circulation.

Target-territory here is connected to limitations on circulation in a colonial setting that were noted earlier in this chapter. García de Sena anticipates possible criticism of his style, which would not have been out of the ordinary. We have seen how the Inquisition attacked Santiago de Puglia's use of the Spanish language in *El desengaño del hombre*. Addressing this issue in the translator's preface to the *Historia concisa,* García de Sena emphasizes that he is a translator out of necessity more than desire. The importance of the US Revolution to Spanish America has prompted him to translate the *Historia concisa* despite "poco conocimentos en el idioma Ingles, y aun en el mio mismo" (limited knowledge of the English language and even of my own). He goes on: "Esta sola reflexion parece que debia hacerme desistir de la empresa; y mucho mas siendome sobremanera dificil en un país extrangero procurarme aquellos libros Españoles, que podian ilustrarme, para no cometer los errores en que precisamente ha de incurrir quien como yo está tan poco versado a escribir" (This conclusion in itself should be enough to stop the enterprise, it being excruciatingly difficult in a foreign country to acquire the Spanish books that could instruct me so that I do not commit the types of errors someone like me, so little prepared to write, is likely to commit). García de Sena's prefatory comments are less about modesty and more about deflecting whatever viciousness might come his way via a politically motivated language police. An apology for stylistic limitations was not unusual in late eighteenth- or early nineteenth-century transatlantic letters; J. Hector St. John de Crèvecoeur opens his *Letters from an American Farmer* with a proposition that personal correspondence can lead to "inaccuracies" of "style and manner" "as must unavoidably occur in the rapid effusions of a confessedly inexperienced writer."[133] But for García de Sena the apology is less about rhetorical artifice and more about anticipating critiques from Spanish authorities. He emphasizes that language limitations must give way to the urgency of ushering the book into publication and making his compatriots aware of the history and governmental institutions of the United States. In other words, the apology for "defects" in style and "errors" in the Spanish language only notes that stylistic flair is less important than the urgent political stakes of his project.

The emphasis on target-territory is connected with epistolary elements in the translated books, as García de Sena's paratextual materials suggest a continuum between personal correspondence and printing a book for a public audience. Both of his Philadelphia translations open with an epistolary salutation to his intended readers. *La independencia* includes a two-page note to his brother containing the salutation "RAMON" and dated "Philadelphia, Diciembre 15 de 1810," with the closing "Soy tu afmo. hermano" (I am your most affectionate brother). This letter is followed by a one-page dedication to "los Habitantes de la Costa Firme" (the inhabitants of the Spanish Main), with the opening salutation "AMERICANOS ESPAÑOLES." Like the letter to his brother, the dedication includes an epistolary closing with the fraternal "De vuestro hermano y compatriota" (From your brother and compatriot). In a similar vein, in the *Historia concisa* García addresses "AMERICANOS ESPAÑOLES" and signs with the closing "Tales son los deseos sinceros de vuestro mas afecto conciudadano"[134] (With the sincere hope and greatest fondness of your fellow citizen). The closing shows the affective fraternal connection that I have associated with Filadelfia letters. With the possessive "your" and "fellow citizen," García situates himself in South America as his *tierra firme* even as he sends out his letters from his base of operation via shipping lines. This is a fine example of epistolarity—or its metaphorical invocation—as an attempt to close a distance that cannot necessarily be bridged so easily geographically.

García de Sena is compelled to send his books because he believes the US context is comparable to that of his home country. He emphasizes analogy, arguing that conditions in "América Española" are "tan analogas á las de este país quando trato de substraerse al yugo de Gran Bretaña" (analogous to those of this country when it attempted to separate from the yoke of Great Britain).[135] Analogy shares with translation a cognitive dynamic that involves source and target. When information or meaning from one subject (the source) is transferred to another (the target), analogy proposes likeness. This is also the spirit of translation, even if a translated text inevitable introduces a variety of differences. For García de Sena, the United States provides the language (in English) of the documents as well as the example of republican institutions. At one point, analogy comes close to identification, as García de Sena writes, "Nuestra causa es en todo identica á la que estos defendieron. La union que los hizo triunfar de sus Tiranos, es la unica que puede tambien salvarnos a nosotros" (Our cause is in all ways identical to one defended by these [states]. The union that drove them to triumph over their Tyrants is the only one that can also save us).[136] Thus he calls for replicating the manner in which independence is achieved.

García de Sena's emphasis on target-territory is the reason that for decades historians have debated whether *La independencia de la Costa Firme* was influential in independence movements. Enthusiastic positions have been developed on both sides. Pedro Grases and Alberto Harkness have argued, "Nunca podremos medir con exactitude matemática la influencia que tuvo García de Sena en los primeros proyectos constitucionales de Hispanoamérica. Sin embargo, podemos declarar definitivamente que fué grande" (We will never be able to measure with mathematical precision the influence that García de Sena exerted on the first constitutional projects of Spanish America. Nevertheless, we can declare definitively that it was significant).[137] By contrast, Jaime Rodriguez O. has argued that while García de Sena's books circulated in South American port cities, their influence is not evident.[138] Letters remain showing that political actors in Caracas read and circulated *La independencia de la Costa Firme*. Seven crates containing 125 copies each arrived in that city, and the contents of one crate were sold before authorities seized the remaining copies.[139] In addition, we see references to *La independencia de la Costa Firme* in books by intellectuals who engaged with the Filadelfia circle. The Chile-based writer and political theorist Juan Egaña, for example, cites García de Sena's translation of the US Constitution in his *Memorias políticas sobre las federaciones* (1825), a book that will prompt a rebuttal in *Cartas de un americano*, to which we turn in chapter 4.[140]

Attempts to gauge the influence of one book in the revolutionary space of the Americas are liable to remain circular. How are we to measure the influence of one book? For Latino literary history, the more important consideration is how García de Sena's focus on target-territory was made possible by Filadelfia as a print center with symbolic potential. The

Philadelphia setting also allows us to consider the United States as one of the target-territories considered by García de Sena. Were there potential Spanish-language readers in Philadelphia?

Translation and Early Latino Literature

García de Sena's books show how trans-American production and circulation constituted an important dimension of early Latino literature. At the same time, they show how historical conditions led to the production of books and other materials that do not correlate to contemporary notions of literary texts. I use *literature* in reference to textual production that includes not only novels and poems but also translations, pamphlets, and political philosophy. One of the challenges a book such as *La independencia de la Costa Firme* presents to contemporary readers is how to consider its place in literary history without situating it as derivative of a great original (*Common Sense*). I have been arguing that it is important to avoid the types of evaluation of stylistic accomplishment that reemerge in A. Owen Aldridge's 1982 comparative study of the Americas. Aldridge writes, "Except for parts of *Common Sense,* the contents of the *Independencia* are dry and prosaic, in large part documentary in nature, and in our day they would seem rather forbidding reading."[141] Aldridge is operating with a notion of translation that values the transference from source to target, a point emphasized when he characterizes García's *Historia* as "a rather rough translation."[142] Aldridge's point seems to be that for a critic working comparatively in the Americas, García de Sena's book is at best a copy of something that is available in the original English. The notion of "forbidding reading" does raise an important consideration for those who encounter nineteenth-century Spanish-language materials in the United States: sometimes these texts do not fit easily into existing generic categories, and thus they might come across as forbidding, or difficult to apprehend.

Although García de Sena's translations retain the flavor of the English-language documents and thus are not likely to be forbidding to someone interested in revolutionary pamphlets and constitutional theory, Aldridge's "forbidding reading" is a wonderful phrase to characterize the types of hermeneutic challenges presented by some writings that are part of early Latino literature: how to make sense of texts that do not conform to more recent historical notions of literary value and sometimes call for historical approaches to interpretation? For example, the valorization of original authorship that underwrites much literary criticism, and that we would grant to Paine, is missing in García de Sena's translation work, which prioritized the circulation of ideas over his own individual achievement.

Politically oriented translation projects are an important component of the multiplicity of texts that make up early Latino literature. In a very general sense, they point to the importance of crossing from one language to another (and back) in Latino history, especially in the context of the anticolonial dimensions of these projects. The movement from Spanish to English, and vice versa, and the way that movement is imbricated in social power relations is an important dimension of Latino experiences in various historical moments. But in a more specific way, translations raise the question of how readers today can approach materials that differ in important ways from contemporary examples of Latino literature. Rather than sending us a self-authored book, García de Sena enters the network of translation and inspires not only a Hispanophone but also a Hispanicized Paine—"Tomás"—who speaks about Spanish America long after the US Revolution.

For US history, García de Sena's book registers the circulation of Spanish-language materials in Philadelphia. With a vibrant and competitive book market, Hispanophone publishing was integrated into the commerce of the city, as is apparent in the advertisement for *La independencia de la Costa Firme* that appeared at the top of the front page in the Philadelphia *Aurora General Advertiser* on July 24, 1811. "PUBLISHED TO-DAY" was the headline, followed by "AND FOR SALE BY FERNAGUS, AT HIS FOREIGN BOOK STORE," a reference to the bookseller Jean Louis Fernagus. The bilingual advertisement shifted from descriptions of the content in Spanish to information about the book in English, "The Whole in one Octavo Volume. Price in Boards $2.50." The ad shows that there was a Spanish-language book-buying public in Philadelphia in 1811, and thus the commercial interest in Spanish-language printing was also local. At the start of the nineteenth century, Philadelphia was a city of about seventy thousand people (the largest in the United States), and the enclave of Spanish-speaking residents was small.[143] It is likely that Fernagus expected to sell no more than a few dozen copies. Perhaps more interesting are the claims made by the advertisement about the book's importance: "This work may be properly called the *Vade mecum* of every true Spanish Patriot. It contains all the basis of social contract, and will prove highly beneficial to the cause of that American nation who is so firmly disposed to, and almost mature for, political regeneration." The use of *vade mecum*—Latin for "go with me" and thus suggesting a guide—indicates that this publication was meant to be kept in a pocket. In the ad, the "American nation" is not a specific place but rather any country in the hemisphere that is ready to shift away from colonialism and toward "political regeneration," a term sometimes associated with the US Revolution that in this case situates colonial rule as a backward condition.

The advertisement in the *Aurora* indicates that there was a predilection for change already taking place in García de Sena's target-territories. At the same time, Spanish-language readers in the United States were seen as potentially spreading the word. The belief that people were "disposed to" and ready to embrace republican principles is reiterated in other Filadelfia books. García de Sena's dedication implies that his readers will be acquainted with some of the principles: "Americanos españoles: si os dedico este mi primer ensayo de traducción en las obras de Thomas Paine, no es para inspiraros sentimientos que os sean desconocidos; sino para que agregado a la negra, pérfida, y excecrable administración de justicia de los monstruos que aborta la España para gobernaros, sirva de justificación a vuestra laudable y generosa conducta" (Spanish Americans: I dedicate to you my first attempt at the translation of the work of Thomas Paine not to inspire thoughts that are unknown to you; rather it is meant to justify the laudable and honorable course you have taken in the face of the dark, treacherous, and abominable administration of justice carried out by the monsters that Spain spits out and sends to govern you).[144] Thus the point of the translation is not to introduce something completely new but rather to deploy the writings of Paine as a way to support a rapidly evolving movement. This partly explains García de Sena's urgency.

As part of the history of US Spanish-language publishing, *La independencia de la Costa Firme* is intertwined with hemispheric movements. That is to say, García de Sena's notion of a target-territory is impossible without the source *location* of Filadelfia. In the hemispherically interconnected world of early Latino literature, the advertisement in the *Aurora* and the copies of the book that make their way to Caracas were part of a rapidly changing economy of letters that traversed region, nation, and language. Whatever the success of *La independencia de la Costa Firme* in spreading revolutionary thoughts in Spanish-speaking America, the book certainly helped fuel the rise of Filadelfia as a symbol and print center.

2

The Trans-American Elite

When Manuel Torres, political operative and diplomat, died in 1822, the funeral procession from 355 Walnut Street to St. Mary's Catholic Church in Philadelphia drew an estimated twenty thousand people. Sometimes called the "Franklin of South America," Torres (1762–1822) was the most influential US-based supporter of independence for Spanish America in the first two decades of the century.[1] Not long before his death, Torres had been the first diplomat received from one of the new South American countries by a US president, James Monroe, marking the first formal US recognition of a new Spanish American nation. Torres's funeral procession included two bands of wind instruments and two drum-and-fife corps, Philadelphia politicians, members of the local bar association, officers from the US Navy and Marine Corps, representatives of various Spanish American countries, clergymen from various churches, and youth representing what had by then become his home country of Colombia.[2] The Philadelphia *Aurora General Advertiser* published the following in its lengthy account of the funeral: "There was much due, and much respect was paid to the great qualities and character of the individual—but it was the great cause of all America, and the sympathy produced by the recency of the recognition of the Colombian Republic, and the demise of the man whose devotion to that cause, whose profound views and wisdom had contributed so much to enlighten our own government, and to strengthen the ties which had been formed by his sagacity and moderation, between the two sections of the new world, that operated to produce that generous concourse, which was testified by the solemnity of the last service of his mortal separation."[3] "Sympathy" was invoked not only for Torres but also for independence movements labeled "the cause of all America," bringing together the man with the hemisphere. Touched by a rhetorical enthusiasm occasioned by death, the piece inverted a narrative of US revolutionary influence on Spanish America by proposing that Torres had also enlightened the US government with his belief in hemispheric commonality.

The laudatory obituary reflects Torres's standing in the United States. "It has always been a matter of great pride to those Philadelphians who believe that this city is an inspiration in the advancement of freedom and liberty, to know that Manuel Torres resided in this city for at least twenty-five years," said Philadelphia mayor Freeland Kendrick more than one hundred years after Torres's death.[4] The protagonist in the story of Filadelfia's support for independence in the southern Americas, Torres helped procure arms for the war, and his house in Philadelphia became an independence cauldron for those who passed through on various diplomatic and military missions.[5] "The listening post for politicians, merchants, bankers, writers, editors, and rebel agents, Torres was the most significant figure in the Spanish American diplomacy of his day," Charles H. Bowman Jr. writes.[6] Torres's connections and contacts in the Anglo United States included Secretary of State John Quincy Adams, the banker Nicholas Biddle, and the newspaper editor William Duane, who was a good friend. Fluent in English, Torres published a language-learning book and an economic treatise, *An Exposition of the Commerce of Spanish America* (Philadelphia, 1816), both the result of his participation in the socioeconomic life of the United States.

How and to what extent Torres might have influenced US diplomatic relations with Spanish America has interested historians for decades, and some have connected him to the Monroe Doctrine, a point to which we turn later in this chapter.[7] More recently, scholars of Latino studies have emphasized Torres's influence in Filadelfia's growing Spanish American community, with Emily García writing, "Torres's life and work remind us that Latino and US identities were mutually informed decades before 1898 or even 1848 and that their mutual imbrication was at the heart of national independence in the South as well as the North."[8] But Torres's possible influence on hemispheric independence needs to be preceded by another compelling question: How did Torres, who went into exile in Philadelphia in 1796, reach a position in which such a claim to influence could even be made? Whatever cultural or language shock he may have suffered from moving to the United States, Torres spent twenty-five-plus years integrating himself into the highest ranks of US political culture and Philadelphia's commercial elite, so that he was able to retain his social status through a process of immigration to the United States, where he settled until his death.

Torres's deftness at navigating the new country reminds us of his elevated position in Colombia, where he had owned and run a plantation. According to several sources, Torres was very successful at overseeing indigenous labor. But his involvement in seditious activities against the colonial government forced him into exile. William Duane tells us that Torres was imprisoned for participating in a conspiracy to establish an independent state, but his influence and standing "rendered the walls of his prison feeble."[9] Among the participants in these events was a young aristocrat, Antonio Nariño, whose early activities for independence included translating and printing the French Declaration of the Rights of Man. Anthony McFarlane has argued that the 1794 movement that led to the incarceration of at least twenty-two men (including Torres) was the result of various factors, including changes in education toward a more secular curriculum, increased interest in science, and the emergence of a periodical press.[10] Torres walked away from New Granada with both exposure to new ideas emerging from the Enlightenment and a penchant for periodical work. His financial resources carried him to his new base of operations in Philadelphia, and Torres was able to transfer his socioeconomic position from one country to another. His affiliation with a US revolutionary tradition allowed him to perceive himself not as an outsider but as someone participating in a historical process that stretched from his home country to Philadelphia.

Torres's ability to move from one country to another and make his way in rarefied circles exemplifies the types of cultural and language crossings of those I term the *trans-American elite,* a group of men with impressive educational backgrounds who had the resources to travel through or settle in the northeastern United States and to publish their texts, thus creating much of the work that makes up Filadelfia letters.[11] The trans-American elite included men with tremendous wealth, such as Torres and Vicente Rocafuerte, and prominent priests, such as Félix Varela. Others had tremendous educational attainments, including Juan Germán Roscio, who had doctorates in canon law and civil law and taught at the Universidad Real y Pontificia in Caracas. Still others came from prominent families that could bankroll their stay in the United States. In the case of José María Heredia, his uncle Ignacio Heredia y Campuzano, a coffee plantation owner who became Heredia's guardian after the death of the poet's father, funded Heredia's residency and travel. José María's letters to his uncle regularly mention whether he has drawn on or used the monthly stipend from his benefactor. "Most indulgent and tender of friends," Heredia writes at one point. "How will I ever repay this debt for which I am immensely grateful?"[12] How indeed, when one considers that Heredia's US stay was funded in part through Cuba's slave-based economy.

These men shared many of the social, economic, and educational advantages that allowed Torres to make inroads into important political and print-culture arenas in the United States. In their home societies, the trans-American elite got their money from inherited wealth and family influence; many had been born into the administrative and military upper echelons of the Spanish Empire. Those resources gave them access to a classical education, and as a result of their learning they were able to plug into Filadelfia print culture and produce their texts. What becomes apparent is that the mobile participants in these print-culture formations conceived of themselves as supranational elites who were capable of crossing territories and languages. In contrast to revolutionary elites who participated in local military battles for independence in Spanish America, the trans-American elite moved through various print-culture sites.

My term *trans-American elite* recognizes the influence these intellectuals had in their home societies, but it is also important to remember that *elite* is also the name of a 12-point typeface, which is the standard size for letters (twelve spaces to the inch). This chapter is not about the sociology of Spanish American elites; rather it is about how the resources available to these intellectuals allowed them to produce texts and participate in geographic and political trans-American movements. Elite as a typeface is more than a convenient metaphor; this chapter focuses on the published writing of two very different figures: Félix Varela and Manuel Torres. In committing themselves to sending out their published work as letters, these men encountered social contradictions that led them to politically radical positions and even exile. Coming from upper-class families, they were part of an independence vanguard, challenging colonial rule and in some cases facing prison time for their activities. Writing was an important dimension of the actions they took to prompt governmental change and develop new understandings of political subjectivity. In the United States, they were not always able to retain their economic power. Thus, the term *trans-American elite* is less a reference to a deterministic economic category and more an indication of personal capacity to write and publish material across geographic distance.

The trans-American elite bring forward an important aspect of Latino literary history: many of the figures we consider as the antecedents to contemporary Latino literature were economically empowered and moved across the Americas. Considering that the field of Latino studies has from its emergence taken as one of its primary concerns the racial and economic oppression of people of Latin American descent in the United States, it is important *not* to assume equivalences between subjects or even political positions across centuries. To consider progressive politics in the nineteenth century demands historical specificity. At least since José Aranda called out attempts to claim a subaltern position for María Amparo Ruiz de Burton (herself a type of trans-American elite), Latino literary history has been grappling with the role of socioeconomic background in historical research. The social positions of trans-American figures are not static and can change with time and movement, as Juan Poblete's article about Vicente Pérez Rosales's participation in the California Gold Rush has shown.[13] A person with social privilege in Latin America can experience a different economic and racial dynamic in the United States. So let us begin with the consideration of how the term *trans-American elite* relates to other terminology.

Trans-American Movements: Does *Criollo* Travel?

As the preceding chapter showed, Filadelfia letters were affected by different types of movement: the circulation of texts, the travel and migration of intellectuals, translation and transference from one language and place to another, and the dissemination of ideas across the Atlantic and the Americas. I emphasize an elite position less to note class distinction, which is apparent, than to show how the resources available to these trans-American figures were intricately connected to notions of textual and language exchange and the transmission of writing. Both before and after the rise of national governments, the trans-American elite's desire to publish their writing necessitated travel to print centers in various countries and involved circulation across the hemisphere.

Nowhere is the ease of movement and its connection to thinking more apparent than in a passage from Vicente Rocafuerte's memoir looking back on his travel to Europe years before publishing *Ideas necesarias* in Philadelphia. Rocafuerte had been chosen as a deputy to represent Guayaquil at Spain's national assembly convened in Cádiz after the liberal Constitution of 1812 was put in place:

> Como yo iba a España a defender el derecho constitutional de los pueblos, y a trabajar al mismo tiempo por la independencia de la América, combinándola con los intereses comerciales y bien entendidos de la Península, me era indispensable prepararme a llenar tan importantes deberes. Para estudiarlos, conocerlos bien y llegar a un resultado positivo, me pareció necesario viajar por algunos países constitucionales de la Europa.... Fui a Inglaterra con intención de pasar despues a Suecia.... Salimos de Londres para Haruich; allí

nos embarcamos para Gotemburgo, recorrimos la Suecia, parte de Noruega, y por Abo, capital de Finalandia, llegamos a San Petersburgo en julio de 1813.... La Emperatriz extendió a nosotros su genial benevolencia ... y tuvimos el honor de comer dos vecez con la familia imperial, con el Principe Nicolás, hoy Emperador de Rusia.[14]

(Since I was going to Spain to defend the constitutional rights of the people, and to work at the same time for the independence of America without disavowing the well-known commercial interests of the [Spanish] peninsula, it was indispensable that I prepare myself to take on such important duties. In order to study constitutional rights, understand them well, and accomplish my goals, I found it necessary to travel through various constitutional countries in Europe.... I went to England with the intention of moving on to Sweden.... We departed from London to Harwich; there we sailed to Gothenburg, traveled through Sweden and part of Norway, through Abo [Turku], capital of Finland, and arrived in St. Petersburg in July of 1813.... The Empress extended to us her genial hospitality ... and we had the honor of eating two meals with the royal family, including Prince Nicholas, who is today emperor of Russia.)

What is striking about the passage is its lack of wonder at the ability to move from one country to another. Rocafuerte might as well be talking about a weekend excursion to see a friend near his home. He sees the travel as a *necessity* for his education, and the offhand tone of the travelogue betrays tremendous privilege. Similarly, his taking meals with the highest levels of Russian aristocracy is without wonder. Upon his return, Rocafuerte proclaims, he has new ideas about representative government and is convinced that "all patriots" have a duty to introduce such government in their respective countries. This type of itinerary opens a window onto how trans-American elites saw themselves moving around the world in connection with their intellectual work.

This cosmopolitan sense of being in the world was fueled by the Filadelfia group's reading of eighteenth-century European philosophical writing in the original language, including Montesquieu's *De l'esprit des lois* (1748). The collection *Cartas de un americano* (1826) offers a reading of *The Federalist Papers* and engages with European political theorists. Manuel Lorenzo de Vidaurre was even known as the Peruvian Rousseau, a point to which we turn in chapter 5. The privilege of a classical education opened a path for these intellectuals to think across languages as an inspiration for moving across the territories. Geographic crossings became necessary to philosophical exchange, as we have seen in Manuel García de Sena's translations of Thomas Paine.

The etymology of *elite* goes back to the Latin *electa*, which conveys a sense of the chosen, and indeed many of the Filadelfia writers were chosen to represent their countries in Spain at the Cortes, convened during periods of reform, or to represent independence movements in other countries.[15] Because of their influence, the trans-American elite have some elements in common with what C. Wright Mills called "the power elite," namely "those political, economic, and military circles which as an intricate set of overlapping cliques share decisions having at least national consequences."[16] Mills's argument focuses on the mid-twentieth-century United States and on the "upper circles" of powerful institutions, but his analysis introduces relevant aspects of elite formation when he describes the group as "composed of men of similar origin and education." Mills continues, "In so far as their careers and their styles of life are similar, there are psychological and social bases for their unity," which in turn leads to "easy intermingling."[17] At times, the trans-American elite are such not because of their money but because of shared intellectual interests.

Education is a crucial influence on the trans-American elite because it facilitates communication and allows them to exchange ideas in various countries, including the United States. Given the large numbers of people without access to formal education in Spanish America during the colonial era, the privilege of learning itself indicated distinction. For example, the nineteenth-century historian José Manuel Restrepo estimated that during the colonial period education was not available to 80 percent of the population in Nueva Granada.[18] Even among the literate, the trans-American elite were some of the most respected intellectuals in their societies. Filadelfia writers were educated in one or more of the following settings: through private tutors; at the finest schools available in their home countries, including universities that had been in operation for centuries; and in European schools. Education cannot be extricated from the economic and social resources that allow certain families to situate young men within this privileged system. François-Xavier Guerra is not wrong in categorizing leaders of Spanish America's revolution as a *cultural* rather than an economic class in that what they shared was a common set of assumptions developed from Enlightenment revolutionary ideals; Guerra argues that discussion circles (*tertulias*) among students and clerics gave rise to the most important social movements.[19]

Most Filadelfia writers studied French and Latin, and their entrance into US society was facilitated by an ability to participate in multilingual exchange. A description of the type of education enjoyed by the trans-American elite is offered in the anonymously published *Manual de un republicano* (Philadelphia, 1812), which presents a series of dialogues between a teacher and a "disciple." In a discussion with a student who has returned after "a journey of six months, through several states in the Union," the teacher says, "You understand the Greek language, you speak the Latin tongue, you are learned in sacred, profane, and modern history; in natural history, chronology, geography, astronomy, and mathematicks."[20] As a result of language study, many Filadelfia intellectuals worked as language instructors in the United States, as we will see below with Torres's forays into language education. The movement from one language to another, whether in personal communications or in the translations published, is more than a metaphor for trans-American movement; it is an acquired ability that is intertwined with travel and geographic changes. The importance of crossing the Americas for these figures is one reason why the word *letrado*, invoked often for educated men in Spanish America, is inadequate for describing the trans-American elite. Depending on the context, a *letrado* could be an administrative judge, a notary or a lawyer, or one who took up literary concerns.[21]

If *letrado* is insufficient, then so is *criollo,* which in Spanish America referred to someone of European descent born in the Americas. The term, often translated as "creole," implies access to power, with some historians telling the story of Spanish America's independence in relation to *criollos* fighting for their own interests against European colonial rule. Ralph Bauer and Antonio Mazzotti have argued that the "discourse of creolization and the creole subject" are important for studying both Anglo and Spanish America "as well as for comparative literary analysis of the literatures of the colonial Americas."[22] Under Spanish American taxonomies of race, *criollos* were located toward the top of their societies, even if the most prominent position was reserved for *peninsulares,* whites born in Spain. In some cases, *criollos* were denied the most important colonial posts and kept from certain social prerogatives and political privileges granted to *peninsulares.*[23] From a European perspective, the word *criollo* carried pejorative connotations connected to notions of European superiority over Americans. "The lowest, least educated and uncultivated European believes himself superior to the white born in the New World," wrote Alexander von Humboldt.[24] The logic of European superiority led to an ordering of various forms of identity, so that creoles saw themselves as superior to indigenous and black populations. Bauer and Mazzotti have emphasized the "ambiguous subject positions within the imperial geopolitical and the colonial social order" of creoles, who are not granted the social standing of Europeans.[25] To varying degrees depending on local historical formations, Spanish American societies included a large number of indigenous populations, who were forced to contribute free labor on plantations or in mines. In certain settings, significant black slave populations were also part of the social hierarchy. Free blacks and people of mixed ancestry—including mestizos and *pardos* (mixed African heritage)—were mostly among the lower economic classes.

Bauer and Mazzotti connect the social position of creoles to conceptions of nature in the Americas as inferior to Europe. "The environmental determinism of Enlightenment philosophes such as Montesquieu, Raynal, Voltaire, and Buffon led to the inevitable conclusion that Americans of whatever ancestry were 'destined' (in the words of William Robertson) 'to remain uncivilized' because of New World climates and soils," they write.[26] As noted in the preceding chapter, Thomas Jefferson and José María Heredia wrote about the mastodon in Philadelphia in part in response to European charges that people, animals, and even land in the Americas were inferior. In other words, they battled not only monarchical rule but also notions of European superiority.

The hierarchical racialized effects of empire stretched from Spanish to Anglo colonies and explains why Benedict Anderson invokes the term *creole* across the Americas to argue that "pilgrim creole functionaries and provincial creole printmen played the decisive historic role" in shaping anticolonial nations.[27] Anderson's conclusion draws from the sense among creoles that they were waging a battle of ideas that would ultimately doom the military might of European powers. This potential North-South male affiliation (if not identification) influenced some of the Filadelfia group. Throughout Filadelfia letters we see moments in which the trans-American elite consider themselves to be working in the trajectory or spirit of US anticolonial thinkers, which in part explains the moniker "Franklin of South America" for Torres. As we have seen, Thomas Paine is central to this conception. But for the Filadelfia group, this identification leads less to a common creole experience than to a trans-American self-conception, and thus their adoption of the self-description *americano* in the hemispheric sense.

Seeing themselves in league with US revolutionaries, the trans-American elite believed their political affiliation opened doors to interaction with prominent political and economic operatives in the United States. We see this in a missive by Rocafuerte addressed in full affectionate mode to Josiah Stoddard Johnston, a Louisiana congressman who later became a US senator. The note, written to Johnston in English, is dated Philadelphia, March 1, 1823, and reads,

> I cannot remember Washington without remembering your amiable acquaintance; since I am arrived here, I have been very much engaged in my business which is not yet transacted, only offers a good prospect of success. I believed I could have returned to the federal city before the adjournment of the Congress, but the bad weather and the state of my business prevents me of having the pleasure of going to take leave of you, and to thank you for all the goodness and civilities you have shown me. I expect to have the pleasure to write you now and then, and to inquire for the interesting health of your charming lady and my friend William. I pray you do me the favor of sending me your exact direction.[28]

The use of *direction* as a false friend for the Spanish *dirección* (address) ironically emphasizes what is ultimately the dominant theme in the letter: movement. The document refers repeatedly to Rocafuerte's own travel: his memory of going to Washington, his arrival in Philadelphia, his envisioning a return to the capitol, another impending departure, and a leave-taking. (William was Johnston's son.) The letter also implicitly speaks to the revolutionary movements that had driven Rocafuerte to the United States to lobby for support from Washington. His "business" in the northeastern United States is multiple: political representation for revolutionaries, his economic ventures, and his publishing projects. Johnston would have been an appropriate ally for Rocafuerte because of the congressman's own concerns about bringing Louisiana's creole population under national republican rule.[29] The Rocafuerte-Johnston friendship is in keeping with Anderson's argument about creole American *revolutions* rather than emphasizing the US Revolution as a singular and exceptional event; however, Anderson's turn toward commonality is an invitation to consider particular conditions.

Given the differences in Spanish and Anglo Americas, the term *criollo* does not travel well from southern American countries to the United States, and it even presents problems of translation. While *criollo* is often translated into English as "creole," the English word sometimes has connotations that invoke race mixing in the Caribbean and Louisiana. Critics have called attention to the complex uses of *creole,* with Sean X. Goudie noting that "creole cultures, races, and identities did not always signify in the same ways in their Spanish, French, and British manifestations."[30] All of which is to say that *creole* can note a common mark of colonial difference from Europe across the hemisphere, but *criollo* does not explain the mobility of the trans-American elite. Nor does it begin to explain why affiliation across countries (rather than identity in the contemporary sense) are intertwined with writing and publication. In order to delve into the connection of writing to self, let us consider the work of a prominent priest.

Elite Connections: Félix Varela's *Cartas*

Writing in Spanish to Joel Roberts Poinsett on January 27, 1825, Félix Varela proclaimed, "España amigo mio es un cadaver, y no puede dar de mas que corrupcion, y principios de muerte" (Spain, my friend, is a cadaver and produces nothing but corruption and catalysts for destruction).[31] Father Varela (1788–1853), one of Cuba's major nineteenth-century intellectuals, was in the midst of publishing his periodical *El Habanero* in Philadelphia and New York and mounting an ongoing argument favoring Cuba's independence. Poinsett was a diplomat and US congressman from South Carolina with deep interests in and influence on Spanish American affairs; he had spent years in Buenos Aires and Chile as an agent and was later appointed by James Monroe as a minister to Mexico.[32] The epistolary correspondence between Varela and Poinsett indicates how lettered exchange could help facilitate integration into the United States. Varela's lengthy residence in the United States and his self-description as a resident suggest that his life was that of an immigrant who settles in a country and engages in civic life, and the Poinsett letters show that he jumped in quickly after arriving and entered into a public-sphere dialogue. This had a profound effect on his writing, particularly the book called *Cartas a Elpidio* (1835–38).

Varela's letter to Poinsett continues with a warning that change will not come while Spain rules the island: "Nada hay que esperar. Por el contrario, un Estado Nuevo (ah! si le vieramos en la isla de Cuba!) tiene todo el calor de la naturaleza en su juventud, desplega los germenes del honor y la virtud, y por un impulso irresistible camina al bien y destruye toda planta nociva" (Expect nothing. On the contrary, a new state [if only we saw one on the island of Cuba!] is in its youth warmed by nature, releases the seeds of honor and virtue, and destroys all weeds by walking toward the good with an unstoppable impulse).[33] The image of a new nation-state growing like a vigorous plant in contradistinction to Spain's decrepitude is in keeping with Varela's belief that patriotism was an offshoot of local nature. He often used the word *naturales* to distinguish those born in the Americas from the Spanish *peninsulares*. But more to the point of this chapter, the letter's recipient shows us that Varela had connections with a prominent US politician less than two years after Varela's arrival in the United States. Two letters from Varela to Poinsett in January 1825 are packed with warm phrases, one of them signed from "your affectionate friend" and with "Q.S.M.B." (*que su mano besa,* with a kiss to your hand).

Varela discusses the ongoing US campaign against pirates in the Caribbean, showing himself sensitive to US geopolitical interests (Poinsett's concern), while advocating Cuban independence. Varela argues that the pirates will never be defeated, because Spain fails to move against them and the colonial government looks the other way while merchants in Cuba buy goods from the pirates. An independent Cuba, Varela proposes, would be a partner in combating the pirates. He writes, "Si este gobierno intenta por medios puramente externos contener la pirateria, es perder absolutamente el tiempo, y exponerse al ridiculo, ps. las armas de una nacion respetable seran siempre burladas por una porcion de picaros, sostenidos por otros iguales pero mas codiciosos; y tolerados por un gobierno a quien sólo queda el nombre" (If this government [the United States] attempts to contain piracy outside the island, it will be an absolute waste of time and expose it to ridicule, for a few rogues within can mock the military force of a respectable nation. They receive support from greedy people and are tolerated by a government that is such in name only).[34] By this account, business interests in Havana are in league with the pirates, and the local rulers make money from it.

Varela picks up on the topic of pirates in an article titled "Tranquilidad de la Isla de Cuba" (Calm on the island of Cuba), in the second issue of *El Habanero*. Discussing how hemispheric America should respond to Cuba's colonial situation, Varela writes, "El gobierno de la Isla, débil o indolente, pues no me atrevo a llamarle cómplice como algunos sospechan, no pone remedio a este mal que se aumenta cada día, en términos que los piratas parece que forman ya una nación temida, si no reconocida por aquel gobierno" (Although I do not dare to characterize it as complicit, the island's government, through its own weakness or indolence, does not solve the problem of pirates, which grow in number each day and can be said to form a feared nation with diplomatic relations on the island).[35] As if echoing his letter to Poinsett. Varela writes in *El Habanero,* "Los piratas no son únicamente los que salen al mar, sino los compradores de los efectos, que animan estas empresas con su codiciosa y criminal conducta" (The pirates are not only those who go out to sea but also those greedy and criminal businesses that buy their goods and support the enterprise).[36]

Varela's correspondence with Poinsett depicts the elite connections available to those who brought to the United States a certain economic or intellectual status. Perhaps no other Spanish American making his way to the northeastern United States in the early nineteenth century came with the intellectual pedigree of Varela, whose geo-biography was intricately connected to trans-American movement. His background helps explain how he could integrate himself into political conversations and print culture in the United States so soon after arriving, and a brief sketch of his life shows the importance of movement.

Born in Havana, Varela grew up in St. Augustine, Florida, when it was still part of Spain. His grandfather was the commander of military forces there. Varela returned to the city of his birth to attend the San Carlos Seminary and also took courses at the Real y Pontificia Universidad San Gerónimo, which was then under the influence of the Dominican Order and later became the University of Havana. Ordained a priest at age twenty-three, Varela was appointed to the faculty at San Carlos, where he taught philosophy, constitutional law, and the sciences, becoming perhaps the most influential Cuban educator of his day. From 1818 to 1820, Varela published his *Lecciones de filosofía* (Philosophy lessons). His students included José Antonio Saco, Domingo Del Monte, and José de la Luz y Caballero—all prominent intellectuals whose travels were sustained by personal resources. (Saco and Del Monte, as we will see in the next chapter, also published materials in Philadelphia.) An early proponent of independence and abolition, Varela is venerated in Cuba as one of its great nineteenth-century figures and credited for inspiring generations of anticolonial thinkers.[37]

Varela came to settle in the United States through a series of historical events tied to governmental changes and wars in Spain and the Americas. In 1821, Varela was elected to represent Cuba at the Spanish Cortes in yet another of Spain's attempts to establish a liberal constitution. Like Rocafuerte before him, Varela made his way to Spain. He signed on to a petition for independence and wrote an article calling for the abolition of slavery. When the liberal project collapsed and Ferdinand VII reclaimed his position as absolute monarch, Varela was forced to flee or else face possible execution. He escaped to Gibraltar and landed in New York in 1823.[38] He spent time in Philadelphia and then in 1825 settled in New York, where he carried out his Catholic ministry for decades. Varela returned to St. Augustine late in life and died there. Varela's activity in the United States was never far from the publication of books and newspapers and included significant contributions to a budding Catholic press in New York City in the 1830s and 1840s.[39]

Varela is among the trans-American elite because of resources available to him as a child of a prominent military family and because of his educational attainments, but he did not enjoy financial wealth throughout his life. If anything, Varela helps us unravel the contradictions encountered by the trans-American elite as a result of moving to a new country. Not long after arriving in the United States, Varela committed himself to the life of a parish priest, and he spent much of his energy helping immigrants from Ireland in the gritty Five Points neighborhood of Lower Manhattan. "He worked unselfishly to help educate the poor immigrants and provided pastoral guidance to those needing spiritual care," Juan M. Navia writes.[40] In other words, Varela's commitments are closer to the socially conscious work of an immigrant working among economically disempowered than to preserving an elite lifestyle. In the United States, Varela's spiritual emphasis moved away from philosophical investigations and toward what I would call a preferential option for the poor, to use the language of twentieth-century Latin American Catholic bishops. Carmen Lamas's research on Varela's work as a Catholic priest in New York situates him as a contributor to education and to the democratization of US society through the inclusion of minority populations in the parishes where he worked.[41] By the time of his death, Varela had given away his personal resources (other than an impressive library) and was described by his former pupils as living in poverty.

After he arrived in the United States, Varela became an important figure in US Latino letters as he moved into a trans-American publication circuit. Two of his major publishing projects—*El Habanero* (1824–26) and *Cartas a Elpidio* (1835–38)—illustrate Varela's concern with political self-determination and religious belief. But they do so through a universalist discourse of political rights and religious morality rather than through attention to the racial, economic, and gender hierarchies of Spanish American societies, points to which we will return in the next two chapters. *El Habanero* and *Cartas a Elpidio* both have elements of the elite epistolary exchange that I have associated with early Latino literature. Both are written not primarily to a US audience but to readers in Cuba with a trans-American sensibility as context. Varela makes clear in both texts that his primary audience is young people.[42] He continues his professorial work in print. That pedagogical spirit informs *Cartas a Elpidio,* two volumes made up of eleven "letters" on the themes of irreligiosity and superstition.

Cartas a Elpidio records a profound disconnect between Varela's stated audience, young people in Cuba, and his engagement with the United States as his new home. Varela adheres to a Christian discourse that he views as applicable to Cuba and, presumably, everywhere else. But even as he reaches out to the island, Varela is focused on religious groups and people in his new home and develops his discussion through a series of scenes that place his work directly in northeastern US cities. The US context, as it emerges both in the print-culture conditions influencing the book and in a series of episodes narrated in the letters, contradicts the Catholic claim to a universal religious system that he believes is applicable to Havana readers. Much of the first volume proceeds with a decontextualized discussion of "human" religious practices and belief systems. Varela ruminates on what drives people to atheism, skepticism, and superstitious practices. As the book's full title clarifies, these are *Cartas a Elpidio, sobre la impiedad, la superstición y el fanatismo en sus relaciones con la sociedad* (Letters to Elpidio on irreligiosity, superstition, and fanaticism in their relation with society)—that is, society in general and not a specific place.

In Varela's Catholic cosmology, both truth and damnation are eternal. The first volume opens with the following temporal claim: "Pasan los tiempos, y con ellos los hombres, mas la verdad inmóvil observa los giros de su mísera carrera hasta verlos precipitarse con pasos vacilantes en el abismo de la eternidad, dejando signos indelebles de que solo convinieron en la impotencia" (Time passes, and men with it, but perennial truth watches the cyclical nature of men's miserable struggles and witnesses how they hesitate before plunging into the eternal abyss and leave behind indelible signs of impotent living).[43] Such a salvo in the opening to his letters is Varela's dire warning about the effects of a lack of belief. The subtitle of the letter is "La impiedad es causa del descontento individual y social" (Irreligiosity is the cause of individual and social unhappiness). How religious belief interacts with society is presented in terms of true believers versus those who choose an "irreligious" path, among them liberal intellectuals who prefer their philosophy without the religious associations that Varela proposes.

Not far into the first letter, Varela offers true religion as an antidote to the "unfortunate history of human error, of the ill-fated effects of runaway passions." "Mas, entre tantas ruinas espantosas, se descubren various puntos brillantísimos, que jamás oscurecieron las sombras de la muerte: vense, querido Elpidio, los sepulcros de los justos, que encierran las reliquias de aquellos templos de su almas puras, que volaron al centro de la verdad" (But amid so many horrible ruins we can find bright beacons that were never darkened by the shadows of death: the graves of the just prevail, dear Elpidio, and they contain relics of the temples of truth that were contained in their souls).[44] From this perspective, it is the soul that contains the truth. For Varela, true religion (Catholicism) stands in opposition to superstition. He works in a perennial tradition that associates belief in God with social well-being and eternal salvation. In this tradition, time is not a progression but conflation of past, present, and future under a conception of truth.

Varela's emphasis on transhistorical salvation is evident in his use of the name Elpidio. Scholars going back to the nineteenth century have questioned whether Elpidio was an actual person. Was Varela writing specifically to one of his students?[45] At times he does refer to the actions of a particular person. But the word *elpidio* comes from the Greek *elpis*, which means hope or an expectation of good to come. In a Christian sense, *elpis* can mean hope for eternal salvation. Thus, Varela's *Elpidio* anthropomorphizes a concept. It is possible that the book's many intimate references (e.g., "my dear Elpidio" or "my Elpidio") are rhetorical. Even if Varela had someone in particular in mind, it appears that in the process of composing his book he lost track of his potential readership in Cuba and ended up writing a book to a concept, an imaginary readership, making his *Cartas* a book written primarily to something rather than to someone.

As the letters continue, the discussion of Catholic belief gives way to Varela's thoughts on Protestant denominations, itinerant preachers, and religious figures, all in the United States. This discussion of conditions in the United States is in keeping with the book's connection to northeastern US print culture. The first volume (on irreligiosity) was printed in 1835 in New York at "la imprenta de D. Guillermo Newell" (William Newell's print shop). Varela himself paid for the run with support from his wealthy friends in Havana.[46] The second volume (on superstition) was printed in 1838 in New York at a shop run by G. P. Scott & Co. A third volume (on fanaticism) was never printed because of the apathetic reception (and poor sales) of the first two volumes. While *El Habanero* has been claimed by Cuban national historiography as a major contribution to the island's long struggle for independence, the letters to Elpidio have not enjoyed similar acclaim.

Cartas a Elpidio was a tremendous failure in terms of sales and intellectual influence. Until the publication of *Elpidio,* Varela's work had been widely celebrated. *Lecciones de filosofía* went through four editions in Havana, Philadelphia, and New York between 1818 and 1828. A fifth edition of the *Lecciones* was published in New York in 1841. *El Habanero*'s fiery position on independence caught the attention of Spanish authorities, who banned the publication. By contrast, *Cartas a Elpidio* was neither banned nor widely purchased. The first volume was commended by Havana's bishop, and Varela took that as a positive sign for potential sales on the island.[47] But when the copies did not move, Varela found himself out of the money that he had invested in the printing. Varela's desperation is evident in the following letter to José de la Luz y Caballero:

> En cuanto a las desgraciadas Cartas a Elpidio le suplico a usted encarecidamente que vea cuanto antes al doctor Suárez por si acaso no ha recibido una carta que le escribí hace muy pocos días, y que le diga que sin pérdida de momento me mande todos los ejemplares para ver si puedo venderlos en otra parte o quemarlos, para sacar cualquier cosa con que pagar los gastos de impresión. Estoy apuradísimo (como usted no puede figurarse) y es justo castigo de mi tontería en meterme a escritor, y lo que es más a editor sin fondos. De veras que si hubiera de escribir el tercer tomito que debía tratar del fanatismo me bastaría observarme a mí mismo, pues soy el primer fanático, puesto que casi siempre me he lanzado a hacer el bien sin tener medios para ello. A los cuatro meses o más de haber mandado mi obra a la Habana nada se de ella! Esto me hace creer que ha tenido mala suerte.[48]

> (In reference to the unfortunate Letters to Elpidio, I ask you urgently to visit as soon as possible Dr. Suárez in case he has not received a letter that I wrote a few days ago, and tell him that as soon as possible he should send me all of the copies to see if I can sell them elsewhere in order to get something to pay the printing costs, or incinerate them. I am in strained circumstances [you can't imagine] and it is an appropriate punishment for my foolishness in impersonating a writer, and even worse a publisher without funds. The truth is that if I were to write the third little volume, which is supposed to treat fanaticism, I would have to look at myself for being a major fanatic, considering that I have always committed myself to do good without having the money for it. Four months after sending my work to Havana, I know nothing about it. This leads me to conclude that it has met with bad luck.)[49]

This passage reveals that Varela was captive to the monetary vagaries of print culture. He had exhausted his finances for the print run.

The poor sales of *Cartas a Elpidio* force him to confront the book for what it became: an experiment in coterie publishing. Both the formal epistolary gestures of *Cartas a Elpidio* and the printed material speak to the privilege of his imagined readers. The book's title claims the letter as a form, no doubt because of the intimate tone between Varela and Elpidio, but the *cartas* are closer to essays or even personal essays, depending on whether the focus is a religious question or Varela's experiences in New York. The content does not seem to attract his audience of (elite) young men in Cuba, which explains why Varela is despondent at the lack of sales.

In many ways *Cartas a Elpidio* is a chronicle of a priest's assimilation into US religious society. More than a decade after leaving Cuba, Varela had evolved in a trans-American way that prevented an easy return to Cuban intellectual culture. Instead, he produced US Latino literature and gives us an account of a priest's interaction with people and places in the northeastern United States. Although she does not discount Varela's connection to Cuba, Carmen Lamas argues that "*Cartas* speaks to a desire to find in the United States the values it was supposed to present, with a place there to be found for the poor, non-white religious minority: the Irish who were not yet 'white' . . . and other immigrant and minority groups."[50] At times, Varela seems oblivious to what readers might be facing in Cuba. He situates himself as a permanent resident who is deeply invested in the United States. The following lengthy paragraph spells out his relationship to his adopted country:

> Acaso no hay un hombre más afecto que yo a este país, en el que he permanecido por tantos años, a pesar de haber corrido peligro mi vida en los primeros a causa del clima y de haber sufrido infinitas privaciones por no saber el idioma. He tenido en este tiempo varias y honorificas invitaciones para situarme en otros países, y a ninguna he ascedido. Luego que me fue familiar la lengua de este pueblo me he relacionado en él y adquirido tan buenos amigos, que sin ingratitud jamás podré ser insensible a sus atenciones y favores. Yo soy en el afecto un natural de este país, aunque no soy ciudadano ni lo sere jamás por haber formado una firme resolución de no serlo de país alguno de la tierra, desde que cicunstancias que no ignoras me separaron de mi patria. No pienso volver a ella, pero creo deberla un tributo de cariño y de respeto no uniéndome a otra alguna.[51]

(No other man than I has more affection for this country where I have resided for many years, despite having faced threats to my health upon arrival due to the weather and having suffered so many deprivations for not knowing the language. During my time here, I have received many attractive invitations to relocate to other countries, yet I have not accepted any of them. After becoming familiar with the language of this country, I settled here and made such good friends that I would be ungrateful to take for granted their care and kindness. I feel as if I had been born here, but I am not a citizen and never will be, for I made a firm resolution not to be a citizen of any country when circumstances with which you are familiar separated me from my mother country. I do not plan to return to her, but I owe her the honor and respect not to incorporate myself to another.)

I translate the phrase "Yo soy en el afecto un natural de este país" as "I feel as if I had been born here," which captures the sentiment; however, that translation misses an important implication of the phrase "un natural de este país," which in an awkward English would read "I am a natural of this country." Varela often used the word *natural* to talk about the home-bred patriotism that came with being born in the Americas rather than in Spain. In effect, Varela complicates his affection for Cuba through a naturalized connection to the United States and claims the latter as his home, even as he eschews the formality of citizenship. He thus offers a window into the ability of someone with his intellectual resources to settle in a country while retaining transnational psychological and emotional connections and devotion to the impossible possibility of legal Cuban citizenship.

Varela's affection for the United States and its people must be considered in light of the argument about superstition he develops in *Cartas a Elpidio*. The passage above can be read as an apology for the one that follows: "No hay pueblo en que los impostores religiosos encuentren tan buena acogida como en este. El que quiere formar una secta aun la más ridícula, puede estar seguro de econtrar numerosos partidarios, sin más diligencia que echarse a predicar y darles un aire de piedad que alucine a los oyentes" (There is not a country where religious impostors will find such a warm reception as in this one. Anyone inclined to start the most ridiculous sect can be assured of finding many followers; it is as easy as starting to preach and taking on an air of piety that will impress the listeners).[52] Varela's proclamation of devotion to the United States emerges in a discussion of how people in the United States are susceptible to beliefs about haunted houses, evil omens from owls, and bad luck brought on by knocking over a salt shaker. Varela is forthright: "Hablando con la franqueza que me es característica, debo decirte que, en mi opinion, hay pocos pueblos tan supersticiosos como el de los Estados Unidos" (Speaking with my characteristic frankness, I should tell you that in my opinion there are few countries as superstitious as the United States).[53]

Despite such superstition, or perhaps because of it, *Cartas a Elpidio* records Varela's integration into the social fabric of New York and particularly his interaction with and response to spiritual matters in his new home. The book includes a feisty discussion of "charlatans," implying that people in the United States are susceptible to fortune-tellers, seers, and Protestant preachers. Varela inveighs against several personalities who made their way around the Northeast at the time, including a preacher proclaiming to be the son of Christ. Varela mocks the evangelist Lorenzo Dow, whose energetic speaking style drew huge crowds. An eccentric who was not affiliated with a particular denomination, Dow was at once popular and controversial. "With his long hair, his flowing beard, his harsh voice, and his wild gesticulation, he was so rude and unkempt as to startle all conservative hearers," writes Benjamin Brawley in an interesting article about how Dow was at times denied entry into white churches and turned to preaching among blacks.[54] Varela was not impressed: "Este curioso personaje se metió a profeta y su profecía fue oída con aprecio, o por lo menos sin digusto, porque era contra la iglesia católica, a la cual siempre atacan suponiendo miras de dominar en los papas" (This curious character turned himself into a preacher and his prophecies were received with some enthusiasm, or at least without displeasure, because he was opposed to the Catholic Church, which is regularly attacked for supposedly being a tool of papal domination).[55] Varela ridicules some of Dow's predictions, and he also dismisses people claiming to be healers.

At times Varela retains the position of an outsider looking into a society, and much of the second volume is trained on New York. In turning to Protestant denominations, Varela is more respectful, but he accuses them of hypocrisy, saying that some Quakers and Baptists are deeply invested in making sure that they patronize only businesses run by others in the denomination. Quakers attract Varela because of their dress and beliefs; he sees their pacifism as a misguided abdication of responsibility for military defense. In one funny scene, Varela tells the story of several *españoles* who visited a Quaker silent prayer meeting and remained near the door. When one of the "women impostors" saw them, she jumped on a bench with great alacrity and began to preach against the Spanish Inquisition. Varela continues, "Mi amigo y compañero Gener me contó el hecho y me decía con su natural jocosidad: 'por esta vez, Varela, se equivocó el Espíritu Santo, pues ni hay Inquisición en España, ni es probable que vuelva a haberla; y los españoles que estaban a la puerta, lejos de ser partidarios de la Inquisición la detestaban mucho más que la vieja predicadora'" (My friend and compatriot [Tomás] Gener told me about this encounter with his usual jocularity: "this time, Varela, the Holy Spirit made a mistake, for there is no Inquisition in Spain, nor is there likely to be again; the Spaniards who were at the door, far from being supporters of the Inquisition, detested it much more than the old preacher woman").[56] Varela concludes that Quakers are "the most ridiculous and opportunistic sect,"[57] and he turns petty in pointing out that even though they opt for modesty in dress, the cloth they use for vestments is sometimes as expensive as the fine clothes worn by ostentatious people.

Varela's less than generous account of Quakers indicates that he felt embattled, and he did indeed face the anti-Catholic nativist movements of the 1820s and 1830s. Varela worked as pastor of Christ Church in New York and was named vicar general, the principal administrative representative, to the New York bishop. His time in New York coincided with the Second Great Awakening. As scholars have shown, Varela fielded attacks from Protestant ministers who sought to paint the Catholic Church and Varela as part of a papist conspiracy against US democratic principles. Joseph and Helen McCadden describe Varela as a "pioneer ecumenist" laboring "in an era of blinding religious animosities."[58] Most of the final letter of *Cartas a Elpidio* is devoted to the ways Protestants attacked Catholics in the northeastern United States, whether in print or in person through violence and threats. In one infamous case, a mob burned down a convent in Charlestown, Massachusetts. Varela points out that the convent doubled as a school and many of the students were Protestant.[59] Thus Varela positions the convent as a tolerant school in contrast to the Protestant mob.

The convent incident and others discussed by Varela lead to his ultimate conclusion about religious life in the United States: he draws a distinction between legal and social tolerance. US cities considered themselves and were often viewed as religiously tolerant, he argues. But there was widespread persecution of Catholics. The burning of the convent, Varela continues, was in keeping with the beliefs of people who detest a religion with which they do not agree. "Yo solo culpo en ellos, mi caro Elpidio, la abominable hipocresía de fingir que tienen una tolerancia que no tienen" (My dear Elpidio, I take issue only with the abominable hypocrisy in feigning that they are tolerant when in reality they are not).[60] By contrast, Varela positions himself as tolerant of different denominations socially even if he is doctrinaire on the question of true religion: "Respecto de la vida eterna no hay más que una religión y una moral derivada de ella y meritoria por este sagrado principio; mas, respecto a la sociedad, pueden unas religiones nominales, quiero decir, unas falsas doctrinas religiosas, inspirar una moral correcta; que, como su principio, sólo tiene mérito ante los hombres" (With respect to eternal life there is only one religion and one true morality derived from it; however, with respect to society, it is possible for so-called religions, that is, false religious doctrines, also to inspire correct morality, which in this case is derived from men and thus has merit only among men).[61] Here Varela notes the positive contributions of Protestant denominations while emphasizing a distinction between social effects and metaphysical conditions. He defends the Catholic Church as the source of eternal truth, but in discussing how to navigate differences among various religious beliefs he is tolerant and speaks more to an audience in the United States than to one in Cuba.

"Francisquita" Wright and the Homosocial Elite

In recounting his responses to debates over religion in the United States, Varela was most heated in *Cartas a Elpidio* when he took up the Scottish feminist, abolitionist, and social reformer Fanny Wright. Varela's energetic sexism emerges in the opening sentence of several pages devoted to Wright: "Acaso habrás oído hablar de un diablo vestido de mujer a quien llaman Fanny Wright, o sea Francisquita Wright" (Perhaps you have heard of a devil dressed as a woman whom people call Fanny Wright, that is Francisquita Wright).[62] In Hispanicizing the diminutive of *Frances,* Varela sets up the attack and emphasizes the irony that a woman preaching atheism would share a name with St. Francis. He is offended not only by her atheism but also by the fact that a woman would espouse it publicly. Elsewhere in the *Cartas,* Varela refutes atheism through argument and logic, but it is Wright's body and demeanor, not her ideas, that he targets. Varela writes, "Asegúranme los que la han visto que carece de hermosura y aun prodríamos sin injusticia llamarla fea" (Those who have seen her assure me that she lacks beauty and we would not be wrong in calling her ugly).[63] Since he had not seen her, why such vehemence in the attacks?

Beyond offering an example of a gendered hierarchical perspective in this historical period, Varela's viciousness helps us apprehend the limits of the reformist platforms of the trans-American elite. Calling for an end to colonialism did not come with a concomitant desire to overturn the types of gendered and social hierarchies that sustained their elite positions. Let us step back to consider how the attack on Wright is sustained by the homosocial dimensions of Filadelfia letters and the lack of women participating in the discourse of republican rights promoted by the trans-American elite. Women emerge in Filadelfia letters most commonly as objects of seduction or control. Whether it is the character Teutila in *Jicoténcal,* a novel to which we turn in chapter 4, or Manuel Lorenzo de Vidaurre's sister-in-law in his *Cartas americanas, políticas y morales,* to which I turn in chapter 5, women are not presented as writers or producers of this early Latino print culture. Upper-class women were part of a target audience of certain books, including the gift books published by the Carey house in Philadelphia, but Varela's *Cartas a Elpidio* offers a bleak portrait of how some in his circle may have treated women. The trans-American elite saw themselves participating in a male-centered revolutionary tradition. Their heroes were the likes of Washington.

The affectionate communication that I have argued is at the center of Filadelfia letters is connected to the homosocial dimensions of the trans-American elite. The brotherhood of early Latino letters was driven by a type of intimacy shared by the men who wrote to one another even as they hoped to spread that type of interaction with a broader readership across the Americas. Robert McKee Irwin, in his study of Mexican literature, has shown how homosocial relations are important to the construction of the nation or imagined community. He notes that "women's role in such symbolic nation building is little more than as an object of barter between men."[64] Irwin's analysis delves into how literature also encodes homoerotic elements in tension with homosocial notions of masculinity, and while it is difficult to locate homoeroticism (or heterosexual desire for that matter) in the largely de-corporealized writing of the trans-American elite, the male-centered bonds motivating anticolonial discourse do emerge. Eve Kosofsky Sedgwick argued that there was a coded expression of male homosocial desire within a segment of the English upper class who shared a particular literary education, and we see a similar nexus in the affectionate male bonding created in and by the writing of the trans-American elite.[65] *Cartas a Elpidio* is an example of these homosocial connections in that its speaker is part of an exclusive male group, the priesthood, and proffers his wisdom across the ocean to a young man who can be read as a stand-in for all young men in Cuba. This readership presumably is able to buy the books and is educated enough to keep up with Varela in his theological discussions.

The presumptive audience for Filadelfia letters was made up of men, something that emerges implicitly in the writing as well as in exchanges that display readerly interaction. Evidence of women who were active participants in the book-producing work of the trans-American elite has not yet surfaced. It was rare among the Spanish American colonial upper class for women to travel to places like Philadelphia or New York unaccompanied, although there were exceptions in the colonial period. This lack of travel opportunity is a result of historical roles within a heteronormative family tied to a specific location and a male protective eye that restricted movement. But along with these material and ideological restrictions, women were excluded from trans-American intellectual circles by this discourse of homosocial intimacy. Varela's take on Wright offers an extreme example in that he insults her intelligence.

The hostile tone on Wright and the pages devoted to her suggest that within Varela's book-producing class, men create an intellectual orbit in part through attitudes about women that do not propose, much less promote, equal participation among the sexes in an imagined new society. As Sedgwick emphasized, the homosocial pattern cannot be "understood outside of its relation to women and the gender system as a whole."[66] Thus, the repulsion Varela expresses toward Wright is an effect of a patriarchal system, and despite the priest's revolutionary longings, he cannot envision equality with women.

For Varela, the problem is that Wright enters a public discussion that he assumes should be reserved for men. His main line of attack is that a woman such as Wright, whom he at one point compares to a prostitute, cannot exist without the support of a male patron. He writes, "Esta mujer perniciosa es, y ha sido siempre, un mero instrumento de que se han valido varios impíos y en especial cierto individuo que se supone ser el autor de todas las arengas o lecciones depravadas con que ha causado tanto daño" (This destructive woman is and has always been a mere instrument of several irreligious men and especially a certain individual who is believed to be the author of all the harangues and depraved lessons that she has deployed to cause harm).[67] These types of assertions are in direct contrast to historical evidence, which shows that Wright was perfectly capable of running her own irreligious projects. Those who met her were impressed (or threatened) by her capacity for independent thinking. Walt Whitman, for one, said, "She was a brilliant woman, of beauty and estate, who was never satisfied unless she was busy doing good—public good, private good."[68] Although Whitman shares a predilection with Varela to comment on her looks, his assessment of her work was more honest. Wright, for example, was involved in the founding and running of a utopian project in Tennessee that brought together former slaves and whites in a failed attempt to establish an interracial community based on equality.[69]

Wright offered an important target for Varela because she was notorious for her beliefs, was prominent in the press, and also enjoyed tremendous popularity during her speaking tours. She espoused positions that were anathema to Varela: atheism and hostility to religious groups, including Catholics; sexual freedom; and even opposition to marriage. Possibly the only part of Wright's political thought that Varela would have shared was the opposition to slavery, and he did not bring that up in *Cartas a Elpidio*. Varela framed her as the "mother of irreligiosity," and thus she fit directly into his concerns in the first volume of *Cartas a Elpidio*. But rather than debating her views, Varela focused on her demeanor, suggesting that her public presentations were memorized recitations created for her by men. He even tells a couple of anecdotes, possibly spurious, about Wright not being able to provide adequate answers to questions at her public presentations. This attempt to discredit someone known as a captivating speaker is part of Varela's assertion that she ventriloquizes the thoughts of men: "He aquí probado por experiencia que los impíos, cuando, por desgracia de la sociedad, encuentran una mujer que adopte sus principios y tenga valor para difundirlos, jamás dejan de valerse de ella y consiguen por este medio tan infame lo que nunca hubieran podido conseguir por si mismos" (I can attest from experience that irreligious men harm society when they locate a woman who adopts their views and is able to circulate their beliefs; they will never stop using her and accomplish through this detestable activity what they never would have accomplished themselves).[70] In other words, he does not grant her or women who may join her in that view the agency of choosing to be irreligious.

Varela's attention to Wright shuts down the possibility that his reformist impulse and the anticolonial programs of the trans-American elite would go so far as to create a society in which women could participate politically. Varela is troubled that women are irreligious because "the fair sex" (*el bello sexo*) should not think like that: he actually suggests that they are not capable of thinking on their own. He frames women as passive recipients of men's thinking but also ascribes power to women, characterizing them as the "most dangerous class" because of their influence in the home. He tells Elpidio, "Acaso te causará risa el que yo pretenda dar reglas para manejar las mujeres, que no tienen más ley que su capricho y sólo son constantes en la inconstacia.... A veces se les antoja causar males enormes, y después se quedan tan frescas como si hubieran esparcido un puñado de flores" (Perhaps you will be amused that I propose to give rules on how to handle women, who don't respond to any law other than their whims and whose only consistency is their inconsistency.... At times they get the urge to cause great harm, and afterward they remain as calm as if they had scattered a handful of flowers).[71] Setting up an opposition between laws and whims, Varela characterizes women as both influential and beholden to their emotions. The effect here is the exclusion of women from a pedagogical conversation between the priest and his young male readers.

He suggests that Elpidio take on a new social role that involves not only a religiously inflected consciousness but a mandate to guide and influence women, even as the latter are completely excluded from participation in the types of public exchanges of the trans-American elite. For Varela, the times seem to call for guidance on actions that could buttress patriarchal religious traditions. At one point Varela goes as far as to suggest that Elpidio seduce women through compliments to bring them around to belief and away from irreligiosity. "A veces nos vemos precisados, mi caro amigo, a echar mano, por decirlo así, de las armas del enemigo para defendernos y destruirlo; y ésta nunca será una alevosía, antes debe graduarse por una acción prudente y heroica" (At times we find ourselves pressed, my dear friend, to grab, so to speak, the arms of our enemy in order to defend ourselves and destroy him; and this should never be seen as treachery but rather should be considered a prudent and heroic act).[72] The phrase *echar mano*, which I translate as "to grab," can also mean "to resort to" or "to take," the latter including sexual connotations. This disturbing advice is part of Varela's logic of men using seduction to spread their religious beliefs and women (whose intellectual capacity he has negated) falling for it because of their vanity.

Varela's attitude toward women, which is sustained by the homosocial relations of the trans-American elite, registers the limits of revolutionary thinking among most of these intellectuals. Historically speaking, Varela and others in his orbit are forced into exile because their writing and political views pose a challenge to colonial authorities. Varela's writing opposes slavery, and his ministering to immigrants in New York City situates him among those who work with the poor. He calls for an independent Cuba that will lead to a more just society. But Varela is not ready to overturn gendered social hierarchies, nor is he willing to give up a belief that men will be at the vanguard of intellectual advancements. In fact, the writing of the trans-American elite shows that they believe men of a certain social class will lead the way. To consider which men the trans-American elite believe will be at the vanguard of their anticolonial project, let us return to Torres.

The Poor Richard of South America?

The moniker "Franklin of South America," even if it implies a US-centric perspective that would make Manuel Torres a copy of a distinguished founding father, is important because it registers a view of the type of men who were expected to lead the Spanish American revolutionary efforts. Torres was extremely accomplished on various fronts, able to move easily in influential US circles by drawing on *elite* connections to fashion a leadership position among trans-American intellectuals. His published books are representative of a type of perspective common in letters from Filadelfia: a decontextualized view from above that does not take into account questions of socioeconomic class or the vexed ethnic taxonomies of Spanish America. If Varela's take on Fannie Wright gives us a window into the attitudes of the trans-American elite toward women, Torres's Philadelphia books offer examples of how trans-American intellectuals ignored and even excluded from their view of society the most oppressed classes in Spanish America. That perspective is not separate from the life experiences of the trans-American elite, which becomes clear when we look at Torres's background.

Torres thrived as the owner of a plantation in South America. According to William Duane, Torres ran a prosperous operation in Colombia using indigenous laborers and "collecting all the riches of the botanical regions."[73] Torres had received the plantation as a land grant from the king of Spain because of the Torres family's connections. Born in Spain, Torres belonged to the highest ranks of Nueva Granada, the Spanish colonial administrative territory that encompassed present-day Colombia, Venezuela, and Ecuador. The area where he lived was rural and thus could accommodate the type of plantation with indigenous people working the fields. Torres's uncle Antonio Caballero y Góngora was archbishop of Bogotá and in 1781 was appointed by the Crown to serve as New Granada's viceroy, the highest colonial official and a direct representative of the monarch. Due to his connections, Torres received the land near what is today the town of Tenerife, about 170 miles from the Caribbean in the Magdalena Department of northern Colombia.[74]

Although Duane calls Torres's land an estate, the term *plantation* may be more accurate in that it signals the racial and gendered hierarchies in the Spanish American hacienda system. Historically, the Spanish Crown had owned all lands conquered; it granted lands to institutions such as missions or individuals. The hacienda had its antecedent in the sixteenth-century *encomienda*, which included a grant of indigenous labor along with the land. Under an *encomienda,* the word from the Spanish *encomendar* (to entrust), a "protector" would oversee and Christianize those who worked on his granted land. By the late eighteenth century the *encomienda* system was no longer in operation, but the structural effect of racialized labor under the control of a landowner persisted. As Vincent Pérez has noted in discussing haciendas in Mexico and California, some of the most prominent features of this landholding were its "paternalistic social organization and its system of debt peonage."[75] While Torres received a grant of land, not people, he oversaw workers on the plantation who may not have had other options but to toil for the elite landowner. Duane described Torres's plantation as follows: "Here he had, by his own mild, kind, and consummate temper, redeemed the Indian of the forest, and formed a native population, mild, industrious, ingenious, and, as he himself said, the best gardeners and cultivators in the world."[76] Duane's references to inhabitants of the forest being socialized into an Edenic commercial operation betray notions of civilization and barbarism that stretched across the Americas. Duane, who visited Colombia after his friend's death, lamented that without Torres the plantation no longer had its bountiful production.

Torres and Duane were very close, and thus it is possible to read the passages on the plantation in Duane's *A Visit to Colombia in the Years 1822 and 1823* as ventriloquizing Torres's account of his own work there. Duane waxes eloquent about the plantation, only to reveal that he stopped short on his journey through the Colombian countryside and did not make it to the actual site. Instead, we get a mix of longing for a lost friend with a description of the plantation. Duane writes that the order imposed by Torres was gone, along with "the avenues of cotton trees and oranges, the groves of foreign firs on the lofty peaks, and the palms in the valleys."[77]

> The orange had become bitter and deformed, as if in anger or despair: the poor Indian too had lost his earthly providence; and, when his race was run, the progeny who followed became like their progenitors, ignorant, indocile and wild, little more rational than the monkeys which gamboled on the lofty

branches of the *champaca,* or the mountain cedar. A wilderness was to be seen on all sides; there was no charm left to replace the paradise that had been created by my friend.[78]

The passage is remarkable for its invocation of racialized degeneration after Torres's departure. The "Indian" is listed among plants that had somehow suffered from the departure of the intellectual Torres for Philadelphia. Duane here offers a window into the thinking that sustains the hacienda system: Torres is a protector who cares for the land and its inhabitants, both associated with a wild natural state. Duane is the writer, and it would be hasty to assume that Torres also saw his workers as "monkeys," but we can presume that racial attitudes had crisscrossed the Americas and informed the Torres-Duane friendship.

Duane's perspective was not completely distinct from general Spanish American notions of superiority that situated urbanity at the top of a social hierarchy. In Torres's commercial treatise *An Exposition of the Commerce of Spanish America; With Some Observations Upon Its Importance to the United States* (Philadelphia, 1816), he had counted among the population of Spanish America only "people already civilized" and not the "vast number of aborigines, who are yet in their primitive state of independence."[79] Considering this statement alongside Duane's description of the plantation, we are reminded of the argument by Aníbal Quijano and Immanuel Wallerstein that the hemispheric colonial system, which they call "Americanity," deployed ethnicity as a way to delineate social effects on the division of labor. In this argument, the hierarchy that placed *peninsulares* and *criollos* at the top effectively prevented darker-colored populations from selling their labor power in a free market. Ethnicity "justified the multiple forms of labour control, invented as part of Americanity: slavery for the Black Africans, various forms of coerced cash-crop labour (*repartimiento, mita,* peonage) for Native Americans, indentured labour (*engagés*) for the European working class."[80] Although the coerced labor of indigenous people in Spanish America differed from the extermination and relocation of indigenous people in the nineteenth-century United States, the distinction between populations of European descent and indigenous people came to structure socioeconomic hierarchies across the hemisphere.[81]

Torres carried the investments of his class (and presumably attendant racial views) across the hemisphere. We know that he became involved in a movement against the Spanish Crown and had to escape to the United

States, an event that Duane described as follows: "He was among those who were ordered to be seized, imprisoned, and sent to Europe, but he was too much beloved, wherever he had authority, not to have friends: his escape was connived at; and, after reaching with his funds an island of the West Indies, where he remained some time, he removed to Philadelphia."[82] Torres became taken "with the early dawn of the revolution of North America" and thus "prepared the way for that of the South."[83] Duane's account emphasizes Torres's intellectual gifts, "moral principles," and devotion to human liberty. But the devotion intersected with a perspective that valorized the United States and its own revolutionary brand of racialized hierarchy and veneration of elite leaders such as Franklin, Paine, and Washington.

Torres's published books show that he worked at the level of macroeconomics and language translation and avoided the socioeconomic conditions in specific sites in Spanish America. It is revealing that social hierarchies are largely absent from Torres's 119-page *Exposition of the Commerce of Spanish America*.[84] This book provides a remarkable window into Torres's economic thinking and connects him to a defense of economic liberalism and free-market commerce. Torres advocates trade between North and South America, with little regard for who was doing the trading or how it might affect different populations. The title page elaborates on the full scope of the book: "To which are added, a correct analysis of the monies, weights, and measures of Spain, France, and the United States; and of the new weights and measures of England: with tables of their reciprocal reductions; and of the exchange between the United States, England, France, Holland, Hamburg, and between England, Spain, France, and the several states of the Union." In keeping with that description, much of the second half of the book is made up of tables summarizing various European and American (hemispherically speaking) currencies and measures. This suggests that the book may have appealed to ship captains or others engaged in trade in Spanish ports.

The *Exposition* is first and foremost an economic manual. For Torres, the impending independence of Spanish America offered investment opportunities and opened a new economic approach that would remove colonial mercantilism and usher in the free exchange of goods and currencies. He ignores questions of power and an imbalance in economic resources that would become crucial to understanding imperialist economics in Latin America. He does so because he views North and South as equal trading partners, a fantasy that emerges in conjunction with his move from South

America to Philadelphia. The book opens with a clear statement about its audience, its goals, and its perspective on the relationship between government and economics:

> The different matters of this work, destined to guide merchants in their commercial operations, will also be very useful to every one who buys, sells, or exchanges in any way: to the farmer and to the insurer, to the banker and to the statesman. There is such an intimate connexion between political economy and commerce, that no one can become acquainted with the former, without knowing well the latter; and, in order to acquire this knowledge, the different monies, weights, measures, exchanges, and every thing relative to national as well as foreign commerce, must be well known.[85]

The word *useful* is a reference to US readers, who may benefit from the trade of Spanish America. In order to facilitate such trade, Torres sets out to present "a precise statement of the articles annually exported from the different departments of Spanish America to foreign countries, and their value" (*E* 4) and to provide an accounting of the measures and weights and rates of exchange in various settings.

The *Exposition* seeks to pull the United States toward Spanish America, which it presents as rich with resources. The book's first half argues that Spanish America is a site that can be tapped as a potential market for goods produced in the United States or other countries. Torres writes about Spanish America: "That country consumes yearly, the value of one hundred millions of dollars in articles of foreign manufacturing industry" (*E* 11). He also holds out the area's resources as ripe for the taking. "It is there, and only there, that all nations can obtain, with facility, those precious metals, which have become so necessary to trade throughout the world, and particularly Asia" (*E* 11).

Torres does the work of global capitalism, situating the United States as an exporter nation in search of markets and offering Spanish America as a resource for raw goods. "The United States, more than other nations, have a powerful interest in an extensive participation of it, in carrying thither foreign or domestic mercantile articles, or from those of Europe, where suitable assortments could be procured, to be changed in South America for the precious metals, or for raw materials" (*E* 11), the latter including cochineal, indigo, logwood, and even medicinal plants. By this logic, the United States would become the dominant trading partner, dislodging Spain's colonial mercantile policies.

In order to convince potential investors, Torres argues that important political changes are taking place in Spanish America that will lead to the end of Spanish colonial protectionist policies. The book praises "the efforts of its inhabitants to shake off the yoke of the Spanish government" and "the extraordinary progress of their revolution" (*E* 7). In a curious phrase that echoes Bolívar's dream of a united Spanish America, Torres ventures that it is only a matter of time until complete emancipation and "the establishment of a new, powerful, and independent empire, (probably) under the form of a representative and central government" (*E* 7). Torres's use of *empire* here for the new countries shows both the identification with the United States (Jefferson's "empire of liberty") and the historically attractive usage of a term that at other points in history comes to be associated with domination and oppression. At times Torres presents Spanish America as a single land, much of it attractive to investors. "From . . . its situation between Asia, Europe, and the United States, as well as from the number of its excellent harbours, opening on the Pacific and the Atlantic Oceans, that country seems to have been destined by the Author of Nature, to become the common centre of the commerce of the whole world" (*E* 9).

The *Exposition* calls attention to Torres's movement in the world of bankers and investors; his dominant mode of thinking is exchange. Many pages include tables of exchange rates; the tables show how to convert amounts in US or English money to their Spanish equivalents and how to convert measurements into those of Spanish America. This emphasis on exchange rates and coinage displays the interest of Torres's class.[86] As Carlos Marichal has argued, coinage (particularly silver) in Spanish America and Brazil circulated among merchants, mine workers, and state functionaries. But most slaves and indigenous populations carried on exchange through barter rather than coin. "The result of such a stratified society and economy was that the mass of the population tended to suffer from lack of metallic currency as well as of other fractional currency instruments, and this clearly made for low levels of individual savings."[87] It becomes clear that Torres is writing for the economically privileged, who have access to coins.

Torres's enthusiasm for hemispheric trade with the United States sheds light on the question that started this chapter: how did Torres retain his elite status after settling in Philadelphia? For one, he participated actively in the economic life of the United States, investing his money in various ventures. And Torres mastered English, which allowed him to write the *Exposition* and also to participate actively in the publication of Duane's newspaper, the *Aurora*. The pages of the newspaper showed the influence of Torres, as its pages offered substantial coverage of Spanish America in the second decade of the nineteenth century and early in the third, including updates on military battles. Torres's editorial mark made the *Aurora* arguably the most important source for news on Spanish America in the early nineteenth-century United States.

Both the newspaper work and Torres's financial ventures show that he integrated himself into his new city in many ways, even as he kept an eye on events in South America. Given Torres's abilities, it is not surprising that he was called the "Franklin of South America." That analogy proposes historical and cultural translation. But if Torres is the Franklin of South America, to which of Franklin's personas was he closest?[88] Because Torres published a book about economics, Emily Garcia has suggested that a discussion of Torres and Franklin could be developed via Poor Richard; after all, both share a concern with quantitative matters.[89] Invoking *poor* Richard in relation to Torres may indeed have a resonance since Torres became financially poorer during his time in Philadelphia. In the years following his arrival, some of the wealth Torres had amassed was lost in bad investments. Torres lived, according to Duane, in both "good and evil fortune": "He had entrusted his funds, in order that they should produce a respectable subsistence without waste, to persons in trade; he was fortunate sometimes in the adventures, but in others was defrauded by those to whom he had committed them; by one person, since deceased, he lost 70,000 dollars—it was his all."[90] Torres presents an interesting picture for US immigration history: a wealthy person who ends up poorer in the United States.

But at the level of textual comparison, Poor Richard and Torres are very different. The Richard persona, which emerged in *Poor Richard's Almanac,* became popular because of his economic sayings. The Ben Franklin of *The Way to Wealth,* a collection of Poor Richard's wisdom on frugality and industry, is *homo economicus,* focused on taking care of pennies. Nothing could be further from Torres's *Exposition.* While Franklin's *The Way to Wealth* is a manual for frugal living, and an ironic one at that, the *Exposition* focuses on how to do business on a grand scale and develops the argument through a macroeconomic analysis. *The Way to Wealth* is a humorous wink at humans' inability to live by the types of precepts set out by the finger-wagging Richard.[91] By contrast, Torres's *Exposition* is not in the least ironic in its argument about the possibilities for exchange in the Americas; it is a book that a merchant could use in calculating commercial exchange. The prominent place of tables emphasizes correspondence, a book "with tables of their reciprocal reductions." The goal there is to reduce quantities to a common meaning and to allow merchants to move from one location in the Americas to another. That sense of correspondence and movement is in keeping with Torres's views on how to learn a new language.

The Commerce of Language

Before he published his *Exposition,* Torres adapted into Spanish and English a language-learning system that was published in two thick volumes as *Dufief's Nature Displayed in Her Mode of Teaching Language to Man* (Philadelphia, 1811). Torres's system is based on a notion of language correspondence, word for word and phrase for phrase, that assumes an ease of movement from one language to another. It represents the way he approached the relationship of Spanish to English and the way he made it look easy to move from one to the other. *Dufief's Nature* was in effect a bilingual publication. The title page, for example, was printed in Spanish and English on facing pages. As such, it could have been used by people learning either language.

Dufief's Nature was coproduced by Louis Hargous (who went on to be appointed to the faculty in modern languages at Princeton University in 1830). I say *produced* rather than *written* because this publication was an adaptation of a popular and controversial language-learning manual by Nicolas Gouïn Dufief, who had published his method for learners of the French language in Philadelphia in 1804. Dufief, who caught the interest of Thomas Jefferson, proposed that people should learn vocabulary and phrases before moving on to the study of grammar. Like Torres, Dufief had gone into exile in Philadelphia; but unlike the independence-minded Torres, Dufief was a royalist who fled from the French Revolution via the Caribbean. In Philadelphia, Dufief worked as a bookseller and teacher of French.[92] He was part of the French community that we noted in chapter 1. Influenced by the philosophical writing of Étienne Bonnot de Condillac, Dufief proposed that his approach came closest to the mental process of acquiring a language.

This method was based on what linguists today would call *language acquisition,* the learning of a language in the way that children learn, in contrast to *language learning,* which is associated with the classroom study of grammar. Dufief's method was controversial, Torres noted in his introduction, because it broke from approaches used by teachers in Philadelphia, who emphasized grammar at the start of language learning. According to Torres, Dufief's method "succeeded almost at once, notwithstanding the novelty of the doctrines it inculcates," and teachers warmed to it.[93] The two volumes are organized in accordance with the Dufief method: start with the teaching of vocabulary and phrases and only later delve into grammar and sentence construction. Volume 1 opens with an introduction to vocabulary and phrases: "salt/sal, 'There is too much *salt* in this soup. / La sopa tiene mucha *sal.*'" The four vocabulary sections focus on food and clothing, the town, animals and plants, and the universe. By contrast, volume 2 goes right into grammatical matters, including parts of speech, possessive pronouns, and verb conjugations. The book promises "the most extensive system of Spanish syntax, ever offered to the public."

Torres's language pedagogy resonates in important ways with his views on international commerce. As we have seen in Torres's *Exposition,* Torres was obsessed with commensurability, particularly as it related to measurements and monies. In other words, his notion of exchange proceeded from the proposition of equivalences not only in the exchange of goods but also in specie and notes. We could say that the *Exposition* is about how to translate the terms of economic exchange from English to Spanish. This emphasis has an analogical connection to Torres's approach to language per the Dufief method. While the *Exposition* presents numerous examples of quantitative equivalence (a US dollar equals so many Mexican coins), the method of language learning that Torres presents is driven by a logic of word-for-word correspondence from one language to another.

Torres's method and the notion of word-for-word correspondence display a belief that moving from one language to another is not only feasible but also potentially smooth. The logic is that every word and sentence has its counterpart. The relationship of word-to-word (or literal) translation to approaches that emphasize other aspects such as form or a general content has been debated for some time by translation theorists. As George Steiner pointed out some time ago, "The theory of translation—if there is one as distinct from idealised recipes—pivots monotonously around undefined alternatives: letter or spirit, word or sense," and he called those dichotomies an epistemological weakness.[94] Steiner's point suggests, as others have also noted, that word-for-word translation always lurks in the background of any translation, and it is particularly relevant for all types of language learning, which calls for the acquisition of vocabulary. The movement from one language to another was part of the modus operandi of the trans-American elite, particularly as they navigated Philadelphia. As we saw with García de Sena in the preceding chapter, translation of language was supposed to facilitate the transposing of revolutionary ideas leading to revolutionary actions. In the 1820s, the notion of moving ideas from the United States to the southern Americas took the form of debates over modes of governing, including whether the US federal system could be replicated elsewhere.

Torres's *Dufief's Nature,* when read alongside the economic *Exposition,* shows an extraordinary faith in the transposition of words and concepts from one language to another, a process with an analogy in Torres's views on political systems and economic exchange. This is in part because Torres's Dufief method is not a formal translation in the way of García de Sena's Thomas Paine book. It is a book with a premise that one can say the same thing in two languages. From Torres's vantage point, words in English had their equivalences in Spanish, the governmental organization in the United States could have its similar manifestation in Spanish America, and currencies and goods had equivalent values in between North and South. It is no surprise that a sentence in the *Exposition* ranks language learning among the important aspects of trading: "In order that the trade with Spanish America may be productive of the advantages of which it is susceptible, the foreign agent or supercargo must be acquainted with the Spanish language, with the habits and manners of the inhabitants, and with their way of buying and selling, which differs somewhat from that of other nations" (*E* 17–18). Torres here might be talking about his integration into the United States; his linguistic experience, the rapid switching and ability to speak and write English, informs his approach to commerce.

When it came to language instruction, Torres aspired to nothing less than teaching fluency in both languages and an ability to translate in both directions. The contents of the two volumes of the Dufief book make this clear. Volume 1 concludes with an "English Reader," made up of character sketches and orations, among them "Speech of Demosthenes to the Athenians" and "The Character of Queen Elizabeth." Volume 2 concludes with a Spanish-language reader that contains selections from Spanish poets and accounts of the conquest by the dramatist Antonio de Solís, who is quoted extensively in the novel *Jicoténcal* (1826). The introduction proposes that students of Spanish who have gone through the vocabulary and grammar sections of the volumes can then turn to the Spanish reader to "study the graces of style, and the best models of composition" so that they can rival "the most enlightened natives in the knowledge thereof." But that is not enough. "When that perfection has been attained," the introduction concludes, "the scholar may venture upon translating into Spanish some of the most interesting pieces of the *English Reader.*"⁹⁵ In other words, before moving to stylistic considerations, students needed to become familiar with the types of equivalencies necessary in the learning of vocabulary.

The correspondence between language and commerce becomes clear in a section of *Dufief's Nature* that treats the writing of business correspondence. Volume 2 offers a bilingual version of "The Commercial Secretary, or a Collection of Commercial Letters, Invoices, Accounts of Sale, Bills of Lading and Exchange, for the Use of Merchants, Supercargoes, & c." Like the Dufief model itself, the commercial-letters section is drawn from an earlier publication, *The Commercial Secretary,* published in English in Bordeaux, France, in 1807, presumably for French merchants doing trade with England. The Torres version offers corresponding versions of the letters in Spanish and English. For example, the sixth letter offers the following side by side in two columns to provide easy understanding of the translation, allowing those using the manual to fill in quantities:

> Gentlemen, Confirming our last of the ——we now have the pleasure to inform you, that we have purchased for your account, COFFEE, about 500 cwt., fine ordinary Java, at ——SUGAR, 2 hogsheads fine loaves, at ——, 2 hogsheads lumps, at ——with the quality of which we are confident you will be satisfied.
>
> Muy Señores nuestros: en confirmacion de nuestra última fecha el ——tenemos el gusto de participar á vmds. haber conprado por su cuenta, CAFÉ cerca de 500 quintales fino de Java á ——AZUCAR, 2 barricas en panes finos, á ——, 2 dichas en pedazos, á ——y estamos persuadidos de que vdms. quedarán satisfechos de su calidad.⁹⁶

The point of "The Commercial Secretary" is for a merchant to have handy a set of sample letters to use in correspondence with trading partners.

Here Torres writes from the perspective of the US trader, arguing that language learning will lead to profit for people in the North but will also work in the inverse. The problem with this logic is that the translatability of commerce and language does not account for the types of power imbalances that are all too common in the history of political economy. Or, continuing the analogy, word-for-word translation does not account for style, phrasing, idiomatic expressions, and formal organization. Torres's political economy does not take into account the trans-American racialized labor hierarchies that Quijano and Wallerstein emphasize and that Torres himself had experienced. In addition, Torres ignores how access to capital (monetary and cultural) could affect trading ability. Torres assumes a community of equals that can exchange different forms of value and communication without the type of inequality that structures colonial society and the new hemispheric order that emerges in the years after Spanish American independence. Torres believes that a move away from Spain's protectionist policies can create balance sheets that will benefit US merchants and their counterparts in other parts of the Americas, but he fails to account for the types of labor practices and highly stratified societies that have affected Latin American economic scenarios from the colonial period to the present. This lack of accounting for racialized and economic power imbalances is not confined only to the trans-American elite. Historians have argued that the Latin American wars of liberation led to changes in governmental structures and the end of colonial rule without adequately transforming economic conditions to the benefit of all. As Jaime Rodriguez O. has noted, after independence, liberal leaders abolished privileges for clerical and military personnel, including stripping "the Church of its landed wealth," in an effort to modernize economies, but "most former Indian communities and many other *campesinos* did not consider beneficial the *liberal* efforts to modernize the countryside."[97]

The trans-American elite adopted a belief in free trade to replace the protectionist limits imposed by the Spanish Crown, but at that point in history they were not able to account for neocolonial formations, nor did they conceive of the economic dimensions of US imperialism. This was a historical condition. But at the same time, Torres's integration into US society, combined with his socioeconomic position, gave him confidence that trade between the United States and Spanish America would benefit both. Torres died before he could witness the full change from colony to independence. In the years after independence, the territories that would become Latin America were drawn into a neocolonial world order with European powers, especially England, and later the United States emerging as dominant players in investment that stretched from the Caribbean to Argentina. We see Latin America's continuing participation in a world system that extracts resources from southern countries for the benefit of a dominant metropole.

The geopolitical wing of this neocolonial world system in the Americas came to be known as the Monroe Doctrine. Torres became the most important Spanish American representative, with access to the Monroe administration, and he presented an anti-European hemispheric message in keeping with elements of the doctrine. That he was received as the first ambassador from one of the new American nations was not surprising given his ability to call on the US secretary of state on numerous occasions. Torres would have proposed a horizontal notion of American independence, based not on US exceptionalism but rather on a shared anticolonial position vis-à-vis Europe. A series of proposals presented by Torres to the Monroe administration show that he lobbied for military assistance to Spanish America through a binary opposition between the hemisphere and Europe, arguing that the independence for all was in direct opposition to the meddlesome politics of Europe and its colonial legacy.[98] But Torres did not argue that the United States was the policeman of the hemisphere, which was the ultimate effect of what became known as the Monroe Doctrine. Torres articulated a hemispheric commonality circulating at the time, especially in Filadelfia letters; however, there were too many other factors influencing the discourse to say that he directly contributed to Monroe's 1823 speech.

But despite his connections and learning, Torres could not overcome the assumption of cultural and even racial difference between Anglo- and Spanish America, which would come to influence US–Latin American relations in the future and the treatment of Latinos in the United States. Torres was not immune to hostile Anglo-American responses to his Spanish American background. We see this in a scenario that involved US secretary of state John Quincy Adams. In 1820, Torres made his way into Adams's office, and the latter responded with polite disdain. "Mr. Manuel Torres came to the office and entertained me again nearly two hours with his demand for recognition of the republic of Colombia and a supply of muskets," wrote Adams in his diary on October 17. "Torres is a European Spaniard, and has all the patelinage that belongs to the Spanish character. He is withal not a little vain, and fancies himself very profound."[99] Adams uses the French *patelinage* (wheedling) to connect behavior to national character, and thus he betrays an Anglo prejudice against Spain. And Adams's use of *European Spaniard* shows that his prejudice extended to ascribing European influence to the most accomplished of Spanish Americans in the United States. More than an individual response to Torres, Adams's attitude reflected his belief that new nations to the south could not run democratic institutions.[100] While Torres may have seen himself moving freely throughout the states of the Americas, Adams clearly saw him as different, in a way that we might associate today with a discriminatory attitude toward Latinos. Torres's drawn-out battle to achieve recognition from the United States for the new nations of the Americas was one against notions of US exceptionalism and superiority circulating in the Monroe administration.[101]

Adams's response to the Franklin of the South is a reminder that a friendship based on equivalence in the early Americas was in tension with hierarchical social views about populations. How social hierarchy did or did not make its way into the writing of the trans-American elite is the focus of the next two chapters. Their texts most often avoided the particular conditions of specific locations, whether in terms of social hierarchy, religion, or governmental organization. Elite education and reading informed the creation of a trans-American and transatlantic public sphere that took up questions of how to combat colonialism and organize new governments but often did not consider specific places in the Americas.

 3

Faith in Print

José Antonio Saco's letter dated Filadelfia, December 26, 1828, announced exuberantly that he had bought a printing press and would begin operating it the following week. The letter was written to the illustrious Domingo Del Monte, who had arrived in New York from Cuba and intended to publish an edition of works by one of Spain's poets. The correspondence and the northeastern US setting brought together two men who would become intellectual giants in Cuba's history, Del Monte as a literary impresario and Saco as a controversial essayist and historian. Filadelfia offered a space early in their careers that helped these intellectuals conceive of themselves as participants in a vibrant transnational print culture with political ramifications. Saco (1787–1879) had started printing a weekly newspaper and now hoped to share his knowledge of print to help Del Monte (1804–1853) with his poetry project.

The letter shows how a desire to publish was intertwined with the material reality of the printing process, both the availability of a press and how it would affect their personal coffers. Rather than see Del Monte pay one of Philadelphia's printers for the job, Saco offered to make his press available to him if Del Monte covered the materials. "Yo no especulo con los amigos" (I do not speculate with friends), Saco said. The rest of the letter went into detail about the cost of paper, ink, and setting "manuscripts in a foreign tongue," that is, foreign in the Anglophone United States. Saco continued, "En cuanto al papel, no hay regla fija, por que ya tú sabes que su precio depende de su calidad" (As far as paper, it varies, because you know that its price depends on quality).[1] Saco also told him that Félix Varela, who was also in New York, would be able to provide more information on paper quality and cost, and although Saco did not note it, Varela was familiar with costs as a result of his own publishing projects.

Saco followed up with a second letter on New Year's Eve with the following:

> Mi Querido Domingo: Filadelfia es más barato que New York; así en igualdad de circunstancias vivirás mejor. Hay casa donde por 4 pesos podrás llenarte

bien la panza, y tener tu cuarto solo. El fuego es por separado; mas si quieres tenerlo en tu cuarto, comprarás tu leña que siempre te saldrá más barato. Vente, vente, pues te acomodarémos lo mejor que se pueda, y seguramente que será más barato y más comodo que en esa.[2]

(My Dear Domingo: Philadelphia is cheaper than New York; spending the same amount you will live more comfortably. There are lodgings for 4 pesos where you will be able to fill your belly well and have your own room. Fire is separate, but if you want to have it in your room you can buy your own wood, which always comes out cheaper. Come, come, we will set you up in the best way possible, and surely it will be cheaper and more comfortable than there.)

Saco's use of the informal *llenar la panza* (fill the belly) suggests their close friendship. This intimate communication helps fuel Saco's enthusiasm for shifting from the private communication of a personal letter to a public sphere of print, but one with a price tag. Despite having enough money to travel to the United States and, in Saco's case, purchase a printing press, they were still concerned about the economics of everyday living. Both Saco and Del Monte came from prominent families with connections to plantations, with Del Monte going on to marry the daughter of one of Cuba's most prosperous planters.[3] But the pecuniary resources of the trans-American elite were not unlimited. In the end, Saco affectionately declared himself so enthusiastic about publishing Del Monte's edited collection that he offered to underwrite the printing himself "pues de esa manera (aunque no gane nada) daré ocupación á los dos oficiales que trabajarán en el Mensagero" (since in that case [even if I do not profit] I will provide work to the two men working for *El Mensagero*).[4] The latter was a reference to his periodical *El Mensagero Semanal* (The weekly messenger), which he published in Philadelphia and New York from 1828 to 1831 and which offered news from Europe and the Americas. Saco had hired two men who could set type in a language other than English, and thus at this moment he combined his instincts as a press owner and printer with his affection for a friend from Cuba. Del Monte's collection appeared in 1829 as *Versos de J. Nicasio Gallego, recogidos y publicados por Domingo Del Monte* (Verses of J. Nicasio Gallego, collected and published by Domingo Del Monte). Its title page includes a Filadelfia imprint from the "Imprenta Española del Mensagero."

The difference in these two projects, one a weekly newspaper and the other a poetry book, registers the economic sacrifices made by intellectuals to enter what they conceived of as a public conversation in print. Concern about cost emerges as a factor in what is otherwise a commitment to move words into print and circulate them. Saco's enthusiasm for braving the commercial challenges of paper, ink, and press not only reminds us of the personal investment in publication common in his group but also indicates a strong belief in print's ability to bring about changes in the Americas.[5] While Philadelphia offered the materials necessary to print pages away from colonial censors and royal licenses, the separation from home countries allowed the likes of Saco to enter a world of vibrant and sometimes risky political and literary interaction. The importance of print was in its ability to travel across the distance separating various sites of American independence.

Filadelfia imprints and the faith writers placed in the published word were connected to an emerging translocal view of a public sphere in which arguments about government and social organization after colonialism could be debated; this public sphere touched various sites in the Americas and Europe. Filadelfia writers' aspirations were not far from Michael Warner's characterization of print in eighteenth-century Anglo America: "Articulating a new representation of the political order, this print discourse restructured relations of power."[6] But in this case the shift was connected to the emergence of a secular political order that turned away from the dictates of Spanish colonial belief systems and toward an internationalist vision of the future. In keeping with this vision, Filadelfia was one of numerous sites in the Americas, including Mexico City and Buenos Aires, where different types of public-sphere interactions emerged.[7] For Latino literary history, the sending of texts from one country to another as part of a public sphere shows the extent to which Spanish-language writing in the United States was not local but rather part of a highly educated trans-American conversation ranging far in geographic scope.

The Filadelfia public sphere, with its connection to transatlantic revolutionary-era documents, was geographically broad, in contrast to the more locally based theoretical formulation of public sphere first presented by Jürgen Habermas in his influential work.[8] Nancy Fraser is among scholars who have emphasized that Habermas's argument rested on a contained local context linked to a "Westphalian political imaginary" that assumes a bounded political community within a territorial state. Even as she points out the importance of the public sphere to conceptualizing democratic notions beyond the nation-state, she recognizes that the term *transnational public sphere* sounds "a bit like an oxymoron."[9] Critiques of the local emphasis in public-sphere theory have in some cases pointed out the long history of translocal movements going back at least to the seventeenth century and proceeding through the Enlightenment republic of letters, reminding us "that metropolitan democracy arose in tandem with colonial subjection, which galvanized transnational flows of public opinion."[10] In the case of Filadelfia writers, print was connected to a pedagogical function, namely, the instruction of populations in new forms of political organization, as summed up in the following passage from Vicente Pazos Kanki in this 1819 discussion of public knowledge in the Southern Cone: "Ten years ago they were ignorant of the representative system of government, of the liberty of conscience, and of the press; now they are familiar with all three." He continues, "In Chili and Buenos Ayres, where the art of printing has begun to extend itself, the people have already begun to adopt the republican institutions of the United States."[11]

Two contradictions emerge as a result of tensions between local conditions in home countries and the international networks of Filadelfia letters. The first is that Filadelfia writers conceive of what we can call a public sphere in interlingual and international terms at the same time that they place their faith in print's ability to penetrate local contexts. The second is that these intellectuals help construct an anticolonial discourse of equity and rights across nations without challenging certain forms of social hierarchies and class inequalities in particular (home-front) settings. Filadelfia writers labored under a notion of democratic universalism that was historically revolutionary but ignored or papered over contingent hierarchical conditions in their home countries. As we will see, Filadelfia publications staunchly oppose Spanish colonial structures but do not regularly account for class and social differences that were an integral part of US and Spanish American societies.

This chapter and the next focus on a variety of trans-American publications, from a theological treatise to republican pamphlets, to show that even as these texts sought to unite territories across the Atlantic and the Americas under principles of universal rights, they also inscribed an inadvertent separation between text and the localities the authors hoped to reach. This disjunction is in part the result of an investment in abstract notions of political subjectivity and political organization that are evident in the writings considered in this chapter and the next. We start this chapter with a book that is the most religious example of Filadelfia letters: Juan Germán Roscio's *El triunfo de la libertad sobre el despotismo* (The triumph of liberty over despotism, 1817). In its conception and publication as well as its argument, *El triunfo de la libertad* is a product of a trans-American and transatlantic public sphere that motivates a tension between the local and the catholic; unlike other Filadelfia writings, it develops its argument through a reading of the Bible. We then move to a newspaper editor of indigenous background who attempted to enter Anglophone political discussions in the United States. We then consider two periodicals that claim a local space in Cuba even as they circulate transnationally, and we conclude with a focus on how poetry and the discourse surrounding literary genre create a nationalist position. Let us begin with an intellectual who went from prison to publication.

Roscio's Confession: A Biblical Argument

He was Filadelfia's theologian, his writing forged by years of imprisonment and exile. Roscio's *El triunfo de la libertad* stands out among Filadelfia's imprints because its theological foundation facilitates an intent to connect to Venezuela through the language of Catholicism. The 1817 edition measured 5½" × 3½", which suggests that the book was meant for easy—and possibly clandestine—circulation and could be carried in a pocket. Roscio's faith in print stemmed from the belief that biblical hermeneutic would carry the day in debates over the future of Spanish America. By publishing a book that spoke to the Catholic societies of the southern Americas, Roscio opted to downplay the influence of revolutionary political thought that might have otherwise been associated with a Filadelfia tradition. In contrast to Manuel García de Sena's attempt to *translate* Paine and the US Declaration of Independence to South America, Roscio avoids citing revolutionary thinkers, instead emphasizing his theological training. At the same time, the biblical emphasis creates separation from other aspects of the social conditions of Roscio's home country, namely, the way race and gender are imbricated in the social hierarchy. Although he had suffered persecution because of his family's ethnic background, Roscio in his Filadelfia book chose to forgo addressing social conditions in favor of a discussion of what he viewed as the Bible's political ideals. The result is a text that exemplifies how the trans-American public sphere could facilitate deterritorialized universal precepts.

Roscio's Filadelfia story involves a journey to take advantage of the city's print culture, but it starts with prison time and escape. Roscio (1763–1821) was among supporters of independence who starting in 1810 worked to form a new government known as the First Republic of Venezuela. This effort grew into a full declaration of independence on July 5, 1811, which emerged from a vote the previous day scheduled to coincide with the US independence celebration.[12] The result was temporary local rule of parts of the country. But in 1812, Spain mounted a military counteroffensive, and a major earthquake struck the area, allowing royal forces to take control of the colony again, bringing an end to the First Republic.[13] Roscio was among those arrested and exiled. His incarceration, which lasted almost two years, shows that the educational and economic advantages of the trans-American elite did not offer adequate protection from Spanish authorities bent on silencing political radicals. He was held incommunicado in a cell for seventy days, then placed on a ship to Spain and eventually transferred to a prison in Ceuta, a Spanish colonial holding in North Africa.[14]

In a daring escape, Roscio got himself to Gibraltar, and he ultimately received protection from British authorities there, making it possible for him to begin heading back to the Americas at the end of 1815. His journey took him to Jamaica, then New Orleans.[15] Like others before and after him, Roscio turned to Philadelphia for its printing presses. *El triunfo* was the culmination of several years of thinking about Catholicism and monarchy and in part a product of the years in prison. In an 1816 letter from Kingston, Jamaica, Roscio says he detests the use of Catholicism by Ferdinand VII and calls his government "arbitrary and anti-religion."[16] When Roscio passed through New Orleans, a merchant loaned him two hundred dollars, which he used for travel and for the printing of *El triunfo de la libertad*.[17] Roscio remained in Philadelphia from early 1817 to the end of 1818, and the city allowed him to engage with other exiled intellectuals, including Manuel Torres, Pedro Gual, and Vicente Pazos Kanki, to whom we turn next. After returning to Venezuela and taking a prominent post in the new government, Roscio appointed Torres as "agent," or informal ambassador, to the United States, citing Venezuela's "confianza en que V. es un antiguo y verdadero amigo de la independencia americana" (confidence that you are a longstanding and true friend of the independence of America).[18] For Roscio, Philadelphia not only was a refuge but provided the materials necessary to release an impressive attack on Spanish colonialism.[19] In addition to *El triunfo de la libertad,* he published a translation into Spanish from French of what he called a "republican homily" delivered by Pope Pius VII when he was still a cardinal, *Homilia del cardinal Chiaramonti, obispo de Imola* (Philadelphia, 1817). In his prologue, Roscio makes a move comparable to that of Manuel García de Sena's translation of Thomas Paine and suggests that the pope is speaking about and to the republics of South America and Mexico, arguing that "tendran estos nuevos Republicanos otra prueba de la excelencia del gobierno adoptado en su insurreccion" (these new Republicans will have yet additional proof of the excellence of the government they have adopted through their insurrection).[20]

El triunfo de la libertad was notable in the commercial and public realm, becoming one of the most reprinted publications to come out of Filadelfia. In October 1818, *El Correo de Orinoco,* in Angostura, Venezuela (today Ciudad Bolívar), published an article announcing that the book was for sale in a local shop and reviewing some of the content: "Su objeto es rebatir con la Sagrada Escritura los errores políticos y religiosos con que la tiranía remacha los hierros de la esclavitud" (Its goal is to refute with Holy Scripture the political and religious misreading that the tyranny uses to conjoin the chains of slavery).[21] In addition to the first edition, printed by Thomas Palmer in 1817, a second Philadelphia edition was published by the Carey house in 1821; Carey then shipped the book to Mexico for sale there.[22] *El triunfo* was subsequently printed at least three more times in Mexico in the nineteenth century.[23] Scholars have argued that the book influenced Benito Juárez and can be seen as a precursor to twentieth-century liberation theology, a point to which we will return.[24]

El triunfo de la libertad is the result of a trans-American Catholic perspective created by exilic movement. It is not about a specific country but rather about the Bible's teachings on political organization. Using the Latin Vulgate, Roscio develops a hermeneutic of biblical events, unusual among Filadelfia letters and also offering a novel twist on the Christian political philosophy and religious practices of his South American region. *El triunfo* was influenced by a South American region where religious beliefs pervaded everyday life. Benito Raúl Losada characterizes Caracas in the late eighteenth century as having a distinct religious atmosphere, with prominent churches and convents as well as regular ecclesiastical celebrations.[25] In this context, religious life and education were intimately connected; we can say that for Roscio theology was not separate from philosophical and legal studies. He earned a doctorate in canon law and then a doctorate in civil law from the University of Caracas and went on to teach Latin at the university. Given this background, he could develop arguments based on biblical learning as he worked as a statesman calling for independence and trying to establish a new government. In an excellent article on his engagement with antiliberal Catholic figures, Carmen Ruiz Barrionuevo shows how Roscio in his writings responds to specific reactionary clerics and bishops.[26]

Roscio did not distinguish between Catholic belief and republican politics, a point he stated clearly in a will he drew up while gravely ill in

Philadelphia: "I declare that I profess the holy religion of Jesus Christ; and, as most comfortable [*sic*] hereto, I profess, and wish to die under the system of republican government; and protest against the tyrannical and despotical government of absolute monarchy, like that of Spain."[27] Published in English in the Philadelphia *Aurora*, the will shows how politics as well as religion had become a matter of life and death. The phrase "comfortable hereto," about the republican government, is the *Aurora*'s awkward translation of the phrase *más conforme a ella*, which we can also translate as "most in accordance with" his religious beliefs.[28]

In *El triunfo de la libertad*, Roscio presents himself as both theologian and political opponent of monarchy, attempting to draw the support of Spanish American Catholics through biblical exegesis (in contrast to what Roscio calls the "theologians of tyranny"). In his prologue, Roscio makes explicit that he is attempting to fill a gap in the existing scholarly literature with a book that draws from the Bible to make an argument against monarchical divine right:

> Yo suspiraba por una obra que refutase estos errores, no con razones puramente filosóficas, sino con la autoridad de los mismos libros de donde la facción contraria deducía sofismas.... En vano busqué lo que yo deseaba: No hallé más que discursos filosóficos, tan cargados de razón, que para nada contaban con la Biblia. Yo estaba muy lejos de pensar que faltasen defensores de la libertad, fundados en la autoridad de libros religiosos.[29]

> (I sought a work that would refute those errors, not purely through philosophical reasoning but by drawing on the authority of the same books from which the opposing party deduced its sophistry.... I searched in vain for what I desired: I found nothing more than philosophical treatises so full of reason that they made no use of the Bible. I could not fathom that no one had turned to the authority of religious books to defend the foundations of liberty.)

The passage gives us insight into his work as an intellectual who had read widely in political philosophy. He opens *El triunfo de la libertad* by characterizing the Spanish monarchy as an "idol of tyranny" that had based its empire on the misreading of scripture. With that brief reference to Plato's allegory of the cave, Roscio develops the argument by drawing on his fluency in Latin and French and a depth of biblical knowledge and the classics that allow him to luxuriate in references to both Virgil and Saint Paul.

El triunfo de la libertad attacks the divine right of monarchs through a sustained discussion of passages from the Old and New Testaments. Roscio shows that the Bible provides examples of social and political organization that are at odds with monarchical rule. The theologian and historian Luis Ugalde has called *El triunfo* the most significant example from Latin America's independence movements of a book that reconciles explicitly and systematically a theological Christian and biblical approach with republican government. For Roscio, Ugalde argues, the military war of independence had to be accompanied by a lettered effort to disabuse people of religious teachings that supported monarchy.[30] And indeed Roscio is usually worried about a religious front, as we see in an 1820 letter to Simón Bolívar in which he recommends attempting to secure written support for independence from church figures as a way to draw military fighters away from the royalist side.[31]

The product of a translocal public sphere, *El triunfo de la libertad* navigates tension between, on the one hand, local conditions—Philadelphia print culture and religious life in Caracas—and, on the other hand, the universal bent of an argument about sovereignty via theology. The book presents a dense biblical exegesis in fifty-one chapters plus an appendix. Translating the Latin Vulgate into early nineteenth-century political language, Roscio challenges the Catholic order by taking the Bible directly into the vernacular at a time when no church-approved Spanish translation existed, and when even the most devout layfolk were discouraged from reading the scriptures independently. He also weaves Rousseau and Paine into his analysis, as evident in the numerous uses of the phrases *contrato social* (social contract) and *sentido común* (common sense), although he refrains from naming these political philosophers directly.[32] Roscio's omission of these names suggests that he sought to communicate with Catholic readers, who might otherwise have been distracted by controversial political philosophers.

The influence of Rousseau and Paine is important because it shows how a vehemently Catholic intellectual was engaging with secular writings on political philosophy. For decades, scholars of intellectual history have emphasized that the Spanish American revolutions were influenced to varying degrees not only by secular Enlightenment thinkers but also by changes in late Catholic Scholasticism. Raúl Coronado, for example, has argued that scientific skepticism and rationalism, as integrated into canonical Catholic philosophical writings, "were the harbingers of revolution, not the political philosophy of the eighteenth-century revolutions."[33] Coronado notes a limited circulation of revolutionary ideas out of Europe and the United States in the restricted publishing system of the Hispanic world in the eighteenth century to argue that changes were already under way in Scholastic debates and in the wake of Bourbon reforms. By the early nineteenth century, however, secular political writings were well known among revolutionary Spanish American thinkers. Roscio would have been educated under late Scholasticism while also having access to political revolutionary writing. One of the writings available to him was a translation of the Declaration of the Rights of Man and of the Citizen that circulated in Caracas, and we know that the García de Sena translation of Thomas Paine published in 1811 had made it to Venezuela.

The political dimension of Roscio's theological argument is emphasized through his twist on a repentant mode associated with Augustine's *Confessions*. Roscio follows Augustine by addressing the book to God (opening with a salutation that you might see in a letter) and providing an account of his personal faults. But unlike the sinful life that Augustine narrates, Roscio's self-described sinfulness stems from prior political maneuvering, most importantly his support of the Spanish Crown prior to his turn toward independence. The book is framed as the confession of a sinner repenting for his *political errors*. Roscio writes, "Yo era en otro tiempo uno de los servidores de la tiranía más aferrados a ella" (*T* 3; In the past I was one of the most fervent supporters of tyranny). The book's full title, *El triunfo de la libertad sobre el despotismo en la confesion de un pecador arrepentido de sus errores politicos, y dedicado a desagraviar en esta parte á la religion ofendida con el sistema de la tirania,* calls attention to his own "errors" in both political and religious thought and presents the book as an attempt to repair (*desagraviar*) what he perceives as the damage to religion caused by the Spanish monarchy's tyrannical use of divine right to sustain its power. Roscio's argument is biblical, even if his confession is political, in that he is embarrassed at having supported a system that he grew to believe was despotic and illegitimate. The inclusion of *confesión* in the subtitle could also be a nod to Rousseau's *Les confessions,* although Roscio's book differs in that it does not include autobiographical information.

The book's place in a trans-American public sphere is evident in Roscio's confessional epistolary approach in a book that would never have been licensed for publication in his home country. Indirectly invoking the Caracas religious context, Roscio repents directly to God in the opening line of the introduction: "Pequé, Señor, contra ti y contra el género humano, mientras yo seguía las banderas del despotismo. Yo agravaba mi pecado cuando, en obsequio de la tiranía, me servía de vuestra santa palabra, como si ella se hubiese escrito y transmitido a los mortales para cargarlos de cadenas, para remachar y bendecir los hierros de su esclavitud" (*T* 7; I sinned, Lord, against you and against the human race while I followed the banner of despotism. I exacerbated my sin when, in support of tyranny, I used your sacred word as if it had been your goal in bestowing it upon mortals to weigh it down with chains and use it as blessing and rivet on the irons of slavery). The word *slavery* is at once a metaphor for colonial subjection and a reference to the actual institution, considering that prior to independence Venezuela had a significant slave population. Estimates are that Venezuela in 1800 had more than 110,000 slaves and 400,000 free people of African descent, who accounted for upwards of 60 percent of a population of almost 900,000.[34] Racial politics during the First Republic were troubled, as Peter Blanchard has argued, because even though the new junta passed a law abolishing the slave trade, slavery itself was allowed to persist at first, and efforts were not made to integrate blacks into political participation in a new society. "Many *pardos* consequently opposed the republic and some expressed outright hatred toward its creole leaders," Blanchard writes.[35] Roscio was reluctant to wade into these issues, and as we will see, his references to slavery are in the abstract.

The prologue to *El triunfo de la libertad* establishes three points. Roscio apologizes for a time in his life when out of self-interest and a desire to develop his reputation he defended the divine right of monarchs; he rejoices at having found that scripture does not support monarchial rule; and he thanks God for opening his eyes and allowing him to repent for his previous support of Spain's kings. Roscio writes: "Vos sabéis, Señor, cuáles fueron los raptos de alegría al convencerme que nada existía en las *Escrituras* favorable al poder arbitrario de las monarquías absolutas; en todos los libros santos le vi odiado y reprobado; decidida en todos ellos la soberanía del pueblo, y en sumo grado protegidos los derechos del hombre en sociedad" (*T* 10; You know, Lord, the rapture and joy I experienced upon becoming persuaded that nothing existed in Scripture to support the arbitrary authority claimed by absolute monarchies. All holy books opposed and condemned monarchies, instead favoring the sovereignty of the people while defending to the highest degree the rights of men in society). Roscio counts himself among those who propped up the monarchy "menos con la fuerza de las armas, que con el influjo de las preocupaciones religioso-políticas" (*T* 69; less with the power of arms than with the influence of religious-political arguments). While it might appear that he admits to a rhetorical fluidity and a willingness to use scripture for one side or another, the different positions are reconciled through a claim to divine intervention. It is God that has brought Roscio to his new reading of the Bible, and the address to God in the book reinforces an intimate connection. In a brutally honest passage, Roscio laments that in one case he supported monarchy with the hope of gaining a professorship in Latin at the University of Caracas. "Menos por malicia que por ignorancia, abusaba de la Religion para sostener la servidumbre de mi patria" (*T* 234; More out of ignorance than malice, I would abuse Religion to protect the subjection of my homeland).

Roscio's confession is an exercise in rereading toward a better interpretation. To open his argument against divine right, Roscio goes straight to Old Testament verses that take up monarchical rule: "By me kings reign, and rulers decree what is just" (Prov. 8:15).[36] He quotes the Latin: "Per me reyes regnant, et legum conditores justa decernant" and offers a Spanish translation, "Por mí reinan los Reyes, dice el texto, y los legisladores decretan lo justo" (*T* 13). Again addressing God, Roscio writes, "Yo suponía que tú eras quien aquí tomaba la palabra... y que por esta expresión atribuida erróneamente a tus divinos labios, quedaban constituidos plenipotenciarios tuyos todos los monarcas" (*T* 13; I used to assume that these words were yours... and by attributing erroneously these lines to your divine lips, all monarchs were constituted as your representatives). This false premise, Roscio writes, was the source of his "first shots against the sovereignty of the people" (*T* 14). But he quickly clarifies that the first-person speaker in these verses is not God but "wisdom." To reach this position, Roscio goes back several lines to Proverbs 8:12, "I, wisdom, dwell with prudence," and notes that wisdom is the speaker several lines later where the verse begins, "By me kings reign." Roscio argues that by reading closely, "we can reach this truth and dispel the error introduced in support of absolute monarchy."[37] His numerous references to the word *reading* in this chapter emphasize a hermeneutics of liberation that drives his project.

The idea of returning to scripture, rereading in order to think anew in relation to political organization, is a hallmark of twentieth-century liberation theology, and thus it is no surprise that Domingo Miliani and other scholars have argued that Roscio is a precursor of this religious movement, which spread across Latin America in the late twentieth century. In addition to writings on sovereignty, Miliani argues, Roscio's repeated references to notions of equality in the face of oppressive monarchical forces and, most importantly, his justification of popular revolt in the face of unjust rulers link him to the theology of liberation.[38] Liberation theology centered on the poor and the powerless, drawing attention to the flawed political conditions that brought about their immiseration, through a hermeneutics of reading scripture in relation to history.[39]

Although Roscio's method can be compared to other religion-based liberatory reading practices, *El triunfo* is most deeply engaged with late eighteenth- and early nineteenth-century philosophical debates on the right of people to govern themselves. In chapter 4, titled "Incorrect Idea of Sovereignty," Roscio writes,

> Confieso, Señor, que el concepto que yo había formado de ella no podía ser más ridículo y chocante a la razón. Imaginaba yo que la soberanía era una cosa sobrenatural e invisible, reservada desde la eternidad para cierto individuos y familias, e íntimamente unida con la palabra *Rey* . . . . Otras veces la consideraba como una cualidad espiritual y divina, inherente a tu omnipotencia, de donde se desprendía milagrosamente para indentificarse con los monarcas y caracterizarlos de vicedioses de la tierra. (*T* 25)

> (I confess, Lord, that the concept I had developed of [sovereignty] was ridiculous and at odds with reason. I imagined that sovereignty was something supernatural and invisible, reserved through eternity for certain individuals and families, and intimately connected to the word *King*. . . . At other times I considered it a divine and spiritual quality inherent in your omnipotence, from whence it emanated miraculously to grace monarchs and characterize them as demigods of the earth.)

The passage is notable for depicting Roscio's turn away from thinking that does not take into account the people. Previously, he had viewed sovereignty as a concept tied to a *word* (king) but also as a "spiritual quality" that seemingly emanated from the sky to create another being (demigod) above the everyday conditions of humans. The various abstractions circulating display how the Catholic theology in which Roscio had been trained took heaven as a starting point, as the origin of sovereignty. And that is exactly where Roscio changed his thinking.

Arguing that the power of leaders comes from the people, Roscio marshals numerous episodes from the Hebrew Bible to situate sovereignty in the populace, including the stories of Moses and the Hebrews, Abraham and Lot, and the death of Jacob. He is thorough in offering examples to support his points. For example, he quotes Proverbs 14:28: "In multitudine populi dignitas regis, et in paucitate plebis ignominia principis" (In a multitude of people is the glory of a king, but without people a prince is ruined). Roscio argues that Moses, in preparing to move to the Promised Land, gauged the strength of any people against whom the Hebrews would have to battle. In turn, Moses also based the strength of the Hebrews not on their leaders but on the people themselves. In Roscio's hands, Moses seems to have read *Common Sense* and operated under the light of reason. "Moisés no tenía más idea del poder soberano que la natural y sencilla que inspira el sentido común: guiado de este conocimiento miraba en el pueblo la fuente de la soberanía" (*T* 34; Moses had no idea about sovereign power other than the natural and simple one inspired by common sense: driven by this understanding, he saw in the people the source of sovereignty). Similarly, in Roscio's retelling of the story of Abraham and Lot, Abraham was able to defeat the four kings that have taken Lot captive because Abraham had "the authority and power of the people" (*T* 36).

The episode that best encapsulates Roscio's argument is Jacob's blessing of his sons in Genesis 49. Roscio quotes the following lines in both Spanish and Latin. "The scepter will not depart from Judah, nor the ruler's staff from between his feet, until he to whom it belongs shall come, and the obedience of the nations shall be his." In his analysis he writes:

> Se deja ver en este vaticinio, que el cetro, símbolo de la soberanía, pertenece a la multitud. Si no fuese de la tribu este poder soberano fijado en el cetro, ella no podría perderlo.... En el presente texto hay una profecía dependiente de la revelación, y un aserto político independiente de ella: dos verdades, una civil, otra religiosa: la soberanía de las tribus; y la venida del Mesías.... Quien niega la primera verdad, desacredita el vaticinio, y se mete en un caos de glosas arbitrarias. (*T* 37)

> (It is evident in this prophecy that the scepter, symbol of sovereignty, belongs to the multitude. If this sovereign power in the scepter did not belong to the tribe, it would not be able to lose it.... In the present text there is a prophecy that depends on revelation, as well as a separate political assertion: two truths, one civil and the other religious: the sovereignty of the people, and the coming of the Messiah.... Whoever denies the first also discredits the prophecy and enters a chaos of arbitrary glosses.)

By combining the question of sovereignty with prophecy, Roscio attempts to prevent a reading that would separate theological belief from civil matters. In other words, civil matters are inextricable from the word of God. To separate them is to fall into chaos, which he associates with a type of Scholastic thinking that does not take into account the "light of reason" (*T* 38).

Roscio also turns to the New Testament and offers readings of passages on politics from the epistles of Peter and Paul. As if to preclude the conclusion that their use of *king* and *prince* reflects monarchical intentions, Roscio devotes a chapter to explaining why they did not use the term *emperor* in the context of the Roman Empire. Roman rulers were "all usurpers, immoral tyrants," Roscio writes (*T* 107). To avoid legitimizing the rule of emperors such as Caligula or Nero, the apostles used the more general terms *prince* and *king* so as to signify not a specific person but an abstract reference to someone in the role of leader. The word *king*, he argues, refers not to the "person who holds the scepter but rather to the authority and power of the people and their political capacity" (*T* 108). In doing so, Peter and Paul followed Christ in referencing a general ruler in the line "render to Caesar the things that are Caesar's" (Matt. 22:21). Here Roscio is countering Catholic teaching, which would use the words of Saint Paul to grant divine sanction to absolute monarchs. "Mas ahora desengañado confieso, que no hablaron de personas, sino de la soberanía del pueblo, contraída a cierto sistema de gobierno, cuando los Apóstoles reconocieron en el poder de la administración una vicaría tuya" (*T* 115; But having been undeceived, I now confess that the Apostles did not speak of specific persons but rather of the people's sovereignty as applied to a system of government when they claimed that a particular administration was your charge). Here we see Roscio echoing the notion of *desengaño* (undeceive) adopted by Puglia.

In Roscio's point about the apostles not speaking about specific rulers we see the logic of his argument. Like the apostles, in discussions about sovereignty he does not speak about an actual people but rather about a universalist sense of the people. For much of his book, Roscio avoids references to any particular country in Spanish America. Not even his native Venezuela makes it into the discussion. He also does not mention the United States, although it is likely that he wrote the manuscript prior to making his way to Philadelphia. It is not until the final pages that Roscio adds a context, one that prompted him to include an appendix. That context involves a bishop's sermon, printed and circulated in Spain, impugning the memory of Juan Diaz Porlier, a South American–born general in the Spanish military who came out in support of the Spanish liberal Constitution of 1812. Porlier had been incarcerated and hanged in Spain. Roscio, still disturbed by the sound defeat of the first wave of liberalism to sweep Spain, early in the second decade of the nineteenth century, excoriated the bishop for arguing that Catholicism had been harmed by Porlier's support of independence: "¡Religión medrosa, religión que se estremece cuando sus hijos ejercen el derecho de la naturaleza; cuando cumplen los deberes de la sociedad, resistiendo a la opresión, solamente cabe en la fantasía de un loco que haya perdido enteramente los sesos!" (*T* 245–46; A religion that rests on fear and exists only in the fantasies of a madman who has completely lost his mind is shaken when its children exercise their natural rights and fulfill their responsibility to society by resisting oppression!). Curiously, Roscio does not turn this fiery rhetoric toward a discussion of his home in Venezuela. He continues a theological debate against the madman bishop who has besmirched the reputation of the great Porlier. What are we to make of Roscio's avoidance of his home country in his confession?

Mestizo No More

In *El triunfo de la libertad,* Roscio spoke to Catholics in Venezuela, but he did so through a trans-American public sphere that also called for a universalist take on sovereignty. The result was an emphasis on an abstract politico-religious panorama that avoided the racialized hierarchies of his home and the place where he published his book. In other words, Roscio addressed one local context (Catholicism in Venezuela), while leaving other dimensions of his country untouched. The implications are that Roscio viewed the battle for independence not just in relation to his specific home country but rather as a grand war that extended all the way to Spain and would not end until the Spanish Crown itself had ceased to exist. The Bible offered Roscio an interpretive opportunity to present sovereignty in the people as a universal precept rather than a particular necessity, and thus he wrote to an expansive Americas readership. Roscio deployed a conception of social organization as it appeared in numerous Bible verses, and thus his vision went back to the centuries of the Old Testament and focused on the contemporary period in which he wrote. In effect, Roscio offered Rousseauian social-contract theory in a theological guise.

The problem with omitting conditions in Caracas and other parts of what would become Venezuela was that it cut out the racial-economic dimensions of social hierarchy. And this was no small matter either in the Venezuelan context or for Roscio, whose mother was a mestiza and whose work as a lawyer had been affected by two significant events related to racial construction and the *sistema de castas*. In one, Roscio took on a legal case in which he defended an indigenous woman from discrimination. In 1797, Isabel María Páez had attended church and been denied the option of using a small rug for kneeling. This privilege was reserved for whites who had proven purity of blood and was not open to mestizos, *pardos,* or slaves. Roscio took up her cause in court and railed against the caste system, calling it a disgrace that notions of nobility based on heredity would be preferred to the natural right of all people, including the lower class, which is "celebrated in divine and humanistic letters and is esteemed and loved by God and good people."[40] In his writing, Roscio did not shy away from condemning his "disgraceful country" for such discrimination. Scholars suggest that this rejection of the caste system influenced an attempt by the Colegio de Abogados de Caracas (College of Lawyers) to prevent him from joining the institution.[41]

The racism inherent in his society came at Roscio in the form of discrimination in legal circles. In 1798, the College of Lawyers, functioning not as a degree-granting institution but as a professional organization that granted legitimacy, refused to admit Roscio because of his ethnic background: one of his grandmothers had been indigenous. This event was notorious and is still understood as an important event in Venezuelan race relations, as the following account in the historical section of the college's website indicates: "Los fundadores rechazan la petición de ingreso al colegio, considerando que Juan Germán Roscio, no era digno de ingresar a la corporación, por su indignidad étnica y racial, circunstancia que fue sometida a un largo y lamentable proceso o juicio de sangre" (The founders rejected the petition for entrance to the college, finding that Juan Germán Roscio was not worthy of being admitted because of his racial and ethnic unworthiness, a decision that led to a judgment on purity of blood and a lengthy and unfortunate legal proceeding).[42] Like the woman he had defended, Roscio was caught in a discourse of *limpieza de sangre,* or "purity of blood," a social litmus test that precluded people of indigenous and African descent from participating in civil, military, and ecclesiastical institutions. Angel Rafael Almarza Villalobos has argued that *limpieza de sangre* emerged from the fifteenth century (the Spanish Reconquista); originally intended to show that people were not of Jewish or Muslim descent, it made its way to the Caracas College of Lawyers in the eighteenth century as a way to shore up elite access to centers of power. The notion of pure blood, Almarza Villalobos argues, came to provide a discursive foundation for a system of social hierarchy that influenced the Caracas College of Lawyers.[43] But the application of these purity statutes was uneven throughout the empire, and thus Roscio could do battle in court. The legal question that emerged was whether the college could deny him entry because his mother was a mestiza, and the result was years of legal wrangling that ultimately led to his acceptance into the college. Roscio refuted the college's claims and argued that a mestizo background was not legal ground for excluding him, making a case for legal equality under the law.[44]

Despite having lived through these racially charged experiences, Roscio does not discuss racialized hierarchies in Spanish America or Philadelphia in *El triunfo de la libertad*. Given his background as a well-educated leader in the society, it would have been unusual for him to claim a mestizo identity publicly. The society actually divided most people into whites and Indians. As Sarah C. Chambers has written about the Andes, "Although elites recognized an intermediate category of mestizos, which they often associated with illegitimacy and deviancy, tax structures and dominant racial ideologies discouraged subalterns from publicly embracing this label until the twentieth century."[45] Roscio did not identify as a mestizo even after he became a print-culture warrior for independence.

In *El triunfo de la libertad* he did not discuss slavery in Venezuela or the role of blacks in independence movements, even though, as Christon Archer has noted, people of mixed ancestry "including mulattos and free blacks, fought on both sides during the wars to improve their social, economic, and political status."[46] Instead, Roscio takes up chattel slavery as a transhistorical system rather than as a condition in his home country or in the United States. Invoking the Bible, he writes, "No ha sido de la aprobación de los Apóstoles la Esclavitud. Ninguno de ellos podía aprobar un exceso contrario a la naturaleza" (*T* 158; None of the apostoles ever approved of slavery because none would have approved of such excess against the laws of nature). By turning to the original disciples of Christ, Roscio bypasses New Testament passages that can be taken to justify slavery. He goes on:

> Muy común es entre los juristas honrar con el dictado de *derecho* al uso bárbaro de la esclavitud, al infame tráfico de carne humana. ¿Y quién será capaz de probar que esta práctica es justa y conforme a razón? Derechos y leyes de servidumbre frecuentemente se leen en la antigua y moderna legislación de la parte más culta del globo. Lo más notable es que en la misma definición de

este abuso se le califique de derecho, al mismo tiempo que se reconoce como contrario a la naturaleza. No puede ser derecho, ni ley, lo que carece de justicia y equidad. (*T* 69)

(It is very common among jurists to say the barbaric practice of slavery, the infamous traffic of human flesh, is a legal right. But who would be able to prove that the practice is just in accordance with reason? Laws justifying servitude are seen frequently in modern and ancient legislation in the most developed parts of the globe. Most egregious is that this abuse should be characterized as a right when it is contrary to nature. Neither a right nor a law can stand if it lacks justice and equity.)

Referring to both ancient and modern "developed parts of the globe," Roscio situates the debate in the realm of laws and legal precedent, with no references to his contemporaneous American theater of slavery.

Roscio's refusal to speak about slavery in Venezuela or the United States specifically in *El triunfo* and the lack of reference to his own racial background were not the result of an oversight but of a rhetorical condition of the trans-American public sphere. He developed a writerly ethos that paralleled a universalist position—that of a trans-American anticolonial intellectual devoid of racial markers—and appealed to readers attempting to conceptualize a new political arena and a set of inter-American relations. Roscio's theological politics and their catholic implications can be read as a direct intervention into the socioreligious life of Caracas. In developing that position, which downplays difference, Roscio shares with the trans-American elite an attempt to claim an unmarked racial position in the public sphere. To delve more into that question, let us turn to the work of an Andean intellectual whose selective self-fashioning raises further questions about the relationship of trans-American publication to racial taxonomies of privilege.

An Aymara in Filadelfia

While most Filadelfia writers were *criollos* descended from Spaniards, the trans-American elite were not uniformly white in contemporary racial terms. Filadelfia at one point saw the arrival of an intellectual with indigenous background. Vicente Pazos Kanki (1779–1853) was born in the southern highlands of Peru, in an area that would become part of the country of Bolivia, and his story begins with the Aymara people. Scholars debate the details of his parentage, but Pazos Kanki seems to have spent the first few years of his life speaking the Aymara language and also learned Quechua.[47] In addition to Spanish, he studied Latin and French as part of his early education at a seminary in La Paz, where he began preparing to become a priest. He received a doctorate in theology in 1804 from the University of Cuzco.[48] Although he was ordained, it does not appear that he ever practiced as a priest, and he eventually married an English woman in an Anglican ceremony in London.[49] Instead of following his religious training, Pazos Kanki became a warrior for independence; his work as a newspaper writer and diplomat took him to Buenos Aires, New York, London, and Philadelphia.

We encounter Pazos Kanki in Philadelphia in 1818 with the publication of *The Exposition, Remonstrance and Protest of Don Vincente Pazos, Commissioner on Behalf of the Republican Agents Established at Amelia Island, in Florida, Under the Authority and on Behalf of the Independent States of South America.* (This was one of two publications by Pazos translated and published in the United States late in the second decade of the nineteenth century. The second was an interesting mix of history, geography, and politics titled *Letters on the United Provinces of South America, Addressed to the Hon. Henry Clay, Speaker of the House of Representatives of the United States* [1819].)[50] The pamphlet misspells *Vicente* in the title (as well as in the body of the pamphlet) as *Vincente,* which suggests an attempt to Anglicize the Hispanophone spelling. Along this line, the pamphlet was not published under the indigenous surname Kanki.

In the United States and for much of his early life, he published under the name Vicente Pazos (excluding Kanki), which indicates some fluidity in his ethnic self-fashioning. It is possible that excluding Kanki was an attempt to fend off potential racial bias from readers while participating in the newspaper world of Buenos Aires and in the trans-American public sphere. Yet later, in 1825, he described himself in print as "un Indio de la ciudad de La Paz" (an Indian from the city of La Paz), and he used the name Kanki in writing and diplomatic work after that.[51] In the case of the Filadelfia pamphlet, the absence of a second family name allowed him to publish his work without calling attention to an element of his identity that might have raised questions for his readers or even prompted racist views about his indigenous background. By publishing the *Exposition* without the name Kanki, Pazos struck a persona that would be rhetorically acceptable to his primary audience: the president of the United States. The issue, as we will see, involves the notorious conflict over Amelia Island. In developing his political argument, Pazos Kanki (like Roscio before him) did not touch on his ethnic background in order to enter the kinds of public discourse that elevated universal rights.

Pazos Kanki also shared with Roscio and others in the Filadelfia circle a tremendous faith in print's ability to end colonial subjection. Pazos Kanki described an exhilarating sensation upon seeing a printing press for the first time upon arriving in Buenos Aires in 1810: "Animated with the view of the admirable invention, I fancied I beheld in those mute characters, the types, the fountain of that light, which ere long would burst forth and dissipate the clouds of despotism which darkened the horizon of my beloved country."[52] The sentence infuses type with a magical quality, as if the printed word could shoot arrows that would bring down the colonial government. Pazos Kanki did indeed contribute in significant ways to the development of a lively political press in Buenos Aires during years when the region was moving toward independence. Among his work are fourteen issues he edited in 1811 of the *Gazeta de Buenos Ayres,* a paper supported by an anticolonial junta and intended to spread news about changes in the society proposed after the end of colonial rule.[53] Pazos Kanki founded two additional papers, *El Censor,* which ran for three months in 1812, and *La Crónica Argentina,* which became a major proindependence paper in 1816–17.[54] But some of his positions in writing crossed leaders of independence movements in Buenos Aires, and as a result Pazos Kanki was exiled twice. First, in 1812 he was put on a ship and ended up in London, where he struck up a friendship with José Blanco White. One of his biographers describes Pazos Kanki as eager to Anglicize himself, not only through marriage and his adoption of Protestantism but also by attempting to learn as much as possible about England.[55] He even became noted as a dandy, visiting London's tailors and showing a preference for fine clothes and the color blue.[56]

It appears that Pazos Kanki's moves from indigenous community member to Hispanic priest and then newspaper editor had prepared him for the adoption of multiple identities. Pazos Kanki returned to Buenos Aires to continue the lettered fight for independence, but a second exile landed him in Savannah, Georgia. Given his ability to move in new contexts, it is no surprise that Pazos Kanki quickly became involved, both physically and discursively, in the notorious Amelia Island affair and ended up publishing his pamphlet in Philadelphia. Although little known today, the Amelia Island conflict was a controversial military action and bellwether for US governmental attitudes toward Latin America and the United States' willingness to use force there. Amelia Island presaged what would become a common history of military intervention and disregard for local populations, as would become apparent in the US-Mexico War.

Pazos's belief that print could have an effect is in full display in the *Exposition, Remonstrance and Protest* in that the pamphlet suggests that the circulation of ideas in a US public sphere might have a more significant effect than private diplomatic correspondence he had already sent to the Monroe administration. The thirty-two-page *Exposition,* translated from the Spanish, was printed as a letter addressed to President Monroe following up on Pazos's communications with the administration. Influenced by the language of diplomatic exchange, the *Exposition* opens with rhetorical flourishes that are explicit in their admiration for the United States. The title page quotes from the US Declaration of Independence, and Pazos introduces himself and his compatriots as defenders of independent republican government.

The story of Amelia Island began in 1817, when a group of self-proclaimed Spanish American republicans, including Pazos Kanki, gathered financial support for a military action to take over the island off the coast of Florida, declare its independence from Spain, and claim it for the "independent states of South America." This action was conceived as part of a broader plan to take over East Florida with the participation of the independence fighters Francisco Javier Mina and José Alvarez de Toledo; neither of those military leaders made it to Amelia, prompting Pazos to accuse Alvarez de Toledo of "perfidious desertion."[57] Instead, the Spanish garrison at Amelia fell after an attack led by a Scottish military leader by the name of Gregor MacGregor, working on behalf of a Philadelphia group that included the independence fighter Pedro Gual and called themselves "the deputies of free America, resident in the United States of the North." MacGregor took over the island with fifty-five men after a hasty Spanish capitulation in June 1817.[58] Pazos Kanki was there for part of the operation.

The occupation was by all accounts a mess, with the hired soldiers bucking MacGregor's leadership. In Pazos Kanki's telling, MacGregor tried to institute order on the island but soon faced "the machinations and desperate views of a few individuals, who, destitute alike of means and morals ... soon attempted the subversion of the lawful authorities; and succeeded so far as to subvert military discipline and the public peace" (*E* 13–14). The disorder was such that MacGregor departed, opening the way for the arrival of Louis-Michel Aury (a.k.a. Luis Aury), a French private military contractor involved in Spanish American independence movements. Pazos Kanki described the process as follows: "By the fortunate arrival of Aury, every thing was changed—the Spaniards were repulsed and beaten—the patriots triumphant—and the island pacified" (*E* 15). Aury hoisted the Mexican flag on Amelia Island.

Pazos's *Exposition* offers an interesting perspective on events in Florida and US–Latin America relations and complicates historiography. A US-based perspective has often denigrated the participation of Spanish American independence fighters in Florida prior to the US takeover of the region. Rufus Kay Wyllys, for example, calls the Amelia Island group "mere adventurers, working for the most part under little or no shadow of established authority."[59] In Wyllys's telling, Spanish American and Caribbean fighters, some of them black, brought disease and disorder to Amelia Island. The charge of filibustering has often hung over the MacGregor group, with Frank Lawrence Owsley and Gene Smith framing events from that perspective.[60] Pazos, as we will see, actually makes a case that fighters from South America, because of their belligerent status vis-à-vis Spain, had first dibs on Amelia Island and Florida in general. The subsequent US seizure, he argues, was the result of force, not international right.

Amelia Island was big news in the northeastern United States, where papers covered the event in some detail. The Philadelphia *Aurora*, under the influence of Torres—who in Philadelphia had hosted Pazos Kanki, Pedro Gual, and others involved in the attack on Amelia Island—offered regular articles. The Monroe administration became concerned about Amelia as a result of reports that Aury's men had seized a slave ship and were involved in slave trafficking. Monroe was involved in negotiations with Spain over the future of the Florida territory that would eventually lead to the Adams-Onís Treaty of 1819. If fighters from the independence movements took over a part of Florida, that could complicate US efforts to secure Florida in the future. The Monroe administration came to see the Aury fighters as a nuisance and sent in troops to dislodge them.[61] Although justified as a way to expel an illegitimate force, the US response was nothing less than an expansionist maneuver.

While the United States had bullied its way in, Pazos Kanki sought a rhetoric of friendship and admiration in his public address on the issue, even as he called out the Monroe administration for unlawful seizure of the territory. Characterizing the US action on Amelia as a misunderstanding comparable "to the quarrels of brethren," Pazos Kanki requested that the United States withdraw from the island and return it to the group that had claimed it first. A contradictory tone emerges in the opening section of his *Exposition* when he accuses the United States of "violating the rights of the new republics" (*E* 4) and, on the same page, writes, "I frankly avail myself of this occasion, to assure the chief magistrate, that the feelings and attachments of the patriots of South America, have been always ardent and full of admiration of this nation, which has prepared the way to the emancipation and liberty of the New World, and from whose example and precepts they have been led to break the yoke of their oppressors; and that no man is more impressed with the same feelings than myself" (*E* 4). The translation of Pazos's Spanish-language manuscript approximates Spanish-language construction, thus bringing Hispanophone formal touches to a public conversation about a major foreign-policy situation. But more to the point, Pazos attempted to trade on the identification of the trans-American elite with a US revolutionary tradition.

The *Exposition* is direct in its claim for a right of conquest between two belligerent powers at war (Spain and the independence fighters), depicting the United States as an outside party unlawfully stepping in before it had negotiated the Florida cession. This position suggested that the "independent states of South America" had full rights to acquire the territory and institute republican government. "As long as a Spanish possession has not been openly and lawfully detached from the crown of Ferdinand, it remains liable to all the operations of war, and to be occupied and dismembered by any power at war with Spain" (*E* 18). Here diplomatic language such as "lawfully detached" and "liable to all the operations of war" is presented in the public sphere as part of a reasonable argument. The United States, by contrast, is presented as turning to military strength and mounting an "invasion of the Floridas" (*E* 19). Pazos continues: "The United States have very recently proclaimed their neutrality, and still, notwithstanding their being at peace with both Spain and the new republics, they have invaded a territory which they now possess, neither by virtue of any cession from Spain, nor from the states of South America, the only two powers which have alternately possessed it" (*E* 19). This was no less than an inversion of the accusations lobbed at filibusters; it was the United States that had taken over the territory by force without any rights recognized internationally. Pazos went as far as to accuse US forces of taking "private properties belonging to the citizens of the new republics, captured in the waters of the Floridas, without any other right than that of force" (*E* 28). The phrase "in the waters" implies a piratical action.

Angry at having lost both the island and whatever resources they held there, Pazos and his group attempted to enter the public sphere of the northeastern United States to influence or even embarrass the Monroe administration and rally supporters in the US Congress. But the effort came to nought, and the Monroe administration responded in a letter to Pazos saying that it stood by its actions and saw no need for further answer. Before matters were concluded, Pazos did work with Henry Clay in Congress to bring the matter before that body (also a failed attempt) and also met with Secretary of State John Quincy Adams, who received him in a polite manner.[62] When he left the United States for Buenos Aires in 1818, it was with admiration rather than hard feelings, which Charles Arnade believes influences his *Compendio de la historia de los Estados Unidos de América* (A brief history of the United States of America).[63] Pazos Kanki spent much of the succeeding two decades in Europe.

As one of the trans-American elite, Pazos moved in influential circles of US political life with some ease. That someone of indigenous background could do so is a testament to the way his work in the public sphere had effectively de-emphasized his background at a time when racial animus might have kept him out of certain company. Caitlin Fitz describes the polyglot Pazos Kanki as "at ease in the world of high-minded revolutionary ideals" and "inclined to emphasize the things that he had in common with other expatriates rather than the ancestry that made him unique."[64] But another aspect of his life that made him unique was his ability as a writer and editor who could cross oceans and publish his work. In a short biography, Fernando Molina describes Pazos Kanki as willing at times to adopt racist discourses against indigenous populations to further certain political arguments. Molina writes, "Además Pazos nunca se sintió Aymara sino 'Americano,' lo que equivalía en cierta forma decir, 'ciudadano del mundo'" (In addition, Pazos never felt himself Aymara but rather "American," which was another way of saying "citizen of the world").[65] Molina's judgment about Pazos Kanki's relationship to the Aymara people may be speculative, but Pazos Kanki did not adopt a consistent attitude toward whatever ethnic background was in his past, claiming the name Kanki and calling himself an "Indian" in the decades following his operations in the United States. Like Roscio, he was responding to a public sphere that called for a de-emphasizing of personal identity. Despite his cosmopolitan views, worldly travels, and willingness to shift his identity in different contexts, Pazos attempted to reach local audiences in much of his public-sphere interaction; this was nowhere more apparent than in the discourse of amity toward the United States and James Monroe that he deployed in the *Exposition*. In his *Letters on the United Provinces of South America*, Pazos Kanki celebrates empire and lauds the United States for remaking land inhabited by "savages":

"But the history of the United States teaches the consoling truth, that civil and religious liberty has transformed her trackless forests, which were once the habitation of savages and wild beasts—at time when Peru and Mexico were mighty empires, with cities and monuments equal to those of Roman grandeur, and with laws more or less just and equitable—into the garden of the world, where cities have sprung up; manufactures, arts, sciences, and commerce flourish."[66] In this panorama, Inca and Aztec societies are comparable to the ur-empire, Rome, with the United States gaining its position alongside those successful powers even as the indigenous people of North America are counted among wild beasts. Pazos Kanki had spent time with Torres in Philadelphia, and his views are in keeping with those expressed by Torres and Duane, suggesting that a discourse of barbarism in relation to North America was part of the Filadelfia circle.

Both of Pazos Kanki's US publications show that he was eager to address an English-reading audience in the United States even as he himself had been on a trans-American and transatlantic odyssey. In those publications, he deployed a hemispheric perspective that united North and South, writing, "Aside from considerations of mercantile gain . . . the people of the United States have a powerful interest in establishing a close connexion with their sister republics in the south. . . . It is here in the two Americas that the people, strong in their principles, and rich in resources, and displaying humanity and justice, constancy and courage, should erect a formidable barrier against the encroachments of European tyranny."[67] Even after Amelia Island, Pazos Kanki still held on to the possibility of hemispheric unity, with a common enemy, even though a notion of *two* Americas was already bisecting the hemisphere. Pazos Kanki's US publications depict a tension between a particular audience/context (US readers) and, on the other hand, the theoretical universalist principles motivating trans-American publication and infusing conceptions of hemispheric Americanism. This tension was in full display in the periodical put out by another warrior for the hemisphere, Félix Varela.

Local Hemispheric Americanism: Filadelfia's *Habanero*

While Pazos Kanki attempted to enter a US-based political conversation, others used a trans-American public sphere to reach readers in their home countries. Félix Varela's paper *El Habanero* claimed Havana in a way not unlike the way the *New Yorker* connects itself to New York. But a focus on particular Spanish American territory, in this case Varela's island home, was not enough to overcome the separation from local conditions in Spanish American sites that was inherent in most Filadelfia publication. In other words, Varela's letters to Havana could not close the distance, which had been created in part by print-culture conditions that precluded the publication of the paper in Cuba. That distance and the attendant separation of writer and audience, I argue here, led him to overlook some of the most pressing conditions on the island.

El Habanero is one of the most important periodicals in early Latino literature, among the first of many nineteenth-century transnational Spanish-language papers and magazines in the nineteenth-century United States. It appeared in seven issues from 1824 to 1826 and was printed in Philadelphia and New York; it billed itself as a "papel político, científico y literario" (political, scientific, and literary paper), and it included articles on general political considerations, South American independence movements, and Cuba, as well as scientific topics such as magnets and the measuring of ocean depths. In keeping with Enlightenment philosophical perspectives, scientific learning was not divorced from political philosophy. As I discussed in chapter 2, Varela's work as a professor of philosophy in Havana had meant that he also included science in his pedagogy.[68] (*El Habanero*'s focus on science varies from one issue to the next, and its claim to a "literary" domain referred to philosophical concerns rather than to literary genres.)

The articles in *El Habanero* about Cuba focus on the potential (or specter) of revolution in light of independence movements in Spanish America. This emphasis reflected Varela's desire to see his island home free of colonial rule. Thus, *El Habanero* offers a dose of what Varela calls patriotism but also suggests a budding nationalism. Is it any surprise that Varela has long been singled out as the nineteenth-century thinker who first introduced Cubans to nationalism?[69] But Varela's protonational emphasis as exhibited in *El Habanero* was informed by a hemispheric Americanism that pulled him away from considerations of social conditions on the island.

Hemispheric Americanism, a conceptualization of the self and the countries of the Americas as being different from and even in opposition to Europe, was informed by a trans-American public sphere that at least in theory, although not always in circulation, cut across numerous countries.[70] In Varela's hands, hemispheric Americanism came close to being a prenational ontology. The result was that the local, Havana, was simultaneously American in the broadest sense as well as Cuban. That is why articles in *El Habanero* at times veer away from Cuba toward discussions of self-determination for the Americas and why Varela's call for Cuba's independence is framed as part of American liberation. Thus, Varela's patriotism is informed by a support of hemispheric "American" independence, which has its roots in a universalist view of self-determination. While Roscio went straight to the question of sovereignty, Varela used the language of natural rights in opposition to colonial rule. For Varela, propositions about the rights of territories to be free of colonial subjection are inextricable from beliefs that American nature itself can provide the inspiration for independence. Varela's emphasis on humanity and American nature may explain why *El Habanero* largely de-emphasizes what are arguably some of the most important elements in Cuban society: slavery and race.

Before delving into an article that most clearly articulates Varela's hemispheric Americanism, let us consider the way he organizes his arguments in *El Habanero*. Each issue moves from general topics to articles about something specific, for example, starting with considerations about human behavior and moving to Cuba and then, what is arguably the most specific dimension, natural science. This approach is evident in the first issue, which opens with two general articles about political actors creating appearances in public life, then shifts to three articles about Cuba and concludes with four short pieces on scientific topics. The articles' titles provide an indication of this approach: "Mascaras Políticas" (Political masks) and "Cambia Colores" (Chameleons) open with a discussion of political opportunism; these are followed by three Cuba articles, "Consideraciones sobre el estado actual de la isla de Cuba" (General considerations over the actual conditions on the island of Cuba), "Conspiraciones en la Isla de Cuba" (Conspiracies on the island of Cuba), and "Sociedades secretas en la Isla de Cuba" (Secret societies on the island of Cuba); the issue concludes with pieces under the heading "Natural Sciences" focusing on ocean temperatures, sounds, the effect of magnets on titanium, and experiments carried out by the Yale professor Benjamin Silliman. Varela's method is influenced by empiricism, and his observations extend from human nature to chemicals.

Varela's first targets are hypocrisy and political opportunism. "Mascaras Políticas" criticizes those who use patriotism as a cover to benefit financially or in terms of reputation; Varela calls them *enmascarados,* which can be translated as "masked men" and implies a false front. Varela writes: "Nada hay en ellos de verdadero patriotismo, si el enemigo de la Patria les paga mejor, le servirán gustosos, y si pueden recibirán de ambas partes" (Nothing in them is about true patriotism; if an enemy of the country pays them more, they will serve him gladly, and if possible they will take from both sides).⁷¹ The notion of "true patriotism" that sustains Varela's argument is about self-sacrifice and the virtue of doing what is best for the island.

Varela states specifically early in the run of *El Habanero* that his audience is Havana's youth, and he prompts them to *observe* the actions of men. The article "Cambia Colores," which I translate as "Chameleons," can also be translated as "those who change colors," thus referring to a chemical process as a metaphor to attack opportunists who change positions depending on what benefits them. He opens the article with the following point on *observation:* "En todas la mutaciones políticas se observa que los hombres mudan de conducta porque mudan de intereses" (*H* 10; In all political transformations one sees that men change their behavior because their self-interests change). The context most directly informing this discussion is political changes in Spain as they relate to the Constitution of 1812, which was briefly revived in 1821, when Varela made his way to Spain to represent Cuba at the Cortes. "Aunque los cambia colores son bichos que abundan en todos los países, yo no he podido menos de hablar de los de España, porque verdaderamente han sido los más particulares y descarados" (*H* 11; Although chameleons are beasts that are abundant in all countries, I cannot help but discuss those in Spain, because they truly have been remarkable and shameless).⁷² As the references to Spain show, Varela's propositions about hypocrisy and political opportunism may be relevant to many nations going through political upheaval and facing changes.

The Cubanocentric articles in the first issue provide a window onto the island in light of potential movements for independence; however, their analysis remains at the level of the upper class, whether *peninsular* or *criollo*. Varela opens with an article that frames Cuba in relation to economic conditions, emphasizing that the island is rich in resources and minerals but its growth is stunted by colonial rule. In a particularly sarcastic line, Varela laments the excessive influence of economic interests on the country: "Es preciso no perder de vista que en la isla de Cuba no hay *opinión política,* no hay otra opinión que la *mercantil.* En los muelles y almacenes se resuelven todas las cuestiones de Estado" (*H* 16; It is crucial not to lose sight that on the island of Cuba there is no *political opinion;* there is nothing other than *commercial* opinion. All questions of state are resolved in the warehouses and on the docks). He presents economic interests in light of the widely held expectation that after independence is settled militarily and constitutionally in Colombia and/or Mexico, troops on the mainland will launch an invasion of Cuba and oust Spanish forces. Varela is ambivalent about this possibility, saying that no one wants an invasion of his or her country but also noting that a significant part of the population will welcome the troops as long as they are respectful and do not cause excessive economic harm.

In this discussion we see the ambivalence in Varela's views on independence, simultaneously defending a Cuban protonationalism and cognizant of hemispheric independence movements. In other words, his hemispheric Americanism goes only so far. But ultimately, he cautions that economics will have the final say: "En la isla de Cuba no hay amor a España, ni a Colombia ni a México, ni a nadie más que a las cajas de azúcar y a los sacos de café" (*H* 18; On the island of Cuba there is no love for Spain, nor for Colombia, nor for Mexico, nor for anything other than boxes of sugar and sacks of coffee).

Varela's focus on elites is reflected in the article about "secret societies," political groups that met in Cuba in the early nineteenth century. These included Masonic lodges and also revolutionary groups such as one calling itself the Comuneros, a reference to the Comunero uprising in Spain against Charles V in 1520, and the Soles y Rayos de Bolívar, a conspiracy to overthrow the government whose participants included José María Heredia. These so-called secret societies have trans-American dimensions because Masons supported one another in independence movements throughout the Americas. The island's colonial government pursued these groups, forcing Heredia and others into exile. These various groups are not interchangeable, as Masons formed lodges with rituals, while political groups were active in discussions of an uprising. Although he does not attack the motives of groups that may be trying to change Cuba's colonial status, Varela takes issue with them because he does not believe that secrecy propagates civic virtue. On the contrary, it could lead to a general distrust in society as people wonder what types of personal interests can drive the work of secret gatherings:

> Los hombres que en público carecen de virtudes y talento, sin duda no adquieren estos dones porque se junten en privado, antes al contrario, dan rienda con menos temor a sus pasiones. En un pueblo donde la moral pública aún no esté cimentada no en las leyes, sino en la opinión y carácter de los hombres, no debe esperarse que las reuniones secretas sean de otra naturaleza. (*H* 25)

(Men who lack virtue and talent in public do not acquire these gifts when they gather in private. On the contrary, they give free rein to their passions. In a country where public morality has not been codified in laws but rather in the character and opinion of men, one should not hope that secret meetings are of a different nature.)

The reference to the codification of morality signals a republican model that does not rely on individual virtue but rather on the juridical definitions of proper behavior. Varela makes clear that he does not support secret societies in any context, and he goes so far as to say that when Cubans stop being secretive about their opposition to colonial rule, that will be a true challenge to the governmental powers. (As I show in the next chapter, Varela proclaimed an aversion to anonymous publication, and his position on secret societies seems to correlate with his views that writers should identify themselves in the public sphere of print.)

In the second issue of *El Habanero,* Varela takes a radical position vis-à-vis colonial rule when he calls for a revolution on the island. As a result, *El Habanero* is banned in Cuba and, according to Varela, Spanish authorities send an assassin to try to kill him.[73] Varela's call for internal revolution comes in the context of other events in the Americas and the potential that another power will invade the island to oust Spanish forces. In keeping with his protonational position, Varela argues that it is better to have an internal uprising to prevent outside forces such as the United States, Mexico, or Colombia from having to take action on Cuba's status: *"Si la revolución no se forma por los de casa, se formará inevitablemente por los de fuera, y que el primer caso es mucho más ventajoso"* (*H* 59, emphasis in original; If the revolution is not led by those at home, it inevitably will be led by foreigners, and the first scenario is much more advantageous). Varela does not specify who exactly in society will lead this effort, saying only that the island's "inhabitants" need to take action.

But what is the source of this love of independence, and what does it tell us about the philosophical frame of Varela's argument? In the same issue where he first calls for revolution, Varela publishes an article titled "Amor de los Americanos a la independencia" (Love of Americans for independence), in which he articulates a hemispheric American view of an inherent love of country. To open the article, Varela inverts the notion that American desire for independence is driven by hatred against Europeans; on the contrary, he says, the love of America is what makes European colonialism particularly despicable. "Americans are born with love for independence," Varela writes.[74] The call for independence thus is inspired in part by *nature,* and Varela describes Spanish America as "unas regiones inmensas,

Faith in Print   141

ricas, ilustradas, y fuertes" (*H* 74; vast regions that are rich, abundant, and full of resources). But he quickly combines this natural inherent love with Enlightenment thinking. "Mas la ilustración, que siempre empieza por una pequeña llama, y concluye por un incendio que arrasa el soberbio edificio de la tiranía, ha conducido ya a los pueblos de América a un estado en que seguramente no quisieron verlo sus opresores" (*H* 76–77; But enlightenment, which begins with a small fuse and concludes with a fire that obliterates the haughty edifice of tyranny, has guided the countries of America to a situation that was surely unwanted by their oppressors). Varela spends much of the article railing against Spain's abusive relationship with its colonies and calls colonial rule a tyranny to which the general population has responded. But ultimately he posits something inherent in America as the driving force toward independence:

> El americano oye constantemente la imperiosa voz de la naturaleza que le dice: yo te he puesto en un suelo que te hostiga con sus riquezas y te asalta con sus frutos; un inmenso océano te separa de esa Europa, donde la tiranía ultrajándome, holla mis dones y aflige a los pueblos; no la temas: sus esfuerzos son impotentes; recupera la libertad de que tú mismo te has despojado por una sumisión hija más de la timidez que de la necesidad; vive libre e independiente; y prepara un asilo a los libres de todos los países; ellos son tus hermanos. Sí, no hay que dudarlo, ésta es la voz de la naturaleza, porque es la de la razón y la justicia. (*H* 80)

> (The American hears constantly the imperious voice of nature say, "I have situated you on soil that assaults your senses with its riches and fruits; an immense ocean separates you from Europe, where its tyranny offends me, stomps on my gifts and afflicts pain on my people. Do not fear it; it is impotent. Take back your liberty, which you yourself have given up as a result of a submission that stems more from timidness than from necessity. Live free and independent, and prepare an asylum for free men from all countries; they are your brothers." Do not doubt that this is the voice of nature, because it is the voice of reason and justice.)

The passage is striking in its personification of nature as an agent in the process of people thinking their way to liberty from colonialism. Nature here is so intense that it harasses Americans into love of country; the ocean separating America from Europe becomes a natural barrier. Varela conflates the voice of nature with reason and justice, making the latter a part of the hemispheric American landscape. And he calls on Americans to listen to that voice.

But Varela's analysis does not go into the social conditions created by Spanish colonialism in the Americas. Slavery remains a metaphor in his discussion of an anticolonial call for independence for Cuban and other American countries. In "Amor de los americanos a la independencia," Varela invokes slavery and its related terminology (e.g., *master*) to describe colonial subjection. For example, he notes that some *peninsulares* believe "que el pueblo Americano quiere ser esclavo" (*H* 79; that the American people want to be enslaved). He says that this assumption is based on their view of Americans as "savages" even though the colonial oppressors themselves have condemned the people to live in slavery (*vivir siempre esclava*). Varela then inverts conditions to support independence: "¿Qué harían ellos con los americanos, si fuesen a su país a ayudar a esclavizarlos?" (*H* 81; If Americans went to their country to help enslave them, what would they do?). The effect here is that slavery becomes a metaphor that allows Varela to propose a hemispheric call for independence.

The use of slavery as a metaphor for colonial subjection shows the extent to which chattel slavery informs notions of revolutionary liberation. As scholars of the coloniality of power have argued, principles associated with Enlightenment thought were inextricable from the oppressive mechanisms of colonial expansion. But at the same time, Varela's evasion of chattel slavery in *El Habanero* is surprising considering that in 1822, as a representative to the Spanish Cortes, he had written a document that called for the abolition of slavery in Cuba. Varela had written, "Me atrevo a asegurar que la voluntad general del pueblo de la isla de Cuba es que no haya esclavos, y sólo desea encontrar otro medio de suplir sus necesidades" (*H* IV; I dare to ensure that the general opinion among the people of the island of Cuba is that there be no slaves, and it wishes only to find other means to ensure its necessities). In the 1822 piece, Varela had gone on to discuss the effects of slavery on the more general society: "La introducción de africanos en la isla de Cuba dio origen a la clase de mulatos, de los cuales muchos han recibido la libertad por sus mismos padres, mas otros sufren la esclavitud. Esta clase, aunque menos ultrajada, experimenta los efectos consiguientes a su nacimiento" (*H* V; The introduction of Africans on the island gave rise to a class of mulatos, of whom many have been granted liberty by their own fathers, but others suffer in slavery. This class, although less mistreated, experiences the effects that follow from their birth). This earlier document shows that Varela was all too aware of the importance of slavery and race in Cuba by the time he edited *El Habanero*.

Although we could surmise that Varela thought it was important to take up independence without antagonizing those who may have wanted to retain slavery in a postcolonial Cuba (a position that other Cuban exiled writers in the United States would adopt throughout the nineteenth century), I want to emphasize how the omission sheds light on *El Habanero* and its Filadelfia context. *El Habanero*, first and foremost, attempts to function in a trans-American public sphere where debates about the future of new Spanish American states is the dominant issue. Here Habermasian public-sphere theory is instructive in that it reminds us how this model of communication relies on a notion of a bounded political community and takes as one of its main topics the general interests of a demos so conceived. In this case, that community is both Cuba via Filadelfia and the trans-American elite in Varela's circle. From the Habermasian perspective, the general interests of the community would be translated into laws, or in the case of Filadelfia publications, into the establishment of a new nation-state free of Spanish colonialism. Habermas further emphasized that an important dimension of this discussion would be the relationship of the political community to a national economy.[75] As we saw in the preceding chapter, economic concerns were important among members of the trans-American elite such as Torres. Varela opens *El Habanero* by emphasizing the importance of economic activity in Cuba, and he is sarcastic in proposing that economic interests, particularly among merchants, have more influence than political considerations. The succeeding issues of *El Habanero* attempt to counter that economic influence with discussions that emphasize the political realm on the island in its hemispheric dimensions. Like *El triunfo de la libertad sobre el despotismo*, Varela's *El Habanero* offers a radical critique of Spanish colonial rule but remains within what numerous critics citing Habermas have called the "liberal model of the bourgeois public sphere" in that it emphasized a transformation at the level of the state but did not offer a reparative path for the racial-economic hierarchies that colonialism had established.

A Weekly Messenger

Not long after *El Habanero*, Saco's aforementioned *El Mensagero Semanal* (1828–31) began to circulate. Saco's paper introduced another dimension to Filadelfia's trans-American public sphere, namely, a weekly with a broad interest in international news and inter-American political relations. In other words, it was less focused on the type of political platforms of *El Habanero* and books that addressed colonial rule. While Saco was following in Varela's footsteps by launching a periodical in the northeastern United States with the goal of reaching readers in Cuba, he also opted for a publication with a variety of content rather than a fiery revolutionary pamphlet. *El Habanero*'s sole author identified himself on the title page with the phrase "Redactado por F. Varela." *Redactado por* can be translated as "written by" and also "reported by." By contrast, most of the articles in *El Mensagero Semanal* ran unsigned. Saco's "Weekly Messenger" printed a variety of articles about news in Europe and the Americas, some about politics in the United States, and still others about Cuba. Despite the differences, Saco noted later in life that Varela worked on *El Mensagero Semanal* with him along with other contributors.[76]

The goals of the paper were best articulaed in Saco's response to a letter to the editor that accused *El Mensagero* of failing to address a literary controversy. Here is his description of the paper as a way to explain why it did not delve into literary matters in more depth: "*El Mensagero* no es un papel cientifico ó literario. . . . *El Mensagero* no es otra cosa que una gaceta destinada á dar noticia de los acaecimientos politicos, y á hacer mas variadas su lectura, si las cicunstancias lo permiten, con los progresos mas notables de algunas artes y ciencias, ó con algunos articulos de util aplicacion á la isla de Cuba, ó finalmente con los chistes y agudezas del ingenio" (The *Messenger* is not a scientific or literary paper. . . . The *Messenger* is nothing more than a gazette that sets out to report on political news and, whenever possible, to make reading more interesting, with articles about developments in the arts and sciences, or practical articles with relevance to the island of Cuba, or even with jokes and sharp wit).[77] Rather than taking up questions of colonialism, as Varela had done, *El Mensagero* aimed for a less politically loaded approach with news, features, and entertainment. In other words, it approximated what came to be known historically as a weekly paper. The use of the Spanish *gaceta* (gazette) is important because it implied a periodical that covered commercial and governmental topics. The eight-page paper usually filled the opening pages with news from Europe and the Americas.

As a result of this cautious tone, *El Mensagero* was allowed to circulate freely in Havana. In its final issue, on January 29, 1831, the paper published a list of 144 subscribers in Havana and noted that Cuba's captain general, the island's highest colonial authority, "jamas ha puesto ningun reparo á su libre circulacion" (never had issued the least objection to its free circulation).[78] That Saco would boast about this speaks to his goals of seeking readers rather than emphasizing political argumentation. The list of subscribers included men who would go on to work for Cuba's separation from Spain, as well as members of the military, lawyers, doctors, and foreign dignitaries. The prominent subscribers included Francisco de la Luz, the owner of a sugar estate with slaves; Florentino Armenteros, a colonial authority who descended from a noble family that traced its time in Cuba back to 1619; and the lawyer Santiago Bombalier, who would go on to edit the abolitionist newspaper *El Mulato* in New York in the 1850s.[79] All of this suggests that Saco, rather than publishing a journal with a particular political angle, instead attempted what would become common in the twentieth century: a newspaper that was topically varied for a broad readership.

El Mensagero navigated colonial restriction by filling its pages for the most part with news of the world. Its first issue, published on August 19, 1828, featured a front-page article about the Russo-Turkish War with a lede that placed Russian emperor Nicholas I at the top of a hill surveying his troops.[80] The next two issues also opened with front-page articles on that war, including one piece translated from London's *Quarterly Review*. These articles were not without anticolonial dimensions in that the war had been prompted in part by the Greek War of Independence against the Ottomans. Russia supported the Greeks. But for a reader to extract political content from the articles necessitated several steps in analogical thinking. And lest such an interpretive move become too obvious, *El Mensagero* provided articles such as "Adornos usados en la arquitectura moderna" (Decorations used in modern architecture) and a lengthy piece on the growing of cocoa beans. Most issues included a "Variedades" (Varieties) section that contained anything from a few sentences on the heights of Mount Blanc to advice on the best time of day to write (morning).[81]

But despite its benign appearance, the paper issued its own brand of opposition to colonialism. Although it did not challenge Spain directly in its pages, *El Mensagero* nevertheless struck a radical print-culture position. Rather than deal with licensing from the Spanish Crown or censorship in Cuba, Saco went to the United States and functioned as an independent editor and publisher. By the second year he ran his own press. A crucial part of this work was his emphasis on developing a transnational public sphere connected to Cuba. The commitment to publish articles about Cuba and the clear goal of circulating on the island suggest a protonationalist preoccupation that was implicitly in opposition to colonial rule. The paper's inclusion of articles about various parts of the world and its cosmopolitan flair combined with a focus on Cuba looked toward a future in which the island would be among the free countries of the world. Some of the articles focused on the ongoing conflict in South America as new countries established independent governments. This may have been why the paper did not receive an eager welcome from authorities in the Cuban city of Matanzas, where the paper was embargoed on arrival. Authorities would review the paper for days or weeks and remove anything they considered harmful to Matanzas's population before releasing the issue to readers. Because of this censorship, Saco did not publish the list of subscribers in Matanzas.[82]

The place where we see the full extent of *El Mensagero*'s protonationalist commitments is in a polemic involving poetry. The newspaper featured verses by writers from Cuba and Spain, and with the participation of Domingo Del Monte, the paper published articles celebrating the poetry of José María Heredia, whose Filadelfia letter was discussed in chapter 1. Three years before the appearance of *El Mensagero*, Heredia had published a collection of his poetry in New York, thus becoming one of the poets of independence whose verses would be tied to literary nationalism in years to come. In the 1820s, Spanish-language poetry was still dominated by the Spanish peninsula, and thus *El Mensagero* published two notable pieces about Heredia. The first was a letter to Domingo Del Monte from the Spanish educator and poet Alberto Lista, a prominent literary voice who had a tremendous influence on universities in Spain. Lista's evaluation of Heredia is mixed, and he criticizes the poetry for use of language that is of French origin, for sounding at times like prose, and for verses that are at times "weak and common." Nevertheless, Lista does recognize Heredia's talent and praises his ability to fill his poems with emotion, a recognition of romantic power in Heredia. "El fuego de su alma ha pasado á sus versos, y se transmite á los lectores: toman parte en sus penas, y en sus placeres: ven los mismos objetos que el poeta y los ven por el mismo aspecto que él. Siente y pinta, que son las dos prendas mas importantes de los discipulos del grande Homero: esto es decir que el Señor Heredia es un poeta y un gran poeta" (The fire of his soul has passed into his verses and is transmitted to his readers; they take part in his pain and his pleasure, see the same objects as the poet and see them from his perspective. He feels and paints, which are the two most important qualities of a disciple of the great Homer. This is to say that Mr. Heredia is a poet and a great one).[83]

Four months later, *El Mensagero* reprinted an article about Heredia from *Ocios de Españoles emigrados* (Leisure hours of emigrant Spaniards), a monthly journal published from 1824 to 1827 in London by Spanish liberals who had fled from the repression of Ferdinand VII. As we will see in the next chapter, Filadelfia publications engaged transatlantically with Spanish-language publications from London. *El Mensagero* published selections from *Ocios* in several issues. In an article titled "Poesías de D. José Maria de Heredia," *El Mensagero* included three poems with an evaluation from *Ocios*. Like Lista's letter, the article criticizes the poetry, in this case noting that Heredia's poetic work is "not fully formed" because it draws from too many poetic styles. In the most damning line, the article calls Heredia a "facil imitador" (facile imitator).[84] Nevertheless, the article praises Heredia for taking up the poetic spirit to capture the wonders of the Americas, noting that he wields "la lira americana consagrada á pintar los objetos grandiosos del aquel hemisferio" (the American lyre devoted to painting the magnificent aspects of that hemisphere).[85]

As this line implies, one of the issues at the heart of what would become the Heredia polemic is his position as a notable Spanish-language poet of the Americas rather than of Spain. His poetry turns out to be nothing less than a challenge to literary colonialism, the assumption that great poetry in Spanish can come only from Europe. Despite its criticism of the poems, *Ocios* is willing to recognize the importance of that challenge:

> Cuando Heredia canta las vibraciones del ardiente sol de la isla de Cuba, el estruendo de Niágara, y la boca inflamada de Popocatepec, abre una ancha puerta á la immesa [sic] serie de nuevas imagenes poeticas, que en adelante no dejarán de pintarse y hermanarse con una robustez y altura proporcionada de pensamientos, por los que desde que nazcan podran contemplarlas y discurrir sobre ellas bajo los auspicios de la libertad.[86]

> (When Heredia sings the vibrations of the burning sun of the island of Cuba, the thunder of Niagara, and the flaming mouth of Popocatepec, he opens a door wide to an immense series of new poetic images that in the future will be painted with fortitude and ability by those who contemplate them from birth and devise new perspectives under the cover of liberty.)

Buried in a long sentence, the phrase "auspicios de la libertad" (cover of liberty) assumes that Spanish America (and presumably Cuba) will be free of colonial rule; the passage then proposes that a new poetic tradition will draw from nature in the hemisphere. We see here how early in his relatively short writing career, Heredia as a romantic poet of nature could be claimed by protonationalist movements in the Americas. The conjunction of Heredia and nation will become a hallmark of criticism in the twentieth century, when he is canonized as a poet of Cuba.

Among the poems reprinted in *El Mensagero* is one that is particularly Cuban in its overture toward a specific location, "Fragmento de una oda al sol" (Fragment from an ode to the sun). The speaker opens by noting the "rigid winter" of a place "far from my homeland" (*lejos de mi patria*) and how he suffers from an illness that could lead to a "dark tomb." What saves the speaker is the sun, but not just any sunlight:

> Mi patria: ¡oh sol! mi idolatrada Cuba
> ¿A quien debe su gloria,
> A quien su eterna y virginal belleza?
> Solo á tu amor.[87]
>
> (My homeland, sunlight! To whom
> Does my idol Cuba owe its glory,
> Its eternal and virginal beauty?
> Only to your love.)

Just as the sun fills Cuba with its glory, the speaker is filled with strength to break through "the confusion of clouds." Here Heredia offers an early example of what will become common in Cuban nationalist romanticism, the use of an apostrophe (in this case "¡oh sol!") as an interjection in an ode that celebrates a particular tropical territory. The speaker's longing for his idolized *patria* is possible because of the deterritorialization of his escape to the United States. This poem is about Cuba as much as it is about the sun and offers one example of the ways *El Mensagero* sneaks protonationalist sentiments into a paper that purports to be a chronicle of news and an entertaining read. The paper's support of Heredia emphasizes his position as a writer of the Americas as distinct from the Spanish domains of literature.

Heredia's poetry, its merits and claims, prompted a particularly vicious transnational war of words in the pages of the journal. The assessments of Heredia's poetry published in the paper reached Cuba, where the botanist and professor of natural history Ramón de la Sagra published the scientific journal *Anales de ciencias, artes, agricultura, y comercio*. Sagra published an article critical of Heredia's poetry, only to run head on into Saco's anger. The latter published a tough response and then fueled the polemic in October 1829, when *El Mensagero* published a front-page letter by Sagra writing under the pseudonym "El Hermitaño del Campo de Marte" (Hermit at the Camp of Mars), in which he challenged the editors: "Les tocaba como á periodistas españoles y compatriotes y *camaradas* del poeta, decirnos algo de su mérito, se atuvieron mas bien á la opinion del Sr. Lista y de los editores de los Ocios, que no á la suya" (Considering that as Spanish journalists and compatriots and colleagues of the poet, it was your duty to tell us something of his merit, you stopped at the opinion of Mr. Lista and the editors of the Ocios rather than offer yours).[88] The use of the term *periodistas españoles* (Spanish journalists) shows the broader Hispanicism informing the way writers referred to one another, but the additional *compatriotes* also recognizes their connection to Cuba. I translate *camarada,* italicized in the original, as "colleagues" because such would be the usage in a professional setting, in this case the publishing of a paper; however, the word politically is closer to "comrade" and can also be used to imply close friendship, in this case with an implication of Cuban intimacy. Sagra went on to defend himself (in the third person) and called the editors of *El Mensagero* "hombres obscuros y de mala fé" (unenlightened men of bad faith) for their attacks on him. Not to be outdone, Saco opened with "He manchado una pagina del *Mensagero* con la carta imprimida que precede" (I have stained a page of the *Messenger* by printing the preceding letter). Saco responded that *El Mensagero* was not a literary magazine and the editors were not versed in literature and thus did not have the necessary depth to offer an insightful evaluation of Heredia: "Sabemos muy bien lo que es saber, y lo que cuesta saber, pues no somos como Sagra, que invadiendo todas las artes y las ciencies, y el comercio y la agricultura, y cuantos conocimientos el mundo encierra, habla magistralmente de todo" (We know full well what it is to have knowledge, and the costs of gaining knowledge, for we are not like Sagra, who invades all arts and sciences, and commerce and agriculture, and any understanding the world holds, and speaks imperially of all).[89] The article went on for pages to excoriate Sagra for his lack of understanding of various topics, including botany.

The colonial dimensions of this fight cannot be overstated. Sagra was a peninsular Spaniard who had settled in Cuba, and thus Saco was responding in part as a trans-American creole. Sagra's evaluation was taken as assailing Heredia's literary honor and Cuba's hope for poetic greatness. No unqualified lover of colonial oppression, Sagra had moved to Cuba because it offered him an opportunity to work as an academic with liberal views. But Saco took issue with what he saw as Sagra's attitude of peninsular superiority, and he challenged Sagra for acting as if he were the only one in

Havana with any knowledge. As the exchange progressed, the question of Heredia's poetry got derailed as the two battle in what looked like an intellectual version of "quién es más macho?" The exchange became notorious in Cuban intellectual history. Later in life, Saco looked back on it with some embarrassment, and when he published a collection of his writings, Saco said that while it hurt him to reproduce such harsh words and phrases against Sagra, with whom he had made peace, he did so because the articles were an important part of his papers.[90]

Considered from la famosa Filadelfia, Saco-contra-Sagra shows the influence of the US print-culture context on the development of a trans-American and also particularly Cuban national public sphere that engaged in tumultuous debates. The tensions that I have associated with this public sphere here found a resolution with a particularly Cuban take on matters. In other words, Saco helped develop a public sphere that was at once protonational (Cuban) and trans-American. *El Mensagero* traversed the circulation blockages instituted by Spanish colonialism in an attempt to conceive of Cuba as existing among other independent countries. For Saco, this exchange is an early example of many controversies and an antagonistic periodical style. Saco is best known in Cuban history for returning to the island in 1832 and publishing the *Revista Bimestre Cubana* (Cuban Bimonthly Magazine). The magazine covered a range of topics, from education to culture and science. It also discussed racial relations, and Saco called for abolition. In 1834, Saco was expelled from Cuba for his liberal views and his opposition to slavery. He spent decades in Europe, still keeping up his publishing and polemics. In 1848, he jumped into a battle over efforts to have Cuba annexed to the United States, particularly among groups affiliated with General Narciso López.

An important figure in history, Saco was formed in part by his work as a publisher and editor in Philadelphia. The battle against Sagra was in some ways about self-determination. Could Cubans speak for themselves and become notable in the world of Spanish-language print culture and letters? Although the value of Heredia's poetry was sidelined by Saco's attack on Sagra's work, it was poetry that occasioned *El Mensagero*'s most notorious polemical contribution to trans-American print culture, transnational Cuban history, and Filadelfia letters.

Faith in Poetry

The role of poetry in Filadelfia letters calls for an analysis of print-culture conditions as a context for the poems. Poems did not always come with the type of clear political message that we see in *El triunfo de la libertad* and *El Habanero*. While some poems did clearly express a patriotic fervor that had become increasingly common during the wars of independence, it is also evident that some were published because editors believed the poems were formally and/or linguistically creative. The question whether the publication of poems was anticolonial in nature was complicated by the political dimensions of publication itself. As we saw with *El Mensagero*, for trans-American intellectuals to publish something not approved by the colonial authorities was in itself a challenge to the colonial system.

Del Monte's poetry book, an edition of poems by the Spanish writer Juan Nicasio Gallego, offered an indirect response to colonialism that can be extrapolated through a consideration of print culture and the literary implications of Gallego's writing and life. The publication itself of *Versos de J. Nicasio Gallego, recogidos y publicados por Domingo Del Monte* was a statement: Del Monte was breaking away from restrictions in his homeland on individuals' printing their own books without approval from the Real Audiencia. While Gallego's verses did not call for revolution and he was not a writer of the Americas, the collection gave voice to the work of a poet who had run afoul of Spain's monarchy. In her consideration of Gallego as a translator, Ana María Freire notes his participation in important political events, most notably as a deputy at the Spanish Cortes in Cádiz convened in 1810 to institute reforms and bring American participation into a legislative body and as a member of the committee that drafted the Constitution of 1812. When Ferdinand VII was restored as king, Gallego was among liberals who were imprisoned and persecuted. He was not released until 1820.[91] Del Monte would have been all too aware of Gallego's political suffering, and his Philadelphia edition became the first collection of Gallego's poetry to see print.

Although the volume did not include an introduction by Del Monte, the editor makes several anticolonial intimations through his paratextual material. The book is dedicated "affectionately" to José María Heredia, "poeta Cubano," positioning a Cuban as worthy of Del Monte's poetic admiration (as was Gallego). He follows up with an introductory note proclaiming that he is publishing the book because Gallego's work is not widely available in either Spain or Cuba, and he is explicit about goals:

El primero, ofrecer á nuestros contemporráneos, y á todo el que en América se dedique á la poesía, los pocos, pero clásicos versos que hemos podido reunir, de un poeta cuyo nombre vá al par de los de Quintana, Lista, Martínez de la Rosa, Solís y demás insignes líricos vivos de España; el segundo, presentar á los estrangeros que estudian la literatura Española, una no mezquina muestra de la harmonía suavísima de nuestra lengua, y del carácter particular de los autores modernos que la cultivan.[92]

(The first is to offer our contemporaries and everyone in the Americas who is dedicated to poetry the few but very important verses that we have been able to gather by a poet whose name is on a level with those of Quintana, Lista, Martínez de la Rosa, Solís and other distinguished lyrical writers of Spain; the second is to present to foreigners who study Spanish literature a not inconsequential example of the sweet harmony of our language, and the notable character of authors who work in it.)

As we saw in chapter 1, Del Monte's note shows that he was trying to tap into the US market for books targeted at Spanish-language learners. But the main justification for publishing Gallego is that his poems are comparable in quality to the work of Spain's greatest writers. What becomes apparent is that Del Monte's anticolonial mission—publishing away from censors and connecting to the work of Heredia—is not at odds with an aesthetic view of poetry.

Del Monte's decision to insert into the title a reference to his editorial work (i.e., "collected and published by") is an early indication of his commitment to building a trans-American and transatlantic literary world with himself at the center. Del Monte would become one of Cuba's most prominent men of letters in succeeding decades, helping to establish a literary culture through both salons (*tertulias*) and publications. His penchant for the salon allows us to see the way the trans-American public sphere of Philadelphia made its way to Cuba. Once back on the island, Del Monte was a catalyst for the publication of, among other work, the fiction of Cirilo Villaverde, the poetry of the mulatto Plácido, and the slave narrative of Juan Francisco Manzano. Plácido was considered radical enough that he was executed in 1844 as part of the notorious repression linked to the La Escalera conspiracy, and Villaverde went into exile in New York several years later.

In Del Monte's early project, *Versos de J. Nicasio Gallego,* we can detect not only his commitment as editor but also his taste for writers who challenged the Spanish government in a variety of ways. It is highly unlikely that Del Monte could have gotten the Gallego book past the censors and licensed to publish in Cuba. Gallego's precarious position in Spain and his running afoul of the monarchy explain why it took a Cuban going to Filadelfia to publish his poetry. The Gallego collection included sonnets and elegies as well Gallego's translations of James McPherson's Ossian. Among Gallego's considerable work as a translator, he was involved in a project to translate the fiction of Walter Scott.[93] Gallego never traveled to the Americas; his poems have long been considered to fall between neoclassicism and literary romanticism, even as the latter was becoming connected to nationalist movements in the Americas. E. Allison Peers is among critics who situate Gallego at this in-between point. He writes that he was among a group that remained attached to pseudo-classicism but whose "love of independence, liberty and sometimes liberalism prevents them from being completely antagonistic to the Romantics, whose merits they are both too shrewd and too honest not to recognize."[94]

Movement and migration are inextricable from the formation of Cuban literary nationalism, as we see here in the case of Del Monte and Heredia, two of the most prominent names in the history of Cuban letters. While Heredia's verses have been held up as exemplary of Cuban sensibility, his travels through the United States were important to the formation of a poet who spent his life in different parts of the Americas and ended up in Mexico. Filadelfia, Niagara, Mount Vernon—all of these figure prominently in Heredia's work. In his poem "A Washington," written during a visit to Mount Vernon, Heredia connects his Romantic longing for immortality to the US president:

> Viva imagen de Dios sobre la tierra,
> libertador, legislador y justo,
> Washington inmortal, oye benigno
> el débil canto de tu gloria indigno,
> con que voy a ensalzar tu nombre augusto.[95]
>
> (Vivid image of God on earth,
> liberator, legislator just,
> immortal Washington, listen benevolently
> to the faint, indignant song that exalts
> your glory, your majestic name.)

These lines from the opening stanza to this 1824 paean are driven by Heredia's desire to see his verses repeated. The poem connects to Washington's "indignant" voice against tyranny, and Washington's presumed immortality will carry Heredia's poem. Washington is deployed as inspiration for the countries of the southern Americas struggling to form governments after colonial rule. That type of exchange—Spanish-language poet at Mount Vernon sending verses about a US president in a southern direction—showed the intricate ways that poetry could enter a trans-American public sphere.

For writers such as Heredia, literary genres became a nexus for the consideration of political upheaval, governmental reorganization, economic transformations, and personal exile. In turn, literary productions encode disruption and tumult both at the subjective level of the speaker and in the subject matter. While we have seen that many of the intellectuals who preceded Heredia in Filadelfia published political tracts, Heredia is one of the earliest examples of another trajectory: the politically minded writer who turned to literary forms in the United States without extricating him- or herself from the trans-American revolutionary upheavals of his time. Del Monte and the editors of *El Mensagero* take up the question of literary greatness even at a time when freedom from colonial subjection seems more pressing.

To think of Heredia and other Filadelfia poets in relation to literary greatness emphasizes the individual attainment of mastery and thus elides the lack of mastery (and the discomfort) that is created by exile and conquest at the level of entire populations. This was the concern of Edward Said, writing about the twentieth century: "It is apparent that, to concentrate on exile as a contemporary political punishment, you must therefore map territories of experience beyond those mapped by the literature of exile itself. You must first set aside Joyce and Nabokov and think instead of the uncountable masses for whom UN agencies have been created."[96] This tension between an emphasis on individuation (the great writer) and conditions that disrupt the lives of large numbers of faceless people has an analogy in the historical reading of Latino literature.

To think of Del Monte's Gallego as part of the Latino history of the United States demands the bracketing of the great writer and the consideration of the book itself as a contribution to the Spanish-language literature of Filadelfia and the United States. If we approach this book as part of the Spanish-language literature of the United States, that is, Filadelfia, Gallego inevitably loses the central place. It is a reminder that for every Gallego and Del Monte there were many unknown people who made their way to Filadelfia, and not all left us letters.

Even though this chapter has put together salient names such as Roscio, Saco, and Heredia in presenting a public sphere that is at once trans-American, transatlantic, and national, *El Mensagero Semanal* in its penchant for unsigned articles also is part of another dimension of Filadelfia publishing: anonymous texts. That separation of an identifiable writer and his or her text is another aspect of this public sphere, especially its attraction to abstract models of subjectivity. What do we make of Filadelfia letters that do not carry an identifiable author? That is the topic of the next chapter.

 4

Anonymously Yours: Republican Man

Filadelfia left us a trove of anonymous publications. A significant dimension of Philadelphia's output of Spanish-language materials, from the politically fired *El amigo de los hombres* (1812) to a trio of gift books published in 1828–29, was anonymity. While in the preceding chapters I focused on individual figures who published books under their own names, print-culture processes in Filadelfia also supported the proliferation of books that privileged anonymity. Many tackled questions of political theory before and after Spanish American independence, as evidenced in titles such as *Manual de un republicano, para el uso de un pueblo libre* (The republican's manual for the use of a free people, 1812) and *Memoria politico-instructiva, enviada desde Filadelfia* (An instructive political account, sent from Philadelphia, 1821). As scholars of eighteenth-century English literature have shown, writers turn to anonymous publication for a variety of reasons, everything from the disguise of gender and class to manipulation of the marketplace.[1] Maria Bustillos, writing for the *New Yorker,* describes anonymous publication as "a stark declaration of intent: a wall explicitly thrown up, not only between writer and reader, but between the writer's work and his life."[2] But such a conclusion comes with a historical context, in Bustillo's case related to twentieth-century fiction. What about print-culture conditions in which anonymity is not so much about throwing up walls as it is about building connections with readers by de-emphasizing individuality? Or to put that another way, what if anonymity is deployed to carve out a political position?

Notions of authorship change over time. The Filadelfia context, with its emphasis on translation and transmission, de-emphasized the individual writer, thus challenging a hermeneutics that focuses on authorial intention. Anonymity can emphasize a conversation among participants in a historical situation that does not privilege authorial recognition. Many of the Filadelfia intellectuals were men of letters rather than authors in the twentieth-century sense of the term, and some were intent on getting out ideas rather than books that they could claim as their own contributions to a literary panorama. Filadelfia publication preceded the spread of professional writers, or people trying to live as such, both in the United States and in Latin America, and thus authors would not have been driven financially to put their names on printed material.

In Filadelfia, anonymity often went hand in hand with the creation of an abstract political subject. Deployed within transatlantic and trans-American communications circuits, anonymity helped promote a notion of republican man, gendered as such, as a political actor in territories throughout the American hemisphere and beyond. Not so much a real person, the republican(o) was an imagined political actor in new societies. Filadelfia writers sought to develop a political demos that would succeed colonial rule, but general conceptions about political subjects were not accompanied by a full engagement with specific conditions in Spanish American countries. As we saw in the preceding chapter, at times Filadelfia writers were more intent on developing a *concept of the people* than on discussing actual people.

Anonymous books and pamphlets presented different approaches to racial formation, in one case deploying republican man to call for an end to slavery, while at other times ignoring altogether how racial difference structured Spanish American territories. In most cases, Filadelfia anonymity served to bridge geographic distance and instruct new political actors in various parts of the hemisphere, including in newly formed countries. The influence of the trans-American elite was evident in publications such as *Cartas de un americano* (1826), a book that ignores racial difference and slavery in the Americas altogether to propose a notion of Americanism connected to a dematerialized reading of the US Constitution.

Why some intellectuals chose to publish anonymously is a question that in many cases does not have a clear answer. Anonymity could indicate that the writer feared some type of reprisal. Some historical documents suggest that there were assassination attempts against Filadelfia figures.[3] In the case of Cuba, which remained a Spanish colony through the 1890s, writers may have been concerned about keeping their names off lists prohibiting a return to their home country. But whatever the intention of an anonymous author, one of the textual effects was the de-emphasizing of the individual in an attempt to create a democratic space. Anonymity precluded the association of that space with a particular country, instead making it relevant to a variety of sites.

More than just a way for writers to conceal or protect their identities, anonymity dovetailed with notions of a bodiless political subject and allowed intellectuals to navigate republican principles in newly independent territories. Anonymous Filadelfia writings call attention to a context in which a connection between an author and a text should not be assumed. Scholars, especially those emphasizing the lives and works of individual historical actors or writers, have sought to name the authors of some anonymously published Filadelfia materials, as we will see in the case of the pamphlet *El amigo de los hombres*. Such a move can lead to misattribution and/or the reification of author-centered forms of literary history. The race to attribution is part and parcel of an epistemological system that demands a connection between knowledge and an individual subject. A passage from Michel Foucault offers tremendous insight into this problem, which he describes as an insistence in the history of knowledge to obey a "claim of attribution":

> Each discovery should not only be situated and dated, but should also be attributed to someone: it should have an inventor and someone responsible for it. General or collective phenomena on the other hand, those which by definition can't be "attributed," are normally devalued: they are still traditionally described through words like *tradition, mentality, modes;* and one lets them play the negative role of a brake in relation to the "originality" of the inventor. In brief, this has to do with the principle of the sovereignty of the subject applied to the history of knowledge.[4]

For Foucault, to insist that either scientific or other types of knowledge be attributed to someone is inextricable from a second assumption, that an individual subject discovers truth and knowledge. By this logic, the truth claims of a period (e.g., the early nineteenth century) are neither evident nor produced by the period itself but discovered or *written* by authors. This emphasis on authorship informs critical approaches that desire and even demand the connection author-text, as in the case of the republication of the anonymous *Jicoténcal* (Philadelphia, 1826).

Luis Leal first proposed that the author of *Jicoténcal* was Félix Varela, an attribution that became popularized with the 1992 Arte Público edition of the novel.[5] But there is no incontrovertible proof that Varela wrote the novel. Scholars today accept Leal's argument even as some hold it at a skeptical distance. The payoff of the Varela attribution was that it offered a name and even a face (the latter printed on a US postage stamp in 1997) that could be attached to the novel. And it did so in relation to Hispanic literary heritage.[6] Thus, it created an important dyad (author and literary text) that was standard in twentieth-century literary studies. But what are the problems with imposing an author on an anonymous publication from another century? How does that alter the very print-culture conditions from which these books emerge? We will return to *Jicoténcal* to offer an alternative anonymously inspired interpretation, but for now let us start with one of the early salvos out of Filadelfia.

Man's Best Friend: Trans-American and Transatlantic Anonymity

The year 1812 was an important one in the history of Spanish America's independence movements. Spanish troops were attempting to regain control over rebellious territories after Venezuela had declared independence on July 5, 1811. With Simón Bolívar still coming up the military ranks, the First Republic would suffer a series of setbacks and be crushed. Among intellectuals a debate raged about the implications and merits of this declaration of independence even as the new country's success was on the line. That debate crossed several oceans via print culture and made its way to Spain and the Caribbean as well as the cities of London, Caracas, and Philadelphia. In 1812, the Philadelphia printer Andres Josef Blocquerst Hispanicized his name as Andres José on a title page and printed the anonymous pamphlet *El amigo de los hombres: Á todos los que habitan las islas, y el vasto continente de la America Española* (The friend of man: To all who inhabit the islands and vast continent of Spanish America). The title page specified that Blocquerst was at the corner of Fifth and Spruce Streets, most likely to advertise the shop's bookselling operation.[7]

This pamphlet engaged in a trans-American and transatlantic debate over Spanish American independence and offered one of the most significant statements on race-based slavery to come out of Filadelfia. The writer of *El amigo de los hombres* embraced anonymity as a way to fashion a writing subject with a universalist flair. By proclaiming to be the "the friend of man," he invoked the gendered intimacy and male-centered "humanity" of the revolutionary project that made its way into Filadelfia letters. In *El amigo de los hombres,* print stood in for a name: while the writer was the friend of man, so was the pamphlet itself. The words identifying the author, "El amigo de los hombres," appear at the end of the pamphlet with a city and date—"Washington, &c., &c., &c. 10 de Diciembre de 1811"—a signatory gesture that associates the pamphlet with epistolary communication. By addressing this letter to the islands and the continent of America in the second part of the title, "the friend" also was a speaking subject, a writer claiming a universal connection that allowed him to argue for the right of self-determination. As scholars have shown, the pamphlet was circulated in Texas in support of an anticolonial military effort.[8]

Anonymity in this case creates a moniker that bridges the distance between Washington, DC/Filadelfia and the multiple territories involved in this debate. Conceivably, the pamphlet and its author could be anywhere, bringing his reasonable pen to bear on questions of self-determination for all of humanity. In the last part of the pamphlet, the argument celebrates not only the independence of Venezuela but also a growing movement in Montevideo for Argentinean independence; the pamphlet argues that independence will eventually spread to the entire continent. It also frames Spanish American independence as part of a world history of democracy that includes ancient Greece and, more recently, Switzerland, Holland, and the United States. Raúl Coronado has noted that the pamphlet "invokes a familiar Enlightenment-era trope of universal brotherhood or of philanthropy (in its original denotation of love of mankind)."[9] Coronado argues that the trope of amity engages with wide philosophical speculation on personal responsibility to create a new order that extends to the field of political economy. As we will see, El Amigo is not everyone's friend.

Despite what appears to be the pamphlet's clear attempt to cross geographic distance through anonymity, scholars have tried to identify the author. Nicolás Kanellos and Coronado have attributed this pamphlet to José Álvarez de Toledo, a Havana-born Spanish naval officer who flirted with independence and spent time in Philadelphia during a six-year residency in the United States.[10] But the connections are tenuous. Coronado argues that Álvarez de Toledo's *Manifiesto o satisfacción pundonorosa* (Manifesto or honorable reckoning, 1811) was also published by Blocquerst, but the title pages of the two publications raise a slew of questions.[11] The *Manifiesto* does not have an imprint, while *El amigo de los hombres* has a title-page ornament that might be a printer's mark. Furthermore, the self-focused narrative of Álvarez de Toledo's *Manifiesto,* an attempt to defend himself against attacks, is at odds with the distancing mechanism of anonymous publication in *El amigo de los hombres.*

What do scholars gain by attributing the pamphlet, possibly erroneously, to Alvarez de Toledo? It allows for the presentation of a subject-centered notion of US Hispanic literary heritage and/or buttresses Álvarez de Toledo's prominence in intellectual history. In the case of Kanellos, the emphasis on a Latino/Hispanic writing subject is of paramount importance, especially when such an attribution plays alongside the tune of a historiography that emphasizes what Foucault calls "the sovereignty of the subject applied to the history of knowledge." The emphasis on a specific historical actor de-emphasizes a Spanish-language print-culture context in Philadelphia, where numerous people could have written *El amigo de los hombres*. But my interest is not in disproving that Alvarez de Toledo wrote the pamphlet; rather, I want to ask how anonymity opens a reading that relates to circulation in a trans-American and transatlantic public sphere.

The difference between emphasizing a Latino writer for texts and analyzing Filadelfia letters as part of Latino literature becomes pronounced in the case of *El amigo de los hombres*. Anonymous publication detracts from the *who* of the production process and emphasizes the content of the publication. The historical print-culture conditions of Filadelfia suggest that what *El amigo* says is more important than who says it. To connect that to the broader argument of *Letters from Filadelfia,* early Latino literature as a body of work is less about the identity of individual writers and more about language in a US context, in this case Spanish out of Filadelfia, and its connection to trans-American and transatlantic public spheres.

While it is possible that the writer of *El amigo de los hombres* wanted to hide his identity to prevent retribution from Spanish authorities, the effect is that the pamphlet emphasizes a political perspective that cannot be attributed to one person or country. It is also possible that the writer of *El amigo de los hombres* wanted to keep a name out of the testy transatlantic exchange over independence that preceded the publication. *El amigo de los hombres* opened by positioning itself as a response to two publications: an issue of the periodical *El Español,* published by José Blanco White in London, and a book by Álvaro Flórez Estrada, *Exámen imparcial de las disensiones de la América con la España, de los medios de su reconciliación, y de la prosperidad de todas las naciones* (Impartial study of America's dissent against Spain and possibilities for reconciliation, and of the economic potential of the nations), published in Cádiz in 1812. Flórez Estrada, a political writer and economist in Spain with connections to the monarchy, went into exile in England as a result of his liberal politics and critical views of Spanish monarchial rule.[12] Blanco White, whose name calls attention to the racially charged issues circulating in this debate between the nameless *amigo* and intellectuals based in Europe, was also in self-imposed exile in London. A lapsed priest who engaged widely with Enlightenment philosophy, Blanco White in *El Español* was sympathetic to principles in the US Declaration of Independence and the Declaration of the Rights of Man.[13] Both he and Flórez Estrada were Spanish liberals at odds with absolute monarchy and seeking constitutional reform. And yet they argued against independence for Spanish America. In response, *El amigo de los hombres* defended independence and sounded scandalized that Blanco White and Flórez Estrada would "insult the rights and the supreme dignity of all the countries of the new world" (insultar á los derechos, y á la alta dignidad de todos los pueblos del nuevo mundo).[14]

The exchange between *El amigo de los hombres* and Blanco White shows the importance of London as a site with transatlantic connections to transAmerican print culture. More than a destination for travelers, London as a hub of proindependence work and print released its own slew of contributions to a cosmopolitan network of anticolonial thinking in relation to Spanish America. As María Teresa Berruezo León has shown, proindependence actors, starting with Francisco Miranda in the 1790s and continuing through the 1820s, carried on important work in London print, including the contribution to periodicals and production of pamphlets and books, and did so while engaging with English politics.[15] Berruezo León suggests that William Burke's pamphlet *South American Independence: or, the Emancipation of South America, the Glory and Interest of England* (1807) was influenced by Miranda.[16] Rocafuerte, Fray Servando Teresa de Mier, and Vicente Pazos Kanki were among the transatlantic print warriors who moved not only through Philadelphia but also through London. That city was also important as a transatlantic print center of Anglophone writing and prompts, as Joseph Rezek has argued, a critical frame that moves past nationalist book history and toward a consideration of "book trade as an interconnected system" across territories.[17]

Coming out of London, *El Español* was an important periodical that reached across the Atlantic to develop its articles. It became entangled in numerous debates, at one point prompting Fray Servando Teresa de Mier to publish in London in 1811 his *Carta de un americano a "El Español" sobre su número XIX* (Letter to *El Español* about issue number 19) and another, similar pamphlet. Issue number 16 of *El Español,* published on July 30, 1811, in London, included a letter to its editor from Juan Germán Roscio, whose *El triunfo de la libertad sobre el despotimo* was discussed in chapter 3. Roscio in his letter praised Blanco White for "favoring the just cause" of Caracas, saying that the new country "counts you among its most distinguished citizens."[18] But Blanco White, lest he be associated with a total revolutionary break from Spain, published a lengthy response to Roscio in which he took a sympathetic position toward Venezuela's project but made an explicit case against independence and argued that Spanish America should retain ties to its "mother country." Blanco White wrote, "Jamas me ha parecido que la América española debia separarse enteramente de España en las circunstancias presentes" (I have never argued that Spanish America should separate itself entirely from Spain under the current situation).[19] The basic thrust of his argument (the *circunstancias*) was that Spanish America should not abandon the motherland while the latter was fighting against Napoleonic France, which then still had control over Spain. Blanco White went on: "El gran riesgo que yo concibo en la actual situacion de América, es el que crezca y se confirme el odio entre europeos y criollos; el que se lleguen á mirar como dos naciones distintas" (The great risk that I perceive in America's actual situation is that the hate between Europeans and creoles will grow and solidify, so that they will come to see each other as two distinct nations).[20] He urged the new governments to consider the multiple political positions of people in the colonies, including that of creoles who refused to take up arms against Spain and who could take issue with hasty independence. This line of argumentation, as will become evident in *El amigo de los hombres,* implied that independent territories were not prepared to deal with the *sistema de castas* in the colonies and could set themselves up for a black-led insurrection in the manner of Haiti. Blanco White protected himself from coming off as a monarchist by saying that he was not against the eventual—and to his view inevitable—independence of Spanish America but that to rush into it would be unwise and lead to conflicts in the new countries.

At a time when positions were becoming increasingly polarized between independence and continued colonial subjection, Blanco White tried to carve out a moderate path in the terrain: Spanish America should gain some autonomy but retain its ties to Spain and only eventually move toward total independence. That path appealed neither to Spain nor to revolutionaries in South America. *El Español* was banned in Spain. Then *El amigo* attacked Blanco White as a supporter of Spain because of his moderate position.

What's in a Name? White White versus Man

In Blanco White's response to Roscio we see an increasingly Anglocentric perspective, which he presented in print and performed through a change in name that emphasized whiteness. "Blanco White," which can be translated as either "White White" or "Blanco Blanco," was not his given name at birth but rather the result of his family's bilingual onomastic crossings. Blanco White's Irish father was christened William White and settled in Spain, where he Hispanicized his name to Guillermo Blanco. William's son was then born José Blanco y Crespo, the Crespo from his mother. In 1810, José moved to London, where he lived out his life, and described himself as a "self-banished Spaniard."[21] He reclaimed the English patronymic and turned himself bilingually into Joseph Blanco White, surely one of the whitest names in history and one that reflected his increasing affection for England. Blanco White converted to Protestantism and settled into the print-culture scene of London.

Blanco White titled his response to Roscio "Contextacion," a bilingual portmanteau that combined the Spanish *contestación* (response) and the English *context*, the latter subtly connecting to the London scene from where he was then writing. (The spelling "contextacion" was not unheard of but also not as common as "contestación" in the period.) Blanco White's "Contextacion" proposes that England should be an intermediary in the conflict between Spain and its revolutionary colonies as the power that could bring about reconciliation. In the most immediate context, the historical animus between Spain and England had been replaced by England's opposition to Napoleonic France's takeover of Spain. England was in alliance with the deposed Spanish king against France. Blanco White raised Spain's subjection while also insisting that Spanish America's situation differed from that of the United States and thus revolutionary independence was not the right path. In the following passage, Blanco White reveals his Eurocentric perspective, starting with a reference to the US Revolution:

> Los Estados Unidos podian contar con el interes que Francia y España tenian en abatir el poder de Inglaterra, en caso de la guerra que se siguió a su determinacion de hacerse independientes. La América Española tiene ahora los intereses de Europa divididos mui de otra manera. La tirania de Francia lo ocupa todo: solo Inglaterra está en contra, y esta auxilia á España en sus esfuerzos para sacudir el yugo. Si la América Española se pone en guerra abierta con España, si no dexa abierto el camino á la reconciliacion, si da pasos que Inglaterra no pueda mirar sino como opuestos á su tratado de alianza con España, la pondrá en un compromiso en que . . . se decidirá no por derehos abstractos sino por la circunstancias políticas. . . . Este seria un caso peligrosísimo; porque al chocar con Inglaterra, no queda otro lado á que inclinarse, que á los Estado Unidos, que en dia son como una especia de resvaladero ácia Francia.[22]

(In carrying out its war for independence, the United States could count on France and Spain to pursue their designs on weakening England's position. Spanish America, however, faces a different division of interests in Europe. France's tyranny is the dominant consideration: only England opposes it, and England supports Spain in its effort to throw off the yoke. If Spanish America declares open war on Spain and closes off a path to reconciliation, if it takes steps that England would see as combating its alliance with Spain, it will put England in a compromising position . . . and force it to consider its political situation rather than abstract principles. . . . This will lead to a most dangerous scenario because upon clashing with England, Spanish America will not have another recourse but to turn to the United States, which today is but a type of slide in the direction of France.)

Focusing on the European theater of war, Blanco White filters Spanish American independence through a French-English conflict. In addition, the United States is positioned in relation to Europe, a contrast to Venezuelan revolutionaries' views of the United States as part of a hemispheric American revolutionary process (evident in their July 5 declaration of independence). The suggestion that the United States was in league with France is a result of US attempts at neutrality in the English-French war, which prompted maritime conflicts and eventually led to the War of 1812.

The economic background to Blanco White's Anglocentric position was a growing commercial interaction between England and Spanish American colonial territories. While England did not publicly support Spanish American independence, it was eager to develop its growing trade with the region. As Juan Goytisolo has written, the Spanish monarchy could not defend its immense dominions against "English adventurers and merchants" with business dealings in Buenos Aires, Santo Domingo, and Trinidad.[23] In keeping with this point, we cannot separate the trans-American and transatlantic print exchange from which *El amigo de los hombres* emerges from the growing economic exchange taking place across empires and languages. As I have noted, textual production was part and parcel of economic changes taking place with the movement away from colonial rule.

Blanco White's Eurocentrism and his support of England as mediator constituted one of the sore spots for *El amigo de los hombres*:

> Como la América está firmemente resuelta á sostener y defender la libertad y la independencia que ha recobrado; y como sus ilustres habitantes han jurado

perecer todos cubiertos de gloria en defensa de sus justos derechos antes que someterse otra vez á España, ni á otra alguna Potencia del mundo; es inutil la mediacion del Gobierno Ingles: los Americanos no tienen que esperar ni que temer ya de los Españoles de Europa.[24]

(Because America is firmly resolved to protect and defend the liberty and independence that it has regained, and because its illustrious inhabitants have sworn to perish in glory in defense of their deserved rights rather than submit themselves again to Spain or any other power in the world, the mediation of the English government is futile: Americans do not need to fear or expect anything from the Spaniards of Europe.)

The phrase "los Españoles de Europa" (the Spaniards of Europe) is clearly a distancing from Spanish Americans, or *Americanos Españoles*. The words "of Europe" remind readers that in contrast to those who might view themselves as Spaniards of America (*peninsulares*), these men are situated in, living in, and/or thinking of themselves as of Europe as opposed to the Americas. In addition, the pamphlet emphasizes the American cause as hemispheric.

El amigo de los hombres, sixteen pages long, is first and foremost a refutation, and it develops its argument against what it calls six "propositions" from Blanco White and Flórez Estrada. The sixth, the call for England's mediation, has already been noted. The other arguments to which the pamphlet responds are the following: (1) the newly independent governments of America have usurped authority to rule without the support of the people; (2) Spanish America should not imitate the United States, because its circumstances are different; (3) Spanish America has recognized the sovereignty of (and thus implicitly supports) Ferdinand VII, who was ousted by Napoleonic troops; (4) Spanish America is committed to battling France in support of Spain; and thus (5) it should support Spain militarily, "if only to show its gratitude" (*A* 3). *El amigo de los hombres* dispatches most quickly the third and fourth arguments, saying that the pledge of support for Ferdinand came from Spain's colonial governors rather than from independent Americans. In relation to the fifth argument, it states that Spanish America owes no more allegiance to Spain than "los inocentes esclavos á los que armados con el hierro destructor los despojaron de la libertad, y los cargaron de afrentosas y pesadas cadenas" (*A* 12; the innocent slaves whom, through your use of destructive arms, you stripped of liberty and weighed down with shameful and heavy chains).

The metaphor of colonial subjects as slaves is important in a pamphlet that offers perhaps the most forceful Spanish-language statement on chattel slavery published by the trans-American elite in Philadelphia in the second and third decades of the nineteenth century. In discussing slaves, the pamphlet argues that "men of all classes and status" should be given the opportunity to pursue happiness. Emphasizing that he is the friend of *all* men, the pamphlet's author argues that governments should make a good life available to all, including slaves and free blacks, and offer benefits with "pureza, imparcialidad, y desvuelo generoso" (*A* 8; purity, impartiality, and purposeful generosity). The pamphlet develops this point in response to arguments from the peninsula that independence will lead to black insurrection: "Los negros y los mulatos (dicen los Publicistas superficialies . . .) serán siempre un escollo terrible para la indepencia de la America. Yo no alcanzo el fundamento solido de esta profecia" (*A* 6; Blacks and mulatos, according to superficial arguments . . . will always be a terrible impediment to the independence of America. I do not understand the basis of this prophecy). The argument over the future of blacks in Spanish America had been a major topic of debate in the Cádiz Cortes, a national assembly instituted in Spain in 1810 with representation from the American colonies. Blanco White's *El Español* covered debates over equality and citizenship rights of blacks and *pardos* and helped circulate these questions in the colonies.[25] The points about blacks in *El amigo de los hombres* were aimed at Flórez Estrada more than at Blanco White.

El amigo de los hombres attacks a European discourse promoting fear of black insurrection associated with Santo Domingo. For one, the pamphlet argues, vast stretches of Spanish America did not have enough enslaved people to mount such an insurrection. And it is correct that while countries such as Cuba, Brazil, and Venezuela had significant enslaved populations, estimates for countries such as Mexico, Paraguay, and Ecuador tell a different story. For example, the most populated country, Mexico, in 1800 had about ten thousand enslaved people, accounting for less than 1 percent of the 6 million people living there.[26] The point is not to downplay the importance of slavery but rather to combat the rhetoric of fear used by colonial authorities. *El amigo* argues that even in the place with the largest number of blacks, Cuba, whites are still the majority, and thus the invocation of insurrection is a fear tactic. The second point against promoting fear of insurrection is that should such a revolt be a threat, Americans are just as capable of responding as "a government that resides at a distance of 1600 leagues." And Americans, *El amigo* says, are more capable of treating enslaved people with respect and dignity, with the result that they will become robust contributors to the new society. This last point is developed with a reference to Roman slaves, who *El amigo* suggests were the most important contributors to that republic.

The pamphlet's overt discussion of slavery allows it to emphasize the analogy with the independence project, in which a justifiably angry anticolonial subject asserts itself. After pointing to Spain's intolerable treatment of enslaved people as beasts, *El amigo de los hombres* announces that Americans will not forget "tres siglos de despotismo, violencias, robos, y maldades" (*A* 12; three centuries of despotism, violence, robbery, and evil). The types of racial hierarchies associated with slavery are presented within a process that includes the treatment of American *criollos* as inferior. Spaniards, the pamphlet argues, "desplegaban una vanidad y orgullo insoportables, creeyendose de una especie superior á la de los Americanos" (*A* 9; displayed unbearable vanity and arrogance, thinking of themselves as a superior species to Americans). The result of this racialized hierarchy is Spaniards' usurpation of important posts in the colonies, one of the points of resentment for creoles: "Ellos poseian todos los empleos honorificos, y todos los destinos lucrosos en esta parte del mundo" (*A* 9; They [Spaniards] held all honorific positions and all profitable posts in this part of the world). Thus, the pamphlet responds to a racial caste system by which American-born whites were viewed as inferior to Spaniards even as blacks were viewed as racially inferior to all whites.

The relationship of creole independence leaders to mixed-race populations in Spanish America was complex, at once influenced by conceptions of political equality for all and also marked by racist perspectives on blacks and indigenous populations. Some historians have argued that Spanish American independence was accompanied by a "myth of racial democracy," that is, the institution of political equality and the elimination of caste accompanied by an ongoing practice of racial discrimination. Marixa Lasso has cautioned that despite the characterization of these processes as mythmaking, "the powerful association among republicanism, nationalism, and racial equality that characterized the Spanish American independence period cannot be taken for granted."[27] In response, Lasso has studied the participation of Afro-Colombians in the struggles for independence. She notes, for example, that in the Gual and España republican conspiracy of 1797 in Venezuela, creole leaders attempted to attract *pardo* militia members (free people of African descent).[28] As we saw in the preceding chapter, most but not all of the trans-American intellectuals in Philadelphia were white *criollos* who de-emphasized questions of racial difference. *El amigo de los hombres,* however, situates blacks at the center of its concerns.

While the pamphlet's discussion of slavery does not refer to the United States directly, the topic of slavery appears in a section on the differences between the United States and Spanish America. Implicitly, the point is that unlike the United States, the new countries of the southern Americas will offer opportunities for freedom for slaves, even if the pamphlet cautions against the effects of freeing all slaves at once. This is in keeping with *El amigo's* attempt to differentiate the new countries from the United States:

> La America Española tiene en su mismo seno recursos mucho mas poderosos, y medios mas felices para labrar y sostener su independencia, que los que tenia el pueblo Anglo-Americano en un pais ingrato, desierto, pobre, y asolado. Para saberlo basta tener sentido comun, y conocer la geografia fisica y politica del hemisferio Americano: por esto no puedo menos de reirme de las paradoxas y paralogismos desatinados que hacian los ecritores á que contesto. (*A* 5)

> (Spanish America has more abundant resources and more auspicious means to develop and protect its independence than those that were available to the Anglo-American people, who were living in a country that was harsh, deserted, poor, and blighted. To understand this you need only common sense and knowledge of the physical and political geography of the American hemisphere; that is why I can do no less than laugh at the misguided contradictions and false reasoning deployed by the authors to whom I reply.)

That passage inverts a sense of exceptionalism that might be associated with US independence and celebrates Spanish America as capable of developing its own very bright future.

El amigo's strong statements on class and caste, especially as they relate to slavery, stand out among Filadelfia letters. Anonymity in the introduction of a male-centered subject (El amigo) supported a move toward equality and away from slavery. The pamphlet posited a future when blacks might be considered full citizens, but it also retained paternalistic racial perspectives. Ultimately, *El amigo de los hombres* offers an important tension: the positing of a universalist speaking subject, the friend of man, as a figure who was in keeping with anonymity, while paying close attention to race and status in the Spanish American context. In doing so, it broke with Filadelfia publications that ignored slavery in their veneration of the new US republic.

Manual of Anonymous Republicanism

The year 1812 saw another anonymous pamphlet out of Filadelfia: *Manual de un republicano, para el uso de un pueblo libre*. While *El amigo de los hombres* addressed racial conditions on the ground in Spanish America as an important consideration, the *Manual* reverted back to an eighteenth-century model of republicanism that ignored racial difference and social conditions. In chapter 1, we saw how Filadelfia intellectuals turned to translation to transport concepts across vast distances. In chapter 2, we considered how certain trans-American intellectuals identified with white US revolutionary figures such as Franklin and Paine. The anonymous *Manual de un republicano* brought together those two dimensions. It was a translation of *The Republican's Manual, For the Use of a Free People* (Philadelphia 1806), a book that presented a "conversation with one of the most upright citizens who never deviated, since the American revolution, from the path of Republican government."[29] That pamphlet connected 1806 with 1776, while the translation into Spanish drew a geographic connection with South America. The effect was one of temporal and geographic conjunction along the lines of what we saw with García de Sena's translation of Thomas Paine.

The Spanish-language *Manual de un republicano* added anonymity as a dimension of translation. The English-language version had been published under the name T. B. Smart, possibly a pseudonym. But *Manual de un republicano* was published without a named author, and its title page did not offer a clue that the manual had been translated, thus precluding a connection between the pamphlet and a specific identity.[30] *Manual de un republicano* aimed at a transparent shift from one language to another. The effect is that much of the pamphlet proceeds as if written by a Spanish-language speaker in the United States. It is not until the footnotes at the end of the Spanish-language version that references to Venezuela and its relationship to US constitutional principles clarify that the pamphlet is a translational export for readers in South America. The result is a text with a transnational function, addressing readers in Venezuela and conceivably also in the United States.

The de-emphasizing of the translator's work is possible in part because of the pamphlet's form: a dialogue between a pupil and a teacher. It opens with the following: "¡Que satisfaccion no es para mi volver á ver á un Maestro, á quien tanto debo, despues de un viage de seis meses por los diversos Estados de la Union!" (*M2* 4; After a journey of six months through the diverse states in the Union, how delicious is it for me to see again a master whom I am so much indebted to? [*M1* 4]). In the Spanish version, that passage reads as if a young trans-American elite had traveled through the United States (as some did) and returned for a conversation with a teacher. The pedagogical thrust of the *Manual* is evident in the hunger for knowledge expressed by the pupil, who begins with questions about the implication of politics as a field of study and concludes with brief considerations of Rousseau and republican government. This question-and-answer format allowed the translator to silently shift the text to a budding print-culture development in Spanish America: the rise of the political catechism.

While the English-language *Republican's Manual* was a product of US debates between Federalists and Democratic-Republicans, the Spanish version shifted the form toward other pedagogical contexts. Between the year 1810 and the waning of the independence movements in the late 1820s, numerous catechisms whose goal was political instruction rather than religious education appeared in Spanish America and Spain. Chile saw the publication of the *Catecismo político cristiano* (Christian political catechism, 1810), by one José Amor de la Patria; Buenos Aires saw the *Catesismo público para la instrucción de los neófitos o recién convertidos al gremio de la sociedad patriótica* (Public catechism for the instruction of neophytes recently recruited to the association supporting a patriotic society, 1811); and Nueva Granada saw the *Catecismo o instrucción popular* (Catechism, or popular instruction, 1814), by a priest, Juan Fernández de Sotomayor, who argued against Spanish title to territories in America and excoriated the Crown for its colonial rule.[31] As late as 1827, Paris saw the Spanish-language publication of *Lecciones de politica, segun los principios del sistema popular representativo, adoptado por las naciones americanas* (Lessons in political systems, in accordance with the principles of popular representation adopted by American nations), a 460-page manual that followed the question-and-answer format in teaching political science.[32] (Some scholars have argued that Roscio's *El triunfo de la libertad sobre el despotismo* is part of the political-didactic literature of political catechisms.[33] Formally, however, Roscio's book did not use the question-and-answer format of a catechism and is more argument driven than instructive.) The scholar Rafael Sagredo Baeza has described political catechisms as books deployed to spread and consolidate new ways of thinking about government "por medio de un sistema de preguntas y respuetas, claras, precisas y directas y a través de una retórica sencilla y accesible a las inteligencias menos cultivadas" (through the use of a system of questions and answers presented in clear, direct, and precise language and a plain rhetorical style that was accessible to those with little learning).[34] This description of Spanish-language catechisms could well have applied to *Manual de un republicano*. Its English-language antecedent stated that its goal was to be "adopted as one of the first reading books in our schools" (*M1* 3), a phrase repeated in Spanish as "se adoptará como uno de los libros que deben leerse con preferencia en nuestras escuelas" (*M2* 4). The Spanish version thus echoes the concerns that public schools do not teach political science.

The anonymity of the Spanish-language version helped to consolidate the pamphlet's argument for a form of republicanism that had not yet moved past an abstract concept of the people. The conversation between pupil and master proceeds with a notion of political participation that completely ignores social and racial hierarchies. Anonymous translation allowed the Spanish-language reader to share a political position with US revolutionary and republican subjects without attention to time, place, or social condition. *The Republican's Manual* developed its argument by echoing the Declaration of Independence: "Men are born free, equal in rights, and by their nature they seek for happiness" (*M1* 10). These were presented as "natural and universal principles" (*M1* 10). But in a country in which slaves and indigenous populations were denied opportunity for inclusion in political society, these principles applied to white men. As will become clear, the translator is clearly attracted to the implicit association of equality with European and Anglo-American whiteness.

The English-language pamphlet does not take up race, and it proceeds with a discussion of liberty and government for "men." In one exchange, the master gives the student examples of people who follow a leader or philosopher and rise against tyranny to establish new governments. "Thus you may foretel [sic], that the end of the abuses of power, will always be, sooner or later, a bursting revolution, more or less favourable to the people, according to the views of the leaders" (*M1* 12). The pamphlet holds up Franklin as an example of those leaders. Here we see a return to the type of gendered identification that is common in Filadelfia writing.

While Franklin offered one inspiration, the pamphlet held up another important figure, Rousseau. In the United States, invoking the French philosopher could be taken as a salvo in the debate between the Federalists and Republicans, the latter associated with France. In Spanish America, Rousseau offered a connection to the trans-American elite and other supporters of independence, many of whom had either read him in the French or discussed some of his work. As we saw in the preceding chapter, Roscio integrated Rousseau's thinking into *El triunfo de la libertad sobre el despotismo*. "Rousseau was cited widely, if sometimes anonymously, throughout Spanish America during the wars of independence, in proclamations, political pamphlets, manifestos, newly founded periodicals and even in draft constitutions," writes Nicola Miller, who also notes that this engagement included both supporters and opponents of independence.[35] Miller's reference to anonymous citations shows that translation at times privileged the transporting of ideas across distance and languages over connecting certain texts to an author. Introducing Rousseau, *The Republican's Manual* situates translation as indispensable to the spreading of republican beliefs through education. It argues that *Du contrat social ou Principes du droit politique* (1762) is the ultimate writing on government and praises a recent "genuine translation of so useful a treatise, elucidated by many reflexions of the translator, chiefly appropriated to the government of the American union" (*M1* 7). That English translation is likely the 1797 "first American edition" published in Albany as *A Dissertation on Political Economy; to which is Added a Treatise on the Social Compact; or, the Principles of Politic Law*. The enthusiasm is not only for Rousseau's text but also for an adaptation that could refer to government in an American setting.

The effect of approaching questions on government via Rousseau is that it shifts the discussion toward universalist considerations. Invoking social-contract theory, the master tells the pupil, "In the state of nature, obstacles of various kinds impeded the enjoyment of the full extent of liberty; equality was limitted [*sic*] by the extent of the individual strength, skill, industry, &c. . . . To have them more powerfully displayed, extended and secured, and to have obstacles more certainly removed, men have agreed to be united in a body, to have laws enacted and executed" (*M1* 25). In the first part of the statement, the political subject is understood but unnamed; in the second the subject becomes a general "man." At the end of the pamphlet, the master situates his teaching as an introduction to Rousseau and encourages further reading. "This and many other interesting precepts are fully discussed in the reflexions of the translator of the Social Compact" (*M1* 27). In the Spanish-language version, the references to Rousseau allowed for a European connection that offered an alternative to Spain. And more to the point of this chapter, engaging with a theory of political organization facilitated the circulation of ideas about an anonymous political subject.

Unlike the English-language version, the translated manual touts social-contract theory as a discourse of civilization that stands in contrast to barbarism for the new American nations. *Manual de un republicano* deploys a racialized sense of the new Spanish American countries' needing to join "cultivated people." This point is clear in the notes that appear in the Spanish-language version but not in the English-language version. I quote from a note at length to capture the full effect:

> Si á la Inglaterra, Francia, y demas potencias civilizadas, se les antojase imponer á Venezuela la condicion de que para ser admitida al rango que pretende, sea qual fuere su forma de Gobierno, ó si ella por si misma concociese de que para ser respetada como tal, era necesario que se vistiesen sus habitantes de blanco, que es el uso entre ellas, y no de negro, ni de otro color oscuro ¿que partido tomaria? ¿Declararles la guerra solo por ser una preocupacion? Seria un delirio, quando por ella se procuraria su total ruina. ¿Desentenderse de ellas y alternar con las naciones barbaras del Africa? No es posible: porque en el grado de civilizacion que se halla Venezuela, necesita absolutamente de que aquellas potencias lleven sus mercanciás, y le exporten su producciones.—Este, pues, es vuestro caso, pueblos de la América, ó habeis de acomodaros á las ideas de los demas pueblos cultos de la Europa, ó habeis de resolveros á vivir errantes como los de Arabia; subsistiendo de la caza y de la pesca; y quedando siempre sujetos á sufrir la dominacion pesada del primero de aquellos que se desembarcace, para emprender nuestra conquista, que en este estado no requeriría grandes esfuerzos. (*M2* 32)

> (For Venezuela, whatever its form of government, to be admitted among England, France, and other civilized powers, it would have to meet the following condition: its inhabitants should dress in white, as those countries do, and not in black or some other dark color. What if this were a precondition to gaining respect? What would be the response? Would [Venezuela] declare war over this point? That would be absurd because it would bring about total ruin. Would it separate itself from [European countries] for an alternate alliance with the barbaric nations of Africa? That is not possible, because the level of civilization in Venezuela calls for those [European] powers to send their merchandise and export their products. This is your situation, countries of America, either adapt yourself to the ideas of the cultivated countries of Europe or resolve to live in the errancy of those in Arabia, subsisting on hunting and fishing and remaining always in danger of facing the brutal domination of the first country that clears a way to undertake our conquest, which under the present circumstance would not require tremendous effort.)

The passage is striking in its introduction of racialized conceptions of social organization, replete with Arabic nomads and African barbarians—all the more so because the English-language version of the pamphlet has no references to racial categories. The English-language version privileges Rousseau as a thinker, not as a representative of Europe. If anything, the English-language version goes out of its way to ignore racial and cultural difference. In the passage above, the Spanish-language note emphasizes the importance of economic exchange and the growing trade between South America and Europe. In this particular case, economic conditions become intertwined with the translation's racial position. The notes make a case for the importance of commodities in the shift to modernity that independence will bring about.

Manual de un republicano and *El amigo de los hombres* take radically different approaches to the treatment of Spanish America's racial situation. The manual calls for the institution of a white-led society based on European mores, whereas *El amigo* calls for liberty for slaves and equality for all people regardless of their color. In the first case, anonymity facilitates the assumption of an unmarked white male citizen who could be a US revolutionary figure or a republican in Spanish America in the second decade of the nineteenth century. In the second pamphlet, anonymity helps to spread a notion of humanity that will include all men regardless of racial elements. What they share is an assumption that in new countries an idealized male political subject will be able to participate regardless of social hierarchies or economic advantages. This blind spot, which is not uncommon in the writing of the trans-American elite, will follow intellectuals into the postindependence period, and it is in full display in an 1826 book that relies on an idealized conception of a political actor to discuss constitutional debates. While *El amigo de los hombres* drew its rhetorical power from the general notion of humanity and the *Manual* from an unmarked white "republican," other Filadelfia publications invoked the term *Americano* to bring forward a political actor and speaking subject with trans-American connections between the United States and Spanish America.

X as Hemispheric American(o)

The anonymously published *Cartas de un americano* (Letters of an American, 1826) contained letters signed by an unknown variable: *X*. Published in London and containing nine letters written in New York and Philadelphia and dated from October 2, 1825, to January 16, 1826, this book was a product of transatlantic and trans-American print-culture processes. Its full title, *Cartas de un americano sobre las ventajas de los gobiernos republicanos federativos* (Letters of an American concerning the advantages of federal republican governments), helps us situate the historical changes that had taken place in the decade-plus since the publication of *El amigo de los hombres*. The debates were no longer about independence but about constitution formation after countries had fought militarily to oust Spanish rule. *Cartas de un americano* introduces another important dimension of anonymous publication, a collaborative writing and editing process that Anna Brickhouse identified as an important historical dimension of writing by dissidents and exiles that "depended on secretive transmission as well as coterie circulation and revision for their publication."[36] The letters in the book, written by one or more people, were taken across the Atlantic by Vicente Rocafuerte and then prepared for publication by José Canga Argüelles, a Spanish economist and government minister who had gone into exile in London for his liberal views. Rocafuerte describes the collaborative publication process as the result of his wish to see the large territory of Gran Colombia governed by a federal government along the lines of the US government instead of a centralized unitarian approach or a dispersal into a confederation. Informing the letters were the differing paths followed to constitution formation in the new countries of Spanish America: some (e.g., Mexico) had set up federal governments comparable to that of the United States, while others (e.g., Peru) had followed a unitary system by which a supreme central government delegated powers to provinces. The federal-unitary tension would play an important part in the histories of several Latin American nations, including Argentina. Jaime E. Rodriguez O. has summarized two competing political traditions as follows: "One, forged in more than a decade of war, emphasized strong executive power; the other, based on the civilian parliamentary experience, insisted upon legislative dominance."[37] In response to these debates, Rocafuerte says, he began to write *Cartas de un americano,* "y no permitiéndome concluírla el recargo de mis ocupaciones diplomáticas, se la entregué al señor José Canga Argüelles, quien tuvo la amabilidad de refundirla, terminarla y publicarla" (but my diplomatic activities prevented me from finishing the work, and I handed it to Mr. José Canga Argüelles, who was kind enough to revise, finish and publish it).[38] The Spanish *refundir,* which I translate as "to revise," has several connotations. Its root is *fundación* (foundation) and thus could mean "to recast," and it also could imply a melting or blending.³⁹

The signature *X* in the *Cartas* implies a political actor that could plug into numerous American sites where constitutions were being written and rewritten. As an unknown variable, *X* signals a deterritorialization of the writing subject into a general hemispheric American. In the introduction, I noted the different historical sense of *X* in this text when compared with the contemporary uses of *LatinX,* which proposes a crossing of gender. The contemporary invocation of *X* in *LatinX* or *Latinx* has circulated both as a reference to cross-gender people and as a wholesale ethnic label to refer to all people previously in the Hispanic/Latino demographic grouping. But in certain contemporary theoretical formulations, *LatinX* is invoked to connote indeterminacy. "The X is unknowable—or beyond knowing," writes Claudia Milian. "The classification itself, LatinX, remains unknown, which is to say we have rendered ourselves to the unknown—or the unknowns of unpredictable worlds."⁴⁰ While Milian veers toward the epistemological limits of subjectivity, her usage of the *X* variable resists the type of fixity associated with ethnic labels and thus opens a dialogue with the different historical circumstances in the 1826 *Cartas. Cartas de un americano* offers a different power of *X* for a different time, one in which lack of attention to social position results in republican man as a default gender position.

The effect of an anonymous *X* is the creation of an abstract American(o) subject that is not tethered to one location either by nationality or social position. The decision to sign with the letter *X* is a curious gesture in that it could be the mark of an illiterate person, and this in a document that offers analysis of constitutional theory. But connecting to illiterate people was probably less important than positioning X as a stand-in for all Americanos. While *El amigo de los hombres* had sought a universalist speaking subject that could position himself in many sites through the invocation of friendship and a shared humanity (man), X as the signatory of the letters invites people to fill in the unknown variable while emphasizing hemispheric Americanism, the latter associated with federal governmental organization in the Americas as opposed to Europe, even though the book at times refers to European constitutions. *X* marks a position that is American but without a specific country, even as it implies a trans-American age of independence by dating Spanish-language letters in New York and Philadelphia. As a result, the *X* of the writer or reader is mobile, and an American(o) can be in any of the countries in the Americas, including the United States. The myriad locations through which the book can and does travel are inextricable from the anonymity claimed by *X*.

The book positions itself as engaging with *The Federalist Papers*, published originally in serial form under the pseudonym Publius, a reference to the Roman consul Publius Valerius Publicola. By quoting from *The Federalist Papers*, *Cartas de un americano* connects not only to the constitutional principles in that collection but also to the collaborative writing and publication that is at odds with individual named authorship. In other words, Rocafuerte and company engage with the writers of *The Federalist Papers*, inserting translations of passages that spell out the differences between modern republics and ancient democracies singled out by opponents of independence for their failures. The translations are direct; for example, the line "The efficacy of various principles is now well understood, which were either not known at all, or imperfectly known to the ancients" is translated as "La fuerza de ciertos principios se percibe en el día mejor que en la antigüedad." The latter cuts out clauses to make a clear case for the advancement of political knowledge, which is one of the points of *Federalist* no. 9.

These highly political *cartas* open with salutations such as "Amigo mio" (My friend) or "Mi dulce y apreciado amigo" (My sweet and appreciated friend), emphasizing personal attachment as a condition of political conversation. The letter form, as I suggested in the introduction, exemplifies the male-centered intimacy that motivates epistolary exchange out of Filadelfia. The letters close complimentarily with a variety of suggestive phrases, including "Es de V. afmo. Q.S.M.B" (Yours most affectionately) with the initialism for *que su mano besa* (who kisses your hand). The closing "mande a su afmo. y eterno amigo" includes the phrase "your most affectionate and eternal friend" with the word *mande*, which could be read as "*send* a letter" but also as "*send* me to do something." This type of exchange at times can sound amorous, such as in the opening to letter 5, "Mi dueño y amigo" (My owner and friend), with dueño close to *sueño* (dream), and raises the suggestion of emotional connection. Given Rocafuerte's explanation that the motivation for composing the book was political conditions in Gran Colombia, the affectionate epistolary elements are part of a rhetoric meant to persuade and attract readers but also suggest intimate attachments shared in this homosocial environment of lettered exchange.

The ties that bring together the trans-American elite can be written into the affectionate rhetoric of a public political conversation. In the opening letter, X emphasizes that he enters a print debate "con la franquesa de nuestra amistad, con la concisión propia del estilo epistolar, y con el ardiente deseo que me asiste de contribuír al bien de nuestra patria" (with the frankness of our friendship, with the succinctness of epistolary style, and with the ardent desire that you assist me in contributing to the good of our homeland).[41] In letter 7, the writer again says that epistolary style calls for a concise discussion (*C* 97) of a topic that is extensive, a statement that precedes an instructive accounting of information about the United States. An epistolary rhetorical artifice is evident when X concludes the first letter by assuring his recipient that "mi correspondencia no saldrá del estrecho recinto de nuestra amistad" (*C* 7; my correspondence will not go beyond the guarded confines of our friendship). The friendly tone takes the edge off what is otherwise an attack on another political writer. Just as *El amigo de los hombres* opened with a reference to other publications, *Cartas de un americano* situates its argument as a response to the book *Memorias políticas sobre las federaciones* (1825), by the Peruvian Chilean intellectual Juan Egaña. *Memorias políticas* is a methodical argument in support of centralized or unitary government. Involved in the drafting of a constitution in Chile in 1823, Egaña is not keen on the North American constitution and argues that the United States ultimately mutes the sovereignty that resides in the states by functioning through a strong national government.[42] Egaña's sober consideration of the US Constitution as well as those of Europe contrasts with the more affectionate and rhetorically enthusiastic *Cartas de un americano*. In one of the first salvos, X accuses Egaña of offering a lazy definition of the federal system. "El vacío que se advierte en la definición del Sr. Egaña es tanto más notable cuanto con sólo reconocer la constitución Agloamericana y las de México y Guatemala, tenia lo bastante para reducir sus ideas al punto debido de claridad" (*C* 10; The weakness apparent in Mr. Egaña's definition is more alarming when one considers that knowledge of the Anglo-American constitution along with those of Mexico and Guatemala would have given him enough to bring clarity to his ideas). X then sets out to provide that knowledge.[43]

Cartas de un americano's argument establishes a North-South political affiliation, praising the US model while completely ignoring populations in either the North or the South whose political rights might have been curtailed because of social, racial, or economic position. As a group, the letters offer a celebratory account of political systems in the United States: "La historia nos dice que desde el momento en que éstos llegaron a consolidar el sistema político que los dirije, aparecieron a la faz del mundo como una nación grande, rica y próspera" (*C* 46; History tells us that from the moment they adopted the political system under which they live, they appeared on the face of the earth as a nation large, rich, and prosperous). This type of rhetorical flourish is mixed with discussion of more specific constitutional matters, such as an explanation of which powers reside in the national government and which reside in the states. The numerous passages about the United States most likely come from the pen of Rocafuerte, who had spent considerable time in Washington, New York, and Philadelphia; these passages discuss the US Constitution and also offer information about the population, religious affiliation, and economic conditions of different states in the union. (The influence of Canga Argüelles emerges in letters that discuss how the Spanish monarchy reacted to the Napoleonic invasion of 1808.)

Cartas de un americano holds the United States as exemplary of the success of a federal government, at times adding references to federalist approaches in Mexico and Guatemala, so that federalism becomes a potential for all of the Americas. It is an *American* system, described by an *American* in the hemispheric sense. The United States does no less than provide the evidence for his arguments. One of the letters discussing the United States opens with the saying "callen barbas y hablen cartas" (*C* 97), which can be translated as "silence the beards so that the documents can speak." The point is that documents, particularly written constitutions, have more power than oral testimony or age. In this case the word *cartas* refers to documents while also echoing the book's title, with the letters as part of the evidence.

The argument of *Cartas de un americano* is driven by a presentation of the United States as a country that has advanced on the world stage as a result of the advantages of federal government. Letters 7 and 8 offer both statistical and descriptive information about the United States, such as the territorial area of each state, customs of the states, snapshots of state legislatures, elements of state constitutions, the number of churches by denomination in each state, the size of state militias, agricultural production, the volume of manufacturing, and the number of newspapers in each state. "¿Y si tan felices resultados produce el federalismo republicano entre los angloamericanos, por qué no esperarlos mayores en las naciones hispanoamericanas, en donde la identidad de los hábitos y de la religión de sus habitantes, y las inmensas riquezas que producen los terrenos que les cupieron en suerte, prometen un éxito más rapido y más completo?" (*C* 136; If republican federalism produces such fortunate results among Anglo-Americans, why not expect even more among Hispano-American nations, where the immense riches produced by the fields that nature bestowed upon them promise more success at a faster pace). Like *El amigo de los hombres,* X does not equate US success with exceptionalism but rather presents it as an example that can be superseded in Spanish America.

The enthusiasm for the United States creates an ideal national panorama without taking adequate account of how people are actually living in the states. At times, this ideal remains within the realm of constitutional theory. Letter 3, for example, offers a comparison of the US, Mexican, and Guatemalan constitutions that presents the organization of each country's government but says little about its actual functioning or the people who live in the country. *Cartas de un americano* mostly stays clear of US politics in the early nineteenth century. Nor does it focus on actual people in the United States. Early on, the book is more interested in the writings of Hamilton and Montesquieu than in conditions in the United States. Most alarmingly, the book says absolutely nothing about chattel slavery and invokes the term *slavery* only as a metaphor for Spanish colonial subjection. And very little is said about indigenous populations, although an idealistic reading of the US treatment of tribes emerges in letter 5. Attempting to present federal republics as peaceful, that letter actually says that in its fifty years the United States has not been aggressive toward its neighbors. The United States, the letter argues, did not create a Machiavellian excuse for a military takeover of "las tierras que ocupaban los bárbaros" (the lands occupied by barbarians). X proposes that instead of making war on indigenous people, the United States gained land through "transacciones amistosas" (*C* 68; friendly transactions), a reference to purchases by treaty.

By ignoring racial and economic conditions for people in the United States and Spanish America, *Cartas de un americano* becomes a successful translation of US ideology. Anonymity facilitates that because it deterritorializes the very political subject that is supposed to be governed by a federal constitution. The hemispheric proposal of *Cartas de un americano* is one in which people without a name or place can be shoved to the back of a discussion that remains at the level of constitutional documents. With everyone as Americanos, particular conditions are erased, a process that we see in the most significant novel published in Filadelfia, *Jicoténcal*.

Deterritorialized Subjects: Anonymous *Jicoténcal*

When we consider the numerous political pamphlets and books written and published anonymously in Philadelphia, the anonymous publication of *Jicoténcal* is not unusual. Published in two small volumes, *Jicoténcal* affirms its position as an anonymous text on the title page, which features only the novel's title in bold caps (no accent) and the following: "Tomo primero" (first volume) and "Filadelfia: Imprenta de Guillermo Stavely. 1826." This emphasizes the main character's name, which does not have to share the title page with an author. Filadelfia is given its due, and William Stavely's name is Hispanicized. Anonymous publication is an important dimension of *Jicoténcal*, which displays the pedagogical-political function that we have associated with texts such as *El amigo de los hombres* and *Cartas de un americano*.[44] The novel elaborates on many of the elements in other Filadelfia texts: abhorrence of tyranny, discussions of republican government, critiques of how Catholicism sustains colonial oppression, and a defense of reason in contradistinction to passion. But more importantly, the novel resists an association with a specific national literary tradition, something that would be facilitated by an identifiable author. For those of us reading now, the book emphasizes the alterity of a historical moment when publication is not associated primarily with an author's identity.

As a compendium of ideas and letters circulating in Filadelfia, *Jicoténcal* challenges the insistence in twentieth-century criticism on attributing the book to a single author. The book blends historical romance, a genre that at that point in history was more common in England than in Spain, with political pamphlets, at times providing instruction on proper republican behavior. *Jicoténcal* even exhibits a patchwork quality when it lifts passages (not unusual in the nineteenth century) from Antonio de Solís's *Historia de la conquista de México* (History of the conquest of Mexico), first published in 1684. Solís (1610–1686) was foremost a dramatist who became well known because of his plays, and his history of the conquest blends melodrama into the narrative. Solís's *Historia* circulated in Philadelphia in the early nineteenth century, and readers of Spanish could have picked up a copy at the Carey and Lea bookshop in 1825.[45] In addition, Manuel Torres and Louis Hargous had included lengthy selections from the Solís history in their language-learning book, *Dufief's Nature Displayed in her Mode of Teaching Language to Man* (Philadelphia, 1811). In chapter 1, I noted that *Jicoténcal* was registered by the bookseller Frederick Huttner and thus can be seen as part of a growing US market for Spanish-language books. Most likely *Jicoténcal* was the result of a combination of intentions that drew the Filadelfia group's political goals and booksellers' desire to make money.

Before proceeding with an analysis of what makes anonymous publication an important dimension of *Jicoténcal*, let us consider the misguided insistence of criticism since the early twentieth century on identifying the author of the novel and situating the book in a national tradition.[46] For example, the novel was included in Antonio Castro Leal's 1964 anthology *La novela del méxico colonial,* with the editor noting that he believed it was by a Mexican author.[47] Others have proposed José María Heredia as author.[48] And most recently, the attribution to Félix Varela has gained traction. But the argument that Félix Varela wrote the book tells us more about the critics than it does about the novel. Much of this criticism is driven by an assumption that there is an inextricable connection between author and nation, a supposition that is a historical effect of the twentieth century and the national organization of literary study.

Under that panorama, Félix Varela becomes a two-fer for the book, offering both a Cuban national association and a US Latino (or Hispanic) connection. Luis Leal proposed the Varela attribution in 1960, and the Arte Público Press edition codified it in 1995 with a substantial introduction by Leal and Rodolfo Cortina situating *Jicoténcal* (with the modernized accent of later editions) and Varela in Latino literary history.[49] As we have seen in preceding chapters, Varela was one of Cuba's foremost intellectuals in the early nineteenth century and published under his own name several well-known texts. For conceptions of Hispanic literary heritage, Varela also offered a geo-biographic trajectory of Cuban exile in the United States, where he lived from 1824 until his death in 1853. The Arte Público edition had two simultaneous effects: it positioned Varela as a nineteenth-century Latino subject, and his oeuvre granted a new *Jicoténcal* edition an impressive authority. Other critics have followed that line, with some claiming that it is a "Cuban-American novel."[50]

And yet there is good reason to doubt the Varela attribution. Leal himself says that the evidence points toward Varela but that "no podemos decir con seguridad absoluta" (we cannot say with absolute certainty).[51] The textual record left by Varela should prompt a pause before linking his name to *Jicoténcal*. Here is a passage from Varela's *Cartas a Elpidio* in which he addresses the question of anonymous writing:

> Sea cual fuere la causa, he tenido siempre tanta confianza en todas mis campañas políticas, religiosas y literarias, que lejos de querer desarmar a mis enemigos he procurado siempre proporcionarles nuevas armas o afilar las que poseen si me han parecido embotadas. El placer de la victoria es mucho mayor cuando el enemigo tiene una completa defensa. De aquí viene mi práctica de poner mi nombre en todos mis escritos indicando mi estado y modo de pensar.[52]

(Whatever the cause, I have always had enough confidence in all of my political, religious, and literary battles that rather than trying to disarm my enemies I have always attempted to grant them new arms or help them sharpen the dull ones in their possession. The pleasure of victory is greater when the enemy is able to defend himself adequately. From here stems my practice of putting my name on all of my writings, claiming my views and thought processes.)

It is possible that Varela is addressing primarily debates against US Protestants, which took up his energy in the 1830s, but the phrase *todos mis escritos* (all of my writings) points to a larger body of work.[53] In the preceding chapter, I noted an article from *El Habanero* in which Varela disparages the secrecy of patriotic and Masonic groups, writing that a true challenge to colonial rule must avoid secrecy. While Leal and Cortina propose that Varela may have been reluctant to admit to writing a novel because of his status as a widely respected philosopher and priest, Varela was not the type to hide the truth, nor does he write surreptitiously on other occasions. In addition, Varela does not express a sustained concern with the history of indigenous groups in Spanish America, although he does note the effect of the conquest on indigenous populations in Cuba and also publishes articles by other writers in the *New York Catholic Register* in 1840 dealing with the treatment of indigenous people by "pilgrims" in New England and Maryland.[54] *Jicoténcal* does contain stylistic similarities to Varela's writing and echoes some of his political concerns, but the attribution to Varela discounts the priest's arguments against secrecy and concealment.

Scholars have objected to some of Leal's arguments supporting the Varela attribution. José Rojas Garcidueñas takes a lawyerly approach and notes that much of Leal's argument is circumstantial. For example, the point that William Stavely printed both *El Habanero* and *Jicoténcal* could be a coincidence since Stavely printed other Spanish-language titles. Rojas Garcidueñas also makes the point that some of the stylistic confluences are more circumstantial than indicative of authorship.[55] In the Arte Público edition, Leal and Cortina present twenty-five similarities of phrasing and spelling in *Jicoténcal* and Varela's writing. Rojas Garcidueñas notes that some of these are general enough to be part of common usage: "en las aras del amor" (*Jicoténcal*) and "en aras del poder" (Varela); "Teutila fue ... a recibir los baldones" (*Jicoténcal*) and "y llenan de baldones al ilustre patriota" (Varela); and also "la llama del amor patrio" (*Jicoténcal*) and "el fuego del amor patrio" (Varela). I add to the list of dubious similarities Leal and

Cortinas's "ideas ridículas" (*Jicoténcal*) and "epítetos ridículos" (Varela). Some of the confluences are mere repetitions of word choice (e.g., *ápice, inauditos, perfidia*). Anna Brickhouse has proposed that perhaps *Jicoténcal*, like *Cartas de un americano*, was a product of authorial collaboration.[56]

Anonymous publication is crucial to this novel because it de-emphasizes the importance of the individual self. A good republican, the novel shows, places virtue and the public good above personal attainment; excessive focus on personal aggrandizement leads to greed. Under that logic, Jicoténcal the character can stand in for an anonymous republican subject rather than an indigenous historical person. The result is a complicated relationship, one in which the figure Jicoténcal is connected to 1820s independence fighters through the metonym *el Americano* while simultaneously inhabiting a distant historically specific site.

Anonymity in authorship facilitates a process by which the principles espoused by the character Jicoténcal circulate while the indigenous body is destroyed and expelled from the body politic. Considering that Filadelfia writings rarely take into account living indigenous people, the introduction of a romantic hero who is long dead allows for a representation of a valiant republican who does not differ in principles from the trans-American elite. This places the novel in dialogue with the various efforts in Spanish America during and after the independence period to look back to the indigenous past to formulate conceptions of an anticolonial nation. Rebecca Earle is among scholars who have noted that these claims referred to ancient cultures rather than social conditions in the nineteenth century. "Recognizing this distinction between the pre-Columbian past and the indigenous present is key to understanding the functioning of elite nationalism in nineteenth-century Spanish America," Earle writes.[57] In the case of *Jicoténcal*, the point is not elite nationalism but rather elite trans-American publication.

Like some of the anonymously published books discussed in this chapter, *Jicoténcal* takes up constitution formation, Spain's colonial rule, and proper republican behavior. The novel opens a discussion about republican government without situating it in a specific country in the 1820s. In other words, it allows for a consideration of political organization as it might apply across the Americas without having to confront the ways that living indigenous people in Mexico, Central America, and the Caribbean might respond to contemporaneous efforts to establish republican governments. The historical-novel form offers a distancing mechanism that permits the focus to shift to a noble and novel pre-Columbian republican.

While the plot is driven by violence and drama—battles, men fighting over someone described as a stunningly beautiful woman, the holding of hostages, attempted rapes, and a love triangle—the novel opens with a discussion of a republic. The first nine paragraphs are devoted to a description of Tlascala as a republic, and the word *republic* appears in the opening sentence of the first four paragraphs. Tlascala is not just any type of republic but a decentralized one without an executive branch, described as follows:

> Its government was a confederated republic; sovereign power dwelt in a congress or senate, composed of members elected one for each party of those in the republic. Executive power, and apparently also the judicial, were to be found among the chiefs or *caciques* from the parties or districts which, nevertheless, were subordinate to the congress, and the congress, in judicial cases, also permitted appeals of its sentences.[58]

As we have seen in *Cartas de un americano,* one of the major trans-American debates in the 1820s was about the type of republican government that would be established in the newly independent territories of Spanish America. One of Rocafuerte's stated motivations for publishing *Cartas de un americano* was the fear that Gran Colombia would separate into a confederation. Arguing for a US-style federalism, *Cartas de un americano* simultaneously opposed the extreme decentralization of a confederated approach as well as, on the other end, the centralized governance of a unitary republic without states' rights. *Jicoténcal* enters this debate by presenting Tlascala as vastly superior to the colonial rule that would follow but also a deeply flawed republic. Although the reference to a senate has resonances with the United States, Tlascala is actually the type of republic that *Cartas de un americano* least prefers, a confederated republic that is an association of sovereign territories: "The capital's four neighborhoods were considered to be four independent districts" (*X* 8). The book tells us that this decentralized government was a reaction to a time when a single "*cacique* or king" was overthrown because of the "excesses of his authority" (*X* 8). In Tlascala, an excessive concentration of power in the legislature facilitates the internal conflict between Magiscatzin and Jicoténcal and eventually leads to disintegration. The implication is that without a balance of power among different governmental branches or even between states and a federal government, Tlascala opens itself up to a power struggle, and the result is that Hernán Cortés can take advantage of the discord. In one narratorial interjection that has rhetorical similarities to other anonymous texts, the novel emphasizes the importance of unity for a government: "I call on all nations! If you love your freedom, gather together all your interests and your forces and learn that, if there is no power that will not fail when it collides against the immense force of your union, neither is there an enemy so weak that it will not defeat you and enslave you when you are disunited" (X 79). Those lines speak directly to the 1820s because they were published during a time when the new countries of Spanish America sought to consolidate their independence.

The framing of Tlascala as a republic in emphatic terms at the novel's outset establishes a double political gesture. On the one hand, the pre-Columbian governmental structure presents republicanism as inherent (natural) on the American continent. Tlascala differs from the Aztec and Spanish Empires; the novel stating early on that "it is indeed certain that the spirit which is truly republican has never been a conqueror" (X 33). On the other hand, the novel shows how a certain type of republican government is vulnerable to the machinations of self-interested Machiavellian characters. The republican breakdown in Tlascala takes place in part because Magiscatzin betrays the republic in an effort to strengthen his own position. Even before the arrival of Cortés, Magiscatzin misleads the Tlascalan senate into an unjust war. He attempts to rape a woman from Zocotlan but is beaten back and injured by her. In turn, he appears before the senate and claims that he was attacked within the borders of Tlascala, thus prompting a war. "That sanctuary of liberty had never before been contaminated by untruth and slander," the narrator tells us (X 23). By the time Cortés arrives, Magiscatzin is eager to work with the Spanish conqueror.

The novel performs a pedagogical function regarding proper republican behavior and thus is in dialogue with other anonymous Filadelfia texts. Most directly, the novel shows that a republican must be rational, truthful, and self-abnegating for the commonwealth. This is why William Cullen Bryant, in his 1827 review, noted that Jicoténcal and other characters "are very unprejudiced, enlightened, and philosophic savages, and, in their notions of government and religion, approach very nearly to the modern *liberales* of Spain."[59] Bryant, accepting the distinction between savage and civilized, is correct in connecting the historical story to contemporaneous events in Spanish America, noting that in the wake of independence "more enlightened notions of government are diffusing and perfecting themselves, and a tolerant spirit is fast displacing the old bigotry."[60] In contrast to this change are the actions of Cortés, whose passion and greed lead to the destruction that he inflicts on the people of what will become Mexico. *Jicoténcal* does not situate this type of behavior as inherent in either the Americas or Europe. Despite the association of Jicoténcal with republican virtue and Cortés with colonial deceit, the Magiscatzin character and Diego de Ordaz show that virtue and corruption can emerge from either side of the Atlantic. (The novel does make clear that European monarchy predisposes people such as Ordaz to think in antidemocratic ways.) In other words, certain indigenous characters can be opportunistic and unjust empire builders, and Spanish characters can be virtuous, even if misguided in their loyalty to a monarch. As a result, Magiscatzin becomes crucial in registering a postindependence political analysis, showing that corruption should not be situated solely in Europe but can emerge from the local population.

The story of Tlascala as told in *Jicoténcal* offers an example of what J. G. A. Pocock called "the Machiavellian moment," the confrontation between virtue and corruption at the heart of republican thought going back to the Florentine early modern context. Pocock showed how this conflict reemerged in the eighteenth century and the revolutionary era that followed. The Machiavellian moment, he wrote, "is a name for the moment in conceptualized time in which the republic was seen as confronting its own temporal finitude, as attempting to remain morally and politically stable in a stream of irrational events conceived as essentially destructive of all systems of secular stability."[61] In an interjection at the start of book 3, the narrator of *Jicoténcal* sets up the historical passing of Tlascala as a result of corruption and claims the perspective of a philosopher-historian who sees major social changes as a result of "las virtudes o los vicios" (virtue or vice).[62] *Jicoténcal* serves as a warning to the newly founded Spanish American countries that they need to establish a constitutional system that is least susceptible to the potential tyrannical forces of Spanish colonizers and their creole supporters. As part of this warning, Tlascala is presented as a republic without the checks and balances of executive, legislative, and judicial branches—or a federal system with some states' rights. In practice, Tlascala functions predominantly as a legislature in which deceit and rhetoric can carry the day and military leaders can command the loyalty of troops. When the senate is about to consider whether Jicoténcal has committed treason, the warrior's father tells the deliberative body, "The Senate's justice has always been inflexible, and it must continue to be so as long as its members do not renounce honor and virtue" (*X* 116). But as Magiscatzin plots against Jicoténcal, the recourse to justice reflects an excessive faith in a flawed system.

This Machiavellian moment, the commitment to virtue as a dimension of republicanism even as the senate is hijacked, situates the novel in the context of the constitutional debates raging in Spanish America in the 1820s. In *Cartas de un americano,* the type of republic that is comparable to Tlascala is a Greek amphictyonic league: "Los anfictiones eran diputados de unas ciudades absolutamente soberanas.... De esta base imperfecta dimanó la debilidad de su autoridad, y de ella vinieron los desórdenes que al cabo arruinaron la federación" (*C* 13; The amphistionics were deputies of absolutely sovereign cities.... From this imperfect foundation emanated the weakness of its authority and gave rise to the disorder that destroyed the federation). Without an executive branch, this confederated republic was open to the will of the stronger city-states and their representatives. *Jicoténcal* suggests that as a confederated republic, Tlascala cannot neutralize the type of corruption exhibited by Magiscatzin and Cortés. Thus, the novel holds an implicit preference for the type of balance of power seen in the United States and other newly formed countries with three branches of government.

The antidote to corruption is sensibilities and behavior that the novel associates with the natural (hemispheric) American. Both Jicoténcal and Teutila are often described as "el Americano/la Americana." The latter is objectified as "la hermosa Americana" (beautiful American woman). Teutila originally appears in nature's grotto, and thus nature becomes not an opportunity for the growth of empire along the lines of the United States but a state that allows reason to arise in relation to questions of state and religious belief. This contrasts belief systems founded on an allegiance to monarchy: "a Spaniard's honor is identified with his fidelity to his king" (*X* 57). The self-abnegation of the Americans, Jicoténcal and the fictional creation of Teutila, situate those characters closer to anonymous republican subjects than to the greedy empire builders from Spain.

Jicoténcal retains a classical sense of republicanism by which virtue is located in a nameless individual. Jicoténcal is described as having an "alma republicana" (*J* 106; a republican soul). This would be in contrast to republican virtue as codified in laws that establish the rule of a people. And it is in response to Jicoténcal's virtue that Cortés decides to kill the indigenous leader. Here the narrator speaks from Cortés's perspective: "Jicoténcal debía perecer: su existencia comprometía a cada momento la de las armas españolas en América; el temple de su alma era inaccesible a toda especie de corrupción y abatimiento, la fama de su valor y de sus virtudes era respetada hasta por los mismo tlascaltecas vendidos a la facción traidora" (*J* 106;

Jicoténcal needed to perish: his existence could challenge at any moment the course of Spanish arms in America; the constancy of his soul was out of reach to all types of suppression and corruption, his valor and virtue well known and respected by even those Tlascaltecans who had sold out to the traitorous faction).[63] The passage presents Cortés's thinking about the indigenous figure in terms of ontology: the very existence of a republican soul in an indigenous body must be eradicated. Cortés becomes intent on destroying Jicoténcal both morally and physically.

The result is that indigenous people are destroyed in body, although the spirit of virtue is not. Cortés tortures and mutilates soldiers and ultimately kills Jicoténcal in a public execution. Earlier in the book, when Jicoténcal sends spies into the Spanish camp, Cortés responds in a way so brutal as to be unknown in those parts: "Cortés had the Tlascalan soldiers mutilated, and after having them suffer the torment of having their ears, noses, fingers, and toes cut off, he was so cruel as to send them, thus, to their general so that they might tell him that he was ready to receive them" (X 43–44). As a metaphor for the breakdown of the Tlascalan senate, the dismembered body becomes the emblem of the end of the republic, which withdraws its support of Jicoténcal's troops. This scene also foreshadows the end of Jicoténcal and *Jicoténcal*. The book concludes not long after the Tlascalan republican is gagged and executed.

The indigenous body is lost in the veneration of the republican soul. This is no small matter for independence movements. Debra Castillo describes the process as follows: "The tragedy of the indigenous loss marking the initiation of the colonial period is balanced with and measured against the implicit celebration of the contemporary gain of independence."[64] That turn toward a decorporalized republicanism is one of the points of similarity between *Jicoténcal* and Filadelfia's other anonymous political writings. Leaving very little room for individual identity, a republican is expected to remain virtuous, self-abnegating, and bodiless, that is, anonymous.

What is Latino literature to make of the emphasis on an eternal (or at least recurring) republican soul of the Americas amid dead Indians? Unlike Varela's *El Habanero*, with its connection to a particular city and a link to Cuban nationalism, *Jicoténcal* refuses a national or even transnational connection. In some ways, Jicoténcal is *el amigo de los hombres* and the *verdadero Americano* that drafted the *cartas*. The novel becomes a rallying cry for republicans in various parts of the hemisphere to stand together in unity against Spain regardless of social positions at home. Anonymity, we come to see, is hemispheric and transatlantic rather than national or ethnic. By these terms, the participants in the new republican societies were abstract subjects rather than the people actually living in the new countries. But to say that anonymity is hemispheric reminds us simultaneously that republicanism can be universal, going back to a classical period and into the nations of the world in the early nineteenth century. If we are really following the anonymous track set forth by this book, then political action is connected to virtue, not to an ethnic subject. Without an identifiable author to play up ethnic connections, *Jicoténcal* is part of Latino literature (or Hispanic literary heritage) only if that body of literature includes anonymous publication in the Spanish language, a much different sense of Latino/a/x literature than the contemporary emphasis on social identity. *Jicoténcal* is part of another tradition: Latino literature as writing with a commitment to constitute societies across the hemisphere where a self-abnegating search for justice is the dominant concern. The identity of the author or even a political subject becomes less important.

 5

Leaving Filadelfia, or Archival Dislocations

In Reinaldo Arenas's novel *El mundo alucinante* (1969, translated as *The Ill-Fated Peregrinations of Fray Servando*) we encounter a pilgrim to Filadelfia walking down the street.[1] The character is the historical figure Fray Servando Teresa de Mier, also known as Servandus A. Mier, a Dominican friar who spent much of his life on the run, leaping hemispherically and transatlantically from Mexico to England, Cuba, Spain, the United States, and other countries. In Arenas's imagining of this 1821 Philadelphia scene, Servando is carrying three great sacks of garbage that he had collected for subsistence. Suddenly, he hears "the news that in Mexico at last *independence had been declared*." In the novel's first-person narration, Servando says, "And so with the Constitution in hand (for I had thrown down my sacks of garbage), I leaped for joy and landed (as a result of that same exceedingly joyous leap) on my own yearned-for soil."[2] For Arenas, the bags of garbage substitute for three rolls of bread in a scene from Benjamin Franklin's *Autobiography*, in which Franklin tells of arriving in Philadelphia with little money and purchasing "three great puffy rolls ... walk'd off with a roll under each arm, and eating the other."[3] Arenas emphasizes that the mythology of founding fathers can be rewritten ironically, for both Franklin and Mier. But the scene also points to another act of rewriting. On this particular leap back to Mexico, Servando takes up the pen after he is thrown back in jail: "There, with all the time in the world before me, I again read over the so-wished-for Constitution, and I began to emend it, marking it all over in its margins, for there was hardly anything in it but praise for that cunning rogue Iturbide, the fact of which brought on my first twinge (or fit, rather) of disappointment under independence."[4] Tracing in his novel the physical movement of a colorful figure who was one of the most important interlocutors in trans-American debates over independence from Spain, Arenas draws an analogy between this imaginative leap from Philadelphia to Mexico City and the notion that constitutional principles could be translated.[5]

In this scene as in much of Arenas's writing, it is difficult to decipher where the fictionalizing begins. The historical Servando de Mier had indeed made his way in 1821 to Philadelphia, where he stayed at the home of Manuel Torres, got embroiled in a schism at St. Mary's Catholic Church, and published pamphlets and books. Like the novel's character, Mier did return from Philadelphia to Mexico, and scholars have shown that he carried republican principles developed in heated debates with Manuel Torres's Filadelfia circle over what form of government should be adopted in Mexico.[6] But before returning to Mexico, Mier contributed to the print culture of anonymity that we discussed in the preceding chapter with the publication in 1821 of *Memoria politico-instructiva, enviada desde Filadelfia en Agosto de 1821, á los gefes independientes del Anáhuac, llamado por los españoles Nueva-España* (An instructive political account, sent from Philadelphia in August 1821, to the independent leaders of Anáhuac, called New Spain by the Spaniards). Emphasizing its Philadelphia starting point in the title, this book offered an elaborate argument against monarchy in light of recent historical events. Mier's title also uses the Nahuatl word *Anáhuac* to claim a preconquest name for the region and positions the term *New Spain* as a European imperial imposition. This move was not new for Mier, who often invoked the indigenous past to argue anticolonial positions.

Given Mier's engagement with Mexican politics and religious culture throughout his life, it is no surprise that he is often framed in relation to Mexican history, and some of his work is very relevant for Mexico's national archive, leading one historian to argue that he "embodied the ambiguities and complexities of the first phase of Mexican nationalism."[7] Filadelfia offers another way to consider Mier's work—as this chapter shows, he is a major contributor to Filadelfia letters—and we could well situate his publications in an archive that differs from the nationalist interpretation of Servando's trajectory. What do we lose by attempting (at times unsuccessfully) to bring Servando within the limits imposed by national (Mexican) archival designation? In many ways, Mier's *Memoria politico-instructiva* resists both a Mexican national frame and a Filadelfia reading of the type I have been developing in this book. *Memoria politico-instructiva* is connected to multiple sites, including Mexico, and it is a reminder that Filadelfia is part of a network with links to other sites in the Americas. Just as Servando lands in Mexico from one minute to the next, so do the texts, personal trajectories, intellectual concerns, and economic conditions of Filadelfia letters move toward various countries and contexts.

This chapter follows Servando's movement into an unexpected terrain: love letters. And these letters offer an example of what I call archival dislocation. Archival dislocation is about that which is out of place, out of time, even out of mind. It forces the question how scholarship should respond to items in an archival space (whether an actual archive or a frame conceived as such) that do not seem to correspond with the focus of the archive. The term *archive,* more trendy than a top-40 song and appearing in the titles of a variety of conference panels and papers, here is meant as a metaphor for a way of thinking that imposes a set of limitations on interpretation.[8] Mier's *Memoria politico-instructiva* offers an example of archival dislocation in that the book can seem out of place if approached from the terms of one archival holding. Even if read from Mexico, the title's invocation of Filadelfia prompts a sense of dislocation. Having spent much of his life on the run and trying to escape from confinement, Mier, along with his texts, exemplifies the process of moving away from an archival domicile.

But if *Memoria politico-instructiva* and the love letters in this chapter are examples of archival dislocation, it is important to emphasize that it is not these objects (letters, books, sentences, lines) that are out of place. Archival dislocation is an effect of the inferences prompted by a particular way of organizing knowledge. In other words, it is not the object of study that is out of place; rather, a way of thinking is dislocated from elements within the text. The notion of archival dislocation is informed by an analogy between an archive and a field of study, one of the contributions of Jacques Derrida's *Mal d'archive* (translated as *Archive Fever*). Derrida's book reminds us of the etymological and classical connotations of "the archive" but is trained on commenting about a school of thought, the twentieth-century development of psychoanalysis as a field. Derrida shows that a brick-and-mortar archive organizes materials under the banner of a term (e.g., *national archive*) and thus is comparable to an area of academic study, whether of disciplinary or interdisciplinary orientation. For example, the field of American literature frames the study of literature and culture through a term that implies national understanding. Taking us through a series of relations between an archival imperative and its psychoanalytic counterpart—including a suggestion that the archivist has something in common with a patriarch—Derrida questions the types of organization of knowledge that structure fields of study. In both cases, the archive and the field provide epistemological limitations. US American studies, for example, was founded with a type of archival organization made possible by a set of common texts, keywords, and approaches. The books that make up the field of American studies become its own archive. The same could be said for Latin American studies.

Archives can be sites of constraint because they seem to organize the contents under what Derrida calls "consignation."[9] An archive's holdings and its organizational premise reinforce and grant legitimacy to each other. A national archive, for example, is intricately bound to a nation-state, which helps to buttress the importance of the archive's materials, and vice versa.[10] In a different context, something like the Coca-Cola archives contain items of value to that particular company, and presumably its fans, and that company's value in turn infuses the archive with importance. Archivists or others who construct archives and maintain them try to define an archive's limitations, both physical and conceptual. And it is precisely the delimiting function that gives rise to the archive's own dislocation. Once the purported limits face the actual contents, the archive is out of place, if not out of line.

Philadelphia has its own purported archive. For centuries, *Philadelphia* has named connections to the establishment of the United States and its early statesmen, foundational documents, and major figures. Benjamin Franklin with his loaves of bread is one example of archival circulation. A physical example is his library, now called the Library Company of Philadelphia, which is joined by the Historical Society of Pennsylvania or the American Philosophical Society, repositories that are indispensable to the study of Philadelphia (and Filadelfia). But the international dimensions of Philadelphia's history and, as we see in this study, its hemispheric influence on intellectuals who moved in and out of the city in the early nineteenth century complicate Philadelphia's apparent local and national US emphasis. The premise that Philadelphia represents the founding of the United States is one dimension of a larger story that includes an intellectual conversation with both trans-American and transatlantic textual interchange, as the preceding chapters have shown. If we approach certain material from the nationalist dimensions of Philadelphia, it is possible for the archive to become estranged from its own content, in this case love letters within Filadelfia's archives.[11]

This chapter argues against a Filadelfia archive and instead makes a case for open-ended scholarship through specific textual examples: love letters with their own contexts. The chapter opens with a consideration of hemispheric Americas via the work of Edmundo O'Gorman, whose scholarship led him to Servando Teresa de Mier. Servando's letters then offer the ultimate example of Filadelfia movement and the print culture of affectionate letter writing that is intricately connected to his work and that of others in the Filadelfia circle. The chapter takes up archival dislocation through love letters: a captivating one written to Servando and a curious set of published love letters in Manuel Lorenzo de Vidaurre's *Cartas americanas, políticas y morales*. The chapter concludes with the ultimate dislocation: the letters of a dying man. These shifts in focus maneuver the conclusion of this book through various fields of study: US American studies, Latin American studies, and hemispheric studies. None of those alone is adequate for analyzing Filadelfia publications. My goal is to propose that this interdisciplinary study—and early Latino literature—should not become another archive that will present its own limits. Rather, this conclusion is an invitation for research agendas that do not speak to preestablished concerns. Early Latino literature should not be organized as an existing set of texts or entries in an anthology. It offers an opportunity to draw out the types of connections and movements, some of them hemispheric, that are part of the textual production of Filadelfia. National containment either in the United States or elsewhere will not suffice for considering cultures of movement. Texts may point in unforeseen directions. Archival dislocation is a reminder of this.

On Not Inventing America Again

As we see in the scene above, a tension is evident in Mier's work between his trans-American and transatlantic crossings and a deep engagement with Mexico's independence. This tension may explain why the Mexican historian Edmundo O'Gorman, one of the foremost theorists of the Americas, was drawn to the priest's work. In two collections of Mier's writings published in 1945, O'Gorman introduces Mier's conceptualization of America in relation to Spanish atrocities and European notions of superiority while also noting that Mier turns in 1821 toward specific political conditions in Mexico.[12] Mier's eight months in the United States, including stays in Philadelphia and New York, involve lively conversations with the likes of Vicente Rocafuerte; Mier stayed in Manuel Torres's Philadelphia home. The result is that Mier calls for a US-style federal republic in Mexico. In his *Memoria politico-instructiva*, Mier writes, "Paisanos mios! el fanal de los Estados Unidos está delante de nosotros para conducirnos al puerto de la felicidad" (My countrymen! the beacon of the United States is before us to guide us to the port of happiness).[13] As O'Gorman sees it, Mier took that position because the discourse over Mexico's future was driven by a false dichotomy between neo-monarchy and US republicanism. This dichotomy left out the possibility of a local approach to independence. O'Gorman writes, "La verdad es que la fórmula norteamericana se ofrecía con el carácter de necesaria, como único remedio, y esto sí que es una cosa terrible, una coyuntura trágica, porque implicó la pérdida de la libre y espontánea autodeterminación, precisamente en el momento eufórico en que se creía haber conquistado la libertad" (The truth is that the North American formula was offered under the guise of a necessity, as the only solution, and this is a terrible thing, a tragic situation, because it occasioned the loss of free and spontaneous self-determination, precisely at the euphoric moment when it was believed that liberty had been attained).[14] O'Gorman sees this as an example of the painful history of Latin America's adoption of models from Europe and the United States. From this perspective, the idea of transposing Philadelphia to Spanish America did not address the particular problems of new countries in the former colonies. But O'Gorman's conclusion also points to one of the temporal problems of archival dislocation.

Although correct about the political problems of transporting governmental models from one country to another, O'Gorman's perspective is the result of historical hindsight. A twentieth-century scholar, O'Gorman can offer that analysis only after the United States has developed as an imperialist power and an independent Mexico has failed to sufficiently improve living conditions for its indigenous people. Writing in 1821, Mier could still view US federalism as an antidote to imperial government and its logics. And for all Mier knew, federalism might have been the best approach for Mexico. Mier was influenced by notions of hemispheric Americanism that we have seen in Varela's *El Habanero* and in writings by Rocafuerte.

O'Gorman's interest in Mier and his times speaks to the relevance of movements out of Filadelfia in the early nineteenth century to future debates on hemispheric America's past. As Susana Rotker has written, Servando "looks intently backward, forward, and sideways in time."[15] That is to say, a hemispheric geographic conception of America is temporally relevant in 1821 but wanes and returns in historical cycles, clearly picking up steam from the 1930s to the 1950s and into the Cold War of the 1960s, a period that tracks a shift from the Good Neighbor policy to the Alliance for Progress. A decade after his books on Mier, O'Gorman published *The Invention of America: An Inquiry into the Historical Nature of the New World and the Meaning of Its History* (1958; 1961 in English), one of the most important books ever published on the challenges of conceptualizing hemispheric America. This book is well-trodden ground for scholars of "America," and here it can give us insight into archival dislocation.[16]

O'Gorman's book is about the problems of imposing meaning on an object on the basis of preexisting assumptions. *The Invention of America* opens with a challenge to the popular and historical belief that Columbus discovered America. In what was then a relatively controversial position, O'Gorman argues, "The 'new world' inferred by Columbus was not actually new, but was part of the familiar world of men."[17] That statement comes close to a postcolonial position validating the ontology of people living in the hemisphere before the arrival of Europeans; it is not a reference to arguments about which European reached the Americas first. Instead, O'Gorman seeks to undo the myth of the valiant sailor who bravely embarks on a transatlantic crossing to discover a new continent. O'Gorman reminds us that Columbus set out to find a route to Asia and ended by believing he had accomplished that. Because Columbus never realized where he had landed, he did not discover what came to be America. But this was not solely a matter related to Columbus. O'Gorman argues that Europeans were incapable of discovering America because they could approach it only from the limits of their own knowledge. In other words, they did not have the necessary information to apprehend, much less understand, what it was they had stumbled upon in the first voyages. For O'Gorman, discovery entailed comprehending what was encountered.

The challenge to the existing meaning of America that O'Gorman presents resonates with debates out of Filadelfia in the early nineteenth century. The goal of Filadelfia writers was to move beyond the colonial assumption that territories in the Americas were nothing more than an effect of Europe, the type of thinking that justified colonial subjection. Instead, they proposed a view of America as its own territory with its own history and even, via Filadelfia, its own governmental institutions. This is in part why constitutional debates of the type we saw in the preceding chapter (and which captivated Mier in 1821) are so important. It was not enough to be free of Europe; the Americas also needed to define themselves as independent nation-states.

For my notion of archival dislocation, O'Gorman introduces a scenario that takes us back to work inside an archive. From his perspective, the problem is not only that European colonists and archivists lack the necessary information to conceptualize what they have stumbled onto but also, more importantly, that they bring ways of understanding that may inhibit an independent consideration of the object at hand. Put another way, someone who approaches an archive from the perspective of US American studies sees herself or himself as working predominantly within an Anglophone enterprise and thus is unlikely to take up Spanish-language letters. A similar point could be made about scholars in Latin American studies who defend, sometimes vehemently, the separation of two Americas. This type of limitation is why early in his book O'Gorman introduces his definition of discovery with the example of someone doing research in an archive. "Let us suppose that the caretaker of an archive comes across an ancient papyrus in a cellar," O'Gorman writes. "The next day he brings it to the attention of a professor of classical literature, who after careful study realizes that it is a hitherto unknown text by Aristotle. Who is the discoverer of this document, the caretaker who found it or the professor who identified it?"[18] The analogy here between someone doing research in an archive and an early modern explorer trying to find "new" territories speaks to the challenges of reconceiving America academically. O'Gorman argues for an epistemological necessity: to identify the find, the researcher must have an understanding of what has been found. According to O'Gorman, Europeans coming to a new continent did not have that kind of context for identifying what they encountered. They could never get a new ontology of new lands and people. In turn, they invented America in light of what they knew from Europe. As a result, conquest and destruction followed. The implications of O'Gorman's argument continue to be extremely important: America was invented as an *effect* of Europe.

For O'Gorman the invention of America as a new world for European expansion had tragic consequences. Everything from the development of a discourse of European superiority to the actual conquest and destruction of native populations stemmed from the belief that America was a new territory where Europeans could exert their influence and expand their way of life. The invention of America became a way for Europeans to gain control over territories that they saw only in relation to themselves; as a result, the colonies could never be European enough. For one seeking to study materials across the Americas, O'Gorman's argument becomes a warning against imposing a ready-made frame on the historical alterity presented by texts such as those out of Filadelfia.

The archival scene as described by O'Gorman also helps us elucidate the challenges of archival dislocation. A scholar unable to understand a text because of the limitations of his or her knowledge is one example of archival dislocation. In other words, the starting frame of a field of inquiry is insufficient for texts that might speak simultaneously to multiple countries and contexts. In the case of research across the Americas, archival dislocations are not uncommon. For a scholar of Latin American studies to come across a book such as Mier's *Memoria politico-instructiva* or many of the other texts out of Filadelfia, the imperative, if not the temptation, is to interpret the text only in relation to the terms of a dominant field (or archive), particularly a national history. In this approach, which is common in historiography, Heredia is viewed as a national poet of Cuba, Rocafuerte as a historical figure of Ecuador, and Mier as a contributor to the independence movements of Mexico. We could say that outside of a sprinkling of articles over the years, the full scope of letters from Filadelfia has been hidden in the archive for decades. The challenge becomes how to read Filadelfia materials in relation to multiple territories and contexts, even moving toward unforeseen possibilities. And Mier's work offers such an opportunity.

Servando's (Textual) Indeterminacy

Servando's textual production is likely to be dislocated from any archive because as a group his texts do not fit easily into a particular literary genre or tradition; nor do they as a whole correlate with a particular place or nation. They exemplify the textual variety that I have associated with Filadelfia letters—but are also part and parcel of an Enlightenment way of moving outside of confined spaces—and they reflect his subjective indeterminacy. Mier's body of writing across the Atlantic includes essays, newspaper articles, memoirs, histories, and political books. His publications are in dialogue with a variety of topics, including Mexican history, Catholic history, trans-American journeys, London's Spanish-language print culture, the history of the Inquisition, and Filadelfia. While his publications do not make for a manageable archival foundation (a consignation other than Servando himself), his biographical trajectory is similarly off course. Mier was always on the run, jailed repeatedly and engineering the next escape. From the time when the Catholic Church first decreed his detention in 1794, Mier faced a succession of apprehensions and imprisonments.[19] But each new detention was followed by a new escape. In some ways, his incarceration can be a metaphor for an archive from which he was continually escaping. That explains in part the novelist Arenas's interest: Servando offers the experiences of a figure who cannot be contained. To place Servando in an archive is to lock him up the way authorities did in El Morro Castle.

Mier's work would be dislocated in an archive, considering that he was both fervently nationalist and hemispheric American. For Latino literature, Mier occupies a role similar to that of Heredia and other Filadelfia writers: he passed through the United States but produced writing that contributes to the field's anticolonial dimensions even as it motivates a conversation with a greater conception of America. His publications do not offer impressions of the United States, and thus they differ from the type of travel writing (descriptive accounts of visiting) we find in other letters from Filadelfia. However, Servando's work is deeply imbedded in US print culture, as we will see.

Born in 1763 in Monterrey, Mexico, when it was still under the Viceroyalty of New Spain, Mier entered the Dominican Order, became a priest, and earned a doctorate. Nettie Lee Benson describes him as "rich in knowledge and erudition and of refined manners, ... an orator of no small repute, a man of fire and undaunted courage."[20] The troubles began with his most notorious act, a sermon that shook Mexico's Catholic Church. In 1794, at the anniversary celebration of the Virgin of Guadalupe's apparition, Mier delivered an oration in front of the local archbishop and the Spanish viceroy as well as prominent members of his society. These annual speeches were usually a celebration and veneration of the supposed appearance in 1531 of Guadalupe, Mexico's patron. In what came to be seen by the church as a heretical account, Servando argued that Christianity had preceded the arrival of Spain in the Americas by hundreds of years. Mier's story was the following: the Virgin of Guadalupe had appeared first not to the indigenous boy Juan Diego in 1531 but to Saint Thomas the Apostle, who had come to the Americas to evangelize the indigenous population and was known by the local populations as the Aztec deity Quetzalcoatl, whose manifestation was a feathered serpent.[21] By conflating Saint Thomas and an indigenous deity, Mier's sermon in effect challenged the basis of the Spanish conquest, which was the arrogant belief that a Spanish right to rule the Americas was founded on the conversion of indigenous populations to Catholicism. In other words, Mier argued that Christianity had reached Mexico *before* Spain's arrival, a position that could justify independence on theological grounds. While Juan Germán Roscio, whom Mier called "mi amigo el célebre Dr. Roscio" (*M* 18), later argued for a theologically grounded notion of popular sovereignty, Mier had made a claim for Christianity in the Americas as preceding the Spanish monarchy.

The church responded swiftly to Mier's reconsideration of a theological assumption by banning him from carrying out priestly duties, including preaching. Mier was sentenced to be detained at a convent in Spain for a decade. But he escaped, and over the years he made his way to France and England, then back to the Americas. Scholars have counted at least seven carceral detentions, but he always managed to get away, and for the rest of his life he carried out a war against the Catholic Church. In his memoirs, he writes about the church: "The agents of Rome, in general, are rogues like those in every court. And in the court in Rome matters are dealt with as in others, by virtue of patrons, women and money."[22]

As a spatial story, Mier's life of trans-American and transatlantic movement reflects a relationship of self to territory that is much broader than the local considerations that are integral to the founding of nations (and archives). As Djelal Kadir has written, "Fray Servando's peripatetic way stations serve as historic markers between imperial entropy and postcolonial uncertainty, between orthodox conviction and the incomprehensible threat of heterodox insecurity."[23] Subsuming Mier into Mexico's history can offer only a partial accounting of his work. The print-culture conditions under which he worked were at odds with the nation, and they are at odds with the North/South, Anglo/Hispanic, US/Latin American divisions that are common today. To consider Mier's spatial story is to move beyond place, site, situatedness—toward another space. Michel de Certeau describes place as delimiting a field. By contrast, space, he writes, "exists when one takes into consideration vectors of direction, velocities, and time variables. Thus space is composed of intersections of mobile elements. It is in a sense actuated by the ensemble of movements deployed within it."[24] This takes us back to the discussion of José María Heredia's letter as a spatial practice in chapter 1. Movement scatters a familiar place and opens multiple avenues, and in the case of Mier the movement results in numerous Philadelphia publications.

Like Filadelfia writers who preceded him, Mier was able to publish materials in Philadelphia because he connected to the city's print culture. Here is how he landed in the United States. In 1821, colonial authorities in Mexico captured Mier and sent him to Spain; however, the priest managed to get off the ship in Havana and persuade his captors that he was too sick to continue the trip. Transferred from Havana's Morro Castle to a hospital, Mier escaped with the help of independence fighters in Havana. Vicente Rocafuerte was there and managed to get Mier on a ship to the United States; it is possible that the two traveled together since both were in the United States not long after that.[25] In Philadelphia, Mier participated in four publishing projects. One, articles in the *Aurora* most likely dictated by Mier praised him as a brilliant Mexican priest and freedom fighter. He also published two pamphlets, translated into English, in relation to a schism over church authority at St. Mary's Catholic Church. With the help of Torres, Mier ushered into publication a version of Bartolomé de las Casas's *Breve relación de la destrucción de las Indias Occidentales* (Philadelphia, 1821); and most significantly, he wrote and published the *Memoria politico-instructiva*. Each of these publications shed light on aspects of Filadelfia letters, including the economic relations that facilitated publication, the tension between self-promotion and anonymity, and the geographic flights that help us consider archival dislocation.

Mier's Filadelfia publications were bankrolled by his wealthy friends. As we have seen in chapters 1 and 2, the conjunction between Philadelphia printers and the trans-American elite led to the possibility of self-publication. In Philadelphia, Mier's benefactor was none other than Torres. A receipt in the Nettie Lee Benson collection at the University of Texas at Austin shows that Torres paid $158 for the paper and the printing and binding of the edition of Las Casas's *Breve relación* and $112 for the paper and the printing and binding of Mier's *Memoria politico-instructiva*.[26] The printer of both editions was J. F. Hurtel, who as usual was paid for the printing job rather than for functioning as a publisher of the work.[27] As Christopher Domínguez Michael has shown, Torres became enamored of Mier and saw him as an important publicist in the fight for the liberation of Mexico. Their affectionate relationship is captured in several letters sent from Philadelphia to New York during Servando's brief stay there in which Torres chides his friend for running off with books and copies of newspapers that Torres needs for his work. Torres writes, "Cuando preste a Vd la historia de la revolución de mexico, tube cuidado de advertirle que no me pertencía, Vd. se olvidó sin duda de mi precaución, y se la ha llevado" (When I loaned you the history of the Mexican revolution, I was careful to let you know that it did not belong to me; without doubt you forgot about my warning and have taken it).[28] In a succeeding letter, Torres generously agrees to let Servando keep the history book but demands the return of newspapers from South America that were supposedly also taken by the priest, along with a book belonging to William Duane.

This exchange of publications between Torres and Mier displays the importance of print materials to developing the cause against Spain. Torres's enthusiasm for Mier's edition of Las Casas—a chronicle of abuse against indigenous populations—is not surprising since that book had a history of being lobbed as a bomb against the moral legitimacy of the Spanish Empire. Jeremy Lawrance has described the book as "a weapon to blacken the name of Spain. It was translated into the languages of her imperialist rivals (Dutch, French, English) and furnished with illustrations."[29] Servando's Spanish-language Filadelfia edition included a thirty-five-page introduction by "Doctor" Mier that excoriated Spain for its abuse and murder of indigenous populations, drawing a line from the history of the conquest to the contemporaneous fight for independence. Mier concluded his introduction with the following reference to Las Casas as a saint:

> Americanos! La estatua de este santo falta entre nosotros. Si sois libres, como ya no lo dudo, la primera estatua debe erigirse al primero y mas antiguo defensor de la libertad de América. Alrededor de ella formad vuestros pactos y entonad á la libertad vuestros cánticos; ningun incienso puede serle mas grato. Yo le pondria esta ó semejante inscripcion.
>
> Pára, si amas la virtud,
> Pasagero: esta es su imágen:
> Venera á Casas, que fué
> De nuestros Indios el Padre.[30]

> (Americans! The statue of this saint is missing among us. If you are free, and I do not doubt you are, you should erect the first statue to the first and most ancient defender of America's liberty. Around its base you should work on your resolutions and sing your hymns to liberty; no other homage would be more appropriate. I would place this or a similar inscription.
>
> Stop, if you love virtue,
> Traveler: this is his image:
> Respect Las Casas, who was
> The Father of our Indians.)

In the passage and inscription Las Casas becomes not only a figure to be venerated but a revenant who can inspire the battles for independence in 1821. Like Servando himself, the founders of new countries are to look to Las Casas for the type of inspiration that will lead to new constitutions (*pactos*) and bring respect for indigenous populations. The reference to "our Indians" is at once paternalistic and integrationist; the point is that Mier's contemporaries should fight for the downtrodden. Here we see Mier's willingness to use propaganda, as the Las Casas book was considered to be, for furthering anti-Spanish positions, including the Black Legend, in England and the United States. Mier had already been involved in the publication of an 1812 edition of Las Casas with Blanco White in London.[31] While Las Casas's proposals for alleviating the plight of indigenous populations have been notoriously controversial because of his recommendation that African slave labor be used to ease demands on indigenous populations, the *Breve relación* as deployed by Mier and Torres in 1821 functioned as an attack on Spain by emphasizing the indigenous question as a symbol of colonial subjection.[32] This type of work led John V. Lombardi to argue that Mier's "greatest effort in behalf of independence was his propaganda." Lombardi continues, "It must be emphasized that Fray Servando was not a political theorist, but a propagandist. His purpose was always to convince, to persuade, or to inspire."[33]

Mier's venture into Philadelphia publishing led to a most curious case of translation, the change of his name to Servandus A. Mier. Mier became involved in a heated schism at St. Mary's Catholic Church, which was in the midst of a disagreement between parishioners and church authorities over the governing of the church. In the late eighteenth and early nineteenth centuries, trustees at several churches in the United States demanded greater participation in church administration, including the appointment of priests. Patrick Carey has described this as "an attempt to create an American national church—one identified with American republicanism, incorporating lay and clerical participation in local and national ecclesiastical administration, thereby establishing a constitutional balance of powers within church government."[34] More immediately and mundanely, the conflict at St. Mary's was about a particular priest, William Hogan, who was supported by a number of parishioners but was removed from his position by the local bishop. By the time Mier arrived, the conflict at the church was already heated, bringing to the forefront an ongoing disagreement over the influence of parishioners versus the authority of the church hierarchy. Dozens of pamphlets appeared on both sides of this debate in 1821 and 1822, with the printer and St. Mary's parishioner Mathew Carey contributing enthusiastically. Dale B. Light has described the context for the St. Mary's schism as follows: "At a time when the United States was becoming more nationalistic, more committed to the idea of secular progress, and when an increasing number of Americans accepted as a fundamental tenet the proposition that political authority ultimately resides with the people, the institutional structure of the Roman Catholic Church was becoming more monarchic, more committed to a supernatural interpretation of human affairs, and more imbued with a romantic vision of universal medieval Christendom."[35] In 1822, riots broke out at the church when a "large number of persons armed with clubs said to have been consecrated by the Bishop" squared off against parishioners and their supporters.[36] The schism became so notorious that it gave rise to a song published as *The Battle of St. Mary's: A Serio-Comic Ballad* (1822).

It appears that Hogan and possibly Torres, who was also a parishioner at St. Mary's, rushed into publication *The Opinion of the Rt. Rev. Servandus A. Mier, Doctor of Sacred Theology in the Royal and Pontifical University of Mexico . . . on Certain Queries Proposed to Him by the Rev. William Hogan* (Philadelphia, 1821). Mier explained the change in his name as a result of a double translation. His English being limited, Mier wrote the pamphlet in Latin and changed his name to Servandus and the Spanish inflection *de Mier* to *a Mier*. But once the pamphlet was translated into English, the preposition *a* was changed to an initial, and thus Servandus A. Mier. According to Mier, he had not been to St. Mary's Church and did not know that his responses to Hogan's queries would be published.[37] He also said that the translation he wanted for his last name was "of Meers," so that English speakers would have an easier time pronouncing his name.[38] The first pamphlet inspired a lively response, which in turn inspired a second pamphlet on the subject from Mier: *A Word Relative to an Anonymous Pamphlet Printed in Philadelphia Entitled, "Remarks on the Opinion of the Rt. Rev. Servandus A. Mier"* (1821). The pro-Hogan group responded with enthusiasm and on July 28, 1821, sent an official letter from the congregation thanking Mier: "Considering the great good they may produce on the minds of the Congregation we have the honor to represent, we should be wanting in our duty to you and to them, did we not in this public manner offer you our most cordial and sincere thanks for the honour you have done this Congregation by your learned opinions."[39]

What is most fascinating about Mier's pamphlets is that they interpret Hogan's plight and the schism at St. Mary's in relation to Spanish colonial subjection. Mier replays the controversy as a battle between republicans and monarchists. That is to say, Mier's defense of Hogan and his party is directly related to his views on the Catholic Church in Spanish America and his negative experiences with the church hierarchy. A priest, Mier argues, cannot be removed by a bishop; similarly, the local church administration in Philadelphia should not be dislodged by one situated in Europe.

For Mier (as for other Filadelfia writers), the change in the subjection of colonies to Spain is a spatial story, and his spatial reconsiderations create archival dislocations. At the root of their republican debates is the distinction between hemispheres, especially as that relates to monarchy—or to quote Mier, in a passage inspired by Thomas Paine's *Common Sense*, "La naturaleza no ha creado un mundo para someterlo a los habitantes de una peninsula en un otro hemisferio" (*M* 109; Nature has not created a world in order to submit it to the residents of a peninsula in another hemisphere). As a spatial effect, monarchy creates hierarchy, and in Spanish America that hierarchy comes to be defended through ideologies of divine sanction and genetic predisposition. Republicanism, by contrast, offers a more horizontal organization of society. When Servando returns to Mexico in the 1820s and is active in debates over the new constitution, he will refer back to the United States and argue for an "intermediate federalism" that gives less power to the provinces than the US Constitution gives to states.

The space of the Americas emerges in Mier's *Memoria politico-instructiva*, which offers an argument against the Plan de Iguala, the constitutional outline of the government proposed by the revolutionary leaders Vicente Guerrero and Colonel Agustín de Iturbide in 1821. Much to Mier's consternation, the plan called for a constitutional monarchy, a "monarquía moderada, a la constitución peculiar y adaptable del reino"—with Iturbide as Mexico's emperor. In his *Memoria,* Servando writes that he first learned about the Plan de Iguala while in Havana, where proponents of independence were considering whether Cuba could unite with Mexico in breaking away from Spain. The people in Cuba, Mier writes, became cold at the thought of an emperor in Mexico. "No, decían, así no nos juntamos, porque sería largar las cadenas para volver a tomarlas" (*M* 167; No, they said, under these circumstances we will not join you, because it would mean breaking out of chains only to shackle ourselves again). In the following passage, Servando describes how the plan for a constitutional monarchy in Mexico had been received in the United States:

> Vine á los Estados Unidos, y hallé una desaprobacion general del tal Plan. Los periódicos decian, que era el colmo de la imbecilidad, ó el desenredo digno del entremes miserable, que despues de once años estaba representando la América española, sin haber mostrado conocimientos, dignidad, caracter ni resolucion, como ya se habia deplorado en las discusiones respectivas á nuestra causa en el Congreso de Washington.
>
> El S.or. Dn. Manuel Torres, ministro de Colombia y yo, no hallamos otro arbitrio para volver por el honor de Mexico, sino contestar en los papeles públicos, que bien se podia ver, que la independencia absoluta era el objeto y la base del Plan, y el resto un estratagema politico imperado por la circunstancias para meter en la red á todos los partidos. (*M* 37–38)

(I came to the United States and found a general disapproval of such a plan. The newspapers were saying that it was the height of imbecility, or the confusion of a bad start, and that after eleven years the plan was representing Spanish America as not having understanding, dignity, character or commitment, a point in accordance with deplorable comments made in discussions about our cause in the Congress in Washington.

Mr. Manuel Torres, Colombia's minister, and I saw no option for defending Mexico's honor but to respond in the papers that total independence was the goal of the plan and the rest was a political strategy necessary to bring all of the parties into the system.)

The passage thus begins with Servando's move to the United States and calls attention to the public discussion about the Plan de Iguala. The view from the United States, according to Servando, was that Mexico's revolutionaries were unable to show character and dignity after the prolonged battle. It is not surprising that politicians in the United States opposed monarchy; it was not in the interest of the United States to have such a government as its neighbor. But the statements also contributed to what would become a common thread in the nineteenth-century United States: the proposition that Spanish America could not govern itself. In order to save face, Mier argued that the actual goal was absolute independence.

Keeping in mind the way Mier navigates space, we can see how his movements create what I call spatial dislocation in that he is anything but stationary. Movement, a Rocafuerte-like hopping around, influences not only the publication of his *Memoria politico-instructiva* in Filadelfia (written, as the title makes clear, for readers in Mexico) but also conceptions about governmental institutions.[40] The passage above displays both the movement of the hemispheric subject, Mier, and his participation in a local US print-culture context to discuss a constitutional plan written in Mexico. The book also contains references to Havana, showing how the spaces of independence were in flux at that historical moment. Servando writes for multiple audiences, both in Mexico and in other Americas, and is very aware of his rhetorical site of enunciation.

Mier's colorful life and the various polemics in which he engaged give rise to archival dislocation because no one archive can address the intellectual and print-culture currents of his day: the role and influence of the Catholic Church, the future of monarchy, and the organization of new nation-states. While his detentions and movements present a tension between limitation and escape from restrictions that are part of the revolutionary period, Mier's life is a reminder of how Filadelfia and its textual production were inextricable from various other geographic locations. Among the sites where Mier did his work was London, and in his final years London would make its way to Filadelfia via a letter that spoke to a romantic entanglement.

"For This Letter Is My Writing": Charlotte Stephenson

The letter was full of love. Epistolary exchanges are often about creating intimacy, or at least connection, but this one expressed longing. It came from London and was addressed to Mier from Charlotte Stephenson, the two separated not only by the Atlantic Ocean but also by the vicissitudes of independence movements in the Americas. Not having seen him for five years, Stephenson makes numerous references to the wars of liberation in Spanish America. "My Dear Friend I was glad to hear that Mexico is almost free, Because it will be an Event of Great happiness to you and Earnestly hope it will soon be so," she writes. Having settled in Philadelphia, Servando had gotten word to Stephenson to write to him care of Manuel Torres. The tone and phrasing of her note suggest that Servando and Charlotte had an amorous relationship. And this aspect of their exchange presents an archival dislocation in the public sphere of Filadelfia letters.

Letters from Filadelfia, as I have shown throughout this study, are mostly communications among and about men, and women seem invisible—or at times they emerge as objects of a male gaze. When José María Heredia walks through Filadelfia, he feels compelled to comment that on Chestnut Street he sees "beautiful girls, who are more abundant here than in any other part of the United States" and then says they are more beautiful than those in his hometown of Matanzas.[41] At other times epistolary exchanges include the occasional wish to say hello to a wife or some other relative, but for the most part references to women—either in the abstract, as a category of rights-bearing persons, or in the particular as authors or recipients—are absent from the personal writing or public discourse. In chapter 2, I argued that Félix Varela's insulting comments about Fannie Wright not only registered the importance of language in cementing homosocial bonds among the trans-American elite but also spoke to the limits of revolutionary ideas that stopped short of conceptualizing equality between men and women. In this chapter, we turn to two cases in which trans-American intellectuals did address women in the intimate epistolary form. The rarity of these exchanges in Filadelfia letters, one of them hidden among personal correspondence, makes all the more important the archival presence (and dislocation) of Stephenson's letter to Servando.

Charlotte Stephenson's letter is housed (dislocated) in the Nettie Lee Benson Latin American Collection in Austin, Texas. Its provenance is significant. Servando's papers in the Benson Collection were acquired as part of the Genaro García Collection, a gargantuan archive of papers and rare books acquired by the library in 1920, which put it on the map for its holdings in Latin American studies. The dislocation is not the effect of a wealthy university in the United States acquiring papers that might otherwise be part of a Mexican national archive (although that is the context); rather, the dislocation emerges because Charlotte Stephenson has little to do with Latin American studies (and nothing to do with with Texas). The content of the letter could direct it into other archival formations where it would speak differently: it is a poignant account of an independent-minded English working woman who had acquired literacy as an adult, a woman striving to overcome the limitations of social class and gender barriers. It landed in this collection, however, because of her friendship with a male Spanish American independence fighter.

Stephenson had, per the letter, spent time not only with Mier but also with General Francisco Javier Mina, a Spanish military leader who had been in London at the same time as Mier planning an invasion of Mexico. Christopher Domínguez Michael has shown that Mina and Servando worked closely on this attack, which they hatched in London, then refined during stops in New York and Baltimore and an 1816 visit to Manuel Torres, Pedro Gual, and other Filadelfia warriors. Making their way to Mexico with stops in New Orleans and Galveston to gather material support, Mina and his companions ultimately made it to Soto la Marina, on what is today the northeast coast of Mexico, on the Gulf. There, a battle led to Mina's death and Mier's apprehension and trial before the Inquisition. Domínguez Michael argues that Servando positioned himself as a religious counselor to the expedition so that he would be tried for religious misconduct rather than revolutionary insurrection.[42] Other historians argue that it was Mier's family connections that helped him escape execution.[43] Either way, Mier was imprisoned by the Inquisition in Mexico City, and he remained there for almost five years before he managed to make his way to Philadelphia. During that time, he had been incommunicado with his friends in London and elsewhere, including Stephenson.

Stephenson's letter, dated August 6, 1821, opens with an attempt to renew their acquaintance after five years of absence. It says she had sent multiple letters that had gone unanswered before finally hearing from him again. The lack of communication had led Stephenson to conclude that Servando had been killed. In a sentence that sounds remarkably close to something two lovers would exchange, she writes, "I do not know what sensations you may feel on Reading my Letter after so many years absence but I must say I cannot Describe the joy I felt on once more seeing the Hand writing of my Dear friend and learning you was well and happy and Godsend you may Remaine so will be my constant prayer."[44] The references to sensation and indescribable joy at seeing the handwriting of someone considered "dear" are a rare reminder, among the Filadelfia letters I have been reading, of the powerful emotional effects occasioned by the materiality of epistolary exchange: the actual ink and paper touched and handled by the correspondent, the impression of the writing, can serve as proof of life and a call to a connection. Stephenson's letter is a tour de force that insists on this emotional connection, at once chiding Mier for minor emotional lapses and proclaiming that a deep affection exists between them.

The effect of handwriting was no small matter in the context of Filadelfia's epistolary connections. The flourishes in signatures that mark individuality and authenticity may well have evoked responses, including affection, respect, even admiration. Servando's intricate crisscross flourish is one of the most memorable among those in his circle (see fig. 3). Stephenson, who would have recognized Servando's signature from previous correspondence, displays her newly learned hand in signing off (fig. 4). Vicente Rocafuerte's signature is distinguished, simultaneously serious and flashy (fig. 5).

Handwriting could convey something about the writer, perhaps age, mood, or even health. In the case of Manuel Torres, his execrable handwriting in letters to Servando looked a bit like scribbling, and it is possible that the serious illnesses that plagued him in 1821 (he would die the following year) affected his hand. These flourishes, or the lack thereof, transfer something of the person in the materiality of the letter at a time in history when it was not always possible to ascertain the living presence of someone, especially in the troubled times of the wars of independence. A handwritten letter can attest that the writer is alive. And for lovers it conveys the ongoing presence of an intimate connection, which is the implication of the tone in Stephenson's letter.

In a particularly telling moment that implies that Mier did more than offer Stephenson spiritual guidance, she reproves him for having

Fig. 3. Fray Servando Teresa de Mier's signature, 20 June 1821. (Nettie Lee Benson Latin American Collection, University of Texas Libraries, University of Texas at Austin)

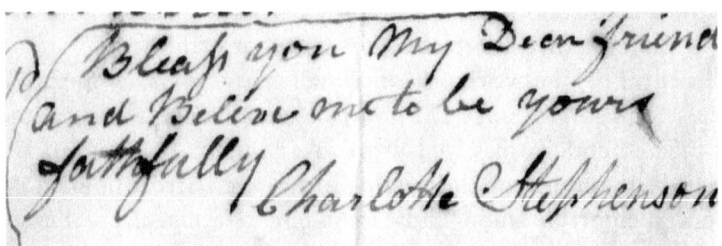

Fig. 4. Charlotte Stephenson's signature, 6 August 1821. (Nettie Lee Benson Latin American Collection, University of Texas Libraries, University of Texas at Austin)

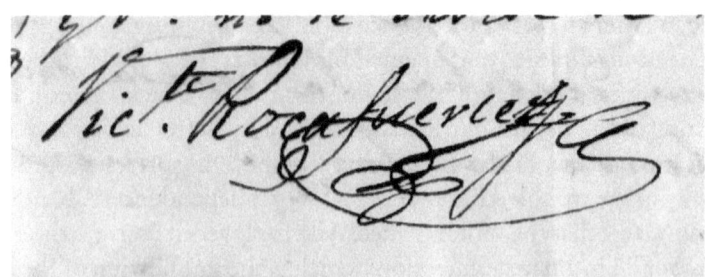

Fig. 5. Vicente Rocafuerte's signature, 31 July 1821. (Nettie Lee Benson Latin American Collection, University of Texas Libraries, University of Texas at Austin)

addressed their correspondence to her sister, Mary. Servando's papers in the Benson Collection include a copy of a letter to "Mi mui amadas Mery y Charlotte," but that letter is not addressed to a particular location and may be a copy of what he actually sent. He writes, "Me agrava que Ust.d Mary y Charlotte estén buenas, padre madre y hermanos á quienes envio muchas mem.a Escribanme dirigiendo las cartas—D.or Mier—at care of Mr. Manuel Torres—Philadelphia. A-dios, mis queridas, y manden á su afmo amigo" (I am concerned that the two of you, Mary and Charlotte, are well, along with your father and brothers, to whom I send many greetings. Write to me by sending the letters to Dr. Mier. . . . A-dios, my beloved ones, and direct your most affectionate friend).[45] Charlotte was having no intrusion of her sister into their epistolary relationship. She responded as follows:

> I have taken the Liberty of answering your letter although you sent it to Mary, which I think is very strange. I do not know that I had offended you in any way that you should write her and not to me. You did once honner me with your Friendship and I Flattered myself you do so still, as I have done nothing to abuse your confidence and Friendship but rather to Deserve it more then [*sic*] before, but 5 years is a very long time, and it may have made a very many alterations in my Dear Friend's Disposition and Heart, but I can lay my hand on my Heart and say with truth that I still think of you with Respect and Gratitude for all your Goodness to me. And if you should never write to me or see me more, you will still be the same Dear friend in my Heart as you was in the first days of your kindness to me.

With a touch of jealousy toward her sister, Charlotte characterizes as "strange" the notion that she would be on the same footing with Mary. "Friendship" here is a code for a level of intimacy that goes beyond what he had with Mary, and we can speculate on "all the Goodness" that they shared. In a sentence that bears the weight of epistolary distance—for if the letter is a bridge, it is also a reminder that London is a long way from Philadelphia—Charlotte faces the real possibility that they may never see each other again and proclaims that he will remain as dear as he ever was. The line "And if you should never write to me or see me more" speaks to a deep emotional attachment, although in this case tempered by the hope inspired by the renewed epistolary connection. The two never did meet again. Mier left Philadelphia for New York in September 1821 and did not return to London before his death in Mexico in 1827.

The power of this letter and the reason why it is ultimately about Charlotte Stephenson's life—and not only about her attachment to the peripatetic priest—is that it gives us a window into the financial challenges faced by a working woman in early nineteenth-century London. Much of the letter is about her money troubles, for example, her attempt to collect on a debt owed to Mier, the money from which he had offered to pass on to her. The letter offers a view into the dire situation she faced: her two options were to "either go to service or live a life of infamy." She says that she could not submit to the latter, and ultimately Stephenson finds a place working for a family, taking on "hard" labor at low wages. But what seems most important to convey to Servando is that she has learned how to write since they last saw each other. She writes, "You may Remember that when you left London I could not write and that Mary used to write my letters for me. Thank God it is not the case now, for this Letter is my writing. I learnt soon after you left. This I am sure you would be glad to hear." (Perhaps Servando had sent the first letter to Mary thinking that she would be the one able to write back.)

Charlotte Stephenson's proclamation that "this Letter is my writing" connects the question of literacy—her triumphant acquisition of a skill that could better her life chances—to the sensuality and intimacy of this exchange. Charlotte's emphasizing that the letter is her writing completes her offer of continuing admiration and presumably the (mutual?) adoration. In this case especially, a correspondent's hand is a substitute for the body. In concluding the letter with the most affectionate *despedida,* "God bless you My Dear friend and Believe me to be yours faithfully," Charlotte emphasizes faith in their connection. While I have argued that other epistolary exchanges among the trans-American elite were intimate in nature, I ascribe an amorous connection in this case not because of Stephenson's gender but because she deploys phrases about not hearing from him for years and about possibly never seeing him again and includes references to her heart, all of which suggest that there was an intense attachment.

None of the archives we are following here have a conceptual space for Charlotte Stephenson's letter. She cannot be framed in terms of Mexican nationalism, US American studies, Latino literature, not even Filadelfia, although her letter is addressed to Mier in Philadelphia. Her letter opens up a new way of seeing Mier as engaged in intimate transformations with people other than the future male Mexican citizen-voters he imagined in his handling of the flawed 1821 constitution. And yet in classifying her letter as significant only because of her connection to Mier, as the preservation of the letter in the Benson Collection implicitly does, we would reiterate the blindness of the trans-American elite to the gendered limitations of their ability to think of a political subject as a man. Stephenson's letter is dislocated, done an injustice, by being buried in the Servando archive, and yet it also helps dislocate that archive in important ways. Another example of the unexpected routes that can be opened by my notion of archival dislocation in relation to the experiences of women can be found in one of the most curious texts out of Filadelfia.

The Wolf and His Sister-in-Law

From the title one would think that Manuel Lorenzo de Vidaurre's *Cartas americanas, políticas y morales* (1823) is another among many salvos on independence and republicanism published in Filadelfia. The texts discussed in the preceding chapters are examples of pamphlets, articles, and books that address independence efforts, the definition of America, republican government, and, in the case of *El triunfo de la libertad sobre el despotismo,* the religious morality of popular sovereignty. The title of Vidaurre's contribution is similar to that of other books and precedes the anonymously published *Cartas de un americano* (1826), discussed in chapter 4. Vidaurre's *Cartas americanas,* totaling almost five hundred pages in two volumes, does offer discussions of political topics. But Vidaurre departs from other Filadelfia books by inserting numerous letters addressed to a female correspondent. This part of his *Cartas* is about Vidaurre's passionate and self-described debilitating love for his sister-in-law, with whom he had an ongoing and semipublic amorous relationship in Peru under the roof he shared with his wife and children.[46]

Vidaurre's *Cartas americanas* takes the intimacy of epistolary forms that I have associated with republican brotherhood into an explicit affective and sexual relationship with a woman. While we have to dig in an archive to read Charlotte Stephenson's tender missive to Mier, Vidaurre paraded his relationship with his sister-in-law across the Americas in a Rousseauian fashion. His doing so reminds us of the gendered privilege that sustains the trans-American elite even as he positions this love relationship within the revolutionary energy that sustains him and that feeds his project to print the letters in Filadelfia. His public parading of this relationship raises questions about the lives of upper-class women in Peru at the same time that the amorous conceit functions as an important dimension of the book. Few Filadelfia texts offer thoughts about the role of women in the Spanish

American context, whether in the present or in the dreamed-of republican future. But the married Vidaurre broadcasts self-involved amorous claims to a younger woman, Josefa Luisa Rivera, who was living in his household. Vidaurre publishes letters by Rivera in *Cartas americanas,* an unusual attempt to bring her voice into a conversation about the preoccupations of men in his circle.

Vidaurre (1773–1841), a jurist and essayist at the center of debates over independence in his native Peru, changed his views about the future of the Americas from the second decade of the nineteenth century to his time in the United States in the 1820s.[47] Although for years he had remained a reformist willing to accept some form of monarchy, Vidaurre eventually became a supporter of Simón Bolívar and called for independence. Like other trans-American elite, Vidaurre came from one of Lima's most established families and was educated in one of the city's most prestigious schools. He was inducted into the equivalent of the bar at age twenty-four, and by the time he was twenty-six he had received a doctorate in law from the University of San Marcos.[48] His financial resources allowed him to travel to the United States twice during the 1820s. In 1821, he was exiled to Spain and then made his way to Philadelphia, where he published *Cartas americanas* and another book, *Plan del Perú* (1823), the latter dedicated to Bolívar. When he returned to Peru, South America had gained independence, and Bolívar appointed Vidaurre chief justice of Peru's Supreme Court. In 1828, as a result of battles with the legislature, Vidaurre was thrown in jail and then put on a ship by his political opponents and expatriated from Peru.[49] He made his way to the United States, where he published, *Efectos de las facciones en los gobiernos nacientes* (The effects of factions on new governments) in 1828, a book with vigorous attacks on his opponents.[50] He also published a meditation on new laws for Peru after colonial rule, *Proyecto de un código penal* (Boston, 1828). His Philadelphia-Boston output is significant, much of it in keeping with the strictly political, legal, and religious discourse of most Filadelfia writing.

What are we to make of his turn from the more politically loaded discussion to the proclamations about his love life in the *Cartas?* Public discussions about personal love were not circulated in letters from Filadelfia, although the romance plot in *Jicoténcal* is in keeping with conventions of the novel. Addressing some of the letters to "Amada mía," Vidaurre opens his *Cartas* in a tortured confessional mode regarding what he portrays as an illicit love relationship. In a letter addressed to his sister-in-law early on, he describes himself as a wolf feasting on the beauty and graces of a younger woman: "Sí, yo soy el criminal, el delincuente. Yo debía ser el custodio de tu inocencia, y como hambriento lobo te sacrifiqué a mi irracional apetito. ¡Pero ah! ¿Eran posible las refleciones delante de tu belleza?" (Yes, I am the criminal, the delinquent. I should have been the custodian of your innocence, but like a ravenous wolf I sacrificed you to my irrational appetite. But wait. Was it possible to be rational before your beauty?).[51]

Vidaurre's published letters to his sister-in-law effectively turn the *Cartas americanas* into a strange hybrid text, part discussion of political issues and part salacious memoir; at times it seems an attempt at epistolary fiction. Influenced by various generic traditions, this book is a prime example of what I am calling archival dislocation, in this case partially dislocated from the archive of politically oriented Filadelfia letters that I have been building in this study. *Cartas americanas* contains enough political content—letters on the Inquisition, slavery, governmental organization—that it would be possible to develop discussion of the book along the political lines of other texts, but the archival dislocation prompts at least two other directions for interpretation. First, the epistolary fiction of eighteenth-century love affairs, particularly via Rousseau, whom Vidaurre emulates. Also, Vidaurre's letters recount experiences living in Lima with Rivera, and thus the memoiristic element is anchored in the social milieu of early nineteenth-century Peru. Vidaurre's movement from South America to Europe and then to Philadelphia (the print culture that allows him to publish this account) creates a text that lends itself to dislocation. While some of the letters in volume 2 were written in the United States, Vidaurre ends his first volume with the following: "All of the letters in this volume were written in Lima." And it is in Lima that he engages with European intellectual traditions.

The hybrid effect of *Cartas americanas* is created in part by the book's conscious engagement with Rousseau's *Julie, or the New Heloise,* published originally in 1761 as *Lettres de deux amans* (Letters of two lovers). (Vidaurre probably read the book in French, thus his use of *cartas* in the title.) Like Rousseau, Vidaurre gave precedence to the authenticity of his love for Rivera over a more rational adherence to social conventions on the institution of marriage. In volume 2, Vidaurre publishes a letter to Rivera written after his departure from Lima:

> Los dioses mismos, dice la Mitología, no fueron siempre constantes: sus amores se suceden, y esta lección consuela al mortal de inferior naturaleza. Sí: yo renuevo al amante de *La Nueva Eloísa.* Oye mi confesión: sincero es mi arrepentimiento, perdóname y compadéceme: da a conocer al universo que

el poema de Rousseau no peca contra la verosimilitud. Nunca te amo tanto como hoy.[52]

(The gods themselves, mythology tell us, were not always constant: their loves come and go, and this lesson consoles a mortal of inferior nature. Yes: I resemble the lover of *The New Heloise*. Hear my confession: my repentance is sincere, forgive me and take compassion: let the universe know that Rousseau's poetry does not stray from verisimilitude. I never loved you as much as today.)

The *Cartas americanas* give Vidaurre a chance to frame his own life alongside and in relation to Rousseau's fiction. Sometimes called the Peruvian Rousseau, Vidaurre compares himself to the Genevan writer at various points. Here an episode from *Cartas americanas* about the Inquisition is instructive. Vidaurre notes that he keeps some books that are prohibited but keeps them locked in his room so that no one has access. One afternoon after he has finished tea and enjoyed a relaxed conversation with a friend, two authorities from the Inquisition arrive at his door to check on him. "No fue tan grande el sobresalto de Rousseau cuando supo que se habia librado un mandamiento contra él, como el que sentí al ver estos dos canes que me figuré con sus colmillos prontos y afilados á destrozarme" (Rousseau's shock at finding that his books had been banned was not as great as the one I felt upon seeing those two canines, who I imagined to be bearing sharp fangs and ready to destroy me).[53] (Vidaurre had at an early age been dragged before the Inquisition and confessed to having read texts by Montesquieu and Rousseau as well as Ovid's *The Art of Love*.)[54] Vidaurre invokes Rousseau at various points in the *Cartas*, including when he says that as a result of social conditioning humans are driven more by greed and self-interest than by attention to public matters and thus many ignore tyrannical government. He claims amity with Rousseau: "Juan Jacobo Rousseau, amigo mío, conocía perfectamente el corazón del hombre" (My friend Rousseau was well acquainted with the hearts of men).[55]

Vidaurre's attempt to incorporate Rousseau's thought into his work, his emulation of elements of *The New Heloise* in *Cartas americanas,* depicts a desire to situate himself alongside European Enlightenment thinkers. Like Rousseau, Vidaurre opens his letters with a departure, a "Farewell to the Beloved." "Ya llegó el momento terrible" (The terrible moment has arrived) is the opening line of Vidaurre's *Cartas*. Rousseau, at least in translation, is less melodramatic: "I must fly from you, Mademoiselle, I know I must."[56] At times, Vidaurre's *Cartas* shares the type of intimate information that is appropriate for epistolary fiction. Unlike Rousseau, however, he rationalizes his feelings with reference to Catholic devotional practice, such as when he imagines Rivera standing before Jesus Christ pleading for the well-being of her lover, Vidaurre himself. Among letters that recount his dreams about Rivera is one in which he sees her wearing "una túnica blanca más que la niebe, coronada de rosas, tus pies de alabastro descalsos, los cabellos de oro tendidos por la espalda" (a tunic whiter than the snow, crowned by roses, your alabaster feet bare, your golden hair flowing down your back).[57] This odd conjunction of intense self-involved romantic involvement and Catholic self-abnegation is part of the panorama of political thinking that informs Vidaurre's US writing. To conclude his lengthy political manifesto, the 1828 *Efectos de las facciones,* Vidaurre compares his political sacrifices to those of the "martirio de los Christianos de la primitiva iglesia" (the martyrdom of Christians in the primitive church). He writes, "Los apostoles de la libertad queremos sellar nuesta [sic] mision con nuestra sangre" (the apostles of liberty want to seal our mission with our blood).[58]

In other letters, he attempts to reconcile the spiritual connection he imagines with the physical union he experiences with Rivera: "Después de ciento veinte nueve días que hacen en esta fecha que unidas nuestras almas aún más que nuestros cuerpos, nos juramos un verdadero matrimonio en el eterno enlace de nuestros corazones" (One hundred twenty-nine days have passed since our souls in addition to our bodies united and we swore a true marriage in the eternal connection of our hearts).[59] At times, he attempts to step back and give her advice for the future, suggesting that she find a nice (single) man to marry: "Elige un joven que sea mayor que tú de ocho a diez años. Esta es una prudente diferencia. Las flores más hermosas se marchitan más pronto. Procura examinar sus pensamientos y su salud. Un hombre corrompido en alma o cuerpo te hará para siempre desgraciada" (Choose a young man who is eight to ten years older than you. This is a prudent age difference. The most beautiful flowers wither more quickly. Seek to examine his thinking and health. A man who is corrupt in soul or body will make you forever unhappy).[60] He is concerned that she will grow old without a husband, something he believes will affect her negatively in Lima society.

While the invocation of Rousseau makes the *Cartas americanas* one of the more literary texts in Filadelfia textual production—Vidaurre positions himself as a character, and in many ways he is—the letters have another effect in that they present an archival dislocation related to real life in colonial society. They point us toward social conditions in Lima, in relation to both Vidaurre's ability to conduct such a relationship under his own roof and how Rivera might live in the wake of its public revelation. Vidaurre was clearly a patriarch whose financial and legal control over the people under his roof, including his sister-in-law, was extreme. It is impossible to know what degree of consent Rivera exercised over their relationship. (I have avoided referring to it as an "affair" because it is unclear how much of it was secretive and at what point patriarchal prerogative gave way to her own agency.) But what is clear is that Vidaurre uses the literary frame of the amorous love letter to validate and exercise control over the way their relationship would be publicly understood. He is self-involved to the extent that the persona in the *Cartas* confesses to Rivera indiscretions with other women, indicating that her role is to accept and discount these experiences and continue to join in venerating their true love together. The ability to publish personal letters (in Filadelfia) is itself indicative of his privilege, which insulated not only him but to an extent also Rivera, who, as an upper-class woman, continued to circulate in Lima society after their relationship became public with Vidaurre's *Cartas* effectively shifting into the realm of published literary nonfiction.

But the question about the relationship between fiction and reality, a mainstay of the novel as form, becomes vexed when Vidaurre's account is read as an inscription of social mores. William Ruschenberger, a US naval officer who in 1834 publishes an insulting travelogue account of South America—its geography, institutions, people, and moral attitudes—delves into the relationship between Vidaurre and Rivera in a lengthy account of Peru and Lima. "The *morale* [sic] of Lima society may be gathered from the fact that females, married or single, who are known to have yielded to amatory intrigues, are received in the fashionable circles," he writes in *Three Years in the Pacific* (1834). "Few people who know anything of Lima," Ruschenberger continues, "have not heard of the celebrated Josepha Luisa, the heroine of a correspondence between herself and a notorious judge, which was printed at Philadelphia in 1823, under the title *Cartas Americanas*."[61] Ruschenberger is shocked that Vidaurre "holds a distinguished place in the government" and that although Rivera is known to have mothered some of his children, she is "seen at the theater, and everywhere with the haut ton [fashionable society]."[62] He is less enthusiastic than Vidaurre's letters about the enduring power of their love. "The passion which suggested the correspondence no longer exists; yet neither of them is ashamed of its publicity."[63] Ruschenberger is all too aware of the literary aspects of the letters and includes a mention of the *Nouvelle Heloise*, but he marshals the episode as evidence for a sociological discussion of attitudes in Lima high society.

But that type of reading, in which Vidaurre's *Cartas* becomes a reflection of society, discounts the possibility that it is an argument against his society (or at least against the limitations of marriage) in the independence period. Historians of Latin America have written about the use of marriage to regulate society during the colonial period and into the early independence period. In 1776, the Spanish Crown had issued a law mandating that whites—mulattoes, blacks, mestizos, and other mixed races were excluded—obtain parental permission before marriage, a form of social control intended to ensure racial separation and social inequality.[64] For Vidaurre the choice of marriage partner would have been influenced by his class position. His wife may not have been entirely his choice. Although Vidaurre was confident enough in his Rousseauian posture to publish an account of the illicit relationship internationally, the tortured letters also show that despite whatever notoriety they may have enjoyed, the two suffer from concerns about the effects of living in a Catholic society. He closes the book with the recognition that he will be criticized for the display of prohibited passions and that he may be called a revolutionary against the church and colonial society. The libertine Vidaurre emphasizes that he is committed to the Catholic Church and does not include anything heretical in his book. While he lives out his desire and love for his sister-in-law in body and in the print culture of Philadelphia, the effects on her are complicated by the intense moral prohibitions of her society. If the word *affair* is not adequate, neither can this be framed as a consensual relationship between equals.

The little sense we have of Rivera's part is mediated by the editorial work undertaken by Vidaurre in *Cartas americanas*. In one of the few examples of published Filadelfia letters written in a woman's voice, *Cartas americanas* includes two letters purportedly written by Rivera. But Vidaurre notes that his priest has made him discard many of the letters from Rivera, and thus the correspondence is one-sided. In one case, she is given a voice taking ownership of the relationship:

> En mi casa, en el pueblo, y tal vez en el mundo pareceré desgraciada. No lo soy: la memoria de tu amor me recompensa de un modo ventajoso todos los bienes que he perdido. Te amaré eternamente y el poder amarte así es una de las causas que me conducen al templo.[65]

(In my house and our town and even before the world I will appear disgraced. But I am not. The memory of your love is ample compensation for all I have lost. I will love you eternally, and the ability to love you in that way will be my safe conduct to the temple.)

The mutual love expressed in these lines is vexed by Vidaurre's novelistic suggestions and his own admission that he does not have enough letters from Rivera to present a more full accounting of her thoughts. How much of her letter is part of Vidaurre's construction of a Filadelfia book?

In a second letter, Rivera takes up directly the political context of Vidaurre's being exiled to Spain as a result of his political views: "¿En fin el gobierno español que has defendido con capricho te expatria injustamente? ¿Obedeces a un decreto tiránico, que te separa de la deliciosa Lima de tus... de mí para siempre? ¿Cómo cumples los juramentos que me hiciste de ser mi guía, mi tutor, mi amigo, mi padre?" (In the end, the Spanish government, which you have defended intermittently, expatriates you unjustly? Are you obeying a tyrannical decree that separates you from delicious Lima... and from me forever? How will you comply with the oaths you made to be my guide, my tutor, my friend, my father?). She entreats him not to go and to instead learn to live in Lima clandestinely, avoiding the polemics that have attracted the attention of Spanish authorities. "Yo me ahogo en mi llanto. Haz este sacrificio, para la que ya no tiene más que sacrificarte" (I drown in my tears. Make this one sacrifice for the one that has sacrificed all for you).[66] The archival dislocation here raises a problem: are we to search for the social conditions of upper-class women in Lima or even to attempt to locate originals of the letters in order to gauge how much purported truth there might be in Rivera's letters? Archival dislocation is often an effect of the challenges of interdisciplinary research, which in this case moves from Filadelfia to Lima and raises questions about gender hierarchies in multiple countries and contexts. What do we make of these expressions of love, which, however fleeting, may contain their own truth?

Despite the heartfelt intrusion of these two letters, the book fails miserably as an epistolary novel in that it largely lacks a two-way correspondence. More often than not, Vidaurre writes without a response, and the letters are regularly interspersed with meditations on various political, social, and religious topics. One particularly passionate letter is followed by another titled "Observations on the English Government." At one point Vidaurre takes up the question of slavery, condemning his own limited views on the issue and the failures of education to adequately address this type of oppression:

"¡Cuántos errores! ¡Cuántos perjuicious! ¡Cuánta ignoracia!" (What errors! What prejudice! What ignorance!).[67] He does not address US slavery specifically but concludes that biological racial difference does not exist and that skin color should not lead to prejudice. "Negros, blancos y amarillos, hombres más o menos oscuros, todos somos de una misa especie: nuestras necesidades y pasiones no se diversifican sino por la educación y las costumbres" (Blacks, whites, and yellow men, men who are more or less dark, we are all of one species: our necessities and passions become different only through education and custom).[68] Men from Africa, he concludes, will be judged at the final hour for their sense of justice and their commitment to beneficence.

The religious elements of Vidaurre's *Cartas* indicate, as do those in Juan Germán Roscio's *El triunfo de la libertad sobre el despotismo*, that the Catholic Church at times looms large over Filadelfia letters because it is so important to Spanish American countries. Vidaurre insists on the inclusion of the word *moral* in his title: "Mesclo la religión y la moral, por que de sus principios bien entendidos depende la felicidad de los pueblos" (I mix religion and morality because the happiness of nations depends on the full understanding of the principles that come from them).[69] All of which points to a necessary connection between religiously inflected morals and political vision, a claim that, in the abstract, could make for dry reading. But Vidaurre does ultimately turn the lens of morality on himself, if only to offer justifications for his actions, as when he spends several pages discussing whether it is acceptable for siblings (as in-laws were construed at this time) to marry. He concludes, as did courts in different countries, that the Bible does not prohibit it.

The family melodrama of *Cartas americanas* and Vidaurre's transposition of elite male privilege from one nation to another reminds us that hemispheric work should be aware of the way movement across countries also raises questions about limitations for women. But the archival dislocations suggested by Josefa Luisa Rivera and Charlotte Stephenson also push us to go further into the terrain of affect in general. What can we say about the emotional life of the trans-American elite and the social limitations of the women excluded from their brotherhood? Should we pathologize the psychically restless Vidaurre—as one of his biographers does in noting that in "his depressions and mystical fervor there was much craziness, even hysterics"[70]—and take the *Cartas* as a record of a prodigious mind with an unstable personal life? Vidaurre's letters suggest that he was depressed (the word he uses is *melancolía*), and his movement to Spain and Philadelphia was accompanied by crises that cannot be readily categorized as solely intellectual, political, social, or emotional but that are affected by all of these factors. This raises a variety of questions that push beyond the various fields of research informing this study: What were the psychological effects of exile and migration, and to what degree can we read them in these texts? Vidaurre concludes the *Cartas* by describing the letters as a repository of his secrets and emphasizing that he went public with his personal life to show that his heart and his deeds were pure and no more sinful than those of other men. Arguing against hypocrisy, Vidaurre seeks (as he does for his nation) to move away from the blemishes of the past and toward a future of proud and public conduct.

Vidaurre's *Cartas* and other letters from Filadelfia remind us that archival research in the Americas at times has to rely less on the structure of a field and more on a process of interpretation and analysis that is open to unforeseen directions, including topics, places, and languages that are not common at the starting line of fields that lead to this research. *Cartas americanas* raises unanswered questions about the emotional life of the people who produced, received, and circulated Filadelfia letters. So too does my final example, which explores the letters of a dying man.

Dying Letters from Filadelfia

One of the early translators of Filadelfia, as we saw in chapter 1, was Manuel García de Sena, whose *La independencia de la Costa Firme, justificada por Thomas Paine* sought to circulate translations of Paine and other US revolutionary-era documents in Venezuela and other parts of South America. García de Sena arrived with his brother Domingo and enough resources to live in the city and publish Manuel's books. But time ate away at their money. By 1815 Manuel García de Sena was back in Cartagena, working as a secretary for Pedro Gual, a leader of independence movements who went on to become president of Venezuela. Domingo, however, stayed behind and ran into financial hardship even as he faced a mortal illness.

Domingo experienced transnational separation from family and friends in his final months. He left a cache of letters from Filadelfia reminding us that separation was an essential part of the connections created by trans-American textual circulation. In this remarkable correspondence, Domingo described his final days as he was overcome by illness. Wishing he could return home, he turned to epistolary writing to bridge the geographic and affective distance between the city where he had lived for six years and the country where his wife, daughters, and siblings still made their home. The letters testify to the different types of physical and economic difficulties affecting Domingo: the disintegration of his body, the obstacles to writing and transmitting letters, and the financial impossibility of his return to Venezuela. They provide a counterexample to the ability to cross intellectual and geographic distance that this study has highlighted as a characteristic of letters from Filadelfia.

The first letter, dated August 2, 1815, opens with a description of how physically taxing it is for the debilitated Domingo to write: "Queridas hermanas mias: ago el mayor esfuerzo pa. volver a escribir a Vs. aunqe. esto no puedo hacerlo sino muy despacio escribiéndo una o dos linias todos los dias por la mañana cuando puedo sentarme con alguna fuersa en el pulso pa. poder sostener la pluma" (My dear sisters: It takes the greatest effort to once again write to you, and I can do this only very slowly, writing one or two lines every morning when I can sit up and muster enough strength in my hand to be able to hold the pen).[71] The use of abbreviations such as *pa.* for *para* usually in this period implied informality and haste, but here it is apparently also a result of the weakness that makes it difficult for Domingo to hold a pen. Suffering from a sustained high fever and difficulty breathing, Domingo can barely get out of bed to write a letter, thus reminding us that while the Filadelfia intellectuals discussed in this study were extraordinary in their ability to write and circulate their texts, the material demands of the process—both physical and economic—were significant.

More than anything, Domingo's letter takes us back to the connection between the physical experience of the body as it composes and reads letters and books and the materiality of their composition on paper. And this bodily connection has important ramifications for American literary history, namely, a reminder that these are letters by forgotten people. Domingo continues, "Mis carnes todas, absolutamente han desaparesido, y solo soy un esqueleto aun todavía con vida" (My flesh has disappeared completely, and I am but a skeleton hanging on to life).[72] He does not have enough energy, he says, to board a ship for a return trip to South America, but the letter becomes a kind of flesh, a testimony to his skeletal life.

Domingo's letters not only display the desperation brought on by physical decay but also remind us of the logistical challenges inherent in the network of letters traveling from Philadelphia to Cartagena. Like the challenges posed by his body, the delivery (circulation) of Domingo's letters is a challenge that must be navigated. At one point he mentions that his courier will be one "William D. Rovinson," most likely William Davis Robinson, a merchant who penned *Memoirs of the Mexican Revolution* (Philadelphia, 1820) and did business in South America. Domingo was writing at a time before international mail delivery was available, and thus he had to send his letters in care of someone traveling via ship. We see similar concerns about circulation and delivery among other writers sending letters, such as when Heredia, writing from Mexico to Cuba, notes that he must send the letters via New York. "Cada ocho dias pienso seguir escribiendo, un sabado á tí y otro á mi mamá, para que se comuniquen mutuamente las cartas. Estas irán á Nueva York para que allí las dirijan, así como de alla me enviarán las suyas a Gener" (I plan to write every eight days, one Saturday to you and the next to my mother, so that you can share the letters. They will go via New York, and will be sent from there, and you should send yours to me through there via [Pedro] Gener).[73] Gener, also in exile, was a friend to Heredia, Félix Varela, and other Cubans moving in the northeastern United States at that time, and he became a part of the letter circuit, which was no easy matter. These circuits attest to the connection between the pain of separation and the difficulty of sending letters: one must anticipate failed deliveries and the possibility that distance will prevent a connection.

For in addition to his physical suffering, Domingo cannot afford to travel. Although the García de Sena brothers had arrived in Philadelphia with a shipment of coffee and other resources sufficient to allow them to settle there for a few years, by this point Domingo does not have enough to pay for a return passage by ship. He writes, "Yo he tenido muchas ofertas de franquearme todo qe. necesitase pa. mi biaje (mis amigos se llamavan) pa. llegado el caso de salir los buques todas las promesas se desvarataban y en esto he estado hasta qe. ya es muy tarde" (I have had many offers to grant me everything necessary for my voyage [from so-called friends] but once the day arrived for the ship to sail the promises evaporated, and that has been my situation, and now it is too late).[74] The phrase "ya es muy tarde" (now it is too late) emphasizes finality.

Manuel is able to respond at one point, and not long after that, Domingo writes what appears to be his final communication:

> Bastante la pesadumbre qe. me causa no poder verte y abrasarte antes de morir. Si Manuel ya no hay remedio yo estoy en un estado qe. yo no soy dueño de mi cuerpo. Hay semanas qe. pr. momentos se espera mi muerte. . . . Pues

hace mucho tiempo qe. las fuersas se fueron de mi de modo qe. he qedado solamente esperando mi ultimo fin.[75]

(I am full of sorrow that I cannot see you and hug you before I die. Yes Manuel, there is no longer any cure I am in such a state that I am no longer owner of my body. There are weeks when I wait for death at any moment.... It has been a long time since I lost all my strength so that I have ended up only waiting for my final end.)

The letter is a metaphor for the frailty of Domingo's body. For us, Domingo's body becomes a metaphor for letters from Filadelfia. A bodily connection with his brother is out of reach, challenging a facile attachment between body and letter. His writing is a last attempt to connect physically prior to "mi ultimo fin" (my final end).

Domingo's letters come to us today as the only remains of a man who, were it not for his better-known brother, would be almost completely forgotten. These letters encapsulate the fragmentary conditions of a history of Latino textuality. They are a partial record of whatever remains of his stay, incomplete evidence of his time in Filadelfia. If Filadelfia was *famosa* in certain Spanish-speaking circles in the early nineteenth century, that Spanish-language flair does not have the same resonance today in the United States. I conclude with Domingo's letters to emphasize the precarious nature of the historical recuperation of materials whose contents would place them in the space between national archives in Latin America and the United States. While all historical recuperation is partial, one of the challenges of approaching early US Latino letters as such is the need to delve into materials that might just as easily have been contained in disparate Latin American archives. Carmen E. Lamas has written of the importance of the Latin American archive for the historical study of Latino writers and their work: "Because they often wrote in Spanish (as opposed to English), their works are published primarily, though not exclusively, in their home countries or in countries where Spanish language is the primary linguistic medium."[76] For Lamas, the Latin American archive is less a location than it is a set of conditions related to epistemologies of Latin American studies and that field's emphasis on nation-based approaches. In the case of Domingo's letters, they were held by his family; the historians Pedro Grases and Alberto Harkness published portions in a study of Manuel García de Sena in relation to Venezuela's history.[77] Thus, Domingo's letters—like Servando

Teresa de Mier's—come to us through the mediation of national historical study. At one point in the history of Venezuela, they seemed to fit into that country's historical archive. And yet it is important to remember that Domingo is first and foremost writing from Filadelfia.

But as Philadelphia texts, Domingo's letters lead to archival dislocation, and they are not easily integrated into US American studies. This is partly because they were written in Spanish, which is often overlooked as a legitimate language of culture and thought in the United States. As late as 2017, the historian Vicki L. Ruiz wrote in *Time* magazine, "U.S. history textbooks typically give only a passing glance to Spanish-speaking settlements, such as St. Augustine (1565), Santa Fe (1610), San Antonio (1718) and latecomer Los Angeles (1781). The first European language spoken in the area that would become the United States was Spanish, not English."[78] Ruiz's intervention offers an educational corrective for readers who have either forgotten or have never known about the multilingual histories of America. The archival imperative related to the Spanish language in the United States for decades has been separation; such works are filed under the heading "foreign language" or in a department that is altogether separate from "American" writing. As a result of these separations, the Spanish language can easily appear out of place in a US setting. In their brittle state and lost direction, Domingo's letters remind us of the ease with which Latino letters can be lost, either physically or epistemologically, and remain at the edge of lost memory.

Historical distance introduces death on several registers: the impending death of Domingo, the potential end of this letter outside of its Filadelfia context, and the possibility of obliteration because of Domingo's minor status as a historical person. Charles A. Porter, writing about the interpretation of historical epistolarity, emphasizes that letters are mediated by temporal distance: "The letter before us, if for no other reason than the passage of time, is *not* identical to the letter that was read by its original addressee, and even that letter was not quite the same as the letter the author thought he or she was sending."[79] Bracketing the witty point about authors losing their intentions at the point of reading, Porter raises questions about an important difference between an epistolary communication among intimate friends and the temporal distance created by historical research. A letter from one brother to another comes to us as the textuality about a history of Latino separation in the United States.

Debates in poststructuralist theory in the 1980s took up the question of how letters are directed, misdirected, and dispersed; this was framed most provocatively by Jacques Lacan when he declared at the end of the seminar on "The Purloined Letter" that "a letter always arrives at its destination."[80] But what about when a letter is fragmented and all we get is a piece? In debates over the letter, those who pointed to lost or diverted letters were said to have given primacy to empirical conditions, even if their point was to negate an opposition between the empirical and the transcendent. But critics who emphasized lost or misdirected letters were intent on the prevention of hermeneutic closure, or a final reading that could indeed lead to a dead letter.[81] What if a letter is always almost reaching its destination? What if letters are not dead but dying? I am less interested here in the debate about a letter and its destination (both singular) than in bringing back *cartas* and their movement throughout the Americas.

Letters, of course, have the potential to revive archival silences. My aim here has been to contribute to Latino literary history while retaining an important skepticism about the ability of something called an archive to fill those silences. In this study, the phrase *early Latino literature* has referred to an anticolonial textuality with connections to hemispheric Americas; however, the people behind the texts are an important dimension of this dynamic reading of letters in the critical panorama of the present day. Latino literary history focuses not only on texts but also on people, not only writers but reading publics, even if people are read through texts. Domingo's reference to blood and bones reminds us that behind Filadelfia letters were actual people who now come back to us at a time of tremendous consternation about Latino subjectivity in the United States. Domingo's dying letters in Filadelfia give us one more window into the variety of voices that emerge, sometimes in little-known corners of history. Because his letters go out to South America, imagining the impossible possibility of a return, they open the question of how Filadelfia is inextricable from various Spanish American contexts. Yet conversely, they insist that what was once Spanish America has never been completely separated from what becomes the United States. *Filadelfia,* I have argued here, was a term that spoke to an imagined collective project of self-determination that attempted to reconcile difference and resisted the divisions created by nations, regions, and ethnic groupings. Letters from Filadelfia bring with them a desire to overcome boundaries, the aspiration for political common ground, and the hope that geographic distance and other types of separation among people can be overcome through letters.

Notes

Introduction

1. Rocafuerte, *Ideas necesarias*, 1. References are to the 1821 edition.
2. Rodríguez O., *Emergence of Spanish America*, 48.
3. The first Mexican edition, *Ideas necesarias a todo pueblo americano independiente, que quiera ser libre*, was published by P. de la Rosa.
4. A copy of the book is at the New-York Historical Society.
5. See, e.g., Altman, *Epistolarity*, 13. For an overview of epistolarity in the Anglophone US nineteenth century, see Bernier, Newman, and Pethers, *Edinburgh Companion to Nineteenth-Century American Letters and Letter-Writing*. For a collection of essays that de-emphasize the formal qualities of letter writing and move toward a social function of communication, see Barton and Hall, *Letter Writing as Social Practice*. For a collection on the historical conditions of letter writing and reading, including the social dimensions of correspondence (including public readings of letters), see Earle, *Epistolary Selves*. Studies focusing on letter writing in the Hispanophone world are cited elsewhere.
6. Quoted in Grases, *Preindependencia y emancipación*, 269.
7. Rocafuerte, *Ideas necesarias*, 1.
8. *Oxford English Dictionary*; *Diccionario de la lengua española*, dle.rae.es.
9. Rocafuerte, *Ideas necesarias*, 1.
10. Furstenberg, *When the United States Spoke French*, 17.
11. Grases, "El círculo de Filadelfia," 280.
12. Leal and Cortina, introduction to *Jicoténcal*, xiii.
13. Guzmán's novella, written in the 1930s but not published until 1960, recounts the story of a Spanish military figure who takes on a false identity to carry out an operation in Filadelfia, only to spend much of his time in taverns and social gatherings.
14. Kanellos, "José Alvarez de Toledo y Dubois," 84.
15. Rojas, "Traductores de la libertad," 46.
16. Coronado, *A World Not to Come*, 139–78; García, "On the Borders of Independence"; Vogeley, *Bookrunner* (focusing on print-culture connections to other parts of the Americas). See also Lazo, "La Famosa Filadelfia."
17. See Nash, *First City* and *Forging Freedom;* Dunbar, *Fragile Freedom;* Rigal, *American Manufactory;* and Otter, *Philadelphia Stories*.
18. Otter, *Philadelphia Stories*, 6.
19. Martí, "Our America."
20. Fitz, *Our Sister Republics*, 9.

21. "President's Annual Message," *Proceedings and Debates of the Senate of the United States,* 18th Cong., 1st sess., 1 December 1823, 14.
22. Kenworthy, *America/Americas,* 2–3, 13–20. Gretchen Murphy emphasizes this interpretive delay in her consideration of Monroe. See Murphy, *Hemispheric Imaginings,* 4–6.
23. Fitz, *Our Sister Republics,* 13.
24. The decades bracketing this study are concurrent with the apparition of Spanish-language materials in Philadelphia (1790s) and a decline in Filadelfia publications after Latin American countries declared independence. The establishment of new countries was accompanied by an increase in the number of presses operating in Central and South America.
25. Numerous other publications use *carta* as metaphor, including Valentín de Foronda's *Cartas sobre lo que debe hacer un príncipe que tenga colonias á gran distancia* (Letter concerning the duties of a prince with colonies at a great distance), a pamphlet presented to Philadelphia's American Philosophical Society in 1804. Foronda was the Spanish general consul in Philadelphia from 1801 to 1807. He represented the Spanish government, against which many Filadelfia writers were fighting. For a recent interpretation of this Foronda pamphlet, see Coronado, "Historicizing Nineteenth-Century Latina/o Textuality," 58–66.
26. Mignolo, *Darker Side of the Renaissance,* 172–73.
27. These types of contradictions by which a shift toward modernity is intertwined with colonial forms of oppression, including racial hierarchies, have been at the center of work by scholars associated with an approach known as "coloniality of power." For a now-classic formulation of this approach, see Quijano, "Coloniality," 533–80. For a formulation in relation to early Mexican American literature, see Aranda, "When Archives Collide," 151–58.
28. Hewitt, "Networks," 4.
29. Debates about which term to use—*literature, writing, texts, discourse*—raged in the 1990s, a historical indication that in literary studies the emphasis on valorizing literary form had given way to an interdisciplinary approach. My use of *literature* is in part an attempt to be in dialogue with the field of Latino literature through the introduction of an important site of literary history.
30. Magnan, "Correspondence," 322–23.
31. Warner argues that the meaning of printedness was crucial for a new political language of an "Anglo-American strand of republicanism" tied to the public sphere. See Warner, *Letters of the Republic,* xi–xiii. In opting for a study of the more capacious "document," Lisa Gitelman questions the efficacy of the phrase *cultural meaning of printedness.* She writes, "But how widely, how unanimously, and how continuously can the meanings of printedness be shared, and what exactly are their structuring roles?" See *Paper Knowledge,* 9. My usage of Warner's phrase recognizes that the texts in question suggest or make explicit a political meaning related to the printing process, which then needs to be read alongside

the structural effects of production. Warner's argument is relevant to Hispanophone publication.
32. Goodman, *Republic of Letters*, 96.
33. Berlant, "Intimacy," 281.
34. Lowe, *Intimacies of Four Continents*, 3. Lowe's intimacies emphasize "the circuits, connections, associations, and mixings of differently laboring people" (21).
35. Earle, "Letters and Love," 29.
36. *Cartas de un americano*, i.
37. For an excellent overview of the problems raised by *Latinx*, see Rodriguez, "X Marks the Spot"; see also De Onís, "What's in an 'x'?" Book titles and courses increasingly use *Latinx*. In this introduction I use *Latinx* in reference to the way the term is being deployed in critical discussions; however, my personal preference is for *LatinX*, which I use elsewhere in this book. The capitalizing of the *X* emphasizes how the use of that letter in this neologism is contested and also that the *X* has numerous implications, including being an unknown variable.
38. See Gruesz, "Errant Latino"; Irwin, "Almost Latino"; and Lamas, "Raimundo Cabrera." See also Lomas, *Translating Empire*, 35–40.
39. Ardao, *Génesis;* Quijada, "Sobre el origen."
40. Chasteen, *Americanos*, 2.
41. See the "Advertencia" in García de Sena's *Historia concisa* and the dedication in his *La independencia de la Costa Firme*.
42. Bryant, review of *Jicoténcal*, 336.
43. Said, *Reflections on Exile*, 382.
44. Coronado, *A World Not to Come*, 8.
45. Mecum, *El idealismo práctico*, 17–23.
46. Bruce-Novoa, *Retrospace*, 26.
47. Lamas, "Raimundo Cabrera," 210.
48. For an overview of the hemispheric turn in American Studies, see Bauer, "Hemispheric Studies." The first major study to bring nineteenth-century hemispheric currents in dialogue with Latino studies was Gruesz, *Ambassadors of Culture*. For a book that displays the epistemological impossibility of separating study of the Americas from European perspectives, see Cañizares-Esguerra, *How to Write the History of the New World*. For a comparative historical approach, see Scott, *Degrees of Freedom*. For a collection that brings together historians and literary scholars, see Shukla and Tinsman, *Imagining Our Americas*. These are representative titles, not a comprehensive listing.
49. Wallerstein, *World-Systems Analysis*, 16–17.
50. Wallerstein, *World-Systems Analysis*, 17.
51. Wallerstein, *World-Systems Analysis*, 21.

1. La Famosa Filadelfia

1. José María Heredia to Ignacio Heredia y Campuzano, 15 April 1824, in Heredia, *Antología Herediana,* 102. Heredia's letter opens as follows: "Diez dias ha que estoy en esta famosa Filadelfia" (Ten days after arriving in this celebrated Philadelphia). Unless otherwise noted, translations are mine.
2. "Esta gran ciudad fundada por Guillermo Penn, habitada al principio por unas cuantas familia cuákeras, hoy presenta el aspecto de unas de las ilustres metrópolis de Europa, con major belleza y muchas mayores esperanzas de prosperidad." Zavala, *Viaje,* 186, my translation. The first edition was published in Paris in 1834. A bilingual edition of this book with an introduction by John Michael Rivera was published as part of the Recovering the US Hispanic Literary Heritage Project in 2005.
3. Mathew Carey Papers, Box 25, Folder 7, American Antiquarian Society, Worcester, MA.
4. Vogeley, *Bookrunner,* 131.
5. García, "Interdependence and Interlingualism," 754.
6. Puglia, *Short Extract,* 15.
7. Simmons, *Santiago F. Puglia,* 20–21.
8. Puglia, *El desengaño del hombre,* v.
9. Puglia revealed this information in a translator's note published in the 1821 translation of Paine, *El derecho del hombre,* 168.
10. Remer, *Printers and Men of Capital,* 18.
11. Remer, *Printers and Men of Capital,* 125.
12. The *ñ* in *año* does not have a tilde on the original title page.
13. Jaksić, *Hispanic World;* Kagan, "From Noah to Moses," 21–25; Vogeley, *Bookrunner,* 42–50; Vilar García, *El Español.*
14. Carey's investment in international markets are discussed in Kaser, *Messrs. Carey & Lea of Philadelphia,* 37.
15. Green, *Mathew Carey,* 17–22.
16. Green, *Mathew Carey,* 25.
17. Carey Letterbook, 1 January–24 June 1822, Lea & Febiger Collection, Historical Society of Pennsylvania, Philadelphia.
18. Kaser, *Messrs. Carey & Lea,* 37.
19. Carey publishing house to Louis Castagnino, 19 February 1822, Carey Letterbook, 1 January–24 June 1822.
20. Carey publishing house to Castagnino, 18 April 1822, Carey Letterbook, w1 January–24 June 1822.
21. Vogeley, *Bookrunner,* 109–47.
22. Vogeley, "Spanish-Language Masonic Books," 337.
23. Manuel Hernández González, "Liberalismo y masonería," 832.
24. *Reflexiones imparciales sobre la franc-masonería,* 29, 28.

25. For a discussion of the US-Mexico connection in relation to Masonry, see Vogeley, "Spanish-Language Masonic Books," 341–43.
26. The title of the Philadelphia edition was *Breve relación de la destrucción de las Indias Occidentales*.
27. The Servando Teresa de Mier Noriega y Guerra Papers in the Nettie Lee Benson Latin American Collection at the University of Texas at Austin include receipts from Hurtel for the printing of Mier's books.
28. Johnson, "Moreau de Saint-Méry," 172.
29. Furstenberg, *When the United States Spoke French*, 108.
30. Blaufarb, *Bonapartists in the Borderlands*, 24–25.
31. Coronado, *A World Not to Come*, 205–6.
32. "Thomas H. Palmer to Thomas Jefferson, 22 February 1813," Founders Online, National Archives, http://founders.archives.gov/documents/Jefferson/03-05-02-0540 (last modified 29 June 2015).
33. "Thomas Jefferson to Thomas H. Palmer, 6 March 1813," Founders Online, National Archives, http://founders.archives.gov/documents/Jefferson/03-05-02-0561 (last modified 29 June 2015).
34. For a discussion of the critical reception of *Jicoténcal*, see below, chapter 4.
35. Leal and Cortina, introduction to *Jicoténcal*, xxviii.
36. "Walks About Town," *Ariel: A Semimonthly Literary and Miscellaneous Gazette*, 8 January 1831, 150, http://search.proquest.com/docview/124476026. The first listing for Huttner's bookstore in the Philadelphia Directory was in 1831.
37. Advertisement in *American Journal of Medical Sciences*, 1 August 1830, http://search.proquest.com/docview/125259672.
38. A copy of the two-volume 1826 edition of *Jicoténcal* is at the American Antiquarian Society, in Worcester, MA. For additional information, see *Philadelphia Directory and Stranger's Guide* (1825).
39. Charvat, *Literary Publishing in America*, 23.
40. Another edition of Iriarte's *Fabulas literarias*, with notes on the difficult and obsolete phrases for students of the Spanish language, was published in Boston by Burdett in 1833.
41. In their introduction to *Jicoténcal*, xvii, Leal and Cortina list many of the books for sale, which include a translation into Spanish of Goldsmith's *The Vicar of Wakefield* and Spanish translations of US history books.
42. Vogeley, *Bookrunner*, 263–65.
43. *Catalogue of an Extensive Collection of Books*.
44. For a discussion of Spanish-language learning in early Filadelfia, see Vilar García, *El Español*, 58–85.
45. In considering Heredia's "Niágara" in relation to US and hemispheric literary culture, Kirsten Silva Gruesz argues that the poem is about Niagara but not of it, because it refuses to release the Caribbean context informing the exile's

longing. In other words, the great Niagara poem is American but not in a nationalistic sense. Gruesz, *Ambassadors of Culture,* 41.
46. José María Heredia, "Advertencia," in Heredia, *Poesías,* 5.
47. The copy of the book in the Special Collections and University Archives, University of Maryland, College Park, has the name A. Behrman written inside the front cover, which implies that it belonged to a nonnative speaker.
48. Del Monte, *Versos de J. Nicasio Gallego,* 7.
49. The copy at the Library of Congress was originally given to "Da Juana de Dios de la Garza," who may have come from a prominent family in Mexico.
50. Thompson, *American Literary Annuals,* 4.
51. Shapiro, *Culture and Commerce,* 40.
52. "El Aguinaldo," in *El Aguinaldo para el año de 1829,* 1–4.
53. Gómez Álvarez, "Lecturas perseguidas," 309.
54. Gómez Álvarez, "Lecturas Perseguidas," 308, 306.
55. Remer, *Printers and Men of Capital,* 156–57.
56. For a more complete list, see Toribio Medina, *Historia de la imprenta,* 1:xxxviii–xxxix.
57. Peralta Ruiz, "La revolución silenciada," 110.
58. Roldán Vera, *British Book Trade and Spanish American Independence,* 13.
59. Febvre, *Coming of the Book,* 208–9.
60. The letter was published two years later in Spanish as *Carta dirigida a los Españoles Americanos.*
61. Berruezo León, *La lucha de Hispanoamérica,* 56–59.
62. For a discussion of Viscardo's pamphlet and Miranda's role in publication, see Racine, *Francisco de Miranda,* 143–47.
63. Racine, *Francisco de Miranda,* 147.
64. Luis Leal and Rodolfo Cortina, in their introduction to the Arte Público edition of *Jicoténcal,* follow the nineteenth-century Cuban historian and bibliographer Antonio Bachiller y Morales, who pointed out that the publisher's name, Teracroef & Naroajeb, was an anagram for Rocafuerte y Bejarano (his full name) and proposed that the book was published in Havana. See Bachiller y Morales, *Apuntes para la historia de las letras,* 3:345.
65. The book gives D. Huntington as the publisher and T. W. Mercein as the printer. Both were based in New York. It would appear that Rocafuerte published the book in New York with a Filadelfia imprint to match the city named in his prologue. *Ideas necesarias* has given rise to speculation that it was published elsewhere. Bachiller y Morales proposes Havana, although he refers to a 194-page edition, which may be a reprint of the 180-page version printed by T. W. Mercein. As I noted in the introduction, *Ideas necesarias* appeared in a second edition in Puebla, Mexico, in 1823. The difficulty of ascribing false imprints is one reason why scholars have been too hasty to follow Bachiller y Morales. Rocafuerte said in a memoir that he published *Ideas necesarias* in the

United States, but some critics have followed Bachiller y Morales's argument and gone so far as to say that Rocafuerte's memory failed him when he wrote the memoir. See Fernández de Castro, *Vicente Rocafuerte*, 73n15.
66. A copy of this broadside, *Nos Los Inquisidores,* is at the Library Company of Philadelphia. I thank James Green for pointing it out.
67. Simmons, *Santiago F. Puglia,* 47.
68. Saborit, introduction to *El desengaño del hombre,* xxvii–xxxiii. Saborit offers details about responses to the pamphlet.
69. Earle, "Role of Print," 24.
70. Peralta Ruiz, "La revolución silenciada."
71. See, e.g., Richardson, "Athens of America," in a comprehensive history of the city.
72. Nash, *First City,* 1.
73. Nash, *First City,* 11.
74. Chasteen, introduction to Rama, *Lettered City,* vii.
75. Rama, *Lettered City,* 6.
76. See, e.g., Dos Santos, "Latin American Underdevelopment." For a collection influenced by dependency theory, see Cockcroft, Grank, and Johnson, *Dependence and Underdevelopment.*
77. Latrobe, *Anniversary Oration,* 17. For a brief overview of the relationship of the arts to the Greek revival in Philadelphia, see Kirtley, "Athens of America."
78. *Viaje por los Estados Unidos,* 99–100, hereafter cited parenthetically as *V.* In this book epistolary exchange comes to the forefront as Reynal presents his letters as a type of gift, written only "para un amigo que sabria perdonar mis yerros y aun advertirmelos" (6; for a friend who would note and know to forgive any errors).
79. Critics have found little information about these two men, and most of what we know about them is recorded in the book. See, e.g., Suárez Argüello, selections from *Viaje por los Estados Unidos,* 87–90.
80. By 1826 the center building of the US Capitol had been built with a copper dome that was later replaced by the larger dome now on the building. See https://www.aoc.gov/history-us-capitol-building, accessed October 2016.
81. Reynal retains the Anglophone spelling "Philadelphia." Perhaps this indicates an emphasis on difference between the United States and Mexico, which some scholars have noted as an important aspect of a book that attempts to sketch a version of Mexican national character. Suárez Argüello, "La mirada en el espejo," 101–2.
82. Heredia, *Antología Herediana,* 103.
83. *Views of Philadelphia and its Environs,* 82.
84. Furstenberg, *When the United States Spoke French,* 94.
85. Heredia, *Antología Herediana,* 103.
86. Vicente Rocafuerte, *Ideas necesarias,* 17–18.

87. This is Wallace Woolsey's translation in Zavala, *Journey to the United States of North America,* 100.
88. Zavala offers an account of the founding of the Bank of the United States, and it is here that we see his comparative impulse: "No debe parecer fuera de proposito en una obra que tiene por objeto principal presentar á los mexicanos las costumbres, los usos, instituciones y establecimientos de los Estados Unidos, modelo nominal, por decirlo así, de los legisladores mexicanos, el dar una idea extensa del sistema de bancos establecido en aquel pais, lo que ademas podrá ser de bastante utilidad para su sistema financiero" (It should not seem out of place to give an extensive account of the system of banks established in this country, which might be very useful for Mexico's financial system, considering that this book takes as its principal goal to present to Mexicans the customs, habits, establishments, and institutions of the United States, which one can call the nominal model of Mexican legislators). Zavala, *Viaje,* 195.
89. Dunbar, *Fragile Freedom,* 48.
90. Zavala, *Viaje,* 37–38.
91. Anderson Imbert, *Spanish-American Literature,* 155. Andrew Bush declares that among Spanish-language writers, Heredia took important steps toward romantic poetry even as "he conceived his national identity—he becomes a national poet—from afar, recognizing the severance without accepting the loss." See Bush, "Lyric Poetry," 393. I argue that he was nationalized in twentieth-century criticism.
92. For a biographical overview of Heredia, see Lacoste de Arufe, "Biografía de José María Heredia."
93. Certeau, *Practice of Everyday Life,* 100.
94. Certeau, *Practice of Everyday Life,* 95.
95. Certeau, Practice of Everyday Life, 93.
96. The *Plan of the city of Philadelphia* was compiled from actual surveys by Thomas F. Drayton in 1824. Historical Society of Pennsylvania. http://digitallibrary.hsp.org/index.php/Detail/Object/Show/object_id/10832#.
97. Heredia, *Antología Herediana,* 102.
98. Otter, *Philadelphia Stories,* 11.
99. Rama, *Lettered City,* 5.
100. Heredia, *Antología Herediana,* 104.
101. Heredia had expressed a similar engagement with urban regularity in a letter written in Boston on 4 December 1823, a few months before he went to Philadelphia: "¡Que hermosa ciudad! Me ha admirado sobre todo el orden que en ella reina. Todas las casas tienen en tarjetas, grabadas de cobre o de madera, el nombre y ocupación de los que las habitan; lo que es excelente y facilita sobremanera el curso de los negocios. Todos parecen ocupados; y aun no he visto un mendigo, ni aun uno que tenga sobre sí la librea de la miseria y desamparo. ¡Afortunado país! ¡favorecido, a pesar de la rudeza de su clima, con las miradas

más benignas del Cielo!" (What a beautiful city! I have been impressed by the order that reigns in her. Every house has a plate made of copper or wood bearing the name and occupation of the inhabitants; this is an excellent way to facilitate commerce. Everyone looks busy, and I have yet to see a beggar or someone beset by misery or poverty. Fortunate country! Despite its weather, it is favored by heaven with kindness!). Heredia, *Antología Herediana*, 101–2.

102. Frank M. Etting writes that Peale's Museum moved into the second floor of the Pennsylvania State House in 1802 and remained there until Charles Willson Peale's death in 1827. Etting, *Historical Account*, 155–56.
103. "Todas mis impresiones anteriores desaparecieron a su vista." Heredia, *Antología Herediana*, 103.
104. Semonin, "Peale's Mastodon." See also Semonin, *American Monster;* and Sellers, *Mr. Peale's Museum.*
105. Laura Rigal has argued that the mammoth, and Peale's collection generally, mediated tensions between Federalists and Jeffersonian Republicans by presenting the labor of incorporation (the skeleton) as a preservation of the union and deflection of class tensions. Rigal discusses the apparatus of presentation surrounding the mastodon, including Charles Willson Peale's painting *The Exhumation of the Mastodon,* as situating labor as the element holding together national nature and culture. See Rigal, *American Manufactory,* 94–95.
106. For a discussion of these debates, see Gerbi, *Dispute of the New World.*
107. Jefferson, *Writings,* 167.
108. Heredia, Antología Herediana, 103.
109. When remains were first discovered in North America, people did not know whether the species was still living, but in time its extinction was verified, and the mammoth's discovery raised questions about the length of life on earth.
110. Heredia, *Antología Herediana,* 103.
111. Quoted in Sellers, *Mr. Peale's Museum,* 146.
112. Jefferson, *Writings,* 165.
113. Heredia, *Antología Herediana,* 104.
114. A. Owen Aldridge proposes that Paine's ideas circulated in Spanish America either in French translation or through writings that discussed Paine prior to the García de Sena book, but the publication put Spanish translations of Paine into circulation. Aldridge, *Early American Literature,* 219–21. In an article comparing García de Sena's translation with two others, Paul Cahen cites another early translation, an 1811 edition published in London under the title *Reflecciones políticas escritas bajo el título de Instinto Común por el ciudadano Tomas Paine y traducidas abreviadamente por Anselmo Nateiu, indígena del Peru.* See Cahen, "Bringing Thomas Paine to Latin America," 209.
115. In the scope of Filadelfia's Spanish-language print culture, *La independencia de la Costa Firme* is a relatively early contribution. García de Sena's book appears roughly concurrent with Venezuela's first declaration of independence.

The number of Spanish-language titles increases in the second decade of the nineteenth century as the wars progress and then become a regular part of Philadelphia's print culture by the 1820s.

116. Langley, *Americas in the Age of Revolution.*
117. Venuti, *Scandals of Translation,* 31.
118. Hassan, "Translational Literature," 1435.
119. Ramón was sentenced to eight days in jail for the fight. Grases, *Preindependencia y emancipación,* 380.
120. "Pennsylvania, Philadelphia Passenger Lists, 1800–1882," *FamilySearch,* image 169 of 512, citing NARA microfilm publication M425 (Washington, DC: National Archives and Records Administration, n.d).
121. A similar conclusion is reached by Georges L. Bastin, Álvaro Echeverri, and Ángela Campo in their article "Translation and the Emancipation of Hispanic America," in which they describe García de Sena's project as "to demonstrate the legitimacy of independence for Hispanic America and the potential benefits of independence for his compatriots, using the sociopolitical and economic situation in the United States as a model" (60).
122. Translator's preface in García de Sena, *Historia concisa de los Estados Unidos,* iv.
123. Brickhouse, *Unsettlement of America,* 18.
124. Bernstein, "Cultura Inquisitorial," 96.
125. Larkin, *Thomas Paine,* 2.
126. García de Sena, *La independencia de la Costa Firme,* 8.
127. Paine, *Collected Writings,* 5–6.
128. Gillman and Gruesz, "Worlding America," 232.
129. Mauro Paez-Pumar offers a study and facsimile edition of Spanish translations of the "Address to the People of Great Britain" (1774) and *An Address from the Delegates of the Twelve United Colonies, to the People of England* (1775). These handwritten translations, dated 1777, were in a personal bound volume belonging to the lawyer Joseph Ygnacio Moreno, suggesting a relatively early (private) circulation of US revolutionary principles in Venezuela. See Paez-Pumar, *Las proclamas de Filadelfia.*
130. Grases and Harkness, *Manuel García de Sena,* 53.
131. Hermans, *Translation in Systems,* 39; see esp. 7–71 for an overview of the descriptive approach to translation studies.
132. Cahen, "Bringing Thomas Paine to Latin America," 220.
133. Crèvecoeur, *Letters from an American Farmer,* 35. I thank Emily García for reminding me of this line.
134. Translator's preface in García de Sena, *Historia concisa de los Estados Unidos,* vi.
135. The phrase "cicunstancias, tan analogas á las de este país," will be echoed in the prologue to Vicente Rocafuerte's *Ideas necesarias* when the latter writes that Philadelphia provides "ejemplos mas análogos a nuestra actual situacion política" (examples more analogous to our actual political situation).

136. Translator's preface in García de Sena, *Historia concisa de los Estados Unidos*, v–vi.
137. Grases and Harkness, *Manuel García de Sena*, 51.
138. Rodríguez O., "Sobre la supuesta influencia," 704. Rodríguez argues that the US revolution had less of an influence than the transformation prompted by the French invasion of Spain.
139. Grases and Harkness, *Manuel García de Sena*, 52–55.
140. Egaña, *Memorias políticas*, 25n.
141. Aldridge, *Early American Literature*, 221.
142. Aldridge, *Early American Literature*, 221.
143. Richardson, "Athens of America," 218.
144. Manuel García de Sena, *La independencia de la Costa Firme*, dedication.

2. The Trans-American Elite

1. "Funeral of the Colombian Ambassador," *Aurora General Advertiser*, 18 July 1822, 2. Torres's friend William Duane, the editor of the Philadelphia *Aurora General Advertiser*, noted that Spanish Americans regularly invoked the "Franklin of South America" reference because of Torres's broad learning and his counsel in matters relating to the wars of independence. "His talents as a mathematician, and his general learning, were transcendent; the writer of this article, who has known, perhaps, the ablest men of three quarters of the globe, never knew among them all his equal," Duane wrote shortly after Torres's death. Duane added that his comparison to the "ablest men" was not meant to denigrate anyone but rather to elevate Torres. See "Death of Mr. Torres," *Niles Register*, 27 July 1822, 348; the article appeared originally in the *Aurora General Advertiser* on 16 July 1822.
2. "The Franklin of South America (From the New York Evening Post)," *Aurora General Advertiser*, 24 July 1822, 2. In other periodicals, Torres was called "the Franklin of the southern world."
3. "Funeral of the Colombian Ambassador," 2.
4. *In Honor of the Patriot Don Manuel Torres, 1764–1822*, 12. This booklet contains several speeches in 1926 honoring Torres and celebrating the placing of a bronze tablet at St. Mary's Church.
5. Miramón, *Diplomaticos de la libertad*, 21. Raúl Coronado writes, "Torres' home became a veritable salon where revolutionary agents gathered, and he introduced them to one another along with U.S. politicians and financiers." Coronado, *A World Not to Come*, 157–58.
6. Bowman, "Manuel Torres, a Spanish American Patriot," 50. On arms, see Bowman, "Activities of Manuel Torres," 237–38.
7. García Samudio, *La independencia de Hispanoamérica*, 149; Miramón, *Diplomaticos de la libertad*, 28–29.

8. García, "On the Borders of Independence," 74.
9. "Death of Mr. Torres," 347.
10. McFarlane, "Science and Sedition in Spanish America," 97, 111.
11. Various scholars have invoked the term *trans-American* or *transamerican* to discuss how nineteenth-century writers developed political and literary cultures that do not fit into either a national sense of Latino-US identity or a Latin American subjectivity (often in national guise) that de-emphasizes the United States and Europe. Two seminal studies are Gruesz, *Ambassadors of Culture* (2001), and Brickhouse, *Transamerican Literary Relations* (2004). Brickhouse, for example, emphasized the trans-American dimensions of the novel *Jicoténcal*, as she presented Philadelphia and New York as a public sphere, "a closely interactive community of hispanophone exiles and expatriates from throughout the Americas" (49). More recently, José David Saldívar adopts the term *trans-Americanity* to cross into the twentieth century and emphasize inequality in the global South and subaltern perspectives in light of North-South economic, literary, and academic interaction. See his *Trans-Americanity* (2012). My argument is that Latino literature in the nineteenth century is inherently trans-American and not just "American" in the hemispheric sense because it involves the crossing of texts and people among various countries.
12. "El más indulgente y tierno de los amigos ¿como podré jamás pagarte la deuda inmensa de gratitud?" José María Heredia to Ignacio Heredia y Campuzano, 4 November 1825, in Cairo Balester, *Jose Mará Heredia: 1803–2003*. The emotional connection, the intimacy, displayed here was without doubt wrapped up in the financial arrangements made by the uncle. Heredia, who ran major decisions by his uncle, at one point wrote, "Te repito lo que te escribí sobre mi absoluta deferencia á tu voluntad" (I repeat what I wrote about my absolute deference to your wishes). Heredia to Heredia y Campuzano, 8 October 1824, in Cairo Balester, *Jose Mará Heredia: 1803–2003*.
13. Aranda, "Contradictory Impulses"; Poblete, "Citizenship and Illegality."
14. Rocafuerte, *Un americano libre*, 18–19.
15. Varela, Cuba's foremost philosopher and a highly regarded professor of constitutional law at the College and Seminary of San Carlos in Havana, was chosen by his compatriots to represent Cuba at the Spanish Cortes in 1822. Rodríguez, *Vida del Presbítero Félix Varela*, 169–70. As I show in the next chapter, Torres was called on to serve as a diplomat for Venezuela and Colombia in the United States. Still others were elected as representatives to the new legislatures being established in various countries, with Roscio taking an important role in establishing the first republic of Venezuela in 1811–12 and later elected to the legislature.
16. Mills, *Power Elite*, 18. In contrast to Mills's power elite, the trans-American elite prior to the 1820s do not have a national base. In place of institutional sites, they opt for political movements and personal geographic movement. Rather

than an institutional site supporting their goals, their mobility, facilitated by inherited family wealth and economic connections, furthers new political conceptions.
17. Mills, *Power Elite*, 19.
18. Restrepo, *Historia de la revolución*, 1:30.
19. Guerra, *Modernidad e independencias*, 98–99.
20. [Smart], *Republican's Manual*, 4. I cite the English-language version of this manual. As I discuss in chapter 4, the Spanish-language *Manual* was a was a translation of an 1806 English-language publication, which suggests a common type of education for upper-class men in the United States and Spanish America.
21. *Letrado* has been used to name educated men who work in various occupations related to writing. Angel Rama used *letrado* in a general sense to name everyone from civil bureaucrats to newspaper writers to wanna-be poets, all doing the work of sustaining the colonial city. Other scholars have a more particular usage of *letrado* to mean a participant in the legal system. Rama, *Lettered City*, 18–25. For the more specific usage, see Malagón-Barceló, "Role of the Letrado."
22. Bauer and Mazzotti, *Creole Subjects*, 8.
23. Lynch, *Spanish American Revolutions*, 16–19.
24. Quoted in Lynch, *Spanish American Revolutions*, 18.
25. Bauer and Mazzotti, *Creole Subjects*, 8.
26. Bauer and Mazzotti, *Creole Subjects*, 6. For a discussion of the various uses of *creole* and bibliographic citations, see Bauer and Mazzotti, *Creole Subjects*, 52–55.
27. Anderson, *Imagined Communities*, 65.
28. Josiah Stoddard Johnston Papers (Collection 0324), Historical Society of Pennsylvania. The letter is included in a collection of Rocafuerte's letters. Rodriguez O., *Estudios sobre Vicente Rocafuerte*, 52–53.
29. Tregle, "Josiah Stoddard Johnston Papers," 328.
30. Goudie, *Creole America*, 8.
31. Félix Varela to Joel Poinsett, 27 January 1825, Joel Roberts Poinsett Papers, Historical Society of Pennsylvania. The letter is transcribed with modernized punctuation in Varela, *Obras*, 2:297–98.
32. For a biographical overview of Poinsett, see Gallardo, *J. R. Poinsett*, 13–76.
33. Varela to Poinsett, 27 January 1825.
34. Varela to Poinsett, 28 January 1825, Poinsett Papers.
35. Varela, *El Habanero*, 49.
36. Varela, *El Habanero*, 49–50.
37. Considerable scholarship on Varela emphasizing his biography goes back to the nineteenth century. The first major biography was José Ignacio Rodríguez's *Vida del Presbítero Félix Varela* (1878). More recent important studies include Antonio Hernández Travieso's *El Padre Varela* (1984), Joseph and Helen

McCadden's *Félix Varela, Torch Bearer from Cuba* (1969), and Juan M. Navia's *Apostole for the Immigrants* (2002).
38. McCadden and McCadden, *Félix Varela*, 49.
39. For an overview of Varela's contributions to the Catholic press of New York, see Lamas, "Father Félix Varela," 159.
40. Navia, *Apostole for the Immigrants*, 175.
41. Lamas, "Father Félix Varela," 165–73.
42. At the end of the article "Mascaras políticas," Varela is explicit that his audience is youth: "la joventud para quien principalmente escribo." *El Habanero*, 9.
43. Varela, *Cartas a Elpidio*, 1:3, my translation. Although there is an English-language translation, *Letters to Elpidio*, which is helpful, I have opted to provide my own translation of selected passages unless otherwise noted.
44. Varela, *Cartas a Elpidio*, 1:4.
45. Rodríguez, *Vida del Presbítero Félix Varela*, 300. One of the persons whom scholars suggest Elpidio stands for is José de la Luz y Caballero, who published a brief review of the first volume of *Cartas a Elpidio* in the newspaper *Diario de la Habana* in December 1835; however, Caballero is mentioned in the third person in the second volume.
46. Varela sent a letter acknowledging his receipt of the money. Félix Varela to José del Castillo, New York, 18 June 1835, in Varela, *Obras*, 3:218.
47. Varela to Castillo, New York, 16 January 1836, in Varela, *Obras*, 3:220.
48. Varela to José de la Luz y Caballero, New York, 5 June 1839, in Varela, *Obras*, 3:224.
49. It is likely that the Dr. Suárez mentioned in the letter is Leonardo Santos Suárez, who had been elected to the Spanish Cortes with Varela in 1821.
50. Lamas, "Father Félix Varela," 172.
51. Varela, *Cartas a Elpidio*, 2:100.
52. Varela, *Cartas a Elpidio*, 2:100.
53. Varela, *Cartas a Elpidio*, 2:99.
54. Brawley, "Lorenzo Dow," 265.
55. Varela, *Cartas a Elpidio*, 2:102.
56. Varela, *Cartas a Elpidio*, 2:104. Tomás Gener was also a friend of José María Heredia's and acted as conduit for the letters between Heredia and his family in Cuba.
57. Varela, *Cartas a Elpidio*, 2:102.
58. McCadden and McCadden, *Father Varela*, 87.
59. "Tenían las monjas gran cuidado en no catequizar sus discípulos ni tocar puntos de religion que podían comprometer la buena armonía con los padres, que todos se demostraban satisfechos de la conducta de las religiosas, y en prueba de ello conservaban sus hijas en el establecimiento" (The sisters took great pains not to catechize their students nor to touch on points of religion that could compromise the good harmony they had with the parents, who were

quite satisfied about the conduct of the nuns, and as proof of this kept their daughters in this institution). Varela, *Cartas a Elpidio*, 2:154. The translation for this passage is from Varela, *Letters to Elpidio*, 270.
60. Varela, *Cartas a Elpidio*, 2:157.
61. Varela, *Cartas a Elpidio*, 1:26.
62. Varela, *Cartas a Elpidio*, 2:129.
63. Varela, *Cartas a Elpidio*, 2:129. In other passages too, Varela refers to women's looks as a factor in irreligiosity, suggesting that "unattractive" women turn away from religion for attention and even acclaim.
64. Irwin, *Mexican Masculinities*, xxvii–xxviii.
65. Sedgwick, *Between Men*, 1–5.
66. Segwick, *Between Men*, 1.
67. Varela, *Cartas a Elpidio*, 2:130.
68. Quoted in Morris Eckhardt, *Fanny Wright*, 189.
69. For a critical view of Wright's communal project, known as Nashoba, see Bederman, "Revisiting Nashoba."
70. Varela, *Cartas a Elpidio*, 2:132.
71. Varela, *Cartas a Elpidio*, 2:122.
72. Varela, *Cartas a Elpidio*, 2:126.
73. Duane, *Visit to Colombia*, 609. The title page notes that the book was printed "for the author."
74. Duane, *Visit to Colombia*, 608; García Samudio, *La independencia de Hispanoamérica*, 151.
75. Pérez, *Remembering the Hacienda*, 32.
76. Duane, *Visit to Colombia*, 609.
77. Duane, *Visit to Colombia*, 610.
78. Duane, *Visit to Colombia*, 609–10.
79. Torres, *Exposition*, 6.
80. Quijano and Wallerstein, "Americanity as a Concept," 551. Far-reaching in its historical scope, their essay emphasizes how ethnicity and racism are part and parcel of colonial systems of subjection, which in turn are integral to capitalism and the world system as it emerges after the European contact with the Americas. The *longue durée* approach of Americanity is important for a consideration of how colonial systems pass into a postindependence hierarchy in Latin America as it moves from mercantilism to the free market envisioned by some of the trans-American elite.
81. José David Saldívar describes the article by Quijano and Wallerstein as bridging the concerns of Latin American and American (US) studies through "an outernationalist approach to the cultures of the Américas in the modern world system." Saldívar, *Trans-Americanity*, x.
82. Duane, *Visit to Colombia*, 608–9. Duane also discusses this in the article "Death of Mr. Torres."

83. Duane, *Visit to Colombia*, 608–9.
84. My reading of the *Exposition* is indebted to the work of Emily García.
85. Torres, *Exposition*, 1, hereafter cited parenthetically as *E*.
86. Torres writes, "The business of the merchant is not confined to the purchase and sale of sugar, coffee, and other similar wares and merchandise; it includes also the purchase and sale of bullion, and the exchange operations with foreign countries" (*E* 4).
87. Marichal, "Money, Taxes, and Finance," 430.
88. Walter Isaacson's biography emphasizes Franklin as inventor, scientist, writer, diplomat, political thinker, printer, and business strategist. "The most interesting thing that Franklin invented, and continually reinvented, was himself," Isaacson writes. *Benjamin Franklin*, 2.
89. García, "On the Borders of Independence," 84.
90. Duane, *Visit to Colombia*, 609.
91. The pamphlet was originally Poor Richard's account of a speech delivered by the fictitious Father Abraham at an auction of merchant goods. Father Abraham borrows liberally from *Poor Richard's Almanack*, so that the pamphlet becomes a compilation of Richard's greatest sayings, such as, "The sleeping fox catches no poultry" and "Lost time is never found again." He calls on his audience to save their money rather than spend it on unnecessary items or ostentations luxuries. One of Abraham's final borrowings from Richard is "We may give advice, but we cannot give conduct," and we learn that at the end of the speech as they moved into the auction, "the people heard it and approved the Doctrine, and—immediately practiced the contrary, just as if it had been a common sermon." Franklin, *Father Abraham's Speech*, 5, 15–16.
92. Carrière, "Mr. Jefferson," 394.
93. Torres and Hargous, *Dufief's Nature Displayed*, xv.
94. Steiner, *After Babel*, 290.
95. Torres and Hargous, *Dufief's Nature Displayed*, xxii–xxiii. The edition has two title pages, one in English and the other in Spanish with "Filadelfia" as the place of publication.
96. Torres and Hargous, *Dufief's Nature Displayed*, 2:253.
97. Rodríguez O., Independence of Spanish America, 245.
98. García Samudio, *La independencia de Hispanoamérica*, 149–69.
99. Adams, *Memoirs of John Quincy Adams*, 5:187.
100. Charles H. Bowman Jr. writes that Adams opposed getting involved politically with Spanish America. See his "Manuel Torres in Philadelphia," 19–20.
101. For an account of the final months of Torres's struggle to receive recognition in 1822, see Bowman, "Manuel Torres in Philadelphia," 24–32.

3. Faith in Print

1. Saco, *Obras*, 5:111.
2. Saco, *Obras*, 5:111.
3. Del Monte was born in Maracaibo, on the northern coast of South America, to a father granted important government positions by the Spanish Crown. He studied at Havana's Seminario de San Carlos, and after the death of his father, Del Monte's mother and family settled in Matanzas, where they ran a sugar plantation. In 1834, Del Monte married Rosa Aldama, the daughter of one of the richest planters in Cuba. See Martínez, *Domingo Del Monte*, 43–57, 189.
4. Saco, *Obras*, 5:111.
5. Some Filadelfia writers, as we saw in the preceding two chapters, saw themselves as the heirs of the US Revolution's combination of letters and republicanism and were driven in part by a notion of causation: documents in the tradition of *Common Sense* and the US Declaration of Independence could lead to independent nation-states. Although publication was driven in part by such a belief, it is difficult to quantify or even gauge the effects of print, particularly as it pertains to individual publications, as we saw in chapter 1 in reference to Manuel García de Sena's translation of Thomas Paine. While one strand of scholarship on print, associated with Elizabeth Eisenstein's work, privileges technologies of print as having a deterministic effect on politics and culture, the Saco–Del Monte letters show how difficult it is to determine which came first. See Eisenstein, *Printing Press*.
6. Warner, *Letters of the Republic*, 36.
7. In Latin American studies, debates about the public sphere have turned to myriad implications of the term, which can encompass everything from public squares to patriotic societies. François-Xavier Guerra's collection *Los espacios públicos en Iberoamérica* proposes the term *public space* as a way to move past what the contributors view as an immaterial abstraction in the public-sphere theory. Victor Uribe-Uran's account of an "incipient public sphere" in the late Spanish colony draws from various types of interactions. See his "Birth of a Public Sphere in Latin America." James E. Sanders has called for a hemispheric approach that reconsiders the public sphere in relation to all classes in society. See his "Democracy in Las Américas," 375, 379.
8. In developing notions of the public vis-à-vis the town, Habermas focuses on three European sites: France, Great Britain, and Germany. See Habermas, *Structural Transformation*, 31–43.
9. Fraser, "Transnationalizing the Public Sphere," 8.
10. Fraser, "Transnationalizing the Public Sphere," 15.
11. Pazos, *Letters on the United Provinces of South America*, 121–22.
12. Grases, *Preindependencia y emancipación*, 276.

13. John Lynch describes competing interests in the First Republic as follows. "The royalists fought for the old order. The independists fought for creole supremacy. The *pardos* and slaves fought for their own liberation. So there were a number of movements and each confronted or exploited the other. These divisions created propitious circumstances for the restoration of royal power." See *Spanish American Revolutions,* 198.
14. Augusto Mijares, prologue to Roscio, *Obras,* 1:xxii; Ugalde, *El pensamiento,* 33.
15. Augusto Mijares, prologue to Roscio, *Obras,* 1:xxiv.
16. Juan Germán Roscio to Martín Tovar, 20 April 1816, in Roscio, *Obras,* 3:41–43.
17. Roscio became gravely ill while in Philadelphia and signed a will in which he requested that the merchant William Watson, of New Orleans, be paid back the two hundred dollars. A translation of the will was published in the Philadelphia *Aurora* upon Roscio's death in 1821. "J. G. Roscio," *Aurora General Advertiser,* 11 June 1821. A Spanish version appears as "Testamento de Roscio" in his *Obras,* 2:136–37.
18. Juan Germán Roscio to Manuel Torres. 14 August 1819, in Roscio, *Obras,* 2:264–65.
19. Once he returned to Venezuela in 1818, Roscio contributed to the periodical *El Correo de Orinoco* and also took on duties of vice president of the newly established country of Gran Colombia. He died in 1821.
20. Roscio, *Obras,* 2:104–5.
21. "Venta de Impresos," in *La prensa heroica,* 33.
22. Vogeley, *Bookrunner,* 110.
23. The editions are as follows: Mexico City: Imp de Martín Rivera, 1824 (abridged); Oaxaca, Mexico: Imprenta de York a cargo de Juan Oledo, 1828; and Mexico City: Imprenta de Juan R. Navarro, 1857. A third Philadelphia edition in 1847 is cited by scholars, but I have not been able to confirm this publication. See Pedro Grases, "Notas del Compilador," in Roscio, *Obras,* 1:iv; and Roscio, *El triunfo de la libertad,* 275–76.
24. Domingo Miliani has noted that an edition of *El triunfo de la libertad sobre el despotismo* was published in Oaxaca in 1828, the same year that Juárez was studying in that city. It's possible that Juárez got a copy, but Miliani stops short of arguing direct influence and calls for other researchers to find more persuasive evidence that Juárez was indeed influenced by *El triunfo*. Miliani, "Juan Germán Roscio," 142–43.
25. Losada, *Juan Germán Roscio,* 12–13.
26. Ruiz Barrionuevo, "Juan Germán Roscio," 187–94.
27. "J. G. Roscio," *Aurora General Advertiser,* 11 June 1821.
28. The Spanish version reads, "Primeramente declaro y confieso que profeso la religión Santa de Jesucristo, y como más conforme a ella, profeso y deseo morir bajo el sistema de gobierno republicano, y protesto contra el tiránico y

despótico gobierno de monarquía absoluta, como el de España." Roscio, "Testamento de Roscio," *Obras,* 2:136.
29. Citations are from the 1996 edition of Roscio, *El triunfo de la libertad,* 3–4, hereafter cited parenthetically as *T.*
30. Ugalde, *El pensamiento,* 25. For an excellent short overview of Roscio's political views, see Cazzato, Piña, and López, "Libertad vs. Despotismo."
31. Ruiz Barrionuevo, "Juan Germán Roscio," 198.
32. How Rousseau came to figure in *El triunfo de la libertad* has drawn the attention of Venezuelan scholars who remark on a vexing passage at the start of chapter 5. Roscio quotes at length writing that is clearly influenced by Rousseau, but the passage's author has not been established. Guillermo Emilio Willwoll first noted that the passage at the start of chapter 5 is a quotation. The following lines start the lengthy quotation: "Soberanía es el resultado del poder y de la fuerza moral y física de los hombres congregados en sociedad: fuera de ella, cada uno es un pequeño soberano porque se halla dotado de facultades intelectuales y corporales, esenciales constitutivos de la soberanía" (*T* 27; Sovereignty emerges from the power and the moral and physical strength of man congregated in a society; outside society, each man is a small sovereign because he is given intellectual and physical abilities that are the essential elements of sovereignty). Ugalde (*El pensamiento,* 78–79) argues that this quoted passage provides insight into Roscio's intertwining of Rousseau and the Bible. Among other scholars who have noted the influence of Rousseau on Roscio is Augusto Mijares in his prologue to Roscio, *Obras,* 1:xxxviii–xxxix.
33. Coronado, *A World Not to Come,* 59.
34. Andrews, *Afro-Latin America,* 41.
35. Blanchard, *Under the Flags of Freedom,* 21.
36. English-language verses are from the English Standard Version, BibleGateway.com.
37. "Con leer siquiera el sumario del capítulo, queda averiguada esta verdad, y disipado el error introducido en obsequio de la monarquía absoluta" (*T* 13).
38. Miliani, introduction to Roscio, *El triunfo de la libertad,* xl.
39. For an example of liberation-theology writing that follows a hermeneutics comparable to that of Roscio's *El triunfo,* see Gustavo Gutiérrez's *Theology of Liberation,* 106, where he writes, "If all that is human is illuminated by the Word, it is precisely because the Word reaches us through human history."
40. Roscio calls the lower class "la más excelente de todas, la real y verdadera, la celebrada en divinas y humanas letras y la estimada y amada de Dios y de los buenos." Quoted in Ugalde, *El pensamiento,* 30.
41. Ugalde, *El pensamiento,* 30–31.
42. See http://www.ilustrecolegiodeabogadosdecaracas.com/quienes-somos/nuestra-institucion-gremial/, accessed December 2018.
43. Almarza Villalobos, "Limpieza de sangre," 306.

44. Documents related to Roscio's application to the College of Lawyers and to the case involving Isabel María Páez are in Parra Márquez, *Historia del colegio de abogados de Caracas*, 1:445–596.
45. Chambers, "Little Middle Ground," 32.
46. Archer, "Introduction," 8.
47. Fernando Molina raises questions about which of his parents was indigenous. See his *Vicente Pazos Kanki*, 15–16.
48. Bowman, *Vicente Pazos Kanki*, 34–35.
49. According to Bowman, *Vicente Pazos Kanki*, 37, he was ordained in Chuquisaca. Charles W. Arnade, in his prologue to Pazos Kanki, *Compendio*, says that Pazos never renounced his priesthood but just did not practice (xxiii–xxiv).
50. These *Letters on the United Provinces of South America* are a hybrid text, offering descriptions of recent independence movements in South America, the oppressive treatment of indigenous populations, religious customs, and social classes. Most of the second half of the book is devoted to geographic accounting and detailed information about mines and the availability of minerals, clearly with the goal of promoting commercial interaction with the United States. In this book, Pazos Kanki is particularly brutal in his treatment of the Catholic Church; passages such as the following, in which he comments on the levying of taxes on indigenous populations for funerals, would have appealed to anti-Catholic sentiment in the United States: "A religion, so abused and transformed into a systematic mode of thieving and robbery, is a calamity more dreadful than a pestilence" (92). Clay was known as a supporter of independence for Spanish America.
51. See the title page of Pazos Kanki, *Compendio de la historia de los Estados Unidos de América* (1825).
52. Pazos, *Letters on the United Provinces of South America*, 18.
53. Bowman, *Vicente Pazos Kanki*, 49.
54. *El Censor* published twelve issues issues from 7 January to 21 March 1812. *La Crónica* published twenty-eight issues from 30 August 1816 to 8 February 1817. Bowman, *Vicente Pazos Kanki*, 57, 90.
55. Bowman, *Vicente Pazos Kanki*, 79–82.
56. Bowman, *Vicente Pazos Kanki*, 88.
57. Pazos, *Exposition*, 11, hereafter cited parenthetically as *E*.
58. Bowman, "Amelia Island Affair, 1817," 277.
59. Wyllys, "Filibusters of Amelia Island," 298.
60. Owsley and Smith, *Filibusters and Expansionists*, 118–40.
61. Owsley and Smith, *Filibusters and Expansionists*, 140.
62. Bowman, "Agent of the Amelia Island Filibusters, 1818," 435.
63. Charles Arnade, prologue to Pazos Kanki, *Compendio de la historia*, xxiv.
64. Fitz, *Our Sister Republics*, 50.
65. Molina, *Vicente Pazos Kanki*, 28.

66. Pazos, *Letters on the United Provinces of South America*, 124.
67. Pazos, *Letters on the United Provinces of South America*, 242.
68. The third volume of Varela's *Lecciones de filosofía* deals almost exclusively with science. Among the topics covered are electrical currents, combustion, gases, chemical properties, and meteors.
69. Cubans often refer to Varela as "el primero que nos enseñó a pensar" (the first who taught us how to think), attributed to José de la Luz y Caballero. Others have called him "el padre de la patria" (father of the country), which is the inscription on Varela's statue at the University of Havana. He has also been called "el primer cubano" (the first Cuban) and "el primer revolucionario" (the first revolutionary). Jorge Mañach calls Varela "primero de nuestros periodistas políticos y precursor del ideal de independencia." See Mañach, *Perfil de nuestras letras*, 115.
70. For more on this concept see Lazo, "Hemispheric Americanism."
71. Varela, *El Habanero*, 6, hereafter cited parenthetically as *H*.
72. In deciding to translate *cambia colores* as "chameleons," I lose the opportunity to translate the word *bichos* as "insects" and thus opt for "beasts," which speaks to the word's etymological antecedent in the Latin *bestius*.
73. Varela writes about these two events in *El Habanero*. In a supplement to the third issue, he says authorities on the island have taken out a bounty and plan to send an assassin to kill him in the United States. "¡Miserables! ¿Creéis destruír la verdad asesinando al que la dice?" (*H* 137; Wretched! Do you believe you can destroy truth by killing the one who delivers it?). Issue 4 opens with the following line: "Todas las cartas que se reciben de aquella isla convienen en que mi pobre *Habanero* sufre la más cruel persecución" (*H* 140; All the letters received from that island agree that my poor *Habanero* suffers from the most cruel suppression).
74. "Los americanos nacen con el amor a la independencia" (*H* 75).
75. Habermas, Structural Transformation, 17.
76. Saco, *Colección de papeles*, 1:220.
77. Response, *El Mensagero Semanal*, 3 October 1829, 50.
78. "Ultimo dia del Mensagero," *El Mensagero Semanal*, 29 January 1831, 192.
79. "Ultimo dia del Mensagero."
80. "Rusia y Turquia," *El Mensagero Semanal*, 19 August 1828.
81. "Variedades," *El Mensagero Semanal*, 27 December 1828.
82. "Ultimo dia del Mensagero."
83. Lista, "Juicio crítico de las poesias de Don José Maria Heredia," *El Mensagero Semanal*, 27 December 1828, 149.
84. "Poesías de D. José Maria de Heredia," *El Mensagero Semanal*, 18 April 1829, 276.
85. "Poesías de D. José Maria de Heredia," 276.
86. "Poesías de D. José Maria de Heredia," 276.
87. "Poesías de D. José Maria de Heredia," 277.

88. "De los Anales de Ciencias, Etc.," *El Mensagero Semanal,* 3 October 1829.
89. José Antonio Saco, untitled response, *El Mensagero Semanal,* 3 October 1829, 51. Most likely here he was talking about Varela and himself and not about Domingo Del Monte, who did study poetry.
90. Saco, *Colección de papeles,* 1:219.
91. Freire, *Entre la ilustración y el romanticismo,* 216.
92. "Advertencia," in Del Monte, *Versos de J. Nicasio Gallego.* Spellings of *conterraneos* and *estrangero* and all accents in the original.
93. Freire, *Entre la ilustración y el romanticismo,* 223–38.
94. Peers, *Short History of the Romantic Movement in Spain,* 138–39.
95. José Maria Heredia, "A Washington," in Heredia, *Antología Herediana,* 40. Published originally in Heredia, *Poesías* (1825).
96. Said, *Reflections on Exile,* 175.

4. Anonymously Yours: Republican Man

1. See, e.g., Griffin, *Faces of Anonymity.*
2. Bustillos, "By Anonymous."
3. Félix Varela wrote in *El Habanero* that after the publication was banned, Spanish authorities sent an assassin to kill him in the United States. See "Suplemento al No. 3 de 'El Habanero,'" in Varela, *El Habanero,* 137.
4. Foucault, "Human Nature," 16.
5. Leal, "Jicoténcal, primera novela histórica."
6. In their introduction to the Arte Público edition, xxxvi, Leal and Cortina provide scholarly and political arguments for situating *Jicoténcal* among Hispanic novels of the United States.
7. I thank Nicolás Kanellos for providing me a copy of this pamphlet years before it became available through databases.
8. Garrett, "First Constitution of Texas," 294–95; Coronado, *A World Not to Come,* 204.
9. Coronado, *A World Not to Come,* 207.
10. Nicolás Kanellos cites as evidence the appearance of *El amigo de los hombres* in Nagadochez, TX, as part of a conspiracy in which Álvarez de Toledo participated. See Kanellos, "José Alvarez de Toledo," 91–92 and n26.
11. Although some of the type on the two title pages is similar, the printer leaves out an imprint on the title page of Álvarez de Toledo's *Manifiesto.* Bibliographical records do not indicate a publisher or printer for the *Manifiesto.* Among evidence presented by Coronado is the publication of the *Manifiesto* in Philadelphia on the same date as the one noted at the end of *El amigo:* 10 December 1811 in Washington. But Coronado also offers competing publication dates, "sometime between late October and early December," for the *Manifiesto.* Coronado, *A World Not to Come,* 207, 164, 176.

12. Llorens, *Liberales y románticos,* 31.
13. For a biographical and intellectual overview of Blanco White and particularly his work in London, see Goytisolo, *Blanco White,* 13–33.
14. *El amigo de los hombres,* 1.
15. Berruezo León, *La lucha de Hispanoamérica,* 21.
16. Berruezo León, *La lucha de Hispanoamérica,* 45–46.
17. Rezek, *London and the Making of Provincial Literature,* 25.
18. "Oficio del Secretario de relaciones exteriores del gobierno de Caracas, al Editor del Español," *El Español* 16 (30 July 1811): 295.
19. Blanco White, "Contextacion," 300.
20. Blanco White, "Contextacion," 301.
21. Goytisolo, *Blanco White,* 26.
22. Blanco White, "Contextacion," 302–3.
23. Goytisolo, *Blanco White,* 30–31.
24. *El amigo de los hombres,* 13, hereafter cited parenthetically as *A.*
25. Lasso, *Myths of Harmony,* 51–52.
26. For estimated populations, including slaves and free blacks, see Andrews, *Afro-Latin America,* 41. Andrews notes the difficulties of tracking racial composition in countries that did not keep such data consistently (203–7).
27. Lasso, *Myths of Harmony,* 9. See also Lasso, "Un mito republicano de armonía racial."
28. Lasso, *Myths of Harmony,* 31.
29. [Smart], *Republican's Manual,* 3. Hereafter the two editions will be cited parenthetically as *M1* (English) and *M2* (Spanish).
30. Emily García proposes that Manuel Torres was involved in the publication of *Manual de un republicano.* "On the Borders of Independence," 84.
31. Sagredo Baeza, "Actores políticos," 505.
32. Rivero, *Lecciones de politica.*
33. See Ruiz, *Las confesiones de un pecador arrepentido,* 62–63.
34. Sagredo Baeza, "Actores políticos," 504.
35. Miller, "Reading Rousseau in Spanish America," 114.
36. Brickhouse, *Transamerican Literary Relations,* 51.
37. Rodríguez O., Independence of Spanish America, 243.
38. Rocafuerte, *Un americano libre,* 50.
39. The notable Ecuadorean scholar Neptali Zúñiga, who edited a multivolume collection of Rocafuerte's writings, proposes that anonymous publication allowed Rocafuerte, while working as a diplomat for Mexico, to justify financial assistance that he passed to Canga Argüelles. Zúñiga, prologue to *Cartas de un americano,* in Rocafuerte, *Colección Rocafuerte,* 4:ii–iii.
40. Milian, "Crisis Management and the LatinX Child," 11.
41. *Cartas de un americano,* in Rocafuerte, *Collección Rocafuerte,* 4:5–6, hereafter cited parenthetically as *C.*

42. Egaña, *Memorias políticas*, 6–27.
43. The nine letters in *Cartas de un americano* are organized as follows: two letters introducing the argument against Egaña and in support of federal governments; a lengthy letter comparing the federal constitutions of the United States, Mexico, and Guatemala, with additional comparisons to unitary governments; three letters engaging with Egaña's arguments and making a case in general terms for federal governments; two letters examining the United States, including a detailed discussion of customs, religious practice, and economic vitality; and a final letter considering the constitution in Chile.
44. The accent was added to the title *Jicoténcal* in later centuries but was not present in the 1826 edition.
45. *Catalogue of an Extensive Collection of Books.*
46. The most complete account of authorship debates on *Jicoténcal* is in González Acosta, *El enigma de "Jicoténcal,"* 119–36. For an English-language account, see Brickhouse, *Transamerican Literary Relations*, 47–51. The earliest positioning of *Jicoténcal* in Mexico's literary history was its inclusion in John Lloyd Read's 1939 study *The Mexican Historical Novel, 1826–1910*. But Read was careful to spell out that its authorship was uncertain and and stated that "its inclusion here must be tentative." See Read, *Mexican Historical Novel*, 82.
47. Castro Leal, *La novela del méxico colonial*, 1:84.
48. José María Heredia's name has always circled around the novel because in 1823 Heredia wrote an unfinished draft of a theatrical play about the historical figure Jicoténcal. See McPheeters, "Xicoténcatl," 405. The most forceful defender of the Heredia attribution is González Acosta. See his *El enigma de "Jicoténcal,"* 119–204.
49. Leal's methodology was impressive. He compared phrases and concepts in the novel with Varela's other writing (at a time when computerized technology could not facilitate that work).
50. Debra Castillo does not say whether she thinks Varela or Heredia wrote the book, but she does propose that colonial Cuba looms large in relation to the book. See *Redreaming America*, 23, 36.
51. Leal, "Jicoténcal, primera novela histórica," 23. In their introduction to the Arte Público edition, Leal and Cortina acknowledge that their argument rests largely on stylistic considerations: "En términos generales, podríamos decir que la prosa de la novela se parece a la de Varela en el estilo discursivo, aforístico, de giro rápido y conciso" (xxx; In general terms, we could say that the prose of the novel resembles Varela's style, which is logical, aphoristic, concise and turns rapidly).
52. Varela, *Cartas a Elpidio*, 2:99.
53. Brickhouse also notes Varela's objection to anonymous publication. See *Transamerican Literary Relations*, 53.

54. I thank Carmen Lamas for the references in the *New York Catholic Register.* See "The Pilgrim Fathers," *New York Catholic Register,* 2 January 1940, 117.
55. Rojas Garcidúeñas, "Otra novela sobre el tema de Xicoténcatl," 102.
56. Brickhouse writes, "There is good reason to suspect that the novel's anonymity disguises not the name of one author but the members of a transnational collectivity that ensured its progress from exilic manuscript to printed book. Anonymity and collaboration often went hand in hand during this period, when controversial writings by dissidents and exiles depended on secretive transmission as well as coterie circulation and revision for their publication." *Transamerican Literary Relations,* 51. She proposes that both Rocafuerte and Heredia may have been involved. But the possibility of collaboration or even single authorship should not remain within the sphere of major figures such as Varela, Heredia, and Rocafuerte. What about other, lesser-known intellectuals in Philadelphia? I am less interested in answering this questioning than in taking the title page at its anonymous word.
57. Earle, *Return of the Native,* 3.
58. Unless otherwise noted, English-language quotations are from Guillermo I. Castillo-Feliú, trans., *Xicoténcatl,* 8, hereafter cited parenthetically as *X.*
59. Bryant, review of *Jicoténcal,* 343.
60. Bryant, review of *Jicoténcal,* 344.
61. Pocock, *Machiavellian Moment,* viii. Pocock also uses the term *Machiavellian moment* to refer to a problem in historical self-understanding that Machiavelli and his contemporaries grappled with during the Florentine Republic.
62. Citations from the Spanish-language version of *Jicoténcal* are from the Arte Público edition, hereafter cited parenthetically as *J.*
63. In cases where I disagree with parts of Castillo-Feliú's translation, I cite the Spanish and provide my own translation.
64. Castillo, *Redreaming America,* 21.

5. Leaving Filadelfia, or Archival Dislocations

1. The word *peregrination* captures the kind of movement and travel undertaken by Servando, in part because of its spiritual connotation.
2. Arenas, *Ill-Fated Peregrinations,* 211.
3. Franklin, *Autobiography,* 32.
4. Arenas, *Ill-Fated Peregrinations,* 211. Agustín de Iturbide was a Mexican army general and politician who assumed the title "Emperor of Mexico" after the country gained independence.
5. The novel also reminds us that independence did not eliminate various problems, and thus Servando's disappointment at the institution of new centralized forms of power.

6. Brading, *Origins of Mexican Nationalism*, 62–65; Benson, "Servando Teresa de Mier, Federalist," 514–17.
7. Brading, *Origins of Mexican Nationalism*, 65; see also 48–65 on Mier and nationalism.
8. My discussion here is influenced by a variety of work on the theory and practice of archives, which has an extensive bibliography. From a theoretical standpoint, see Derrida, *Archive Fever;* Foucault, *Archeology of Knowledge;* and Agamben, *Remnants of Auschwitz*. Among historical and postcolonial studies, see Stoler, *Along the Archival Grain*. In library studies, see Jimmerson, *Archives Power*.
9. "*Consignation* aims to coordinate a single corpus, in a system or a synchrony in which all the elements articulate the unity of an ideal configuration," Derrida writes. *Archive Fever*, 3.
10. The establishment of nation-states went hand in hand with the construction of archives. A revolutionary break from monarchy in the nineteenth and twentieth centuries was often the catalyst for the establishment of a national archive, including those of France in 1790 and Mexico in 1823. In the case of the latter, independence from Spain shifted the frame of the archive from a colonial holding in Europe to the Archivo General de la Nación in Mexico City. In national archives, the archive and nation came together to grant each other authority and credibility: the holdings contained documents and records that supposedly spoke to and about the state, while the nation granted a certain cachet to an archive, elevating it above its local and regional counterparts. For a longer discussion of this issue, see Lazo, "Migrant Archives."
11. This is a problem of knowledge organization and goes far beyond the scope of this book. In many ways the term *archive* is marshaled today (and so overused as to become comical) as a way to maneuver through changes in academic disciplines and their interdisciplinary heirs as well as institutional formations. That is why the use of the phrase *my archive* is so telling; it speaks to a radical subjectivity that informs debates over fields of study and the future of humanistic inquiry.
12. O'Gorman, *Fray Servando Teresa de Mier;* O'Gorman, *Mier: Escritos y memorias*.
13. Mier, *Memoria politico-instructiva*, 46, hereafter cited parenthetically as *M*.
14. O'Gorman, *Mier: Escritos y memorias*, xxi.
15. Rotker, introduction to Mier Noriega y Guerra, *Memoirs of Fray Servando*, xxxv.
16. O'Gorman was one of the main contributors to the influential collection *Do the Americas Have a Common History?*, edited by Lewis Hanke. Among collections on O'Gorman's work is *La obra de Edmundo O'Gorman*. Works by US-based scholars who have been influenced by O'Gorman's work include Mignolo, *Idea of Latin America*, and Rabasa, *Inventing America*. O'Gorman has also been

discussed in US American studies for decades. See Rozwenc, "O'Gorman and the Idea of America."
17. O'Gorman, *Invention of America*, 103. O'Gorman did his own translation of the English edition.
18. O'Gorman, *Invention of America*, 15.
19. For a perceptive and interesting biographical study, see Domínguez Michael, *Vida de Fray Servando*.
20. Benson, "Servando Teresa de Mier, Federalist," 514.
21. O'Gorman, preface to Mier Noriega y Guerra, *Ideario político*, xiii.
22. Mier Noriega y Guerra, *Memoirs of Fray Servando*, 65.
23. Kadir, *Memos from the Besieged City*, 110.
24. Certeau, *Practice of Everyday Life*, 117.
25. Domínguez Michael, *Vida de Fray Servando*, 593–96.
26. José Servando Teresa de Mier Noriega y Guerra Papers, 1808–1823, Nettie Lee Benson Latin American Collection, University of Texas Libraries, University of Texas at Austin. Drawing from research by Yael Britan Goren, Domínguez Michael discusses the receipts in *Vida de Fray Servando*, 600–601.
27. The Mier Noriega y Guerra Papers include receipts from Hurtel dated 16 July and 30 July 1821.
28. Manuel Torres to Servando Teresa de Mier, 16 October 1821, Mier Noriega y Guerra Papers.
29. Lawrance, *Spanish Conquest, Protestant Prejudice*, 12.
30. Mier, "Discurso Preliminar," in Mier, *Breve relación*, xxxv.
31. Las Casas, *Breve relación*.
32. For a discussion of Las Casas and the proposal on slavery, see Castro, *Another Face of Empire*, 71–74. For a reconsideration of Las Casas's attitude toward slavery and the argument that his sense of slavery was influenced by the life of slaves in Seville, Spain, rather than the later plantation system, see Clayton, "Bartolomé de las Casas," 1527–29. (I would disagree with Clayton's suggestive argument because the labor conditions for indigenous people that Las Casas had witnessed in Cuba and elsewhere were abysmal.)
33. Lombardi, *Political Ideology of Fray Servando*, chap. 1, p. 17. In chapter 2 of his book, Lombardi outlines the various political positions taken by Mier in his writing.
34. Carey, "Arguments for Lay Participation," 43.
35. Light, *Rome and the New Republic*, 106; for context on the schism at St. Mary's, see 97–127.
36. *Graphic Account of the Alarming Riots*, 6–7.
37. Mier, *A Word Relative*.
38. Mier Noriega y Guerra, *Obras completas*, 4:240.
39. Joseph Dugan et al. to Servando Theresa de Mier, 28 July 1821, Mier Noriega y Guerra Papers.

40. Mier's spatial story makes us aware of how the constitutional debates are driven in part by a spatial metaphor. The notion of a unitary or strong central government was termed *centralism*, which marks where power will be situated. Constitutions raise questions about the relationship between provinces and the seat of government, for example, whether power resides in the capital or in the states. At the point in history when *Memoria politico-instructiva* was published, the maps of nations in the Americas had not been completely drawn, and neither were their constitutions. Because the space of Spanish-language writing such as Servando's *Memoria* moves toward transatlantic crossings and hemispheric spaces—and those spaces are always changing—it is necessary to shift the location from where one reads Mier repeatedly. Neither the limited national US or Mexican approach would be sufficient, and his texts are bound to prompt archival dislocation.
41. The passage is as follows: "La calle de moda, y por lo mismo más concurrida, es la de Chesnutt [*sic*], donde se hallan paseando las muchachas bonitas, que aquí abundan más que en ninguna otra parte de los Estados Unidos. ¡Cuánto me he acordado al verlas de tus lamentaciones sobre la escasez que de ellas se sufre en M . . . !" The *M* is a reference to Matanzas. Heredia, *Antología Herediana*.
42. Domínguez Michael, *Vida de Fray Servando*, 490–505.
43. Brading, *Origins of Mexican Nationalism*, 55–56.
44. Charlotte Stephenson to Servando Teresa de Mier, 6 August 1821, Mier Noriega y Guerra Papers.
45. Servando Teresa de Mier to Mary and Charlotte Stephenson, 20 June 1821, Mier Noriega y Guerra Papers. It is unclear why a Spanish-language copy of this letter (presumably sent) is in the Mier Papers. Could it be that what he actually sent was an English-language version of this letter?
46. Leguía, *Manuel Lorenzo de Vidaurre*, 155–56.
47. Leguía, *Manuel Lorenzo de Vidaurre*, 207.
48. Lohman Villena, "Manuel Lorenzo de Vidaurre," 200.
49. Vidaurre, *Efectos de las facciones*, 266.
50. In *Efectos de las facciones*, Vidaurre describes himself on the title page as *citizen* Vidaurre, a Supreme Court justice, diplomatic minister, and congressional legislator. The title page promises an account of his expatriation: "El Cuidadano M.L. Vidaurre, presidente de la Corte Suprema de Justicia de la Republica del Peru, Ministro plenipotenciario en el gran congreso de Panama, ministro de estado y de relaciones interiores y exteriores, diputado por la provincial de Lima en el congreso constituyente; resulta de su Expatriacion" (Citizen M. L. Vidaurre, chief justice of the Supreme Court of the Republic of Peru, diplomatic envoy at the congress of Panama, minister of foreign and domestic affairs, deputy for the province of Lima in the congress, effects of his expatriation). Vidaurre is brutal in his attacks on congressional opponents and includes in the book speeches that he delivered in Peru. He also publishes writings by

the opposition, suggesting that he wants a dialogue, or at least a concrete text against which to argue.
51. Vidaurre, *Cartas americanas*, 13. Quotations are from the 1973 Peru edition, which modernizes the use of accents and corrects spelling errors.
52. Vidaurre, *Cartas americanas*, 219.
53. Vidaurre, *Cartas americanas*, 37.
54. Lohman Villena, "Manuel Lorenzo de Vidaurre," 205.
55. Vidaurre, *Cartas americanas*, 122.
56. Rousseau, *La nouvelle Héloise*, 25.
57. Vidaurre, *Cartas americanas*, 14.
58. Vidaurre, *Efectos de las facciones*, 277.
59. Vidaurre, *Cartas americanas*, 97.
60. Vidaurre, *Cartas americanas*, 15.
61. [Ruschenberger], *Three Years in the Pacific*, 270–71.
62. *Haut ton* here refers to the most fashionable people. For an interesting gloss, see Knowles, "What is the haut ton?"
63. [Ruschenberger], *Three Years in the Pacific*, 271.
64. Socolow, "Acceptable Partners," 210.
65. Josefa Luisa Rivera to Manuel Lorenzo Vidaurre, in Vidaurre, *Cartas americanas*, 19.
66. Josefa Luisa Rivera to Manuel Lorenzo Vidaurre, in Vidaurre, *Cartas americanas*, 207–8.
67. Vidaurre, *Cartas americanas*, 52.
68. Vidaurre, *Cartas americanas*, 52.
69. Vidaurre, *Cartas americanas*, 3.
70. Leguía, *Manuel Lorenzo de Vidaurre*, 165.
71. Grases and Harkness, *Manuel García de Sena*, 27–28.
72. Grases and Harkness, *Manuel García de Sena*, 28.
73. José María Heredia to Ignacio Heredia y Campuzano, 4 November 1825, in Cairo Balester, *Jose Mará Heredia: 1803–2003*.
74. Grases and Harkness, *Manuel García de Sena*, 28.
75. Grases and Harkness, *Manuel García de Sena*, 29.
76. Lamas, "Raimundo Cabrera," 210.
77. According to Grases and Harkness, Domingo's letters are held by his family. See Grases and Harkness, *Manuel García de Sena*, 27n24.
78. Ruiz, "7 Things People Get Wrong."
79. Porter, foreword to "Men/Women of Letters," 7.
80. Lacan, "Seminar on 'The Purloined Letter,'" 53. I thank the late Marshall Grossman for his interventions.
81. Derrida, "Purveyor of Truth," 187, responded to Lacan.

Bibliography

Archives, Rare Book Libraries, and Special Collections

American Antiquarian Society, Worcester, MA.
American Philosophical Society, Philadelphia.
Carey, Mathew. Papers. American Antiquarian Society, Worcester, MA.
Historical Society of Pennsylvania, Philadelphia.
Huntington Library, San Marino, CA.
Rocafuerte, Vicente. Letter to Josiah Stoddard Johnston. 1 March 1823. Josiah Stoddard Johnston Papers. Historical Society of Pennsylvania, Philadelphia.
Lea & Febiger Collection. Historical Society of Pennsylvania, Philadelphia.
Library Company of Philadelphia.
Library of Congress, Rare Book and Special Collections, Washington, DC.
Mier Noriega y Guerra, José Servando Teresa de. Papers, 1808–1823. Nettie Lee Benson Latin American Collection, University of Texas Libraries, University of Texas at Austin.
New-York Historical Society, New York.
Poinsett, Joel Roberts. Papers. Historical Society of Pennsylvania, Philadelphia.
University of Maryland Special Collections and University Archives, College Park, MD.

Filadelfia Imprints and Other Cited Early Nineteenth-Century Publications

El Aguinaldo para el año de 1829. Philadelphia: Carey, Lea & Carey, 1828.
El Aguinaldo para 1830. Philadelphia: Carey, Lea & Carey, 1829.
Álvarez de Toledo y Dubois, José. *Manifiesto ó satisfaccion pundonorosa, á todos los buenos españoles europeos, y á todos pueblos de la America.* Philadelphia, 1811.
El amigo de los hombres: Á todos los que habitan las islas, y el vasto continente de la America Española: Obrita curiosa, interesante, y agradable. Philadelphia: Imprenta de Andres José Blocquerst, 1812.
Blanco White, José. "Contextacion." *El Español* 16 (30 July 30 1811).
Bosquejo ligerisimo de la revolucion de Mégico, desde el grito de Iguala hasta la proclamacion imperial de Iturbide. Por Un Verdadero Americano. Philadelphia: Imprenta de Teracrouef y Naroajeb, 1822.
Bryant, William Cullen. Review of *Jicoténcal*. *United States Review and Literary Gazette,* February 1827, 336–46.
Carta dirigida a los Españoles Americanos. London, 1801.

Cartas de un americano sobre las ventajas de los gobiernos republicanos federativos. London: M. Calero, 1826.

Catalogue of an Extensive Collection of Books, in the English, French, Spanish, and Italian Languages, Sporting Prints, Books of Caricatures, &c. &c. Recently Imported and for Sale. Philadelphia: H. C. Carey & I. Lea, 1825.

Compendio de la historia de los Estados Unidos de América: Puesto en castellano por un Indio de la ciudad de La Paz. Paris: Imprenta de E. Pochard, 1825.

Del Monte, Domingo, ed. *Versos de J. Nicasio Gallego, recogidos y publicados por Domingo Del Monte.* Philadelphia: Imprenta Española del Mensagero, 1829.

El director de los niños para aprender á deletrear y leer. Philadelphia: En la Imprenta de Matio Carey, 1811.

Duane, William. *A Visit to Colombia in the Years 1822 and 1823.* Philadelphia: Thomas H. Palmer, 1826.

Egaña, Juan. *Memorias políticas sobre las federaciones y legislaturas en general y con relación a Chile.* Santiago, Chile: Imprenta de la Independencia, 1825.

Flórez Estrada, Alvaro. *Exámen imparcial de las disensiones de la América con la España, de los medios de su reconciliación, y de la prosperidad de todas las naciones.* Cádiz, 1812.

[Foronda, Valentin de]. *Cartas sobre lo que debe hacer un principe que tenga colonias á gran distancia.* Philadelphia, 1803.

Franklin, Benjamin. *Father Abraham's Speech to a Great Number of People, at a Vendue of Merchant-Goods.* Boston: Benjamin Mecom, 1758.

García de Sena, Manuel, trans. *Historia concisa de los Estados Unidos, desde el descubrimiento de la América hasta el año de 1807.* By John M'Culloch. Philadelphia: Imprenta de T & G Palmer, 1812.

García de Sena, Manuel, ed. and trans. *La independencia de la Costa Firme justificada por Thomas Paine treinta años ha.* Philadelphia: T. & J. Palmer, 1811.

A Graphic Account of the Alarming Riots at St. Mary's Church, in April of 1822. N.p., 1844.

Heredia, José María. *Poesías.* New York: Libreria de Behr & Kahl, Imprenta de Gray & Bunce, 1825.

Jicoténcal. 2 vols. Philadelphia: Imprenta de Guillermo Stavely, 1826.

Las Casas, Bartolomé. *Breve relación de la destrucción de las Indias Occidentales.* London: Schulze & Dean, 1812.

Latrobe, B. Henry. *Anniversary Oration Pronounced Before the Society of Artists of the United States.* Philadelphia: Bradford & Innskeep, 1811.

Manual de un republicano, para el uso de un pueblo libre. Philadelphia: Imprenta de T. & J. Palmer, 1812.

Mier, Servando Teresa de, ed. *Breve relación de la destrucción de las Indias Occidentales.* By Bartolomé de Las Casas. Philadelphia: J. F. Hurtel, 1821.

[Mier, Servando Teresa de]. *Memoria politico-instructiva, enviada desde Filadelfia en agosto de 1821, á los gefes independientes del Anáhuac, llamado por los españoles Nueva-España.* Philadelphia: Juan F. Hurtel, 1821.

[Mier, Servando Teresa de]. *The Opinion of the Rt. Rev. Servandus A. Mier, Doctor of Sacred Theology in the Royal and Pontifical University of Mexico . . . on Certain Queries Proposed to Him by the Rev. William Hogan.* Philadelphia, 1821.
[Mier, Servando Teresa de]. *A World Relative to an Anonymous Pamphlet Printed in Philadelphia Entitled, "Remarks on the Opinion of the Rt. Rev. Servandus A. Mier."* Philadelphia, 1821.
Morales, Benigno. *Carta de Benigno Morales a Felix Megia.* Philadelphia: Imprenta de Guillermo Stavely, 1825.
Nos los inquisidores apostolicos, contra la herética pravedad, y apostasia en la ciudad de Mexico. Mexico City, 1794.
Paine, Thomas. *El derecho del hombre.* Translated by Santiago Felipe Puglia. Philadelphia: Matías Carey & Hijos, 1821.
Pazos, Vicente. *The Exposition, Remonstrance and Protest of Don Vincente Pazos, Commissioner on Behalf of the Republican Agents Established at Amelia Island, in Florida, Under the Authority and on Behalf of the Independent States of South America.* Philadelphia, 1818.
Pazos, Vicente. *Letters on the United Provinces of South America, Addressed to the Hon. Henry Clay, Speaker of the House of Representatives of the United States.* Translated by Platt H. Crosby. New York: Printed by J. Seymour, 1819.
El pequeño director de los niños, para aprender á deletrear y leer. Philadelphia: M. Carey, 1811.
Presente las damas. Philadelphia: Carey, Lea & Carey, 1829.
Puglia, James Ph. *A Short Extract (Concerning the Rights of Man and Titles) From the Work Entitled Man Undeceived.* Philadelphia: Printed by Johnston & Justice, 1793.
Puglia, Santiago Felipe. *El desengaño del hombre.* Philadelphia: Imprenta de Francisco Bailey, 1794.
Reflecciones políticas escritas bajo el título de Instinto Común por el ciudadano Tomas Paine y traducidas abreviadamente por Anselmo Nateiu, indígena del Peru. Lima: Imprenta de Rio, 1821.
Reflexiones imparciales sobre la franc-masonería. Philadelphia: Imprenta de Thomas H. Palmer, 1818.
Reflexiones sobre el comercio de España con sus colonias en America en tiempo de guerra. By "Un Español en Philadelphia." Philadelphia: Imprenta de Jaime Carey, 1799.
Rivero, Luis Fernando. *Lecciones de politica, segun los principios del sistema popular representativo, adoptado por las naciones americanas.* Paris: Imprenta de Gaultier-Laguionie, 1827.
Rocafuerte, Vicente, ed. *Ideas necesarias a todo pueblo Americano independiente, que quiera ser libre.* Philadelphia: D. Huntington, 1821.
Rocafuerte, Vicente. *Ideas necesarias a todo pueblo americano independiente, que quiera ser libre.* Puebla, Mexico: P. de la Rosa, 1823.

[Roscio, Juan Germán], trans. *Homilia del cardenal Chiaramonti, obispo de Imola, actualmente sumo Pontifice Pio VII. Dirigida al pueblo de su diocesis en la republica Cisalpina, el dia del nacimineto de J. C. año de 1797.* Philadelphia: J. F. Hurtel, 1817.
Roscio, Juan Germán [J.G.R., Ciudadano de Venezuela en la America del Sur, pseud.]. *El triunfo de la libertad sobre el despotismo.* Philadelphia: Thomas H. Palmer, 1817.
Roscio, J. G. *El triunfo de la libertad sobre el despotismo.* Philadelphia: En la imprenta de M. Carey & Hijos, 1821.
Ruschenberger, William [An Officer of the US Navy]. *Three Years in the Pacific; including Notices of Brazil, Chile, Bolivia, and Peru.* Philadelphia: Carey, Lea, & Blanchard, 1834.
Saco, José Antonio. *Colección de papeles científicos, históricos, políticos, y de otros ramos sobre la isla de Cuba.* 3 vols. Paris: Imprenta de D'Aubusson & Kugelmann, 1858.
Salazar, José María. *Observations on the Political Reforms of Colombia.* Translated by Edward Barry. Philadelphia: Printed by William Stavely, 1828.
Salazar, José María. *Observaciones sobre las reformas politicas de Colombia.* Philadelphia: Imprenta de Guillelmo Stavely, 1828.
T. B. Smart [pseud.?]. *The Republican's Manual, For the Use of a Free People.* Philadelphia: Printed for the author by R. Cochran, 1806.
Torres, Manuel. *An Exposition of the Commerce of Spanish America; With Some Observations Upon Its Importance to the United States.* Philadelphia: G. Palmer, 1816.
Torres, Manuel, and Louis Hargous. *Dufief's Nature Displayed in Her Mode of Teaching Language to Man.* 2 vols. Philadelphia: Printed by T. & G. Palmer, 1811.
Varela, Félix. *Cartas a Elpidio, sobre la impiedad, la superstición y el fanatismo en sus relaciones con la sociedad.* Vol. 1, New York: Imprenta de Guillermo Newell, 1835. Vol. 2, New York: G. P. Scott, 1838.
Viaje por los Estado Unidos del Norte, dedicado á los jovenes mexicanos de ambos secsos. Cincinnati: Imprento por E. Deming, 1834.
Vidaurre, Manuel de. *Cartas americanas, politicas y morales, que contienen muchas reflecciones sobre la Guerra civil de las Americas.* 2 vols. Philadelphia: Juan F. Hurtel, 1823.
Vidaurre, Manuel de. *Plan del Perú, defectos del gobierno Español antiguo, necesarias reformas.* Philadelphia: Impresa por Juan Francisco Hurtel, 1823.
Vidaurre, M. L. *Efectos de las facciones en los gobiernos nacientes. En este libro se recopilan los principios fundamentales del gobiero democratico constitucional representativo.* Boston: W. W. Clapp, 1828.
Vidaurre, M. L. *Proyecto de un código penal; contiene una explicacion prolija de la entidad de los delitos en general, y de la particular naturaleza de los conocidos. Se señalan las penas que parecen proporcionadas. Al ultimo se agrega una disertacion sobre la necesaria reforma del clero.* Boston: Hiram Tupper, 1828.

Views of Philadelphia and its Environs from the Original Drawings Taken in 1827–1830. Philadelphia: C. G. Childs, 1830.
Villavicencio, Joseph Manuel. *Constitucion de los Estados Unidos de América traducida del Ingles al Español por Don Jph. Manuel Villavicencio.* Philadelphia: Smith & M'Kenzie, 1810.
[Viscardo y Guzmán, Juan Pablo]. *Lettre aux Espagnols-Américains.* By "un de Leurs Compatriotes." Philadelphia, 1799.
Webster, Daniel. *Discurso pronunciado al poner la piedra angular del monument de Bunker Hill.* Translated by José María Heredia. New York: Wilder & Campbell, 1825.
Zavala, Lorenzo de. *Viaje a los Estados-Unidos del Norte de América.* Merida de Yucatán: Imprenta de Castillo y Compañía, 1846.

Secondary Sources

Adams, John Quincy. *Memoirs of John Quincy Adams, Comprising Portions of His Diary from 1795 to 1848.* Edited by Charles Francis Adams. 12 vols. Philadelphia: J. B. Lippincott, 1875.
Agamben, Giorgio. *Remnants of Auschwitz: The Witness and the Archive.* New York: Zone Books, 2012.
Aldridge, A. Owen. *Early American Literature: A Comparatist Approach.* Princeton, NJ: Princeton University Press, 1982.
Almarza Villalobos, Angel Rafael. "Limpieza de sangre en el Colegio de Abogados de Caracas al fin del siglo XVIII." *Fronteras de la Historia* 10 (2005): 305–28.
Altman, Janet Gurkin. *Epistolarity: Approaches to a Form.* Columbus: Ohio State University Press, 1982.
Anderson, Benedict. *Imagined Communities.* Rev. ed. New York: Verso, 1991.
Anderson Imbert, Enrique. *Spanish-American Literature: A History.* Translated by John V. Falconieri. Detroit: Wayne State University Press, 1963.
Andrews, George Reid. *Afro-Latin America, 1800–2000.* New York: Oxford University Press, 2004.
Aranda, José. "Contradictory Impulses: María Amparo Ruiz de Burton, Resistance Theory, and the Politics of Chicano/a Studies." *American Literature* 70, no. 3 (September 1998): 551–79.
Aranda, José. "When Archives Collide: Recovering Modernity in Early Mexican American Literature." In Lazo and Alemán, *Latino Nineteenth Century*, 146–67.
Archer, Christon I. "Introduction: Setting the Scene for an Age of Warfare." In *The Wars of Independence in Spanish America*, 3–42. Wilmington, DE: Scholarly Resources, 2000.
Ardao, Arturo. *Génesis de la idea y el nombre de América Latina.* Caracas: Centro de Estudios Latinoamericanos Rómulo Gallegos, 1980.

Arenas, Reinaldo. *The Ill-Fated Peregrinations of Fray Servando*. Translated by Andrew Hurley. New York: Penguin, 1994.
Arenas, Reinaldo. *El mundo alucinante*. Madrid: Cátedra, 2011.
Bachiller y Morales, Antonio. *Apuntes para la historia de las letras y de la instrucción pública en la isla de Cuba*. 3 vols. Havana: Cultural, 1937.
Barton, David, and Nigel Hall. *Letter Writing as Social Practice*. Philadelphia: John Benjamins, 2000.
Bastin, Georges L., Álvaro Echeverri, and Ángela Campo. "Translation and the Emancipation of Hispanic America." In *Translation, Resistance, Activism*, edited by Maria Tymoczko, 42–64. Amherst: University of Massachusetts Press, 2010.
Bauer, Ralph. "Hemispheric Studies." *PMLA* 124 (January 2009): 234–50.
Bauer, Ralph, and José Antonio Mazzotti, eds. *Creole Subjects in the Colonial Americas*. Chapel Hill: University of North Carolina, 2009.
Bederman, Gail. "Revisiting Nashoba: Utopia, and Frances Wright in America, 1818–1826." *American Literary History* 17, no. 3 (Fall 2005): 438–59.
Benson, Nettie Lee. "Servando Teresa de Mier, Federalist." *Hispanic American Historical Review* 28, no. 4 (November 1948): 514–25.
Berlant, Lauren. "Intimacy: A Special Issue." *Critical Inquiry* 24 (Winter 1998): 281–88.
Bernier, Celeste-Marie, Judie Newman, and Matthew Pethers, eds. *The Edinburgh Companion to Nineteenth-Century American Letters and Letter-Writing*. Edinburgh: Edinburgh University Press, 2016.
Bernstein, Harry. "Cultura Inquisitorial." *Historia Mexicana* 2, no. 1 (July–September 1952): 87–97.
Berruezo León, María Teresa. *La lucha de Hispanoamérica por su independencia en Inglaterra, 1800–1830*. Madrid: Ediciones de Cultura Hispánica, 1989.
Blanchard, Peter. *Under the Flags of Freedom: Slave Soldiers and the Wars of Independence in Spanish South America*. Pittsburgh: University of Pittsburgh Press, 2008.
Blaufarb, Rafe. *Bonapartists in the Borderlands: French Exiles and Refugees on the Gulf Coast, 1815–1835*. Tuscaloosa: University of Alabama Press, 2005.
Bowman, Charles H., Jr. "The Activities of Manuel Torres as Purchasing Agent, 1820–21." *Hispanic American Historical Review* 48, no. 2 (May 1968): 234–46.
Bowman, Charles H., Jr. "Manuel Torres, a Spanish American Patriot in Philadelphia, 1796–1822." *Pennsylvania Magazine of History and Biography* 94, no. 1 (January 1970): 26–53.
Bowman, Charles H., Jr. "Manuel Torres in Philadelphia and the Recognition of Colombia Independence, 1821–22." *Records of the American Catholic Historical Society of Philadelphia* 80, no. 1 (March 1969): 17–38.
Bowman, Charles H., Jr. "Vicente Pazos, Agent of the Amelia Island Filibusters, 1818." *Florida Historical Quarterly* 53, no. 4 (April 1975): 428–42.
Bowman, Charles H., Jr. "Vicente Pazos and the Amelia Island Affair, 1817." *Florida Historical Quarterly* 53 (January 1975): 273–95.

Bowman, Charles H., Jr. *Vicente Pazos Kanki: Un Boliviano en la libertad de América.* La Paz, Bolivia: Editorial Los Amigos del Libro, 1975.
Brading, D. A. *The Origins of Mexican Nationalism.* Cambridge: Centre of Latin American Studies, 1985.
Brawley, Benjamin. "Lorenzo Dow." *Journal of Negro History* 1, no. 3 (1915): 265–75.
Brickhouse, Anna. *Transamerican Literary Relations and the Nineteenth-Century Public Sphere.* Cambridge: Cambridge University Press, 2004.
Brickhouse, Anna. *The Unsettlement of America: Translation, Interpretation, and the Story of Don Luis de Velasco, 1560–1945.* New York: Oxford University Press, 2015.
Bruce-Novoa, Juan. *Retrospace: Collected Essays on Chicano Literature.* Houston: Arte Público Press, 1990.
Bush, Andrew. "Lyric Poetry of the Eighteenth and Nineteenth Centuries," In *The Cambridge History of Latin American Literature,* edited by Roberto González Echevarría, 375–400. New York: Cambridge University Press, 1996.
Bustillos, Maria. "By Anonymous: Can a Writer Escape Vulnerability?" *New Yorker,* 18 November 2013.
Cahen, Paul. "Bringing Thomas Paine to Latin America: An Overview of the Geopolitics of Translating Common Sense Into Spanish." In *New Directions in Thomas Paine Studies,* edited by Scott Cleary and Ivy Linton Stabell, 207–27. New York: Palgrave Macmillan, 2016.
Cairo Balester, Ana, ed. *Jose María Heredia: 1803–2003, bicentenario de su natalicio: Un homenaje de la Biblioteca Nacional José Martí a su vida y obra.* Havana: Biblioteca Nacional José Martí, 2003. CD-ROM.
Cañizares-Esguerra, Jorge. *How to Write the History of the New World: Histories, Epistemologies, and Identities in the Eighteenth-Century Atlantic World.* Stanford: Stanford University Press, 2001.
Carey, Patrick. "Arguments for Lay Participation in Philadelphia Catholicism, 1820–1829." *Records of the American Catholic Historical Society* 92 (March–December 1981): 43–58.
Carrière, J. M. "Mr. Jefferson Sponsors a New French Method." *French Review* 19 (May 1946): 394–405.
Cartas de un americano sobre las ventajas de los gobiernos republicanos federativos. In Rocafuerte, *Colección Rocafuerte,* vol. 4.
Castillo, Debra. *Redreaming America: Toward a Bilingual American Culture.* Albany: State University of New York Press, 2005.
Castro, Daniel. *Another Face of Empire: Bartolomé de Las Casas, Indigenous Rights, and Ecclesiastical Imperialism.* Durham, NC: Duke University Press, 2007.
Castro Leal, Antonio, ed. *La novela del méxico colonial.* 2 vols. Mexico City: Aguilar, 1964.
Cazzato, Salvador, Raiza Piña, and Luis López. "Libertad vs. Despotismo: Sobre el ideario político de Juan Germán Roscio." *Agora Trujillo: Revista del Centro*

Regional de Investigación Humanística, Económica y Social 11, no. 22 (December 2008): 133–49.

Certeau, Michel de. *The Practice of Everyday Life*. Berkeley: University of California Press, 1984.

Chambers, Sarah C. "Little Middle Ground: The Instability of a Mestizo Identity in the Andes, Eighteenth and Nineteenth Centuries." In *Race and Nation in Modern Latin America*, edited by Nancy P. Appelbaum, Anne S. Macpherson, and Karin Alejandra Rosemblatt, 32–55. Chapel Hill: University of North Carolina Press, 2003.

Charvat, William. *Literary Publishing in America, 1790–1850*. Philadelphia: University of Pennsylvania Press, 1959.

Chasteen, John Charles. *Americanos: Latin America's Struggle for Independence*. New York: Oxford University Press, 2008.

Chasteen, John Charles. Introduction to Rama, *Lettered City*.

Clayton, Lawrence. "Bartolomé de las Casas and the African Slave Trade." *History Compass* 7, no. 6 (2009): 1526–41.

Cockcroft, James D., André Gunder Grank, and Dale L. Johnson. *Dependence and Underdevelopment: Latin America's Political Economy*. Garden City, NY: Anchor Books, 1972.

Coronado, Raúl. "Historicizing Nineteenth-Century Latina/o Textuality." In Lazo and Alemán, *Latino Nineteenth Century*, 49–69.

Coronado, Raúl. *A World Not to Come: A History of Latino Writing and Print Culture*. Cambridge, MA: Harvard University Press, 2013.

Crèvecoeur, Hector St. John de. *Letters from an American Farmer*. New York: Penguin, 1986.

De Onís, Catalina M. "What's in an 'x'? An Exchange about the Politics of 'Latinx.'" *Chiricú Journal* 1, no. 2 (Spring 2017): 78–91.

Derrida, Jacques. *Geneses, Genealogies, Genres and Genius: The Secrets of the Archive*. Translated by Beverley Bie Brahic. New York: Columbia University Press, 2006.

Derrida, Jacques. *Archive Fever: A Freudian Impression*. Translated by Eric Prenowitz. Chicago: University of Chicago Press, 1995.

Derrida, Jacques. "The Purveyor of Truth." Translated by Alan Bass. In Muller and Richardson, *Purloined Poe*, 173–212.

Domínguez Michael, Christopher. *Vida de Fray Servando*. Mexico City: Ediciones Era, 2004.

Dos Santos, Theotonio. "Latin American Underdevelopment: Past, Present, and Future." Translated by Paulo Frank. In *The Underdevelopment of Development*, edited by Sing C. Chew and Robert A. Denemark, 149–70. Thousand Oaks, CA: SAGE, 1996.

Dunbar, Erica Armstrong. *A Fragile Freedom: African American Women and Emancipation in the Antebellum City*. New Haven, CT: Yale University Press, 2008.

Earle, Rebecca, ed. *Epistolary Selves: Letters and Letter-Writers, 1600–1945.* Brookfield, VT: Ashgate, 1999.
Earle, Rebecca. "Letters and Love in Colonial Spanish America." *Americas* 62, no. 1 (July 2005): 17–46.
Earle, Rebecca. *The Return of the Native: Indians and Myth-Making in Spanish America, 1819–1930.* Durham, NC: Duke University Press, 2007.
Earle, Rebecca. "The Role of Print in the Spanish American Wars of Independence." In *The Political Power of the Word: Press and Oratory in Nineteenth-Century Latin America,* edited by Iván Jaksić, 9–33. London: Institute of Latin American Studies, 2002.
Eisenstein, Elizabeth. *The Printing Press as an Agent of Change.* Cambridge, MA: Harvard University Press, 1979.
Etting, Frank M. *An Historical Account of the Old State House of Pennsylvania Now Known as the Hall of Independence.* Boston: James R. Osgood, 1876.
Febvre, Lucien. *The Coming of the Book: The Impact of Printing, 1450–1800.* Translated by David Gerard. London: NLB, 1976.
Fernández de Castro, José Antonio. *Vicente Rocafuerte: Un Americano libre.* Mexico City: Secretaría de Educación Pública, 1947.
Fitz, Caitlin. *Our Sister Republics: The United States in an Age of American Revolutions.* New York: Norton, 2016.
Foucault, Michel. *The Archeology of Knowledge.* New York: Pantheon, 1972.
Foucault, Michel. "Human Nature: Justice vs. Power, a Debate between Noam Chomsky and Michel Foucault." In *The Chomsky-Foucault Debate on Human Nature.* New York: New Press, 2006.
Franklin, Benjamin. *The Autobiography of Benjamin Franklin.* New York: Pocket Books, 1950.
Fraser, Nancy. "Transnationalizing the Public Sphere: On the Legitimacy and Efficacy of Public Opinion in a Post-Westphalian World." *Theory, Culture & Society* 24, no. 4 (2007): 7–30.
Freire, Ana María. *Entre la ilustración y el romanticismo: La huella de la Guerra de la independencia en la literature Española.* San Vicente de Raspeig: Publicaciones de la Universidad de Alicante, 2008.
Furstenberg, François. *When the United States Spoke French: Five Refugees Who Shaped a Nation.* New York: Penguin, 2014.
Gallardo, Guillermo. *J. R. Poinsett, agente norteamericano, 1810–1814.* Buenos Aires: Emecé Editores, 1983.
García, Emily. "Interdependence and Interlingualism in Santiago Puglia's El desengaño del hombre (1794)." *Early American Literature* 53, no. 3 (2018): 745–72.
García, Emily. "On the Borders of Independence: Manuel Torres and Spanish American Independence in Filadelfia." In Lazo and Alemán, *Latino Nineteenth Century,* 71–88.

García Samudio, Nicolás. *La independencia de Hispanoamérica.* Mexico: Fondo de Cultura Económica, 1945.
Garrett, Kathryn. "The First Constitution of Texas, April 17, 1813." *Southwestern Historical Quarterly* 40, no. 4 (April 1937): 290–308.
Gerbi, Antonello. *The Dispute of the New World: The History of a Polemic, 1750–1900.* Translated by Jeremy Moyle. Pittsburgh: University of Pittsburgh Press, 1973.
Gillman, Susan, and Kirsten Silva Gruesz. "Worlding America: The Hemispheric Text-Network." In *A Companion to American Literary Studies,* edited by Caroline F. Levander and Robert S. Levine. Malden, MA: John Wiley & Sons, 2011.
Gitelman, Lisa. *Paper Knowledge: Toward a Media History of Documents.* Durham, NC: Duke University Press, 2014.
Gómez Álvarez, Cristina. "Lecturas perseguidas: El caso del Padre Mier." In *Empresa y cultura en tinta y papel (1800–1860),* edited by Laura Beatriz Suárez de la Torre and Miguel Ángel Castro. Mexico City: Instituto Mora, UNAM, 2001.
González Acosta, Alejandro. *El enigma de "Jicoténcal": Estudio de dos novelas sobre el héroe de Taxcala.* Mexico: Instituto Tlaxcalteca de Cultura, 1997.
Goodman, Dena. *The Republic of Letters: A Cultural History of the French Enlightenment.* Ithaca: Cornell University Press, 1994.
Goudie, Sean X. *Creole America: The West Indies and the Formation of Literature and Culture in the New Republic.* Philadelphia: University of Pennsylvania Press, 2006.
Goytisolo, Juan. *Blanco White, "El Español" y la independencia de Hispanoamérica.* Madrid: Santillana Ediciones, 2010.
Grases, Pedro. "El círculo de Filadelfia." In Grases, *Preindependencia y emancipación.*
Grases, Pedro. *Preindependencia y emancipación: Protagonistas y testimonios.* Barcelona: Seix Barral, 1981.
Grases, Pedro, and Alberto Harkness. *Manuel García de Sena y la independencia de Hispanoamérica.* Caracas: Secretaría General de la Décima Conferencia Interamericana, 1953.
Green, James N. *Mathew Carey, Publisher and Patriot.* Philadelphia: Library Company of Philadelphia, 1985.
Griffin, Robert J., ed. *The Faces of Anonymity: Anonymous and Pseudonymous Publication from the Sixteenth to the Twentieth Century.* New York: Palgrave Macmillan, 2003.
Gruesz, Kirsten Silva. *Ambassadors of Culture: The Transamerican Origins of Latino Writing.* Princeton, NJ: Princeton University Press, 2001.
Gruesz, Kirsten Silva. "The Errant Latino: Irisarri, Central Americanness, and Migration's Intentions." In Lazo and Alemán, *Latino Nineteenth Century,* 20–48.
Guerra, François-Xavier, ed. *Los espacios públicos en Iberoamérica.* Mexico City: Centro de Estudios Mexicanos y Centroamericanos, 2008.
Guerra, François-Xavier. *Modernidad e independencias: Ensayos sobre las revoluciones hispánicas.* Madrid: Editorial MAPFRE, 1992.

Gutiérrez, Gustavo. *A Theology of Liberation*. Rev. ed. Maryknoll, NY: Orbis, 1988.
Guzmán, Martín Luis. *Filadelfia: Paraíso de conspiradores*. Mexico City: Compañía General de Ediciones, 1960.
Habermas, Jürgen. *The Structural Transformation of the Public Sphere*. Translated by Thomas Burger. Cambridge, MA: MIT Press, 1991.
Hanke, Lewis, ed. *Do the Americas Have a Common History? A Critique of the Bolton Theory*. New York: Knopf, 1964.
Hassan, Waïl S. "Translational Literature and the Pleasures of Exile." *PMLA* 131, no. 5 (2016): 1435–43.
Heredia, José María. *Antología Herediana*. Edited by Emilio Valdés y de Latorre. Havana: Imprenta El Siglo XX, 1939.
Heredia, José María. *Niagara y otros textos: Poesía y prosa selecta*. Edited by Angel Augier. Caracas: Biblioteca Ayacucho, 1990.
Hermans, Theo. *Translation in Systems*. Manchester: St. Jerome, 1999.
Hernández González, Manuel. "Liberalismo y masonería en la América de las guerras de la independencia: Cabral de Noroña y sus reflexiones sobre la masonería." In *Masonería, revolución, y reacción*, edited by J. A. Ferrer Benimeli, 829–36. Alicante, Spain: Instituto de Cultura "Juan Gil-Albert," 1990.
Hernández Travieso, Antonio. *El Padre Varela*. Miami: Ediciones Universal, 1984.
Hewitt, Elizabeth. "Networks of Nineteenth-Century Letter Writing." In *The Edinburgh Companion to Nineteenth-Century American Letters and Letter-Writing*, edited by Celeste-Marie Bernier, Judie Newman, and Matthew Pethers, 1–10. Edinburgh: Edinburgh University Press, 2016.
In Honor of the Patriot Don Manuel Torres, 1764–1822. Washington, DC: Colombian Legation, 1926.
Irwin, Robert McKee. "Almost-Latino Literature: Approaching Truncated Latinidades." In Lazo and Alemán, *Latino Nineteenth Century*, 110–23.
Irwin, Robert McKee. *Mexican Masculinities*. Minneapolis: University of Minnesota Press, 2003.
Isaacson, Walter. *Benjamin Franklin: An American Life*. New York: Simon & Schuster, 2003.
Jaksić, Iván. *The Hispanic World and American Intellectual Life, 1820–1880*. New York: Palgrave Macmillan, 2007.
Jefferson, Thomas. *Writings*. Edited by Merrill D. Peterson. New York: Library of America, 1984.
Jimmerson, Randall C. *Archives Power: Memory, Accountability and Social Justice*. Chicago: Society of American Archivists, 2009.
Johnson, Sara E. "Moreau de Saint-Méry: Itinerant Bibliophile." *Library and Information History* 31, no. 3 (2015): 171–97.
Kadir, Djelal. *Memos from the Besieged City: Lifelines for Cultural Sustainability*. Stanford: Stanford University Press, 2011.

Kagan, Richard L. "From Noah to Moses: The Genesis of Historical Scholarship on Spain in the United States." In *Spain in America: The Origins of Hispanism in the United States,* edited by Richard L. Kagan, 21–48. Urbana: University of Illinois Press, 2002.

Kanellos, Nicolás. "José Alvarez de Toledo y Dubois and the Origins of Hispanic Publishing in the Early Republic," *Early American Literature* 43, no. 1 (2008): 83–100.

Kaser, David. *Messrs. Carey & Lea of Philadelphia: A Study in the History of the Book Trade.* Philadelphia: University of Pennsylvania Press, 1957.

Kenworthy, Eldon. *America/Americas: Myth in the Making of US Policy toward Latin America.* University Park: Penn State University Press, 1995.

Kirtley, Alexandra Alevizatos. "Athens of America." In *Encyclopedia of Greater Philadelphia.* Accessed February 2018. http://philadelphiaencyclopedia.org/archive/athens-of-america/.

Knowles, Rachel. "What is the haut ton?" *Regency History* (blog). 20 December 2014. https://www.regencyhistory.net/2014/12/what-is-haut-ton.html.

Lacan, Jacques. "Seminar on 'The Purloined Letter.'" Translated by Jeffrey Mehlman. In Muller and Richardson, *Purloined Poe,* 28–54.

Lacoste de Arufe, María. "Biografía de José María Heredia." In *Poesías, discursos y cartas,* by José María Heredia, xiii–clxxiv. Havana: Cultural, 1939.

Lamas, Carmen E. "Father Félix Varela and the Emergence of an Organized Latina/o Minority in Early Nineteenth-Century New York City." In *The Cambridge History of Latina/o American Literature,* edited by John Morán González and Laura Lomas, 157–75. New York: Cambridge University Press, 2018.

Lamas, Carmen E. "Raimundo Cabrera, the Latin American Archive, and the Latina/o Continuum." In Lazo and Alemán, *Latino Nineteenth Century,* 210–29.

Langley, Lester D. *The Americas in the Age of Revolution.* New Haven, CT: Yale University Press, 1996.

Larkin, Edward. *Thomas Paine and the Literature of Revolution.* New York: Cambridge University Press, 2005.

Lasso, Marixa. "Un mito republicano de armonía racial: Raza y patriotismo en Colombia, 1812–1820." *Revista de Estudios Sociales* 27 (August 2007): 32–45.

Lasso, Marixa. *Myths of Harmony: Race and Republicanism during the Age of Revolution, Colombia, 1795–1831.* Pittsburgh: University of Pittsburgh Press, 2007.

Lawrance, Jeremy. *Spanish Conquest, Protestant Prejudice: Las Casas and the Black Legend.* Nottingham: Critical, Cultural and Communications Press, 2009.

Lazo, Rodrigo. "La Famosa Filadelfia: The Hemispheric American City and Constitutional Debates." In *Hemispheric American Studies,* edited by Caroline F. Levander and Robert S. Levine, 57–74. New Brunswick, NJ: Rutgers University Press, 2008.

Lazo, Rodrigo. "Hemispheric Americanism: Latin American Exiles and US Revolutionary Writings." In *A Companion to the Literatures of Colonial America,* edited by Susan Castillo and Ivy Schweitzer, 306–20. Malden, MA: Blackwell, 2005.

Lazo, Rodrigo. "Migrant Archives." In *States of Emergency: The Object of American Studies,* edited by Susan Gilman and Russ Castronovo, 36–54. Chapel Hill: University of North Carolina Press, 2009.

Lazo, Rodrigo, and Jesse Alemán, eds. *The Latino Nineteenth Century.* New York: New York University Press, 2016.

Leal, Luis. "Jicoténcal, primera novela histórica en castellano." *Revista Iberoamericana* 25 (January–June 1960): 9–31.

Leal, Luis, and Rodolfo Cortina. Introduction to [Varela?], *Jicoténcal.*

Leguía, Jorge Guillermo. *Manuel Lorenzo de Vidaurre: Contribución a un ensayo de interpretación sicológica.* Lima, 1935.

Light, Dale B. *Rome and the New Republic: Conflict and Community in Philadelphia Catholicism between the Revolution and the Civil War.* Notre Dame, IN: University of Notre Dame Press, 1996.

Llorens, Vicente. *Liberales y románticos: Una emigración española en Inglaterra.* 2nd ed. Madrid: Editorial Castalia, 1968.

Lohman Villena, Guillermo. "Manuel Lorenzo de Vidaurre y la Inquisición de Lima." *Revista de Estudios Políticos* 52 (1950): 199–216.

Lomas, Laura. *Translating Empire: José Martí, Migrant Latino Subjects, and American Modernities.* Durham, NC: Duke University Press, 2009.

Lombardi, John V. *The Political Ideology of Fray Servando Teresa de Mier, Propagandist for Independence.* Cuernavaca, Mexico: Centro Intercultural de Documentación, 1968.

Losada, Benito Raúl. *Juan Germán Roscio.* Caracas: Fundación Eugenio Mendoza, 1953.

Lowe, Lisa. *The Intimacies of Four Continents.* Durham, NC: Duke University Press, 2015.

Lynch. John. *The Spanish American Revolutions.* London: Weidenfeld & Nicolson, 1973.

Magnan, André. "Correspondence." In *Encyclopedia of the Enlightenment,* edited by Michel Delon. Abingdon, Oxon: Routledge, 2013.

Malagón-Barceló, Javier. "The Role of the Letrado in the Colonization of America." *The Americas* 18 (July 1961): 1–17.

Mañach, Jorge. *Perfil de nuestras letras.* Edited by Carlos Espinosa Domínguez. Barcelona: Red Ediciones, 2017.

Marichal, Carlos. "Money, Taxes, and Finance." In *The Cambridge Economic History of Latin America,* edited by Victor Bulmer-Thomas, John H. Coatsworth, and Robert Cortés Conde, 423–60. New York: Cambridge University Press, 2006.

Martí, José. "Our America." In *Selected Writings,* edited and translated by Esther Allen, 288–96. New York: Penguin, 2002.

Martínez, Urbano. *Domingo Del Monte y su tiempo.* Havana: Ediciones Unión, 1997.

McCadden, Joseph, and Helen McCadden. *Félix Varela, Torch Bearer from Cuba.* New York: U.S. Catholic Historical Society, 1969.

McFarlane, Anthony. "Science and Sedition in Spanish America: New Granada in the Age of Revolution, 1776–1810." In *Enlightenment and Emancipation*, edited by Susan Manning and Peter France, 97–117. Lewisburg: Bucknell University Press, 2006.

McPheeters, D. W. "Xicoténcatl, símbolo republicano y romántico." *Nueva Revista de Filología Hispánica* 10 (1956): 403–11.

Mecum, Kent. *El idealismo práctico de Vicente Rocafuerte*. Puebla, Mexico: Editorial Cajica, 1975.

Mier Noriega y Guerra, Servando Teresa de. *Ideario politico*. Caracas: Biblioteca Ayacucho, 1978.

Mier Noriega y Guerra, Servando Teresa de. *The Memoirs of Fray Servando Teresa de Mier*. Edited by Susana Rotker and translated by Helen Lane. New York: Oxford University Press, 1998.

Mier Noriega y Guerra, Servando Teresa de. *Obras completas*. Edited by Jaime Rodríguez O. 4 vols. Mexico City: Universidad Nacional Autónoma de México, 1988.

Mignolo, Walter. *The Darker Side of the Renaissance: Literacy, Territoriality, and Colonization*. Ann Arbor: University of Michigan Press, 1995.

Mignolo, Walter. *The Idea of Latin America*. Malden, MA: Blackwell, 2005.

Milian, Claudia. "Crisis Management and the LatinX Child." *English Language Notes* 56, no. 2 (October 2018): 8–24.

Miliani, Domingo. "Juan Germán Roscio, vigencia de su pensamiento: Posibles influjos en la formación intelectual de Benito Juárez." In *Bolívar y el mundo de los libertadores*, edited by Charles Minguet. Mexico: Universidad Nacional Autónoma de México, 1993.

Miller, Nicola. "Reading Rousseau in Spanish America during the Wars of Independence." In *Engaging with Rousseau: Reaction and Interpretation from the Eighteenth Century to the Present*, edited by Avi Lifschitz, 114–35. Cambridge: Cambridge University Press, 2016.

Mills, C. Wright. *The Power Elite*. 1956. Reprint. New York: Oxford University Press, 1999.

Miramón, Alberto. *Diplomáticos de la libertad*. Bogóta: Empresa Nacional de Publicaciones, 1956.

Molina, Fernando. *Vicente Pazos Kanki*. Bolivia: Editorial Gente Común, 2011.

Morris Eckhardt, Celia. *Fanny Wright: Rebel in America*. Cambridge, MA: Harvard University Press, 1984.

Muller, John P., and William J. Richardson, eds. *The Purloined Poe: Lacan, Derrida, and Psychoanalytic Reading*. Baltimore: Johns Hopkins University Press, 1988.

Murphy, Gretchen. *Hemispheric Imaginings: The Monroe Doctrine and US Narratives of Empire*. Durham, NC: Duke University Press, 2005.

Nash, Gary B. *First City: Philadelphia and the Forging of Historical Memory*. Philadelphia: University of Pennsylvania Press, 2002.

Nash, Gary B. *Forging Freedom: The Formation of Philadelphia's Black Community, 1720–1840*. Cambridge, MA: Harvard University Press, 1991.

Navia, Juan M. *An Apostle for the Immigrants: The Exile Years of Father Félix Varela y Morales*. Salisbury, MD: Factor, 2002.
La obra de Edmundo O'Gorman: Discursos y conferencias de homenaje en su 70 aniversario. Mexico: Universidad Nacional Autónoma de México, 1978.
O'Gorman, Edmundo, ed. *Fray Servando Teresa de Mier*. Mexico City: Imprenta Universitaria, 1945.
O'Gorman, Edmundo, ed. *Fray Servando Teresa de Mier: Escritos y memorias*. Mexico City: Universidad Nacional Autónoma, 1945.
O'Gorman, Edmundo. *La invención de America*. Mexico: Fondo de Cultura Económica, 1958.
O'Gorman, Edmundo. *The Invention of America: An Inquiry into the Historical Nature of the New World and the Meaning of Its History*. Translated by Edmundo O'Gorman. Bloomington: Indiana University Press, 1961.
O'Gorman, Edmundo. Preface to *Ideario político*, by Servando Teresa de Mier Noriega y Guerra. Caracas: Biblioteca Ayacucho, 1978.
Otter, Samuel. *Philadelphia Stories: America's Literature of Race and Freedom*. New York: Oxford University Press, 2010.
Owsley, Frank Lawrence, Jr., and Gene A. Smith. *Filibusters and Expansionists: Jeffersonian Manifest Destiny, 1800–1821*. Tuscaloosa: University of Alabama Press, 1997.
Paez-Pumar, Mauro. *Las proclamas de Filadelfia de 1774 y 1775 en la Caracas de 1777*. Caracas: Centro Venezolano Americano, 1973.
Paine, Thomas. *Collected Writings*. New York: Library of America, 1995.
Parra Márquez, Héctor. *Historia del colegio de abogados de Caracas*. 3 vols. Caracas: Imprenta Nacional, 1952.
Pazos Kanki, Vicente. *Compendio de la historia de los Estados Unidos de América*. Prologue by Charles W. Arnade. La Paz: Academia Boliviana de la Historia, 1976.
Peers, E. Allison. *A Short History of the Romantic Movement in Spain*. Liverpool: Institute of Hispanic Studies, 1949.
Peralta Ruiz, Victor. "La revolución silenciada: Hábitos de lectura y pedagogía política en el Perú, 1790–1814." *Anuario de Estudios Americanos* 54, no. 1 (1997): 107–34.
Pérez, Vincent. *Remembering the Hacienda: History and Memory in the Mexican American Southwest*. College Station: Texas A&M University Press, 2006.
Poblete, Juan. "Citizenship and Illegality in the Global California Gold Rush." In Lazo and Alemán, *Latino Nineteenth Century*, 278–300.
Pocock, J. G. A. *The Machiavellian Moment: Florentine Political Thought and the Atlantic Republican Tradition*. 2nd ed. Princeton, NJ: Princeton University Press, 2003.
Porter, Charles A. Foreword to "Men/Women of Letters." Special issue, *Yale French Studies* 71 (1986): 1–14.
La prensa heroica: Selección del "Correo del Orinoco." Caracas: Ediciones de la Presidencia de la República, 1968.

Quijada, Mónica. "Sobre el origen y difusión del nombre América Latina." *Revista de Indias* 43, no. 214 (1998): 595–616.
Quijano, Aníbal. "Coloniality of Power, Eurocentrism, and Latin America." *Nepantla: Views from the South* 1, no. 3 (2000): 533–80.
Quijano, Aníbal, and Immanuel Wallerstein. "Americanity as a Concept, or the Americas in the Modern World-System." *International Social Science Journal* 134 (November 1992): 549–57.
Rabasa, José. *Inventing America: Spanish Historiography and the Formation of Eurocentrism.* Norman: University of Oklahoma Press, 1993.
Racine, Karen. *Francisco de Miranda: A Transatlantic Life in the Age of Revolution.* Wilmington, DE: SR Books, 2003.
Rama, Angel. *The Lettered City.* Translated by John Charles Chasteen. Durham, NC: Duke University Press, 1996.
Read, John Lloyd. *Mexican Historical Novel.* 2nd ed. New York: Russell & Russell, 1973.
Remer, Rosalind. *Printers and Men of Capital: Philadelphia Book Publishers in the New Republic.* Philadelphia: University of Pennsylvania Press, 1996.
Restrepo, José Manuel. *Historia de la revolución de la República de Colombia en la América Meridional.* 1827. 2 vols. Medellín, Colombia: Editorial Universidad de Antioquia, 2009.
Rezek, Joseph. *London and the Making of Provincial Literature: Aesthetics and the Transatlantic Book Trade, 1800–1850.* Philadelphia: University of Pennsylvania Press, 2015.
Richardson, Edgar P. "The Athens of America." In Weigley, Wainwright, and Wolf, *Philadelphia,* 208–57.
Rigal, Laura. *The American Manufactory: Art, Labor and the World of Things in the Early Republic.* Princeton, NJ: Princeton University Press, 1998.
Rocafuerte, Vicente. *Colección Rocafuerte.* Edited by Neptalí Zúñiga. 16 vols. Quito: Gobierno del Ecuador, 1947.
Rocafuerte, Vicente. *Vicente Rocafuerte: Un americano libre.* Edited by José Antonio Fernández de Castro. Mexico City: Secretaría de Educación Pública, 1947.
Rodríguez, José Ignacio. *Vida del Presbítero Félix Varela.* New York: Imprenta O Novo Mondo, 1878.
Rodriguez, Richard T. "X Marks the Spot." *Cultural Dynamics* 29, no. 3 (2017): 202–13.
Rodríguez O., Jaime E. *The Emergence of Spanish America: Vicente Rocafuerte and Spanish Americanism, 1808–1832.* Berkeley: University of California Press, 1975.
Rodríguez O., Jaime E. *Estudios sobre Vicente Rocafuerte.* Guayaquil: Archivo Histórico del Guayas, 1975.
Rodríguez O., Jaime E. *The Independence of Spanish America.* New York: Cambridge University Press, 1998.

Rodríguez O., Jaime E. "Sobre la supuesta influencia de la independencia de los Estados Unidos en las independencias Hispanoamericanas." *Revista de Indias* 70 (2010): 691–714.

Rojas, Rafael. "Traductores de la libertad: Filadelfia y la difusión del republicanismo en Hispanoamérica." In *Ecuador: Relaciones exteriores a la luz del bicentenario*, edited by Beatriz Zepeda, 45–76. Quito: FLACSO, 2009.

Rojas Garcidueñas, José. "Otra novela sobre el tema de Xicoténcatl." *Anales del Instituto de Investigaciones Estéticas* 8, no. 30 (1961): 101–12.

Roldán Vera, Eugenia. *The British Book Trade and Spanish American Independence*. Burlington, VT: Ashgate, 2003.

Roscio, Juan Germán. *Obras*. Edited by Pedro Grases. Prologue by Augusto Mijares. 3 vols. Caracas: Secretaría General de la Décima Conferencia Interamericana, 1953.

Roscio, Juan Germán. *El triunfo de la libertad sobre el despotismo*. Edited by Domingo Miliani. Caracas: Biblioteca Ayacucho, 1996.

Rousseau, J. J. *La nouvelle Héloïse*. Translated by Judith H. McDowell. University Park: Penn State University Press, 1968.

Rozwenc, Edwin C. "Edmundo O'Gorman and the Idea of America." *American Quarterly* 10, no. 2 (1958): 99–115.

Ruiz, Nydia M. *Las confesiones de un pecador arrepentido: Juan Germán Roscio y los orígenes del discurso venezolano*. Caracas: Fondo Editorial Tropykos / Facultad de Ciencias Económicas y Sociales, 1996.

Ruiz, Vicki. "7 Things People Get Wrong about American History." *Time*, 26 September 2017.

Ruiz Barrionuevo, Carmen. "Juan Germán Roscio y el pensamiento antiliberal." *Philologia Hispalensis* 25 (2011): 181–200.

Saborit, Antonio. Introduction to *El desengaño del hombre*, edited by Antonio Saborit. Mexico City: Fondo de Cultural Económica, 2014.

Saco, José Antonio. *Obras*. Edited by Eduardo Torres-Cuevas. 5 vols. Havana: Imagen Contemporánea, 2001.

Sagredo Baeza, Rafael. "Actores políticos en los catecismos patriotas y republicanos americanos, 1810–1827." *Historia Mexicana* 45 (January–March 1996): 501–38.

Said, Edward. *Reflections on Exile, and Other Essays*. Cambridge, MA: Harvard University Press, 2000.

Saldívar, José David. *Trans-Americanity: Subaltern Modernities, Global Coloniality, and the Cultures of Greater Mexico*. Durham, NC: Duke University Press, 2012.

Sanders, James E. "Democracy in Las Américas." *J19* 5, no. 2 (Fall 2017): 374–81.

Scott, Rebecca J. *Degrees of Freedom: Louisiana and Cuba after Slavery*. Cambridge, MA: Harvard University Press, 2008.

Sedgwick, Eve Kosofsky. *Between Men: English Literature and Male Homosocial Desire*. New York: Columbia University Press, 1985.

Sellers, Charles Coleman. *Mr. Peale's Museum*. New York: Norton, 1980.

Semonin, Paul. *American Monster: How the Nation's First Prehistoric Creature Became a Symbol of National Identity.* New York: New York University Press, 2000.
Semonin, Paul. "Peale's Mastodon: The Skeleton in Our Closet." *Common Place* 4, no. 2 (January 2004). http://www.common-place-archives.org/vol-04/no-02/semonin/.
Shapiro, Stephen. *The Culture and Commerce of the Early American Novel: Reading the Atlantic World-System.* University Park: Penn State University Press, 2008.
Shukla, Sandhya, and Heidi Tinsman, eds. *Imagining Our Americas: Toward a Transnational Frame.* Durham, NC: Duke University Press, 2007.
Simmons, Merle E. *Santiago F. Puglia: An Early Philadelphia Propagandist for Spanish American Independence.* Chapel Hill: University of North Carolina Press, 1977.
Socolow, Susan M. "Acceptable Partners: Marriage Choice in Colonial Argentina, 1778–1810." In *Sexuality and Marriage in Colonial Latin America,* edited by Asunción Lavrin, 209–51. Lincoln: University of Nebraska Press, 1989.
Steiner, George. *After Babel.* Oxford: Oxford University Press, 1975.
Stoler, Ann Laura. *Along the Archival Grain: Epistemic Anxieties and Colonial Common Sense.* Princeton, NJ: Princeton University Press, 2009.
Suárez Argüello, Ana R. "Imaginar a la patria en la distancia: Cuatro viajeros Mexicanos en Estados Unidos a fines de la primera república federal." In *La construcción del discurso nacional en México, un anhelo persistente,* edited by Nicole Girón, 71–107. Mexico City: Instituto Mora, 2007.
Suárez Argüello, Ana R. "La mirada en el espejo: El viaje de Manuel Payno a los Estados Unidos (1845)." *Anuario de historia* 1 (2009): 101–12.
Suárez Argüello, Ana R. Selection from *Viaje por los Estados Unidos.* In *Republicanos en otro imperio,* edited by Vicente Quirarte, 87–90. Mexico City: UNAM, 2009.
Thompson, Ralph. *American Literary Annuals & Gift Books, 1825–1865.* New York: H. W. Wilson, 1936.
Toribio Medina, José. *Historia de la imprenta en los antiguos dominios españoles de América y Oceania.* 2 vols. Santiago, Chile: Fondo José Toribio Medina, 1958.
Tregle, Joseph G., Jr. "The Josiah Stoddard Johnston Papers." *Pennsylvania Magazine of History and Biography* 69 (October 1945): 326–29.
Ugalde, Luis. *El pensamiento teológico-político de Juan Germán Roscio.* Caracas: La Casa de Bello, 1992.
Uribe-Uran, Victor M. "The Birth of a Public Sphere in Latin America during the Age of Revolution." *Comparative Studies in Society and History* 42, no. 2 (April 2000): 425–57.
Varela, Félix. *Cartas a Elpidio sobre la impiedad, la superstición y el fanatismo en sus relaciones con la sociedad.* 2 vols. Havana: Editorial de la Universidad de la Habana, 1944.
Varela, Félix. *El habanero: Papel político, científico y literario.* Miami: Ediciones Universal, 1997.

[Varela, Félix?]. *Jicoténcal.* Edited by Luis Leal and Rodolfo J. Cortina. Houston: Arte Público Press, 1995.
Varela, Félix. *Lecciones de filosofía.* 3 vols. Havana: University of Havana, 1962.
Varela, Félix. *Letters to Elpidio.* Translated by Felipe J. Estévez. New York: Paulist Press, 1989.
Varela, Félix. *Obras.* Edited by Eduardo Torres-Cuevas, Jorge Ibarra Cuesta, and Mercedes García Rodríguez. 2nd ed. 3 vols. Havana: Ediciones Imagen Contemporania, 2001.
Venuti, Lawrence. *The Scandals of Translation: Towards an Ethics of Difference.* New York: Routledge, 1998.
Vidaurre, Manuel Lorenzo de. *Cartas americanas.* Lima: Comisión Nacional del Sequicentenario de la Independencia del Perú, 1973.
Vilar García, Mar. *El Español, segunda lengua en los Estados Unidos: De su enseñanza como idioma extranjero en Norteamérica al bilingüismo.* Murcia, Spain: Universidad de Murcia, 2000.
Vogeley, Nancy. *The Bookrunner: A History of Inter-American Relations—Print, Politics, and Commerce in the United States and Mexico, 1800–1830.* Philadelphia: American Philosophical Society, 2011.
Vogeley, Nancy. "Spanish-Language Masonic Books Printed in the Early United States." *Early American Literature* 43, no. 2 (2008): 337–60.
Wallerstein, Immanuel. *World-Systems Analysis.* Durham, NC: Duke University Press, 2004.
Warner, Michael. *The Letters of the Republic.* Cambridge, MA: Harvard University Press, 1990.
Weigley, Russell R., Nicholas B. Wainwright, and Edwin Wolf, eds. *Philadelphia: A 300-Year History.* New York: Norton, 1982.
Wyllys, Rufus Kay. "The Filibusters of Amelia Island." *Georgia Historical Quarterly* 12, no. 4 (December 1928): 297–325.
Xicoténcatl: An Anonymous Historical Novel about the Events Leading Up to the Conquest of the Aztec Empire. Translated by Guillermo I. Castillo-Feliú. Austin: University of Texas Press, 1999.
Zavala, Lorenzo de. *Journey to the United States of North America.* Edited by John Michael Rivera. Translated by Wallace Woolsey. Houston: Arte Público, 2005.

Index

Adams, John Quincy, 108–9, 134, 246n100
Adams-Onís Treaty, 132
"Aguinaldo, El" (poem), 40–41
Aguinaldo para el año de 1829, El, 40–41
Aguinaldo para 1830, El, 40
Aldridge, A. Owen, 67–68
Alvarez de Toledo, José, 131, 160
Amelia Island, 130–33
Americanism (hemispheric): and anonymity, 177; and architecture, 49, 50; and geography, 206–7; and government, 180, 258n40; and nature, 141, 147; in opposition to Europe, 7, 46, 49, 136–37, 140–42; —, and *americano,* use of, 16, 65, 69, 78, 179–80; —, and *Spanish American,* use of, 17; and public sphere, 136–37. *See also* hemispheric American studies
Americanity, 98, 106, 142
American Philosophical Society, 195
American studies (field), 194, 198
Amigo de los hombres, El, 156, 158, 170, 176, 177, 182, 190; and anonymity, 161; argument of, 166–67; printing of, 34, 252n11; slavery discussed in, 167–68; and transatlantic debate, 159–63
Anderson, Benedict, 78, 79
anonymity, 156, 160, 169, 170; and collaborative writing, 255n56; and early Latino literature, 189–90; and political subjects, 157, 177; and Jean-Jacques Rousseau, 173; and *X,* use of, 177, 178–79
anonymous publication, 156, 157, 170, 193; and attribution of authorship, 160, 183; and *Jicoténcal,* 158–59, 181, 182; and translation, 172
archival dislocation, 194, 196, 210, 217, 219, 228; definition of, 198–200; and gender, 214–15
Archive Fever (Derrida), 194
archives, 17, 199, 256n11; definition of, 194; and epistemology, 21, 227; and limitations, 195, 215; and nation formation, 193, 194, 256n10; and omission, 35, 210, 225, 227, 229; and research questions, 224

Arenas, Reinaldo, 192–93
Armenteros, Florentino, 145
Aurora General Advertiser (Philadelphia), 68–69, 70, 102, 117, 132, 202
Aury, Louis-Michel, 131–32
"A Washington" (poem), 153–54

barbarism, discourse of, 97, 135, 174–75, 181
Behr, Charles de, 36
Behr & Kahl (booksellers), 38, 39
Berlant, Lauren, 11–12, 13
Biddle, Nicholas, 71
Black Legend, 30, 204
black populations: in Cuba, 142, 167; and fear of insurrection, 167; and identification terms, 78; and labor, 98; in Mexico, 167; in United States, 52; in Venezuela, 120, 127, 167, 168
Blanco White, José, 130, 161–65, 204
Bolívar, Simón, 101, 118, 159, 216
Bombalier, Santiago, 145
book market, Northeast United States: changing conditions of, 27–29; international expansion of, 27, 30–32; —, and exchange methods, 32; and Spanish-language books, 35–40. *See also* printers
Bowman, Charles H., Jr., 71, 246n100
Breve relación de la destrucción de las indias (Las Casas), 33, 203–4, 205
Brickhouse, Anna, 61, 176, 185, 233n37
Bryant, William Cullen, 16–17, 39, 187

Cabral de Noroña, Miguel, 33
Canga Argüelles, José, 176–77, 180
Caracas College of Lawyers, 126–27
Carey, Mathew (printer), 31, 205; as Carey & Lea, 32; as Carey & Sons, 32; and international trade, 32, 33; and Masonic titles, 33; and Spanish-language titles, 38
Cartas a Elpidio (Varela), 7, 80, 83, 84–96, 183; and homosocial connections, 92; and the name Elpidio, 85, 244n43; and sales, 85–87

281

Index

Cartas americanas, políticas y morales (Vidaurre), 7, 34, 196, 215–16, 217–20

Cartas de un americano sobre las ventajas de los gobiernos republicanos federativos, 7, 13, 75, 157, 181, 182, 254n43; and federal constitutions, 179–81, 186; and *The Federalist Papers,* 178; and transatlantic publishing, 175–76; and X as signatory, 14–15, 177

Carta sobre lo que debe hacer un principe que tenga colonias á gran distancia (Foronda), 29–30

Castagnino, Louis, 32

Catholic Church (Rome), 41–42, 44, 61, 89, 221, 223

Catholic churches, 83, 116, 193, 200, 201, 205–6

Catholicism, 114, 182; and Vicente Pazos Kanki, 129–30; and Servando Teresa de Mier, 201, 205–6; and *El Triunfo de la libertad,* 116–17, 125; and US anti-Catholicism, 90–91, 244–45n59; and Félix Varela, 83–85

censorship, 41, 43, 153

Certeau, Michel de, 54, 202

Chasteen, John Charles, 16, 47

circulation (publications): in Caribbean, 32; and distance, 10; and Freemasons, 33; in Mexico, 1–2, 116; and restrictions, 66, 140; and size of books, 2, 31, 114; in South America, 1, 28, 32, 66, 116; and Spanish-language books in the United States, 68–69; and transatlantic crossing, 33–34, 159–63

Clay, Henry, 129, 134

colonialism, opposition to, 113, 136, 137–38; and cities, 47–48; and the Monroe Doctrine, 108; and newspapers, 144, 145–46; and poetry, 151–55

Constitucion de los Estados Unidos de América traducida del Ingles al Español por Don Jph. Manuel Villavicencio, 63

Constitution (US), 1, 25, 35, 47, 52, 60, 63, 66, 180, 192, 197

Constitution of 1812 (Spain), 74, 138

Coronado, Raúl, 5, 18, 118–19, 160

Cortina, Rodolfo, 4, 183–84

creoles (*criollos*), 77, 78, 79–80, 138, 168

Declaration of Independence (US), 1, 47, 60, 131

Declaration of the Rights of Man and of the Citizen, 52, 119, 161

Del Monte, Domingo, 39, 82, 110–11, 146, 151–52, 247n3

dependency theory, 47

Derecho del hombre, El (Paine), 27

Derrida, Jacques, 194, 228–29

Desengaño del hombre, El, 27–29; and the Inquisition, 44–45, 64; and subscribers, 28

Diaz Porlier, Juan, 124

Director de los niños, El, 31

Domínguez Michael, Christopher, 203, 210

Dow, Lorenzo, 89

Dufief, Nicolas Gouïn, 103

Dufief's Nature Displayed in Her Mode of Teaching Language to Man (Torres), 38, 103–6

Duane, William, 71–72, 96–98, 99, 135, 203

Dunbar, Erica Armstrong, 5, 52

Earle, Rebecca, 13, 185, 231n5

early Latino literature, 9, 17–18, 83; and anonymous publication, 156–59, 161, 189–90; and anticolonial printing, 154–55, 200–201; and archives, 196; and hemispheric movements, 10; and indigenous people, 189; and literary aesthetics, 146–47, 154; and multiplicity of texts, 68; and periodicals, 136, 143–46; and Philadelphia, 31, 229; and trans-American production, 67; translation, importance of, 26–27; and use of Latinx, 14–15

economic trade, 99, 100; across the Americas, 99–103, 107; and England, 165; and liberal policies, 107; and protectionism, 101, 107; and translation, 106

Egaña, Juan, 66, 179

epistolarity: and books called *cartas,* 7–9; and bridging nations and languages, 8, 13; and elite men, 8, 82; and the Enlightenment, 9–10, 11, 141, 200; and fiction, 2, 222; and geographic distance, 2; and intimacy, 11–13, 81, 215, 242n12; letters (*cartas*), 8–10; and love, 209–214, 215, 216; and salutations and signatures, 11–13, 81, 178, 211–12, 214, 216; and writing style, 178–79. *See also* letters

Español, El (London), 161, 162, 167

Exámen imparcial de las disensiones de la América con la España (Flórez Estrada), 161
Exposition of the Commerce of Spanish America, An (Torres), 30, 71, 98, 99–103
Exposition, Remonstrance and Protest of Don Vincente Pazos, The (Pazos Kanki), 129, 131, 132–34, 135

Federalist Papers, The, 13, 178–79
Filadelfia: as anticolonial site, 53; as center of conspiracy, 5; and "circulo de," 4; and false imprints, 43–44; as "la famosa," 25, 53, 57; as inspiration for other cities, 25–26, 46, 240n135; and newspapers, 143–44; and printing, 43, 46, 115, 202, 232n24; and public sphere, 19, 112; and separation from Spanish America, 5, 57, 113, 190; as symbol of independence, 3, 6, 26, 43, 229; as trans-American city, 25, 47; and translation, 3–4
Filadelfia, paraíso de conspiradores (Guzmán), 5, 231n13
First Bank of the United States, 49, 50
Fitz, Caitlin, 6–7, 134
Flórez Estrada, Álvaro, 161, 167
Florida, 131–33
Foreign and Classical Book Store, 35–36
Foronda, Valentín de, 29
Foucault, Michel, 47, 158, 161
Franklin, Benjamin, 51, 96, 102, 170, 172, 192, 195, 246n88
Franklin Institute, 36, 37
Freemasonry, 33
French Atlantic, 4, 10–11, 34
Furstenberg, François, 4, 49

Gallego, Juan Nicasio, 151–54. See also *Versos de J. Nicasio Gallego*
García, Emily, 5, 28, 71
García de Sena, Domingo, 59, 224–29
García de Sena, Manuel, 26, 58–69, 114, 224, 226–27; and arrival in Philadelphia, 59; biographical background of, 59–60; and *Common Sense* translation, 61–62; and translation, 58–59, 104–5. See also *Independencia de la Costa Firme, La*
Gener, Tomás, 89–90, 226
Genet, Edmund-Charles, 28
gift books, 40–41, 156

Gillman, Susan, 62
Gran Colombia, 176, 178, 190
Grases, Pedro, 4, 59, 66, 227
Greek War of Independence, 145
Gruesz, Kirsten Silva, 62, 233n37, 235–36n45, *212*
Gual, Pedro, 115, 131, 210, 224
Guayaquil, 1, 45; compared to Philadelphia, 51
Guerra, François-Xavier, 76, 247n7
Guzmán, Martín Luis, 5

Habanero, El, 36, 80, 81, 83, 135, 144, 184, 190; and Cuban independence, 136, 138–39; and organization of articles, 137–38; and hemispheric Americanism, 140–43; and revolution, 140; and secret societies, 139
Habermas, Jürgen, 10, 12, 112–13, 143
Hamilton, Alexander, 28, 44, 181
Hargous, Louis, 103
Harkness, Alberto, 66, 227
hemispheric American studies, 233n48, 242n11. *See also* Americanism (hemispheric)
hemispheric revolutionary movements, 7, 46, 165; and Latino literature, 19, 69; and US Revolution, 5, 58. *See also* trans-American movements
Heredia, José María, 7, 25, 38, 41, 49, 58, 139, 183, 209; as Cuban poet, 53–57, 146–48, 151, 200; and Filadelfia letter, 53–55, 202; and letter writing, 38–39, 53, 72, 226; and literary history, 53; and poem "Niágara," 38–39; and preface to *Poesías,* 39; and trans-American elite, 72; and travel in the United States, 53, 238n101
Heredia y Campuzano, Ignacio, 72
Historia concisa de los Estados Unidos, desde el descubrimiento hasta el año de 1807 (M'Culloch), 60, 64
Historical Society of Pennsylvania, 195
Hogan, William, 205–6
Humboldt, Alexander von, 77
Huttner, Frederick, 35–36, 182

Ideas necesarias á todo pueblo americano independiente, que quiera ser libre (Rocafuerte), 1–4, 8, 18–19, 25, 27, 74; printing of, 44, 236–37n65

immigration: to Philadelphia, 5; and printing, 34, 36; and Manuel Torres, 102; and trans-American elite, 71; and Félix Varela, 83, 87, 89
imperialism, US, 6, 18, 130–33
Independencia de la Costa Firme justificada por Thomas Paine treinta años há, La (García de Sena), 26, 58, 60–69, 224
indigenous body, 189–90
indigenous people: and attitudes of trans-American elite toward, 97–98; and empires, 135, 187; and labor, 96–97, 98; and self-identification, 128–29, 134
indigenous populations: across the Americas, 98; and independence, 204; and mythical past, 57, 193; overlooked by intellectuals, 57; in the United States, 51–52, 181, 184
Inquisition, the, 42, 44, 90, 210, 218
intimacy, 11–13; and epistolary signatures, 12, 13; and gift books, 40–41; and homosocial dimensions, 92–93
Invención de América, La (The Invention of America; O'Gorman), 197, 198–200
Iturbide, Agustín de, 192, 207

Jefferson, Thomas, 28, 35, 56, 103
Jicoténcal, 4, 105; advertisement in, 37; and authorship, 35, 158–59, 183, 254n46, 254n51; and comparison to Varela's writing, 184–85; and copyright, 35–36; and Machiavellian moment, 187, 188–89; printing of, 37; publication of, 182; and republicanism, 186, 189; and Spanish-language book sales, 35–36
Johnson, Sara E., 34

Kanellos, Nicolás, 5, 160

Lacan, Jacques, 229
Lamas, Carmen, 20, 83, 87, 227
language acquisition/learning, 38–39, 103–4
Lanuza & Medía (bookseller), 36, 37, 38
Las Casas, Bartolomé de, 33, 203–4, 257n32
Latin American studies, 17, 20–21
Latino/a: community in Philadelphia, 5, 16; literary history, 73–74; literature, 17; and racism, 108–9; and *la raza Latina*, 16; studies (field of research), 19; as term of identification, 14–16, 19–20

Latinx, 14–16, 177, 233n37
Latrobe, Benjamin Henry, 48
Laval, John, 36, 37
Leal, Luis, 4, 183–84
LeBrun, Charles, 38
Lecciones de filosofía (Varela), 82, 86
letters: and *cartas* (usage), 8–10, 232n25; and difficulty of transmission, 225–26; and early Latino literature, 199; and gender, 209; and love, 194, 209, 211, 216, 219–220; and theory of, 228, 229. See also epistolarity
Letters from an American Farmer (Crèvecoeur), 10, 64
Letters on the United Provinces of South America (Pazos), 129, 134–35, 250n50
letrado, 77, 243n21
liberation theology, 83, 121–22, 249n39
Library Company of Philadelphia, 195
Lista, Alberto, 146–47, 152
literacy, 76, 213, 214
London, 10, 44, 147, 161, 162, 204
López, Narciso, 150
Luz, Francisco de la, 145
Luz y Caballero, José de la, 82, 86

Machiavellian moment (J. G. A. Pocock), 187, 188–89
MacGregor, Gregor, 131–32
Manual de un republicano, para el uso de un pueblo libre, 34, 156, 170–75
Martí, José, 6, 20
Masonic groups, 139, 184. See also Freemasonry
mastodon skeleton, 55–57
Memoria politico-instructiva, enviada desde Filadelfia en agosto de 1821 (Mier), 42, 156, 192–93, 200, 208
Memorias políticas sobre las federaciones (Egaña), 179
Mensagero Semanal, El, 36, 111, 143–45, 146–49
Merino, Félix, 36, 37
Mexico (independence of), 1–2, 192–93, 207, 208
Mexico City, 44
Mier, Servando Teresa de, 25, 34, 192–93; biographical background of, 200–201, 202; and *Breve Relación* (Las Casas), 203–4; and *Carta de un americano a "El*

Español," 162; and incarceration of, 201, 202, 210; and love letter to, 209–215; and movement, 162, 201–2; and Philadelphia publications, 202–3; and seizure of his books, 41–42; and signature, 212. See also *Memoria politico-instructiva, enviada desde Filadelfia en agosto de 1821*
Mills, C. Wright, 76
Mina, Francisco Javier, 42, 131, 210
Miranda, Francisco de, 1, 43–44
monarchy: allegiance to, 189; divine right, 118; and Mexican independence, 207, 208; opposition to, 1, 5, 125, 193; and federalism, 196–97; and sovereignty, 122–24; and *liberales* (Spain), 161
Monroe, James (administration), 71, 107–9, 132–34
Monroe Doctrine, 6–7, 107–8
Moreau de Saint-Méry, Médéric-Louis-Élie, 34
Mulato, El (newspaper), 145

Nash, Gary B., 5, 47
naturales, 81, 88, 189
newspapers, 136, 143–44, 145–46
"Nuestra America" (two Americas), 6, 20, 135

O'Gorman, Edmundo, 195, 196–97, 256–7n16. See also *Invención de América, La*
Otter, Sam, 5, 55

Paine, Thomas, 25, 51, 114, 170; and *Common Sense* (*El sentido común*), 58, 121; and name Hispanicized, 63, 68; and *The Rights of Man*, 27, 32; in Spanish translation, 1, 58, 119, 239n114; and *El triunfo de la libertad*, 118. See also *Independencia de la Costa Firme justificada por Thomas Paine, La*
Palmer, Thomas H., 27
paratextual writing, 1–2, 60–61, 64, 65, 203–4
Pazos Kanki, Vicente, 113, 115, 128–35
Peale, Charles Willson, 56
Peale's Museum, 55–57
peninsulares, 77, 81, 138, 149, 166
Pequeño director de los niños, para aprender á deletrear y leer, El, 31

Pérez Rosales, Vicente, 74
Philadelphia: and architecture, 48–50, 234n2; as asylum, 3–4; as Athens of America, 46–49, 51; as banking center, 49–50, 51, 238n88; and cost of living, 110–11; as economic model, 3, 46, 50, 51; French emigrés in, 34; French language in, 4, 34; and immigration, 5; Latino community in, 5, 16, 68; and mythmaking, 47, 195; as Spanish-language print center, 2–3, 5, 21, 36, 115, 150; and street grid, 55; as urban model, 46, 47, 54–55, 58; and world-systems theory, 21, 22. See also printers
pirates, 81–82, 133
Plan de Iguala, 207, 208
Poesías (Heredia), 38, 39
poetry: and Filadelfia publishing, 151–54; and nationalism, 139, 146; and opposition to colonialism, 41, 147, 154
Poinsett, Joel Roberts, 80–81
political catechisms, 171–72
Poor Richard's Almanac, 102, 246n91
Presente las damas, 40
presses in Spanish America, 42, 43, 45–46, 110–12, 130
printers: Andrés Josef Blocquerst, 34; Hispanicized names of, 27, 34, 37, 85; Jean-François (Juan F.) Hurtel, 33–34, 203; Médéric-Louis-Élie Moreau de Saint-Méry, 34; William (Guillermo) Newell, 85; number in Philadelphia, 42; George Palmer, 30, 34–35, 58; Thomas H. Palmer, 27, 34–35, 58; José Antonio Saco, 110–12; G. P. Scott & Co., 85; and Spanish-language publishing, 26, 27, 30, 35, 110–11; William (Guillermo) Stavely, 37, 182. See also Carey, Mathew
printing: and false imprints, 43–44, 236nn64–65; and prohibitions in Spanish America, 45–46, 140, 153; and republicanism, 113, 130; Spanish America, in, 42; and subscriptions, 28
public sphere, Spanish America, 42; and Buenos Aires, 112, 129, 130, 171; and Caracas, 63, 66, 69, 119; and Havana, 32, 44, 85–86, 144–45; and Lima, 43, 46, 217; and Mexico City, 112; and restrictions, 42–43

public sphere, trans-American, 10, 112–13, 247n7; and English language, 99–100, 131; and Filadelfia, 112; and homosocial connections, 92; and liberal bourgeois approach, 143; and racial identification, 129; and religious writing, 118, 120–25; and women, exclusion of, 92–93, 172
Puglia, Santiago Felipe, 27–28, 44–45

Quijano, Aníbal, 98, 106

racial formations, 6, 52, 126–27, 128, 163, 172; and anonymous publication, 157; and barbarism, discourse of, 174–75; and *limpieza de sangre,* 126; and *sistema de castas,* 126, 163; and skin color, 223; and social hierarchies, 97, 168
Rama, Angel, 47, 55
readers: in Cuba, 83–84, 85; and disconnect from US-based writers, 84, 85, 86, 96, 136; in Ecuador, 1; and gender, 92–93; in Mexico, 1–2, 116, 208; in Venezuela, 65–66, 116
Reflexiones imparciales sobre la francmasonería, 33
republicanism, 5, 69, 92, 113, 140, 168, 196; and anonymous publication, 157; and behavior, 185, 187, 188, 189–90; and federal/unitary tension, 176, 179, 180; and forms of government, 171, 182; and racial conditions, 170
Republican's Manual, For the Use of a Free People, The, 170–73
Revista Bimestre Cubana, 150
Revolution, US, 170; and analogy, 65–66; and gender, 92; and historical conflation, 58; and influence on Americas, 70, 247n5
Rivera, Josefa Luisa, 216, 223; and letters published, 221–22; and Lima society, 220; and relationship with Manuel Vidaurre, 218–19
Robinson, William Davis, 226
Rocafuerte, Vicente, 1–4, 11, 25, 27, 79, 196, 197, 202; and *Cartas de un americano,* 178–81; and economic resources, 18–19; as Ecuador's president, 1, 200; and family background, 19; and geographic movement, 74–75, 162; and Philadelphia's economy, 50–51; and signature, *212.* See also *Ideas necesarias á todo pueblo Americano independiente*
Rodriguez O., Jaime, 1, 66, 107, 176
Rojas, Rafael, 5
Roscio, Juan Germán, 17, 201; biographical background of, 114–15; and *El Español,* 162, 164–65; *Homilia del cardinal Chiaramonti,* 115; and racial background, 125–28; and theology, 117–18, 119; as trans-American elite, 72. See also *Triunfo de la libertad sobre el despotismo, El*
Rousseau, Jean-Jacques, 19, 118, 125, 171, 172–73, 217–18, 249n32
Ruschenberger, William, 220–21
Russo-Turkish War, 145

Saco, José Antonio, 82, 110–12, 143–50
Sagra, Ramón de la, 148–50
Said, Edward, 18, 154
Saint Domingue, 34, 58
Saint Mary's Catholic Church, 193, 202, 205–6
Sedgwick, Eve Kosofsky, 92
slavery, 6, 52–53, 127–28; and *El amigo de los hombres,* 159, 167, 169; and *Cartas americanas, políticas y morales,* 222–23; and Cuba, 137; as metaphor, 120, 142, 166, 181; and the United States, 169
Soles y Rayos de Bolívar, 139
Solís, Antonio de, 105, 152
"Spanish America," usage, 17
Spanish language: printing, 2–3, 5; —, and US culture, 5, 228; learning and instruction of, 38–39, 103–6; and trade, 106
Spanish-language books: as commodities, 40–41; as gifts, 40; and language instruction, 38, 103, 152; and poetry, 39; and readers in the United States, 68–69; sales, 38
Spanish-language publishing: and book sales, 38, 85–86; and changes in the US book market, 27–30; growth of market, 35–40; profit from, 27; and trans-American elite, 73
Steiner, George, 104
Stephenson, Charlotte, 209–15, 223
Stoddard Johnson, Josiah, 79

target-territory (translation), 58, 59, 63, 65, 66

tertulias, 76, 152
Torres, Manuel, 7, 30, 203, 207, 209, 211, 213; and John Quincy Adams, 108–9; and *Aurora General Advertiser*, 70, 102; and economic resources, 101; as "Franklin of South America," 70, 96; funeral procession for, 70, 241n1; and handwriting, 211; as host of revolutionaries, 71, 115, 135, 193, 196, 210; and language acquisition, 103–4; and Latino literature, 71; and Monroe Doctrine, 71, 107–8; and his plantation, 97; and economic trade, 99, 100; and trans-American elite, 72. See also *Dufief's Nature Displayed*; *Exposition of the Commerce of Spanish America, An*
trans-American elite: and cosmopolitanism, 75; defined, 72–73, 76; and economic resources, 18–19, 74–75, 101, 110–11; and education, 76, 77, 170–71, 172; and geographic movement, 71, 74, 75; and homosocial aspects, 92–93; and immigration to the United States, 83; and indigenous populations, 97–98; and Latino literary history, 73–74; as leaders, 95–96, 142, 242n15; and letters, 79, 82; and literary history, 73–74; and paying for printing, 42, 110–11; and racial formations, 174–75; and women, 91–95, 172, 189, 215–16, 223
trans-Americanicity, 101, 242n11, 245nn80–81
trans-American movements, 20–21; and anticolonial battle, 108; and censorship in Spanish America, 41; and circulation of books, 74; and Cuban literary nationalism, 153; and Freemasons, 33; and US Revolution, 58, 78–79
translation, 4, 170; and anonymity, 172; and evaluation of quality, 59, 67; and political goals, 60, 116–17; as response to political crisis, 59, 133; and republican pedagogy, 173, 178; and target-territory, 58–59, 133; and text-network, 62–63; and theory of, 104–5. *See also* Paine, Thomas
Triunfo de la libertad sobre el despotismo, El (Roscio), 17, 113–14, 120–21, 151; and Catholicism, 116–17, 125; and circulation, 116; and confessional mode, 119–120; editions of, 248n23; and liberation theology, 121–22; and political catechisms, 171; and race, 126; and sovereignty, 122–24

underdevelopment, 46, 52
US-Mexico War, 6

Varela, Félix, 7, 80–81, 82–83; and anonymous publication, 183–84; and *Cartas a Elpidio*, 80, 83, 84–96; and Cuban history, 251n69; and *El Habanero*, 80, 83, 135–43, 144, 197; and hemispheric Americanism, 140–42; and indigenous populations, 184; and *Lecciones de filosofía*, 82, 86; and presumed authorship of *Jicoténcal*, 158–59, 183–84; and Protestant denominations, 89–91; and slavery, 142; and trans-American elite, 72; and United States, views of, 87–89; and women, attitude toward, 93–95; and Fanny Wright, 91–95
Versos de J. Nicasio Gallego, recogidos y publicados por Domingo Del Monte, 39, 111, 151–54
Viaje a los Estados Unidos del Norte de América (Zavala), 26, 52–53
Viaje por los Estado Unidos del Norte, dedicado á los jovenes mexicanos de ambos secsos, 48–49, 237n78
Villaverde, Cirilo, 152
Visit to Colombia in the Years 1822 and 1823, A (Duane), 97–98
Vidaurre, Manuel Lorenzo de, 34, 196; biographical background of, 216, 258n50; and Catholicism, 219, 223; and mental health, 223–24; and Jean-Jacques Rousseau, 217–19; and sister-in-law, 215–17; as trans-American elite, 75
Viscardo y Guzmán, Juan Pablo, 43–44
Vogeley, Nancy, 5, 27, 30, 33

Wallerstein, Immanuel, 21, 22, 98
Warner, Michael, 10, 112, 232n31
Washington, George, 45
Way to Wealth, The (Franklin), 102
Whitman, Walt, 93
world-system theory, 32, 48
Wright, Fanny, 91–95

X (as signature), 13, 14–15

Zavala, Lorenzo de, 26, 51, 52

WRITING THE EARLY AMERICAS

Spanning the broad chronological territory between contact and colonization through the long nineteenth century, this series publishes scholarship that amplifies, challenges, and regrounds the study of literary culture in the United States by highlighting the varied spaces, temporal periods, and forms of language of the early Americas.

Letters from Filadelfia: Early Latino Literature and the Trans-American Elite
  Rodrigo Lazo

Sifilografía: A History of the Writerly Pox in the Eighteenth-Century Hispanic World
  Juan Carlos González Espitia

Creole Drama: Theatre and Society in Antebellum New Orleans
  Juliane Braun

The Alchemy of Conquest: Science, Religion, and the Secrets of the New World
  Ralph Bauer

www.ingramcontent.com/pod-product-compliance
Lightning Source LLC
Chambersburg PA
CBHW021347300426
44114CB00012B/1114